I0009052

Suite

markup your mind!

User and Reference
Manual Version 4.3

© 1998-2002 Altova GmbH & Altova Inc.

ALTOVA

www.altova.com

XML Spy Suite 4.3

All rights reserved. No parts of this work may be reproduced in any form or by any means - graphic, electronic, or mechanical, including photocopying, recording, taping, or information storage and retrieval systems - without the written permission of the publisher.

Products that are referred to in this document may be either trademarks and/or registered trademarks of the respective owners. The publisher and the author make no claim to these trademarks.

While every precaution has been taken in the preparation of this document, the publisher and the author assume no responsibility for errors or omissions, or for damages resulting from the use of information contained in this document or from the use of programs and source code that may accompany it. In no event shall the publisher and the author be liable for any loss of profit or any other commercial damage caused or alleged to have been caused directly or indirectly by this document.

Published: 2002

©Copyright 1998-2002 Altova GmbH & Altova, Inc.

Printed in the United States of America

5 4 3 2 1

ISBN 0-595-21902-0

Table of Contents

Part III User Reference

Part I

1   Introduction

Introduction to XML

The eXtensible Markup Language (XML) is a subset of SGML (the Structured Generalized Markup Language) that has been defined by the World Wide Web Consortium (W3C) in 1998 (see http://www.w3.org/TR/REC-xml). Its goal is to enable generic SGML to be served, received, and processed on the Web in the way that is now possible with HTML. XML has been designed for ease of implementation and for interoperability with both SGML and HTML.

The XML Spy online help and printable documentation contain a Tutorial section that give you a general overview of XML and XML Spy.

To learn more about XML and its associated protocols, please also visit our list of recommended links to various XML-related information resources on the XML Spy web server.

We will take a short tour to discuss the various aspects of XML and the other related W3C standards, before explaining the various features of XML Spy that will help you make the most of XML.

If you are already familiar with XML, you may wish to skip to the Using XML Spy section.

Welcome to XML Spy

XML Spy Suite is a comprehensive and easy-to-use product family that facilitates all aspects of XML Application Development.

The product family consists of the XML Spy Document Framework and XML Spy IDE. XML Spy **Document Framework** consists of **XSLT Designer** and **XML Spy Document Editor**. Help on each member of the product family is available using the Help menu option.

XSLT Designer is a new approach to automate the writing of complex XSLT Stylesheets using an intuitive drag-and-drop user interface. XSLT Designer creates advanced electronic forms for use with XML Spy Document Editor.

XML Spy Document Editor is a word processor type editor, supporting electronic form-based data input, graphical elements, tables, as well as real-time validation using XML Schema.

XML Spy IDE is the industry-leading solution for XML-based application development, allowing easy creation and management of XML documents, XML schemas, as well as XSLT Stylesheets.

XML SPY Suite includes a Tutorial that shows you how to use XML Spy for the major aspects of XML:

- **XML editing & validation**
- **Schema/DTD editing & validation**
- **XSL editing & transformation**

The Reference section explains each window and menu command in detail and can easily be accessed through the Contents, Index and context-sensitive help (F1) from any menu or dialog box.

You may also want to periodically check our XML Spy web-server for news, updates, and new examples.

If you encounter an occasional error or, perhaps, some incomplete information in this online help or the printed documentation and you need help with XML Spy, please don't hesitate to visit our Support Center on the Internet, where you'll find additional links to the FAQ pages as well as our online Support Form. Also, please feel free to send us any feedback regarding the new documentation.

We will also be providing periodic free updates to the online help system and the printable documentation on the Download page on our web server.

What is XML

If you are new to XML, perhaps the most confusing aspect is it's similarity to HTML, which makes XML seem familiar at first, but also tends to obscure the view for the finer details of what makes XML tick.

We will, therefore, start by looking at what XML really is and why you need XML.

The XML Specification

The W3C specification defines XML as a subset of SGML, so to properly understand XML, it is useful to take a closer look at SGML first.

SGML stands for Standard Generalized Markup Language, and was developed for large scale applications, aircraft maintenance or power plant documentation, and intended to be maintained over the long term .

The reason why XML seems to be so similar to HTML lies in the fact that HTML is defined as a subset of SGML. XML is actually a lot more similar to SGML than to HTML, because HTML is only one specific subset of SGML used to describe web pages.

As XML was created to simplify SGML, it is no wonder that the W3C has now decided to redefine HTML 4.0 as an XML application, thereby creating XHTML 1.0. But this shall be of no concern for us at the moment, because we are still faced with the fundamental question "What is XML?".

To answer this, let us define what XML is **not**:

- It is **not** a programming language.
- It is **not** the next generation of HTML.
- It is **not** a database.
- It is **not** specific to any horizontal or vertical market.
- It is **not** the solution to all your problems, but it can be a very powerful tool in building such a solution.

XML is a clearly defined way to **structure, describe,** and **interchange data.**

Data in this context really means every conceivable kind of data! You can use XML for such diverse things as describing mathematical formulas, chemical compounds, astronomical information, financial derivatives, architectural blueprints, annotating Shakespearean plays, collecting Buddhist wisdoms, or voice-processing in telephone systems!

To get a feeling for XML, let us take a look at a simple XML document:

```
<product>
  <name>Apple</name>
  <price>0.10</price>
</product>
```

The < and > angle brackets are used to distinguish between the so-called "markup" (between the brackets) and the actual data of the document (outside of the brackets).

The XML document consist of individual *elements* that are marked by start- and end-tags (hence the term markup). Tags contain the name of the element, so that they can be distinguished from one another more easily.

The start-tag is bracketed by `<  >` and the end-tag by `</  >` - both the start- and end-tag must always occur in pairs. The example XML document contains one element called "product", which consists of two elements: "name" (which contains the data "Apple") and "price" (which contains the data "0.10"). Unlike HTML, XML does **not** enforce a predefined set of element names (such as "body", "h1", and "p") - you can make up your own to suit the particular needs of your data.

This simple XML document also shows a very important aspect of XML - it is "self-describing". In addition to structuring the actual data, the XML element names (sometimes also called *tag names*) serve to describe the information provided in the document (in our case the price of an Apple). If you compare this to the way such data is traditionally exchanged between different applications (e.g. comma-separated value or CSV files), you can easily see the benefit:

> "Apple";0.10

This is even more obvious, if you look at a slightly more complicated XML example document (as shown as in the Text View of XML Spy):

```
<invoice due="2000-09-22">
  <product>
    <name>Apple</name>
    <price>0.10</price>
  </product>
  <product>
    <name>Orange</name>
    <price>0.08</price>
  </product>
  <product>
    <name>Strawberries</name>
    <price>0.20</price>
  </product>
  <product>
    <name>Banana</name>
    <price>0.14</price>
  </product>
  <total currency="US$">0.52</total>
</invoice>
```

You can immediately see another crucial property of XML here: the elements can be nested in any way that is useful to show the semantic structure of the data contained, and elements can be repeated, if more than one item of data of the same kind needs to be listed. Our example now describes an invoice with four products and a total.

Also note that some elements contain additional information within the start-tag: *attributes* always have a name and a value and are written as `name="value"` (E.g. `currency="US$")`. Attributes are used to further specify additional information that augments the data of the element (in our example, the currency of the total).

A disadvantage of XML is that the bigger an XML document is, the more markup it contains. This can make it difficult to find the data contained in the document. This slight disadvantage is typically more than compensated by the flexibility of XML, and by the fact that XML is inherently suitable for reading by both humans and machines.

XML Spy offers a concise presentation of a XML document - called the Enhanced Grid View. This view allows you to see and directly manipulate elements in your XML document, such as the actual data it contains:

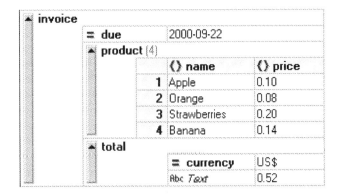

This is the same XML document as show in the Text view above. The product names and respective prices are shown as columns of a table - just as you would expect to see in a grid view.

Editing in this view is infinitely more comfortable, since you can simply:
• drag & drop elements
• insert new rows
• copy/paste your data to and from other applications (e.g. Excel, etc.) and
• manipulate data in a graphical way that is not possible in views offered by other products

You now have a first impression of an XML document and have learned about the two most important features of XML: **elements** and **attributes**. We will explain the other concepts of XML in the tutorial when we look at the specific features offered by XML Spy.

Before we continue, let us first consider the ever-important "why" question...

Why XML

The reasons for using XML typically are as diverse as the different forms of data that exist today. We will, therefore, not consider specific benefits for certain vertical markets - such as engineering, e-commerce, mathematics, or others - but will instead try to focus on several individual properties of XML that are of universal advantage to all applications.

XML is easily readable by both humans and machines

Until now, most formats for storing data were either suitable for interpretation by software programs (e.g. dBase, GIF, etc.), or human readable (text or CSV files) - but not both.

XML defines a set of rules that make interpretation by computer very simple. It thus satisfies both needs, because XML documents remain text-based and can still be easily manipulated by a human being.

XML is object-oriented

While the relational data model is very successful for processing large amounts of table-like data, manipulation of other kinds of data - such as hypertext (i.e. text plus hyperlinks), multimedia, graphics, mathematical or chemical formulas, hierarchical information - are not so straightforward.

In contrast, XML is object-oriented in the sense of being suitable for describing objects of the real world or any abstract problem domain by modeling their properties as they are, instead of enforcing a normalized decomposition into various tables linked by relations. This makes XML documents more intuitively understandable and thereby reduces both the time required to design and implement computing systems based on XML.

XML is being widely adopted by the computer industry

One key factor in the success of the Internet was the wide adoption of the TCP/IP protocol suite by many corporations. This resulted in huge sales volumes and consequently ever decreasing prices for all network components used.

XML is widely accepted and implemented by many vendors, this fact will result in higher volumes and lower prices for software components. This is why XML's predecessor, SGML, was never successful on a broad scale. SGML products were typically priced in the ten-thousand dollar range, whereas XML products are today priced in the hundreds.

XML is global

To better understand the attention that XML has received, it is useful to recall another widely-adopted data standard that everybody takes for granted today: ASCII, the American Standard Code for Information Interchange.

While ASCII was restricted to a certain alphabet and writing system, it was still crucial in allowing different computer types and operating systems to freely exchange data. With the adoption of Unicode 1.0 and its continuing evolution. The idea of ASCII was expanded to encompass *all* languages and writing systems of the world.

Today, it is taken for granted that computers are capable of reading and processing text documents based on ASCII or Unicode. XML takes this approach one step further, by building on Unicode and defining a universal way to describe *structured* data for all different purposes.

All XML documents are per definition Unicode-based, but may be stored on disk or transmitted over the network in various different "encodings", such as ISO-8859-1 or UTF-8 . This is, why some people today call XML the "ASCII of the future".

Now that we have investigated some of the reasons why XML makes sense, we will turn to the XML "Acronym Puzzle".

The XML Standards Puzzle

In addition to XML, you will also encounter one or more of the following standards or acronyms closely associated with XML:

DTD

The "Document Type Definition" is a part of the original XML 1.0 specification that allows a developer, or standards body, to specify what elements and attributes may be used in a particular type of XML document and what their structure and nesting may be. This is also called the *content model* or *schema* of an XML document.

If an XML document conforms with the content model defined by a DTD, it is said to be *valid* with respect to that DTD.

XSLT

The "eXtensible Stylesheet Language Transformation" is a programming language that allows XML documents to be transformed from one schema to another or into entirely different forms, such as HTML pages, WML cards, or PDF files.

XPath

The "XML Path Language" is a language for addressing and querying the content of XML documents.

XLink

The "XML Linking Language" describes hyperlinking in XML documents and extends the hyperlinking concepts of HTML.

XPointer

The "XML Pointer Language" is a companion standard to Xlink and describes mechanisms for addressing particular parts of a document.

XML Schema

The "XML Schema" is an ongoing effort by the W3C to supplant DTDs with a more flexible and powerful system to describe the structure of conforming XML documents, including provisions for defining datatypes.

XHTML

The "Extensible HyperText Markup Language" is the reformulation of HTML 4.0 based upon XML and will soon supplant HTML as the de-facto standard of the Internet.

WML

The "Wireless Markup Language" is used for WAP phone systems to enable a mobile Internet environment and is entirely based on XML - it is described by one particular DTD, which is part of the WML specification.

SVG

Scalable Vector Graphics. SVG is an XML application used to describe 2D vector graphics, text and raster images. This enables vector graphics to be defined solely in XML.

SMIL

The "Synchronized Media Integration Language" is a XML document type designed to describe multimedia presentations.

DOM

The "Document Object Model" describes how some XML parsers return the information contained in an XML document. The elements of the XML document are described as nodes of a tree that can be traversed by a programmer.

SAX
The "Simple API for XML" provides another programming model used by some parsers, which is based on events instead of a traversable tree.

This list does not attempt to be a complete list of all XML-based standards, as there are new proposals emerging on an almost daily basis and many standards are very specific to a certain market or problem domain. Please feel free to visit our XML Spy Home Page to learn about recommended links, news, and other XML related information.

XML Spy user interface

This screen shot shows the XML Spy application window.

The Enhanced Grid View [icon] is enabled, and the Altova.xml file is the active document.

The Database/Table view has been activated for the Division element. This view is available wherever the **Enhanced Grid view** can be activated, and can be used when editing any type of XML file - XML, XSD, XSL etc.

Clicking the "Display as Table" icon, [icon] activates the Database/Table view.

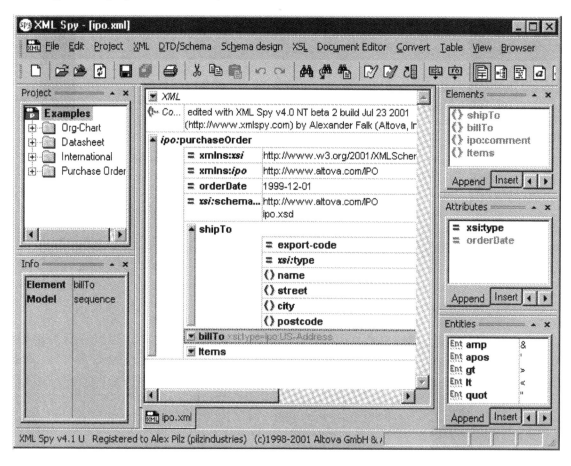

XML Editing

This screen shot shows the main window containing a XML document, and the same document in Browser view.

Click on the Browser view icon, 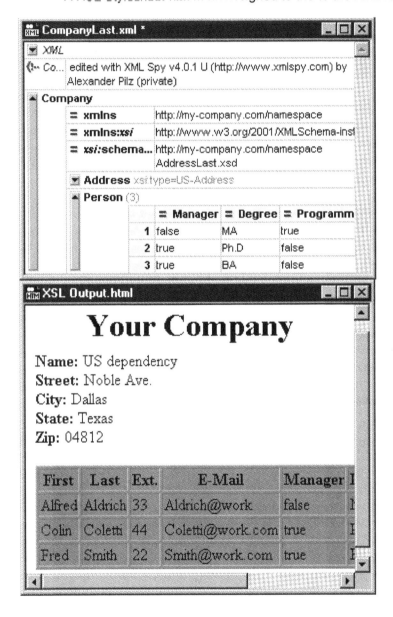 to open the Browser view of an XML Document.

For the Browser view to display/render a XML document correctly:
- The XML Document must contain a reference to a XSL stylesheet, or
- A XSL Stylesheet has to be assigned to the to the XML folder or project.

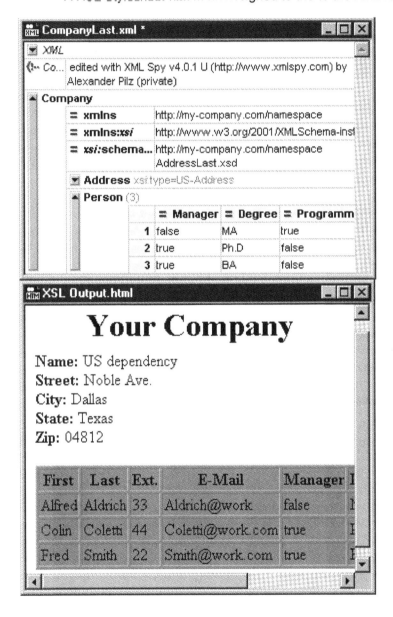

Schema Editing

This screen shot shows the main window containing an XML Schema document (XSDL - XML Schema Definition Language).

Click on the Schema Design View icon 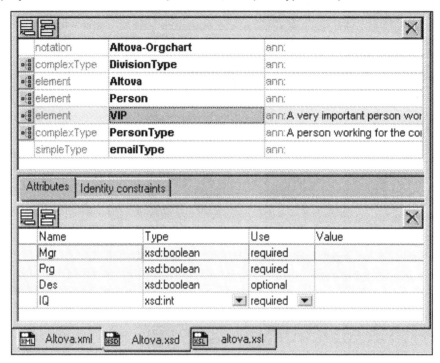 to open Schema Overview. The main window then displays all Global "definitions" (elements, complex types etc.) in list form.

notation	**Altova-Orgchart**	ann:
complexType	**DivisionType**	ann:
element	**Altova**	ann:
element	**Person**	ann:
element	**VIP**	ann: A very important person wor
complexType	**PersonType**	ann: A person working for the co
simpleType	**emailType**	ann:

Attributes | Identity constraints

Name	Type	Use	Value
Mgr	xsd:boolean	required	
Prg	xsd:boolean	required	
Des	xsd:boolean	optional	
IQ	xsd:int	required	

Altova.xml   Altova.xsd   altova.xsl

To see the content model in graphical form:

1. Click on the icon next to the definition you want to display.
   The *content model* for that component appears in a tree view.

To return to the Schema overview:

- Click the "Show Globals" icon to return to the Schema Overview.
- Select the menu option **Schema design | Display All Globals** to return to the Display All Globals view.

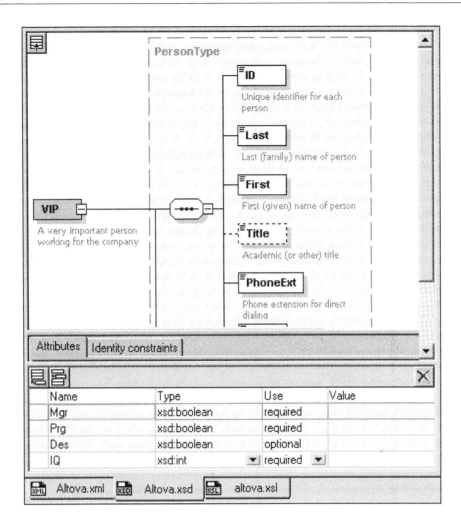

XSL Editing

This screen shot shows the main window containing a XSL (eXtensible Stylesheet Language) document, in Text view.

```
<?xml version="1.0" encoding="UTF-8"?>
<xsl:stylesheet version="1.0"
xmlns:xsl="http://www.w3.org/1999/XSL/Transform"
xmlns:xsi ="http://www.w3.org/2000/10/XMLSchema-instance"
xmlns:my="http://my-company.com/namespace">

<xsl:template match="/">
    <html>
        <head> <title>Your company</title></head>
            <body>
                <h1><center>Your Company</center></h1>
                <xsl:apply-templates select="//my:Address"/>
                <table border="1" bgcolor="lime">
                    <thead align="center">
                        <td><strong>First</strong></td>
                        <td><strong>Last</strong></td>
                        <td><strong>Ext.</strong></td>
                    </thead>
                    <xsl:apply-templates select="//my:Person"/>
                </table>
            </body>
```

ipo.xml   CompanyLast.xml   Company.xsl

Clicking on the Enhanced Grid View icon, ▤ displays the same XSL document in grid form.

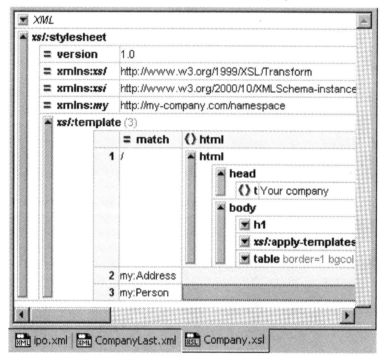

Project Management

XML Spy uses the familiar tree view display to manage your XML projects.

Project folders allow you to:
- Group XML files by their extension
- Assign XSL transformation parameters to specific folders, enabling you to view XML documents with "default" stylesheets
- Validate XML files by assigning DTDs or Schemas to specific folders.

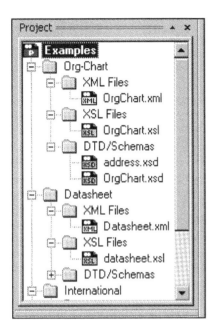

Part II

2   XML SPY Tutorial

This tutorial gives a short overview of XML, and takes you through several tasks which provide an overview of how to use XML Spy to its fullest.

You will learn how to:
- Create a **simple schema** from scratch
- **Generalize** the schema using simple and complex types
- Create schema **documentation**
- Create an **XML document** based on the schema file
- Copy data XML data to a **third party product** (Excel) and reinsert it in XML Spy
- **Validate** the XML document against its schema
- **Update** Schema settings while editing the XML document
- **Transform** the XML document into HTML using XSLT, and see the result in the Browser view
- **Import** and **export** database data to and from XML Spy
- Create a **schema** from a MS Access database
- Create an XML Spy **project** to organize all your XML documents

XML Spy installation and configuration
This tutorial assumes that you have successfully installed XML Spy on your computer and received a free evaluation key-code, or are a registered user of XML Spy.

The evaluation version of XML Spy is fully functional but time-limited to 30 days. You can request a regular license from our secure web server or through any one of our resellers.

Tutorial example files
The tutorial files are available in the **...\XML Spy Suite\Examples\Tutorial** folder.

Tutorial example files:
AddressFirst.xsd
AddressLast.xsd
CompanyFirst.xml
CompanyLast.xml
Company.xsl
Company.html
Company.mdb
DB2schema.mdb
DB2schema.xsd
Person-import.xml

The **Examples folder** contains various XML files for you to experiment with, while the **Tutorial** folder contains all the files used in this tutorial.

The **Template folder** contains all the XML template files that are used whenever you select the menu option **File | New**. These files supply the necessary data (namespaces and XML declarations) for you to start working with the respective XML document immediately.

XML Spy Overview

XML Spy provides several windows that show various aspects of your XML document:

- The left area consists of the **Project** and **Info** windows.

- The central area, called **Main** window, is where you edit and view all types of XML documents.
  You can choose from different views: Enhanced Grid view, Schema view, Text view, Document Editor view or Browser view. The Enhanced Grid view incorporates a special view, called the Database/Table view, which collapses recurring XML data into table form.

- The right area contains the three **Entry helper** windows which allow you to insert or append: elements, attributes, and entities.

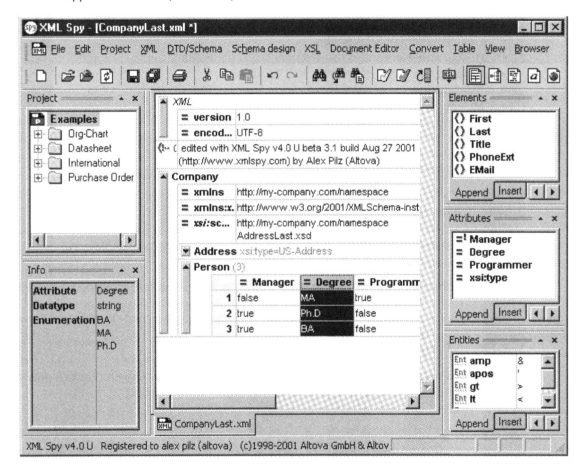

Creating a schema from scratch

A Schema describes what one or more XML documents can look like,
and defines:

- The elements the document contains, and the order in which they appear
- The element content, and element attributes if any

The purpose of a schema is to allow machine validation of document structure. Instead of using the syntax of XML 1.0 DTD declarations, schema definitions use XML element syntax. A correct XML schema definition is, therefore, a well-formed XML document.

Goal of this section:
The goal of this section is to **create a simple schema** describing a company and its employees. The company is to consist of an **address** and an unlimited number of **persons**.

This will be achieved by:

- **Adding** elements to the schema
- Defining element **sequences**
- Adding **sub-elements** to an element (child elements)
- Creating elements using **drag and drop**
- **Configuring** the schema view
- Making an element **optional**
- Defining an element **facet**

Functions (and their icons) in this section:

 File | New, creates a new type of XML file.

 Schema design | Display diagram, the component icon displays the content model of the active global component.

 Schema design | Display all globals, takes you back to the schema overview.

TAB Takes you to the next field and automatically opens a drop-down list if one exists.

CTRL + **Drag&Drop**, enables you to copy existing elements.

 Append icon, allows you to append an element to the schema or add a new line in the "View config." dialog (**Schema design | View config.**)

Creating a new Schema file

To create a new schema file:

1. Start XML Spy by double clicking on the XML Spy icon.
   You are presented with an empty environment. There are no XML documents in the main window.

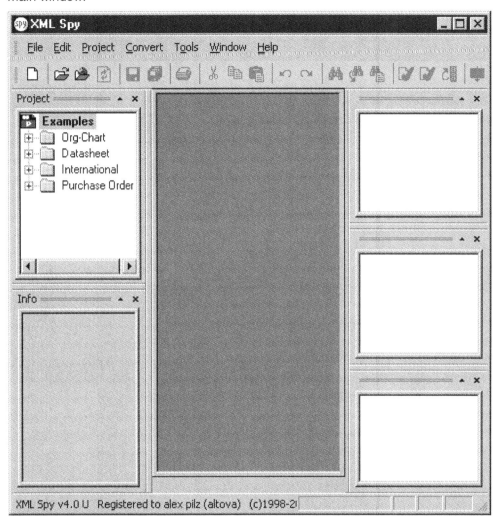

2. Select the menu option **File | New** and select the **.xsd W3C Schema** entry from the dialog and confirm with OK.

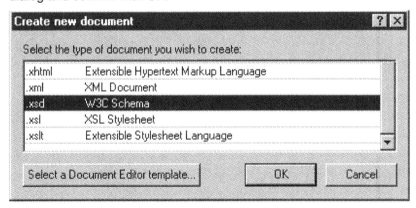

An empty schema file appears in the main window. You are prompted to enter the name of the root element.

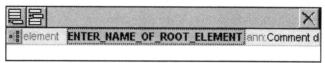

3. Click in the highlighted field and enter "Company", confirm with Enter.
   Company is now the "root" element of this schema and is automatically a "global element" as well.

   This view is the **Schema overview** and displays the **global components** in the top window and the **attributes** of the currently selected component, in the lower one.

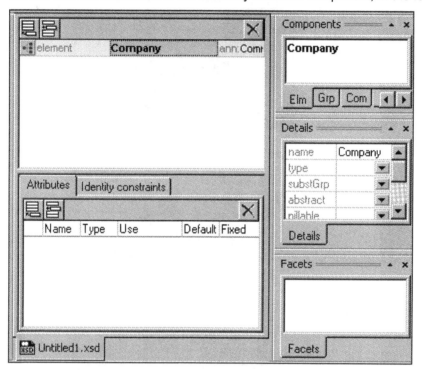

The top entry helper window, the **Component Navigator**, displays Company in the "Elm" tab. The entries in these tabs can be used to navigate your schema by double clicking on them.

4. Click the menu option **File | Save as**, and name your schema (**AddressFirst** for example).

Defining your own namespace:
1. Select the menu option **Schema Design | Schema settings.**
2. Click the Target namespace radio button, and enter **http://my-company.com/namespace.**

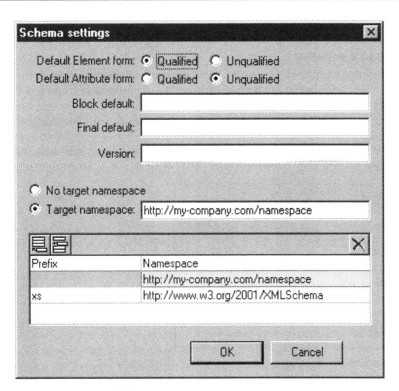

3. Confirm with the OK button.

Adding elements to a schema

To add elements to a schema:

1. Click the component icon ▪▪ next to the **Company** element, in the main window, to display the content model (or double click on the Company entry in the Component Navigator).
    The text below the company element is annotation text. Double click the text if you want to edit it. (shortened to "Root element" here.)

2. Right click the Company element to open the context menu, and select **Add Child | Sequence**.

This inserts the **Sequence compositor**, and defines that the following elements must appear in the same sequence (in the XML document).

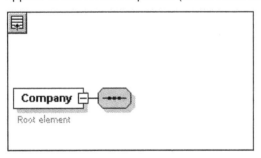

3. Right click the Sequence compositor and select **Add Child | Element**.
4. Enter "Address" as the name of the element, and confirm with the Enter key.

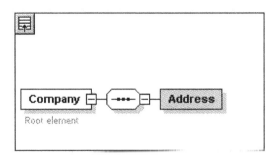

5. Right click the Sequence compositor again, select **Add Child | Element**, and enter "Person" as the name of the element.

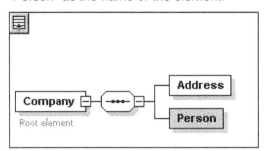

We have now defined a schema which allows for one address and one person per company. As this is too restrictive, we want to make sure that we can include as many persons per company as necessary.

6. Right click the Person element, and select **Unbounded** from the context menu.
    The Person element changes at this point, showing the range in which it can occur, in this case 1 to infinity.

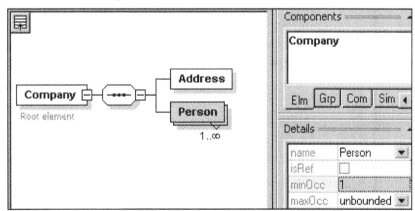

Please note:
    You can also edit the **minOcc** and **maxOcc** fields in the Details entry helper directly.

We will now add the sub-elements which define the address structure.

To add sub-elements to an element:
1. Right click the **Address** element to open the context menu, and select **Add Child | Sequence**.
2. Right click the **Sequence** compositor, and select **Add Child | Element**. Enter "Name" as the element name.

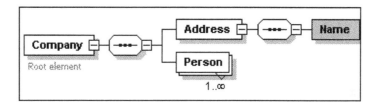

Defining element parameters:
At this point we want to define that the Name element is to occur only once, and contain only textual data.

1. Click the Name element, if not currently selected.
2. Click on the **type** combo box of the middle entry helper, and select the entry **xs:string** from the drop down list.

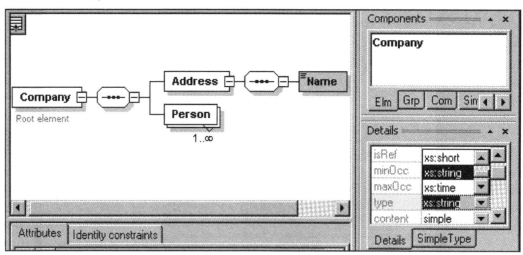

This entry helper is called "**Details**" in the Schema view, and provides information on the currently selected element. **All data can be edited directly in the Details window!**

An icon appears in the top left of the element ▔**Name**, indicating that this element contains text.

Both "minOcc" and "maxOcc" fields contain 1, showing that there is only one occurrence of this element (this is the default setting when creating a new element).

Adding elements with drag and drop

To add elements using drag and drop:
There is a quicker method of adding new elements to a schema, which avoids multiple menu commands:

1. Click the Name element, hold down the **CTRL** key, and **drag** "slightly" with the mouse. A marquee with a small "plus" icon appears, showing that you are about to copy the element.

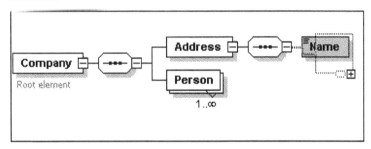

2. Release the mouse button to create the new element. If the new element appears somewhere else, just drag it near to the Name element and drop it there.
   This method creates an element of the same type, with the same settings as the one copied.

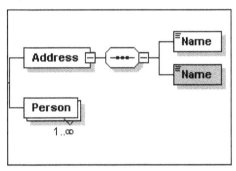

3. Type "Street" to change the element name.
4. Use the same method to create a third element, "City".
   The content model should now look like this:

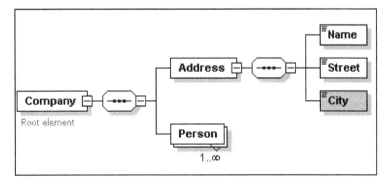

Configuring the schema view

Configuring the Schema view enables you to see specific settings in the content model, and also edit them directly.

To configure the schema view:

1. Select the menu option **Schema Design | View config**.
   A dialog opens at the bottom right of XML Spy, giving you room to see your selections appear in the content model immediately.

2. Click the **Append** 🗒 icon to add a line, and use the combo box to select "**type**" from the drop-down list (or double click in the line and enter "type").

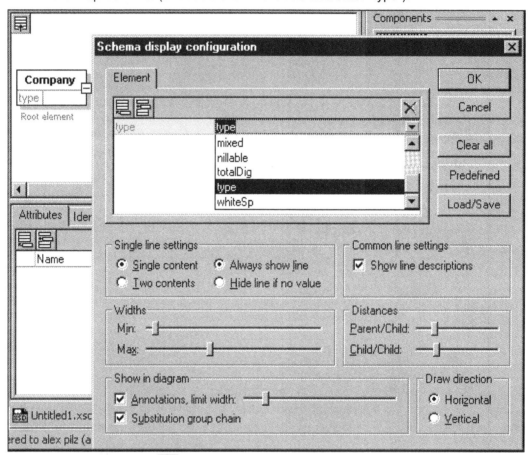

The delete button 🗙 deletes a line from the dialog.
The dialog remains open, and each element symbol has been enlarged by a "type" field. The type field displays the element "type".

3. Click **OK** to confirm the changes.

Please note:
The settings you define here, apply to the schema documentation output as well the printer output.

Completing the basic schema

At this point we want to add those sub elements to the Person element, which make up the personal data. All these elements will be **simple types** (with **simple content** models).

Person sub-elements: First, Last, Title, PhoneExt, and Email.

Requirements:
Title element: should be **optional**
PhonoExt: should be an integer and limited to **99 digits**

1. Right click the Person element to open the context menu, and select **Add Child |**
   Sequence. This inserts the Sequence compositor.
2. Right click the **Sequence** compositor, and select **Add Child | Element**.
3. Enter "**First**" as the name of the element, and hit the "**Tab**" key. This automatically places you in the **type** field.

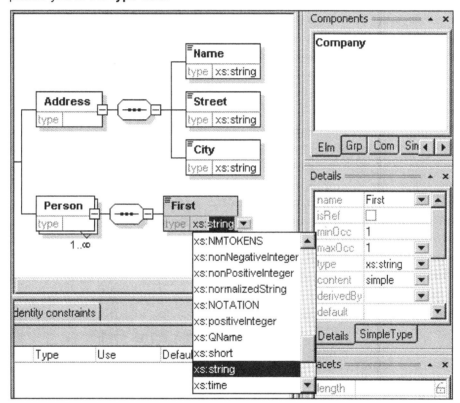

4. Select (or enter) the **xs:string** entry from the drop down list.
5. Use the drag and drop method to create **four more elements**, and name them: Last, Title, PhoneExt, and Email respectively.

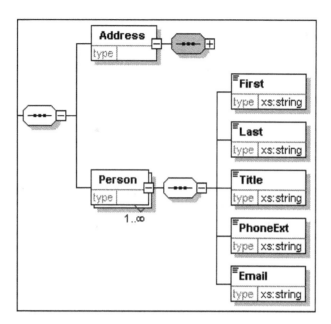

Please note:
> You can select multiple elements by holding down the CTRL key, and clicking each one.

To make an element optional:

1. Right click the **Title** element, and select **Optional** from the context menu.
   The solid element frame changes to a dashed one; this is the visual display that an element is optional.

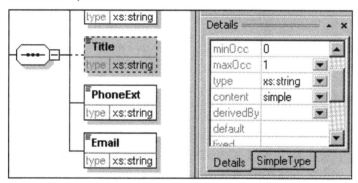

The "Details" fields have also been updated **minOcc=0** and **maxOcc=1**.

To limit the content of an element (Facets):

1. Double click in the **type** field of the PhoneExt **element**, and select (or enter) the **xs:integer** entry from the drop down list.

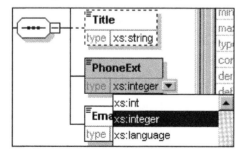

The items in the Facets tab (in the lowest entry helper) change at this point.
2. Double click in the "**maxIncl**" field of the Facets tab (in the lowest entry helper) and enter **99**, confirm with Enter.

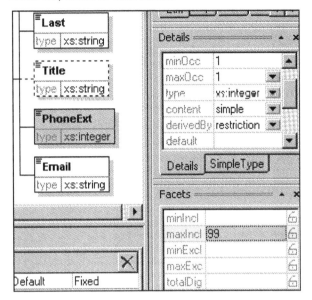

This defines that all phone extensions up to, and including 99, are valid.
3. Select the menu option **File | Save** to save the changes to the schema.

Please note:

- Selecting a predefined simple type "text" (i.e. xs:string, xs:date etc.) for an element, automatically changes the content model to: content = simple, in the Details entry helper.

- Adding a compositor to an element (selection, choice or all), automatically changes the content model to: content = complex, in the Details entry helper.

- This schema is available as '**AddressFirst**' in the ..\Tutorial folder.

Making schema components reusable

Goal of this section:
To create generic **schema** components which can be reused by other elements.

This will be achieved by:
- Creating a global **AddressType** component, which will be the basis for specific country addresses (a complex type)
- Creating two specific address templates for UK-, and US Adresses by **extending** the global address element (extend the complex type)
- Creating a global US-State element, by **restriction** (simpleType)
- Creating a global person element by **reference**
- Defining person **attributes** that supply information about the persons position in the company
- **Limiting** the **attribute contents** to a predefined set of attribute values (enumeration)

Functions (and their icons) in this section:

 Schema design | Display all globals, takes you back to the schema overview.

 Append icon, allows you to append an element, attribute or enumeration to a schema.

 Schema design | Display diagram, the component icon displays the content model of the active global component in the schema overview.

Globals, extending simple and complex types

Having defined an element, you may then realize that you want to reuse it somewhere else in your schema. In XML Spy this is achieved by creating a **global component**.

To create a global component:
1. Right click the Address element, and select **Make Global | Complex type**.
   The Address elements appear in a yellow box.

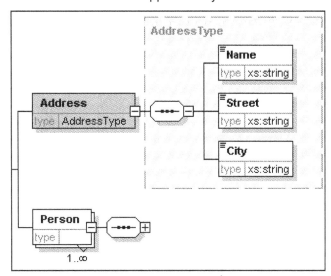

2. Click on the "Display all Globals" 🔲 icon.
   The schema overview now displays two global components: the Company element and the complexType "AddressType".

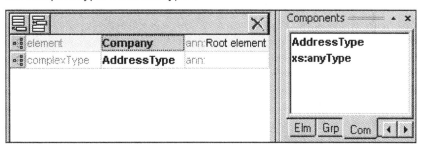

Click on the **Com**(plex) tab of the **Component Navigator** to see that AddressType is also visible there.
3. Click on the AddressType component icon ▪️, to see the content model.

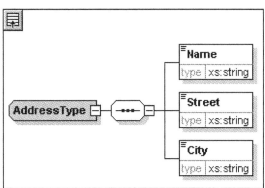

4. Click the "Display all Globals" icon to return to the schema overview.

Extending a "complex type" definition
We now want to use the global AddressType component, to create two kinds of country specific addresses. For this purpose we will define a **new** complex type **based** on the AddressType component.

To extend a "complex type" definition:
1. Switch to the schema overview, if not already visible (Display all globals).
2. Click the **Append** icon, at the top left of the component window.
3. Select **ComplexType** from the context menu.

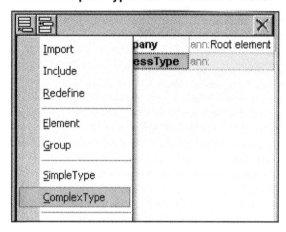

A new line appears in the component list, and the cursor is set for you to enter the component name.
4. Enter "US-Address" and confirm with Enter. (If you forget to enter the hyphen character "-", the element name will appear in **red,** signalling an illegal character.)

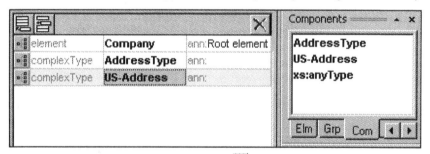

5. Click the **US-Address** component icon to see the content model.
6. Click the "**base**" combo box in the Details entry helper, and select the "AddressType" entry.

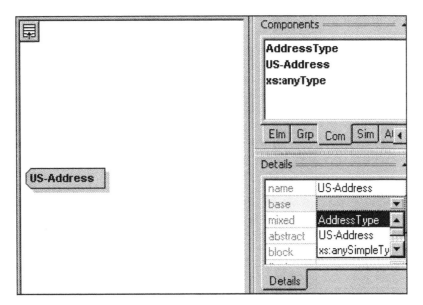

The content model view changes immediately and displays the previously defined generic address.

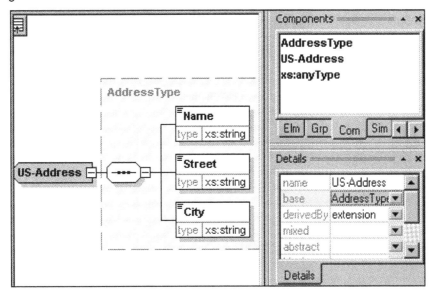

7. Right click the US-Address **element**, and select **Add Child | Sequence**.
    A new sequence compositor is displayed **outside** of the AddressType box. This is a visual indication that this is an **extension** to the element.

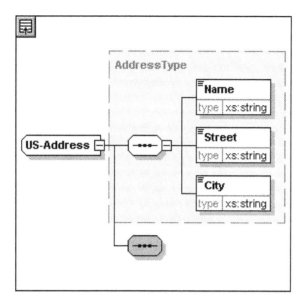

8. Right click the new **sequence** compositor, and select **Add Child | Element**.
9. Name the element "Zip", and hit the "**Tab**" button.
10. Select (or enter) **xs:positiveInteger** from the "type" field combo box, and confirm with Enter.

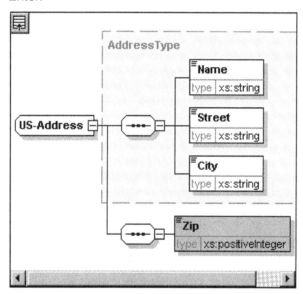

Creating reusable "simple type" elements

Simple type elemets can also be made generic. In this case we want to make the State element reusable, so that an abbreviated version could also be included in address labels at a later time (GA for Georgia, for example).

To create reusable "simple type" elements:

1. Switch to the Schema overview ▦ (Display all Globals).
2. Click the **append** icon, select SimpleType, and enter "US-State" as the element name (Enter to confirm).
3. Select **xs:string** in the "**restr.**" value field of the Details entry helper.
    This completes the definition. This element can now be used in the US-Address definition.

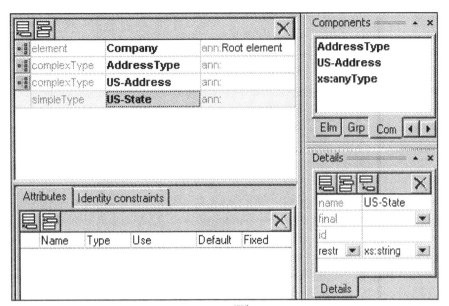

4. Click the US-Address component icon , then right click the lower sequence compositor and select **Add Child | Element**.
5. Enter "State" for the element name, and hit the "Tab" key.
6. Select (or enter) "US-State" from the "type" combo box (click Enter to confirm).

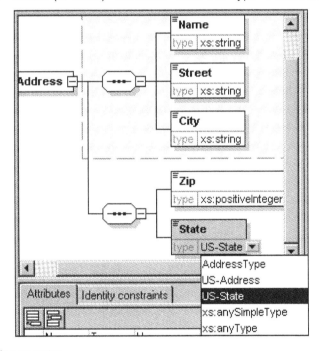

Please note:
   Global simple types can only be created from the schema overview.

Creating the second Address template

Using the method described above, define the global complex type "**UK-Address**".

   1. Create the global **complex type** "UK-Address", with the **base**="AddressType"
   2. Add a new Postcode element to the content model of UK-Address.

Your UK-Address content model should finally look like this:

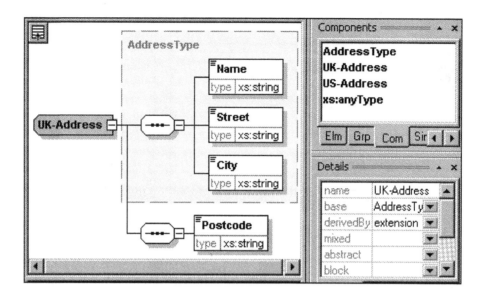

References, attributes and enumerations

To finish off the schema definition we will make the Person element global, define specific element attributes and limit the attribute selection.

To create a reference:

1. Switch to the Schema overview 📇 (Display all Globals).
2. Click on the component icon of the ▪️ **Company** element.
3. Right click the Person element, and select **Make Global | Element**.
    A small "link" icon appears in the Person element, showing that this element now references the globally declared "Person" element. The "**isRef**" field in the Details entry helper is set active.

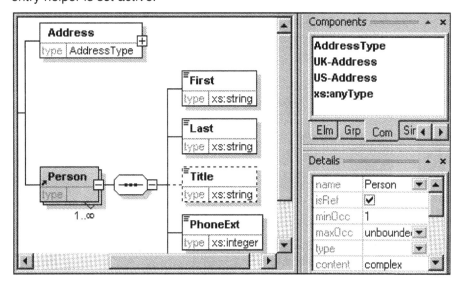

4. Click the "Display all Globals" icon 📇 to return to the schema overview.
    The Person element is now also visible in the component list, as well as in the "**Elm**" tab of the Component navigator. Click the Elm tab to see the global elements.

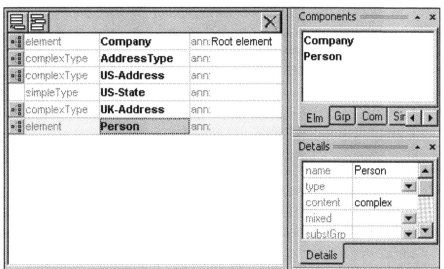

Please note:
>   **Global declarations** do not describe where an element is to be used in an XML

document, they only describe what it contains. Global definitions have to be referenced from within a complex type, or another element, to determine their position in the XML document.

To define Element attributes:

1. Click the Person element to make it active.
2. Click the Append icon, in the top left of the **attribute** tab (the lower window of the schema overview), and select the "Attribute" entry.

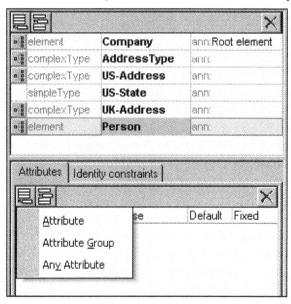

3. Enter "**Manager**" as the attribute name in Name field.
4. Use the **Type** combo box to select "xs:boolean".
5. Use the **Use** combo box to select "required".

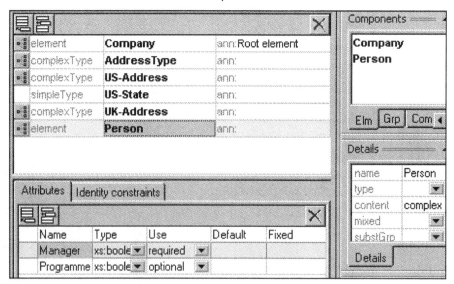

6. Use the same method to:
   Add a "Programmer" attribute in the Name field (type="xs:boolean), and set its Use to "optional".

To limit the contents of an attribute (Enumerations):

1. Click the **Append** icon in the top left of the attribute window, and select the "**attribute**" entry.
2. Enter "**Degree**" as the attribute name, and select "xs:string" as the attribute type.
3. Click the **Enumerations** tab of the Facets entry helper.

4. Click the Append icon 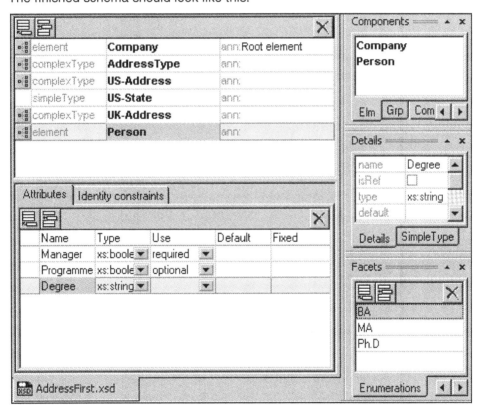of the Enumerations tab and enter "BA", confirm with Enter.
5. Use the same method to add two more items to the enumerations list ("MA" and "Ph.D").

The finished schema should look like this:

6. Select the menu command **File | Save**, and save the file as **AddressLast.xsd**.

Please note:
      This schema is available as '**AddressLast.xsd**' in the Tutorial folder.

Navigation shortcuts in schema documents

This section is designed to show you how you can navigate the Schema view efficiently.

Displaying the content model of any element:

* Select the **element type** you want to see by clicking the specific Component navigator **tab** e.g. Com(plex).

  Elm=global elements, Grp=element group, Com=Complex type, Sim=Simple type, Att=Attribute, AGrp=Attribute group. The Component navigator entries are independent of the content model currently visible in the main window.

* **Double click** the element name in the Com tab e.g. **UK-Address**.

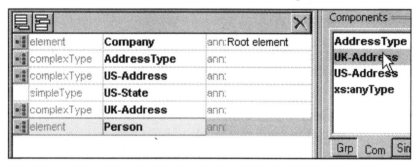

The content model of the UK-Address element is displayed. The specific settings are shown in the Details tab.

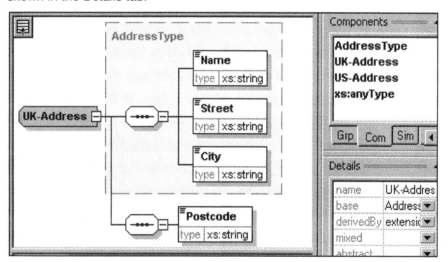

Go to "ElementType" definition:

E.g. While viewing the **Company** content model:

* Double clicking the *AddressType* **text** in the yellow box, takes you to the AddressType definition.

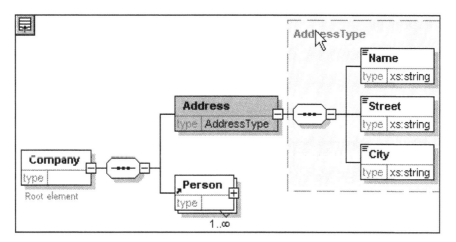

The AddressType definition:

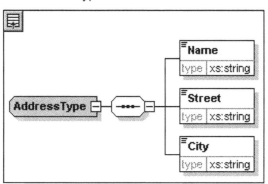

Go to element definition:

E.g. While viewing the **Company** content model:

- Press and hold down the **CTRL** keyboard key, and
- **Double click** on any element definition you want to see (here, the element **Last**).

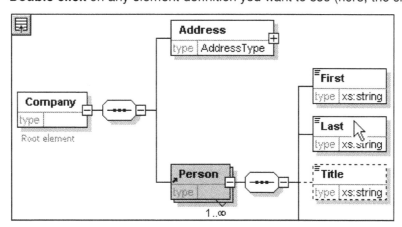

The element Last, which is a sub-element of the Person element, is displayed. The specific settings are shown in the Details tab.

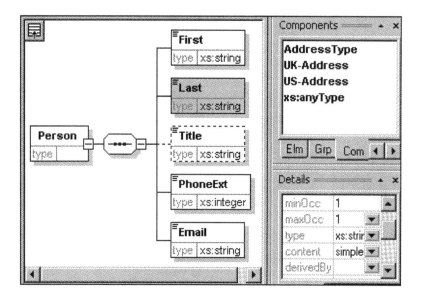

Generating Schema documentation

Goal of this section:
To generate detailed documentation on our current schema and select the specific elements we want to include in it.

You can generate an HTML or Word document, whereby related schema elements (child elements, complex types etc.) are hyperlinked, enabling you to navigate from element to element.

To generate Microsoft Word documentation, you have to have Microsoft Word installed on your computer (network).

To create schema documentation (of the AddressLast schema):
1. Select the menu option **Schema design | Generate documentation**.
2. Select the **Output format**, HTML or Word, and confirm with OK.
3. Select the folder and enter the name of HTML file you want to output, in the Save as... dialog, then click the Save button.

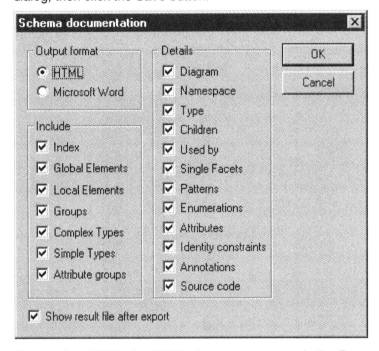

If you select HTML, the HTML document appears in the Browser view of XML Spy. Selecting Microsoft Word creates and displays the Word document.

Schema **AddressLast.xsd**

schema location: **C:\Program Files\Altova\XML Spy**
                  Suite\Examples\Tutorial\AddressLast.xsd
targetNamespace: **http://my-company.com/namespace**

Elements   Complex types Simple types
Company AddressType US-State
Person   UK-Address
           US-Address

element **Company**

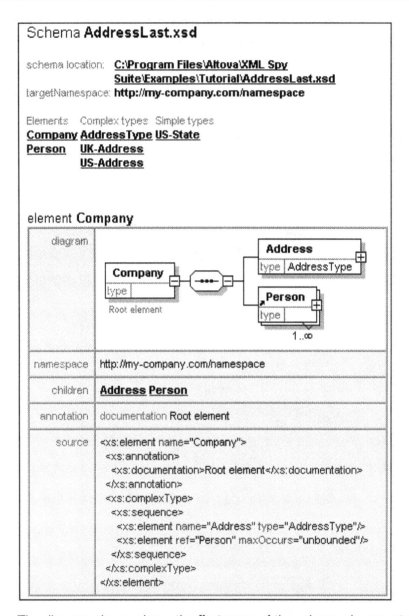

namespace	http://my-company.com/namespace
children	**Address Person**
annotation	documentation Root element
| source | ```xml
<xs:element name="Company">
 <xs:annotation>
  <xs:documentation>Root element</xs:documentation>
 </xs:annotation>
 <xs:complexType>
  <xs:sequence>
   <xs:element name="Address" type="AddressType"/>
   <xs:element ref="Person" maxOccurs="unbounded"/>
  </xs:sequence>
 </xs:complexType>
</xs:element>
``` |

The diagram above, shows the **first page** of the schema documentation in HTML form. If components from other schemas have been included, then those schemas are also documented.
```

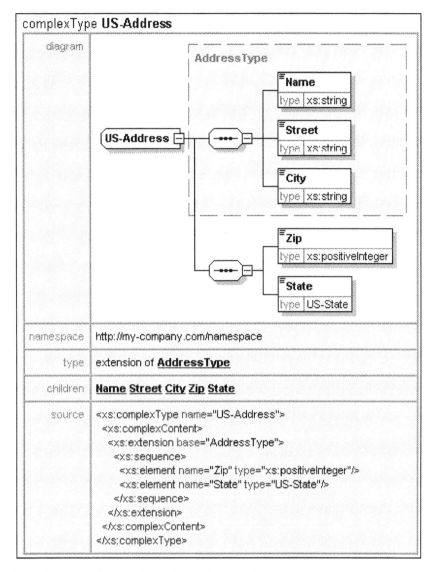

The diagram above, shows how ComplexTypes are documented.

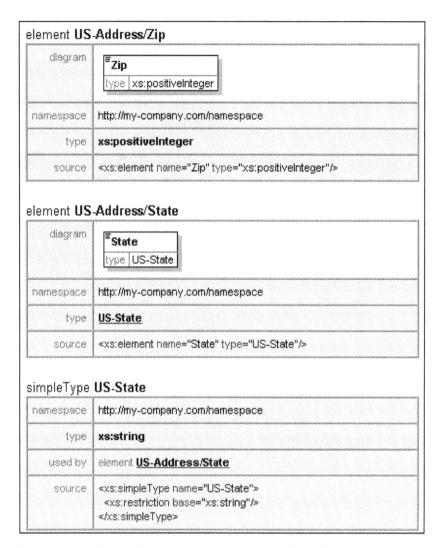

The diagram above, shows how elements and simpleTypes are documented.

Creating an XML document

Goal of this section:

To create a new XML document and use the various XML Spy views and intelligent editing capabilities, to rapidly enter and validate data.

This will be achieved by:

- Creating a new XML document based on the **AddressLast** schema
- Making **elementType** definitions available to an XML document
- Adding elements using **intelligent entry helpers** in the Text and Enhanced Grid view
- Copying **XML data to Excel**, adding new data there, and pasting it back to XML Spy (Enhanced Grid-, and Database/Table view)
- **Sorting** table data by Last name in the **Database/Table** view
- **Validating** the XML document
- **Updating** the **schema definition** to allow for three digit phone extensions

Functions (and their icons) in this section:

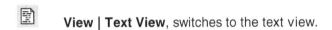 **File | New**, creates a new type of XML file.

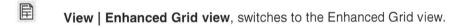 **View | Text View**, switches to the text view.

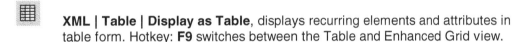 **View | Enhanced Grid view**, switches to the Enhanced Grid view.

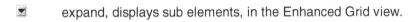 **XML | Table | Display as Table**, displays recurring elements and attributes in table form. Hotkey: **F9** switches between the Table and Enhanced Grid view.

 expand, displays sub elements, in the Enhanced Grid view.

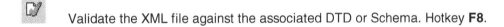 Checks for well-formedness. Hotkey: **F7**.

Validate the XML file against the associated DTD or Schema. Hotkey **F8**.

 Opens the associated DTD or Schema file.

Creating and completing a new XML file

To create a new XML document:

1. Select the menu option **File | New**, and select the **.xml XML Document** entry from the dialog, then confirm with OK.

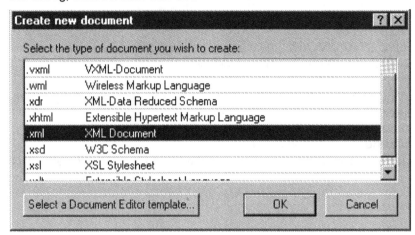

A prompt appears, asking if you want to base the XML document on a DTD or Schema.

2. Click the **Schema** radio button, and confirm with OK.

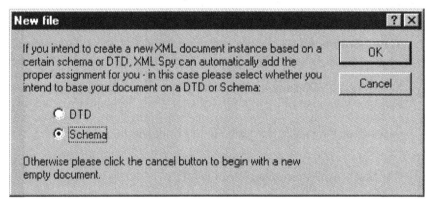

A further dialog appears, asking you to select the schema file your XML document is to be based on.

3. Use the Browse or Window buttons to find the schema file, in our case the **AddressLast** schema, and confirm the selection with OK.

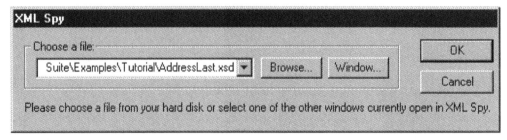

An XML document containing the main elements defined by the schema, opens in the main window. XML documents are automatically opened in the Enhanced Grid View.

Please note:
XML Spy tries to find the root element of a schema automatically. The "Select a root

element" dialog box is opened, if it is unclear which is the root element. You can then select the root element manually.

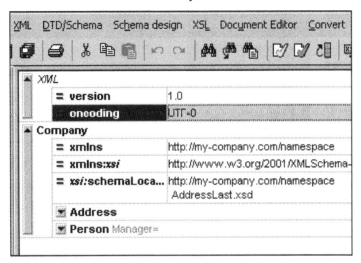

4. Click on any element to deselect the data.
5. Click on the ☒ icon next to Address, to view the Address sub-elements.

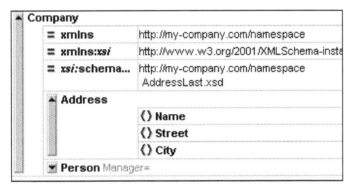

Making elementType definitions available in XML documents
The Address elements we see in the grid view are those that were defined by the global complex type "AddressType". We would, however, like to access the specific AddressTypes we defined: UK- and US-Address.

1. Right click the **Name** element, and select **Insert | Attribute** from the context menu. An attribute field is added to the Address element, and a popup containing **xsi:type** automatically opens.

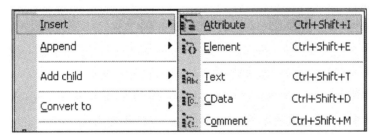

2. Hit the "Tab" key to move into the next field.
3. Select **US-Address** from the drop-down list, and confirm with Enter.

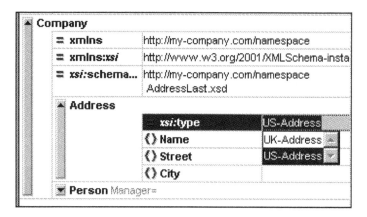

Please note:
> The *xsi* prefix allows you to use special XML Schema related commands in your XML document instance. Please see the W3C website at http://www.w3.org/TR/2001/REC-xmlschema-0-20010502 for more information.

Entering (and deleting) data

1. Double click in the **Name** value field (or use the arrow keys) and enter "US dependency", confirm with Enter.

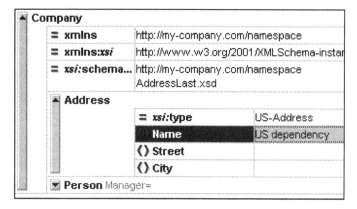

2. Use the same method to enter a **Street** and **City** name (e.g. Noble Ave. and Dallas).
3. Click the **Person** element, and hit the "**Del**" key to delete it (we will add it again in a few moments in the Text view!).
4. Click on any Address element to deselect the elements.
   Your XML document should look like this:

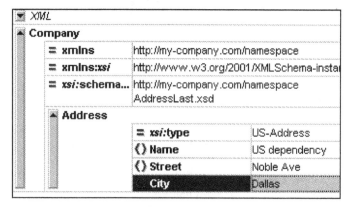

Editing in Text- and Enhanced Grid view

XML Spy Text view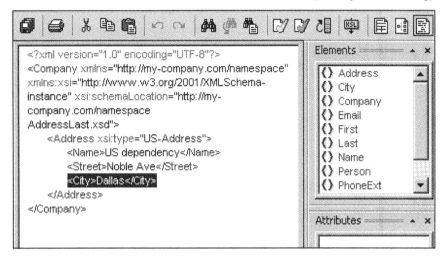
When it comes down to low-level work, the text view of XML Spy is suitable for editing any type of XML files in textual or source code form, and provides **intelligent editing** capabilities if you are working with an XML document based on a DTD or XML Schema.

Viewing and entering data in the Text view

1. Select the menu item **View | Text view**, or click on the Text view icon.
   You now see the XML document in its raw text form (with syntax coloring).

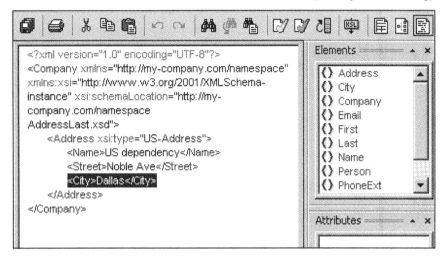

2. Place the text cursor after the </Address> | **end tag**, and hit Enter to add a new line.
3. Enter the "less than" angle bracket **<** at this position.

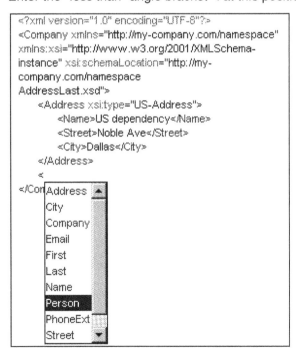

4. A drop-down list appears; select the **Person** entry.
   The element name "Person" as well as the attribute "Manager", are inserted.

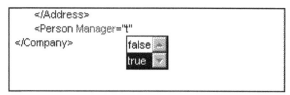

5. Enter the letter "**t**" and hit Enter.

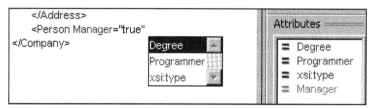

This opens a drop down list where "true" is highlighted. Enter, inserts the value (true) at the cursor positon.

6. Move the cursor to the end of the line (End key), and hit the space bar.
    This opens the drop-down list again. There are now fewer entries available in the list; "Manager" is grayed out in the Attribute entry helper.

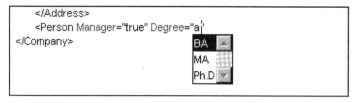

7. Select "Degree" with the Down arrow key, and hit Enter.

```
  </Address>
  <Person Manager="true" Degree="|"
</Company>
```

8. Enter any character. This opens another list box from which you can select one of the predefined enumerations (BA, MA or Ph.D).

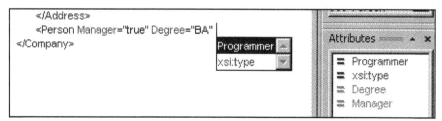

9. Select "BA" with the Down arrow key (confirm with OK), move the cursor to the end of the line (End key), and hit the space bar. Manager and Degree are now grayed out in the Attribute entry helper.

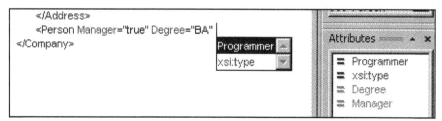

10. Select "Programmer" with the Down arrow key, and hit Enter.

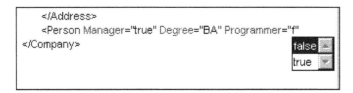

11. Enter a "**f**" character and hit Enter.
12. Move the cursor to the end of the line (End key), and enter the "greater than" angle bracket **>**.

XML Spy automatically inserts all the Person element tags. Each element is supplied with start and end tags.

You could now enter the Person data here in the text view, but why do so? The Enhanced Grid view is a lot more comfortable, and contains a special view enabling recurring data to be presented in tabular form: the Database/Table view.

Enhanced Grid view

- Select the menu item **View | Enhanced Grid View,** or click the Enhanced Grid view icon. The Person attributes (and data) entered in the Text view, are also visible in the Enhanced Grid view.

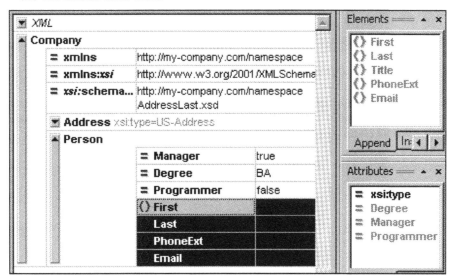

Validating and entering data

At this point let's check if the document is well-formed and valid, there might still be work to do.

To check for well-formedness:

1. Select the menu option **XML | Check well-formedness** or hit the **F7** key.
    A message appears at the bottom of the main window declaring that the document is
    well formed. Click OK to confirm and close the message.

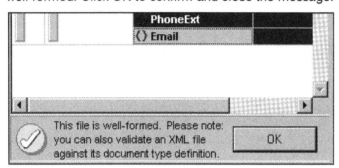

Being well-formed, means that the XML document **syntax** is correct (i.e. there is a root
element, each start tag has a corresponding end tag, all elements are nested correctly
etc.).

This check does not check against a schema file (or any other external file). Element
sequence or element content are not checked either.

To check for validity:

1. Select the menu option **XML | Validate** or hit the **F8** key.
    An **error message** appears: "This file is not valid: Mandatory elements expected after
    'City' (Zip, State).
    The error message describes in detail what is currently wrong with our XML document.

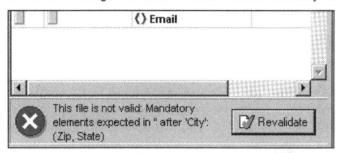

Fixing the invalid document (intelligent help):
At this point the element which is the "cause" of the error message is highlighted (City).
Take note of the **Element entry helper** (top right). The Zip element is prefixed by an
exclamation mark. This is the symbol for a **mandatory** element, and means that the US-
Address element must contain the Zip sub-element.

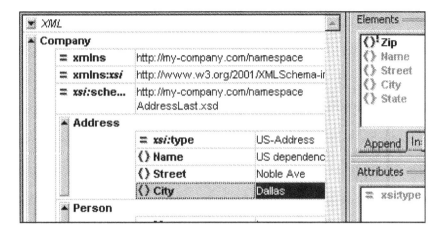

1. Double click the **!Zip** element in the **Element entry helper**.
   This inserts the Zip element under the City element (Append tab is active by default).
2. Hit the **Tab** key, enter the Zip Code of the State (04812), and confirm with Enter.
   The Element entry helper now contains the **!State** entry, which is also a mandatory element and must also appear with the Zip element.

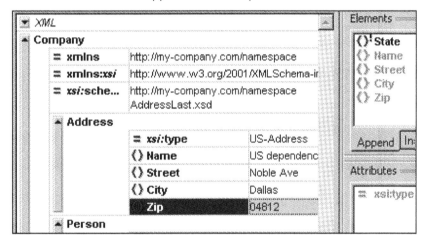

3. Double click the **!State** element, hit the Tab key and enter the name of the state (e.g. Texas), confirm with Enter.
   The Element entry helper now contains only grayed-out elements. This shows that all the required Address sub-elements have been inserted.

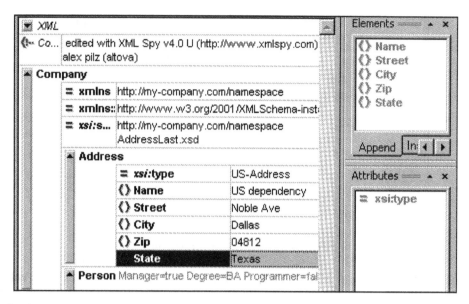

Filling in the rest of the XML document data & revalidating

1. Click the empty element content field (right of element name) of the element **First**, enter the persons first name (e.g. Fred), and hit the Enter key.

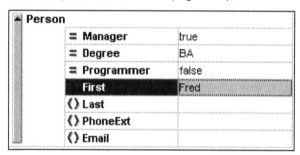

2. Hit the Down arrow key, and fill in the next field, **Last** (e.g. Smith)
3. Use the same method to enter PhoneExt (e.g. 22) and the persons e-mail address (e.g. smith@work.com). You XML document should look like this:

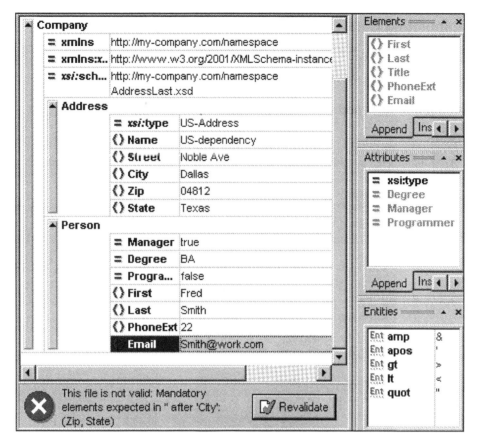

4. Click the **Revalidate** button to check if the document is valid.
   The "This file is valid" message appears. The XML document is now valid against its schema. Click OK to confirm and close the message.

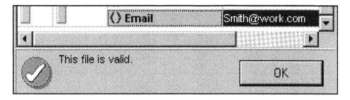

   Being valid, means that the XML document adheres to the assigned schema i.e. the elements and the sequence they appear in is correct, as well as the element "contents" and their attributes.

5. Select the menu option **File | Save As...** and name the XML document (e.g. **CompanyFirst.xml**)

This XML document is available as 'CompanyFirst.xml' in the Tutorial folder.

Please note:
   An XML document does not have to be valid in order to save it. Saving an invalid document causes a prompt to appear which then allows you to select "**Save anyway**", the document is then saved in its current state.

Manipulating data - Entry helpers

At this point we want to enter more person data in our XML document. XML Spy incorporates a special view (within the Enhanced Grid view), which allows you to enter data in tabular form - the **Database/Table view**.

Inserting elements and attributes (intelligent entry help):
We now want to add a new Person element to the document, as well as define specific person attributes.

1. Click the gray **side bar** to the left of the Address element, to collapse the Address elements.
2. Click on or below, the "**Person**" element text in the grid view.
   This marks the Person and all its sub-elements. Notice that **!Person** is now available in the Element entry helper.

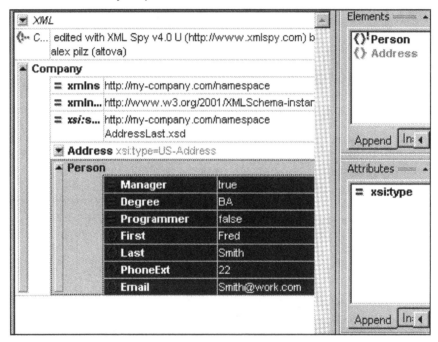

3. Double click the **!Person** element in the Element entry helper (Append tab active).
   A new Person element with all **required** sub-elements is appended.
4. Click on the **Manager** attribute of the new Person element. Notice the attributes available in the **Attribute entry helper**.

The underlying schema document delivers information to the Entry helpers, specifically the elements or attributes that can be inserted at specific points in the XML document.

Clicking the Update Entry Helpers icon, refreshes the Entry helper contents.

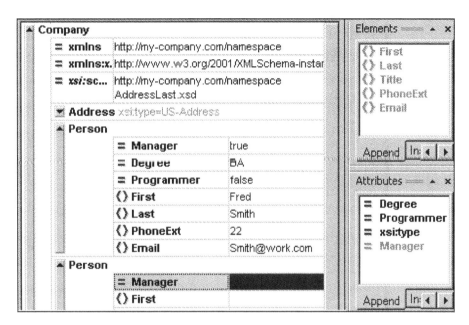

The "Manager" attribute has been **grayed out**, as it already exists in the Person element. Looking in the **Info** window, you can see all the Manager attribute information: Datatype=boolean, Occurrence=required (which means mandatory).

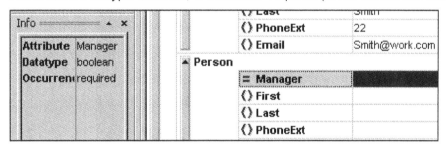

5. Double click the **Programmer** attribute in the Attribute entry helper.
This inserts an empty **Programmer attribute** after the Manager attribute (append tab is active).

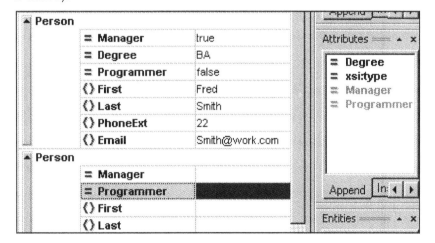

The Programmer attribute is now grayed out in the Attribute entry helper.
We could continue entering data here, but let's be more efficient and activate the Database/Table view.

Database/Table view

Database/Table view:
The Database /Table view is available wherever the Enhanced Grid view can be activated, and can be used when editing any type of XML file - XML, XSD, XSL etc.

Advantages:
- Drag and drop column headers
- Sort column (table) data using the menu command **XML | Table | Ascending Sort**
- Append (or insert) rows using the menu command **XML | Table | Insert Row**.
- Copy and paste **structured data** to and from third party products
- Intelligent entry help

Activating the Database/Table view:
1. Click on or near, Person element text in the grid view (this marks the person element).

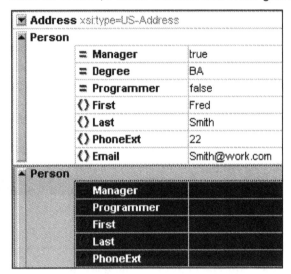

2. Select the menu option **XML | Table | Display as table**, or click the Display as table icon (Hotkey F9).
   The Person elements have now been combined into a single table. The Element and Attribute names are now the column headers, and the element contents (values) are now the rows of the table.

3. Select the menu option **View | Optimal widths**, or click the Optimal widths icon, to optimize the table view.

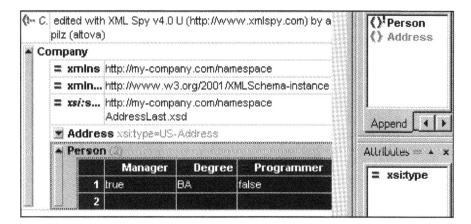

Please note:
   The element and attribute entry helpers also function in the Database/Table view. The
   element entry helper now displays the mandatory **!Person** element; double clicking it
   would add a new row to the table.

4. Double click in the "Manager" cell of row 2, and select "false". Use the Tab key to get
    to the next cells, and select the following data: Degree=MA, Programmer=true,
    First=Alfred, Last=Aldrich, PhoneExt=33 and EMail=Aldrich@work.

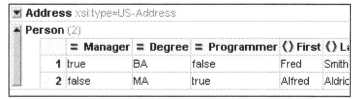

Please note:
   The **F9** key switches between Grid view and Database/Table view, of the currently
   selected table or recurring element.

Copying XML data to and from third party products

XML Spy allows you to easily copy data to and from third party products. The copied data can
be used within XML Spy as well as third-party products, enabling you to transfer XML data to
spreadsheet-like applications (e.g. Microsoft Excel).

Copying XML data to and from Excel:

1. Click on the row label 1, hold down the CTRL key and click on row label 2.
    This marks both rows of the table.

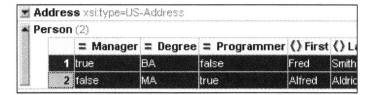

2. Select the menu option **Edit | Copy as Structured text**.
    The "Copy as Structured Text" command, copies elements to the clipboard as they
    appear on screen.
3. Switch to Excel and **paste** the XML data in an Excel worksheet.

A	B	C	D	E	F	G	H
TRUE	BA	FALSE	Fred	Smith	22	Smith@work.com	
FALSE	MA	TRUE	Alfred	Aldrich	33	Aldrich@work	

4. Enter a new row of data in Excel. Make sure that you enter a three digit number for the PhoneExt element (e.g. 444).

A	B	C	D	E	F	G	H
TRUE	BA	FALSE	Fred	Smith	22	Smith@work.com	
FALSE	MA	TRUE	Alfred	Aldrich	33	Aldrich@work	
TRUE	Ph.D	FALSE	Colin	Coletti	444	Coletti@work.com	

5. Mark the table data in Excel, select **Edit | Copy**, and switch back to XML Spy.
6. Click in the top left cell of the table data in XML Spy, and select **Edit | Paste**.

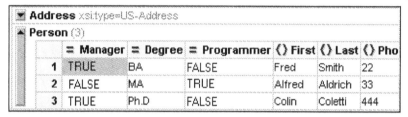

Address xsi:type=US-Address
Person (3)

	= Manager	= Degree	= Programmer	() First	() Last	() Pho
1	TRUE	BA	FALSE	Fred	Smith	22
2	FALSE	MA	TRUE	Alfred	Aldrich	33
3	TRUE	Ph.D	FALSE	Colin	Coletti	444

The updated table data is now visible in the table.

7. Change the uppercase boolean values, "TRUE/FALSE", to lowercase "true/false" using the menu option **Edit | Replace** (Hotkey CTRL+H).

Sorting data in the Database/Table view
The Database/Table view allows you to sort your XML table data by any column you wish. In this case we want to sort our table by last names.

1. Click on the **Last** column header. This marks the whole column.

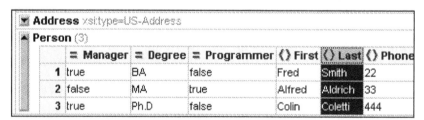

Address xsi:type=US-Address
Person (3)

	= Manager	= Degree	= Programmer	() First	() Last	() Phone
1	true	BA	false	Fred	Smith	22
2	false	MA	true	Alfred	Aldrich	33
3	true	Ph.D	false	Colin	Coletti	444

2. Select the menu option **XML | Table | Ascending sort,** or click on the "Ascending sort" icon.
    The column and **whole table** are now been sorted alphabetically (the column remains marked).

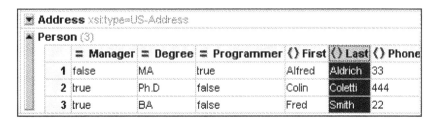

This sorting procedure affects your data at source level. (Click the Text view icon if you want to see the changes there.)

3. Select the menu option **XML | Validate**, or hit the **F8** key.
An **error message** appears: "This file is not valid: Value does not match facet **maxInclusive="99"** in element '**PhoneExt**'.

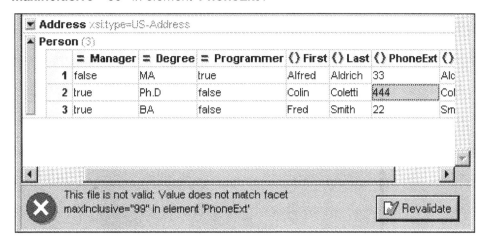

The offending element is automatically marked in the Database/table view. We need more telephone extensions!

Updating a schema definition
At this point that we realize that two digit phone extensions are definitely not enough, and that we would like to allow for three digits. To do this we have to make a change to the underlying schema document.

1. Select the menu option **DTD/Schema | Go to definition** or click the "Go to definition" icon.
The associated schema document, in this case **AddressLast.xsd**, is opened in the Schema overview.

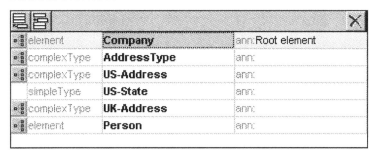

2. Click the "component" icon of the global **Person** element, and then click the PhoneExt element. You can now see the facet data in the facets tab.

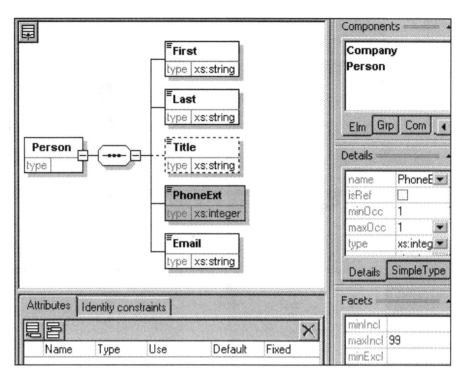

3. Click the "**maxIncl**" cell containing the facet data, enter **999**, and confirm with Enter.

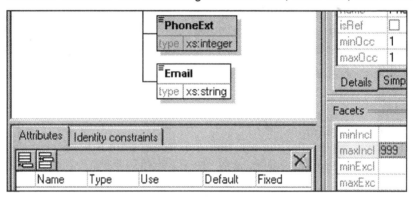

4. Hit CTRL+TAB to switch back to the XML document.
5. Click the "**Revalidate**" button to revalidate the XML document.

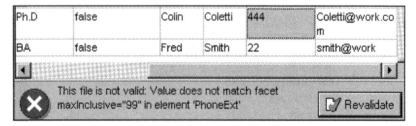

The "This file is valid" message appears. The XML document now conforms to the changed schema definition!

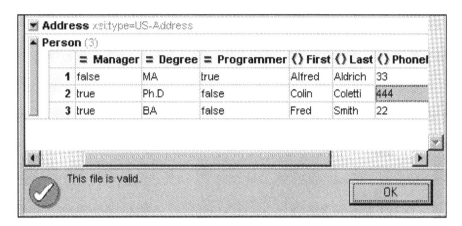

6. Select the menu option **File | Save As...** and name the XML document (e.g.
    CompanyLast.xml).
7. Hit CTRL+TAB to switch back to the schema document, and save the schema
    document.

    The XML document is available as 'CompanyLast.xml' in the Tutorial folder.

XSL Transformation

Goal of this section:
To generate a Company HTML document which can then be posted on the corporate web site.

This will be achieved by:
- **Assigning** a predefined Company.**xsl** file to the XML document
- Using the XSL file to **transform** the XML file into an HTML document

Functions (and their icons) in this section:

XSL | Assign XSL, assigns an XSL file to an XML document.
XSL | Go to XSL, opens the XSL file referenced by the XML document.

 XSL | XSL Transformation, transforms the XML document(s) into the files specified by the XSL Transformation document, in this case into an HTML file. Hotkey: **F10**.

Please note:
If you encounter a problem while generating the HTML file, you only see the table header and no XML data, please download and install the **MSXML Parser 3.0** (649 kB) from the component download center at http://www.xmlspy.com/download_components.html.

Transforming XML to HTML

To assign an XSL file to the CompanyLast XML file:

1. Click the **CompanyLast.xml** tab on the main window, to make it the active document.
2. Select the menu option **XSL | Assign XSL**.
3. Click the Browse button, select the **Company.xsl** file, and confirm with Open.

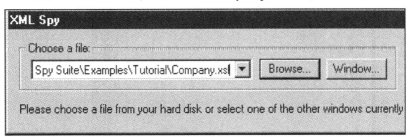

4. Click the OK button to assign the XSL file to the XML document.

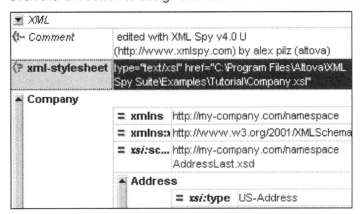

A XML-stylesheet reference is placed in the XML document.

To transform the XML document into HTML:

1. Select the menu option **XSL | XSL Transformation** or click the 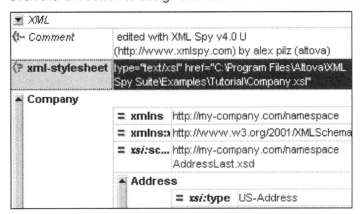 icon (Hotkey: **F10**)
   This creates a new document in the **Browser view** with the name **XSL Output.html**. It shows the Company data in one block down the left, and the Person data in tabular form below.

Changing the output of the HTML file:
You can change the appearance/output of the HTML file by editing the underlying XSL file. In this case, we want to change the table background color from lime to yellow.

1. Click the **CompanyLast.xml** tab to make it the active document.
2. Select the menu option **XSL | Go to XSL**.

The command opens the Company.XSL file referenced in the XML document.

3. Find the line <table border="1" bgcolor="lime">, and change the entry bgcolor="**lime**" to bgcolor="**yellow**".

```
<h1><center>Your Company</center></h1>
<xsl:apply-templates select="//my:Address"/>
<table border="1" bgcolor="yellow">
    <thead align="center">
        <td><strong>First</strong></td>
        <td><strong>Last</strong></td>
```

4. Select the menu option **File | Save** to retain the changes made to the XSL file.
5. Click the **CompanyLast.xml** tab to make the XML file active, and select **XSL | XSL Transformation,** or hit the **F10** key.

Your Company

Name: US dependency
Street: Noble Ave
City: Dallas
State: Texas
Zip: 04812

First	Last	Ext.	E-Mail	Manager	Degree
Alfred	Aldrich	33	Aldrich@work.com	false	MA
Colin	Coletti	444	Coletti@work.com	true	Ph.D
Fred	Smith	22	Smith@work.com	true	BA

A **new** XSL Output.html file appears in the Browser view. The table background now appears in yellow.
6. Select the menu option **File | Save**, and save the document as **Company.html**.

Importing and exporting database data

Goal of this section:
To export Person data from our address list to MS Access, and reimport the Person table into XML Spy.

This will be achieved by:

- using the menu option **Convert**, and then selecting the export or import process.

Functions (and their icons) in this section:

Convert | Export to Text files / Database, enables you to export XML data as text or for use in third party databases.

Convert | Import Database data, enables you to import database data into XML Spy.

Exporting XML data to external databases

To export data to a database:

1. Click the **CompanyLast.xml** tab on the main window, to make it the active document.
2. Select the menu option **Convert | Export to Text files / Database....**
   The default settings in this dialog export all elements, attributes, and generate primary and foreign keys.

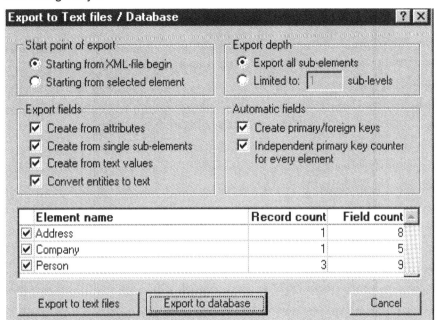

3. Click the **Export to Database** button.

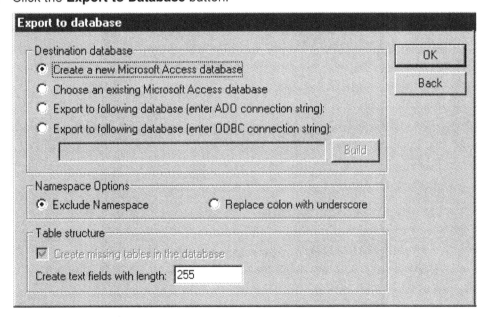

This dialog allows you to select if you want to create a new Access table, export data to an existing one, or export to a third party database. The namespace option, "Exclude Namespace" is active per default.

4. Click the **Create a new Microsoft Access database** entry, and confirm with OK.
5. Enter the name of the new database in the "Save as..." dialog (e.g. Company.mdb),

and confirm by clicking the Save button.
A progress indicator displays export progress and a message box appears when the process has been completed successfully. Click OK to confirm.

6. Open the **Company.mdb** file you just saved. The export process automatically created a table for each exported element.

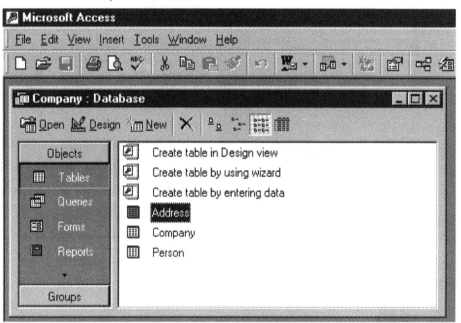

7. Double click the **Person** icon to open the Person table.
The table shows all the Person data from the XML file and includes the "Automatic fields" PrimaryKey and ForeignKey, which can be used to index the database data.

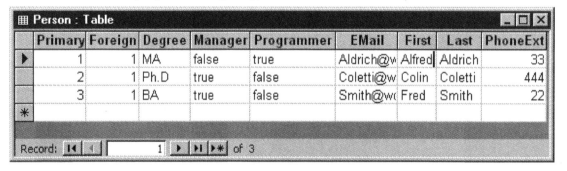

Primary	Foreign	Degree	Manager	Programmer	EMail	First	Last	PhoneExt
1	1	MA	false	true	Aldrich@w	Alfred	Aldrich	33
2	1	Ph.D	true	false	Coletti@w	Colin	Coletti	444
3	1	BA	true	false	Smith@wc	Fred	Smith	22

Record: |◄| ◄ | 1 | ► | ►| | ►* | of 3

Please note:
    If you select the "Create a new Microsoft Access database" option when **exporting** database data, XML Spy creates a new Access 2000 database!

    If you want to export data to an Access 97 database, please create an empty Access 97 database first, and then select the export option "Choose an existing Access database". There are no restrictions when **importing** data from any Access database.

Importing database data

To import data into XML Spy:
1. Select the menu option **Convert | Import Database data....**

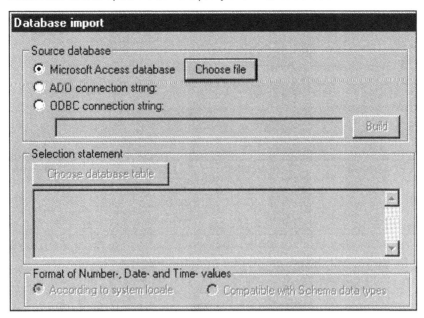

2. Click the **Choose file** button, and select the **Company.mdb** file.
    The cursor is placed in the Selection statement text box.
3. Click the **Choose database table** button, select Person and confirm with OK.
    The *SELECT * from [Person]* statement is now visible in the text box. You can extend
    the select statement, using standard SQL statements, to further filter the imported
    data.

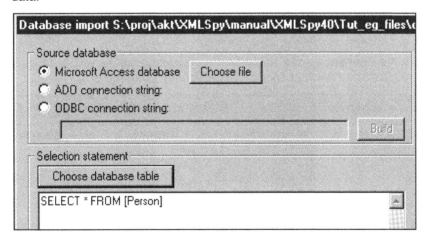

4. Click the **Preview** button to see an example of the table data you intend to import. The
    Preview window displays only those records that fulfill the select criteria.

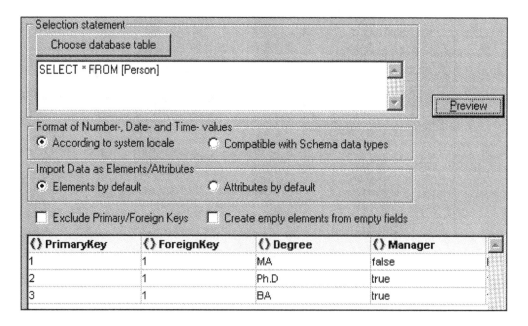

Importing fields as: attributes, elements, or skip import
The preview window allows you to directly select and define the field data you want to import.

Clicking repeatedly on the **element symbol** () to the left of the element name, cycles through the available possibilities:

()   Define and import this field as an **Element**.

≡   Define and import this field as an **Attribute**.

✕   **Skip**, do not import this field.

5. Click the **Element** symbol of the PrimaryKey column, until the **skip** symbol appears. Do the same for the ForeignKey column.
6. Click the **Element** symbol of the Degree column, until the **attribute** symbol appears. Do the same for the Manager and Programmer columns.

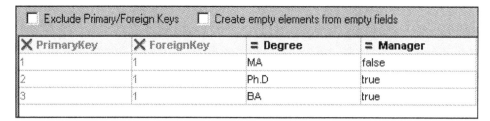

7. Click the **OK** button to start the import process.
8. Select the menu option **File | Save** and name the XML document (e.g. **Person-Import.xml**)

XML Spy creates an **untitled XML file** containing the Person table data. The **root element** is called Import, and each Person element has become a Row element.

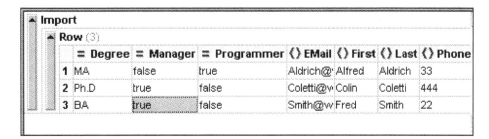

Click on the Text view icon, to get another view of the imported data.

```
<Import>
    <Row Degree="MA" Manager="false" Programmer="true">|
        <EMail>Aldrich@work.com</EMail>
        <First>Alfred</First>
        <Last>Aldrich</Last>
        <PhoneExt>33</PhoneExt>
    </Row>
    <Row Degree="Ph.D" Manager="true" Programmer="false">
        <EMail>Coletti@work.com</EMail>
        <First>Colin</First>
        <Last>Coletti</Last>
        <PhoneExt>444</PhoneExt>
    </Row>
    <Row Degree="BA" Manager="true" Programmer="false">
        <EMail>Smith@work.com</EMail>
        <First>Fred</First>
        <Last>Smith</Last>
        <PhoneExt>22</PhoneExt>
    </Row>
</Import>
```

For more information on importing data, please see the following sections in the reference section under **Menus | Convert Menu | Convert How to...**

- Setting up an ADO or ODBC connection
- Importing a table using ODBC
- Importing hierarchical data - ADO Data shaping
- Shape string examples

Creating a database schema

XML Spy enables you to create a schema based upon an external database file. Microsoft Access databases, as well as ADO and ODBC compatible databases, are supported.

Goal of this section:
To convert an existing MS Access database into a schema file, having the same table structure.

This will be achieved by:

- Using the menu option **Convert | Create Database Schema**, to create the schema in XML Spy.

- This example uses the **DB2Schema.mdb** file supplied with this tutorial. The Relationships view of the DB2schema.mdb file is visible in the diagram below. Use the menu option **Tools | Relationships** in MS Access, to view the relationships.

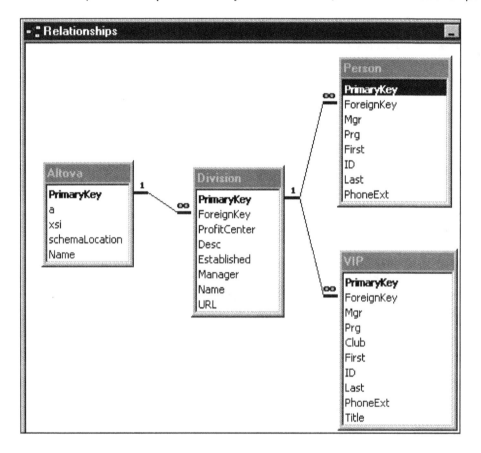

Converting a database to a schema

To create a schema from a database file:

1. Select the menu option **Convert | Create Database Schema.**

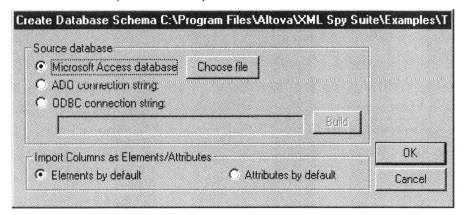

2. Select **Microsoft Access database**, and click the Choose file button.
3. Select the **DB2schema.mdb** file supplied with XML Spy, and click the **Open** button.
4. Click the **OK** button of the Create Database Schema dialog, to start the conversion process.

   The generated schema appears in the Schema Design View. Click the "Identity constraints" tab, to see the keyref and key fields of the respective elements.

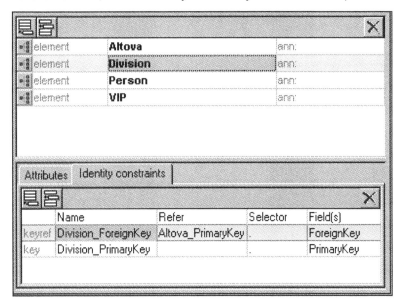

5. Click the component icon ▣ next to the **Altova** global element, to see the content model.

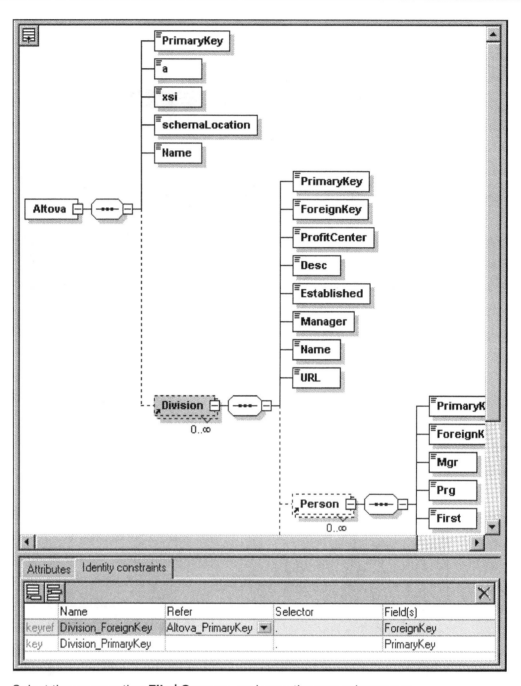

6. Select the menu option **File | Save as**, and save the new schema e.g.
    DB2schema.xsd.

7. Click the Display all globals icon ▦, to return to the schema overview.

Please note:
  When generating the schema, all namespace prefix colons are automatically
  converted into underscore characters.

Databases currently supporting the key and keyref fields:
MS Access and several other databases are able to automatically provide the key and keyref
information for the ADO driver, used to create the database hierarchy.

  Please note:

The following text describes in condensed form, how to create a database schema using other types of databases. This text is added for the sake of completeness, and is not a tutorial task. Please contact your database administrator for further information regarding the setup and use of these databases!

To create relationships for NON MS Access databases:

1. Click the "**ADO connection string**" radio button in the Create Database Schema dialog box.

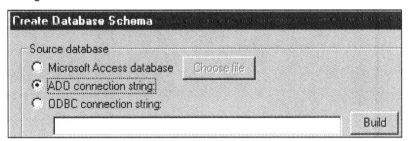

2. Click the **Build** button that has now become active.
   This opens the Data Link Properties dialog box.
3. Select the corresponding **Microsoft OLE DB Provider** (or vendor specific provider) for the database you use, do not select one of the generic drivers. Please see the "To convert from..." list at the end of this section.

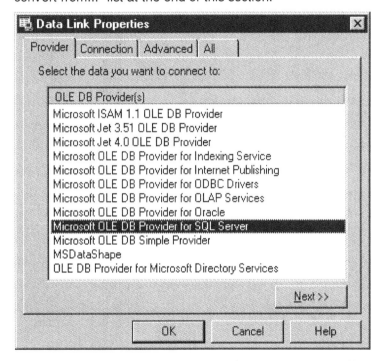

4. Click the **Next** button to switch to the Connection tab and fill in the required information: the data source, the user name and password, and activate the **Allow saving password** check box.
5. Click the Test Connection button to test the connection, and Click OK to confirm the settings.

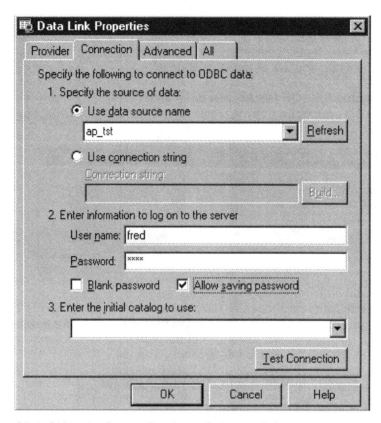

6. Click OK in the Create Database Schema dialog box, to create the schema.

To convert from... SQL server databases:
*   Select the **Microsoft OLE DB provider for SQL server** provider.

To convert from Oracle... databases:
*   Select the **Microsoft OLE DB provider for Oracle** provider.

To convert from... MS Access:
*   Click the **Microsoft Access Database** radio button in the Create Database Schema dialog box. This selects the correct provider, there is no need to use the ADO connection string and Data Link Properties dialog box.
*   If however, you want to build the connection string yourself, please use the **MicrosoftJet 4.0 OLE DB** provider.

To convert from... Other databases:
*   Select the corresponding Microsoft OLE DB, or vendor specific provider, from the Data Link Properties dialog box.

To convert from... databases without a specific provider:
Other databases will create a flat structured schema, including all tables and their corresponding datatypes.

*   Use drag and drop in the schema overview, to create the necessary relations between the imported elements.
*   To create an element hierarchy you have to directly edit the key and keyref fields, visible in the Identity constraints tab. Please see "Creating Identity Constraints" in the Reference manual for more information.

Creating a project

Goal of this section:
To create an XML Spy project that includes all the files currently open in the main window.

This will be achieved by:
- using the menu option **Project** to create a project folder
- using the specific Project commands to add files to the project

Functions (and their icons) in this section:

Project | New Project
Project | Add active and related files to project
Project | Add active file to project

Advantages of Projects:
- Files and URLs can be grouped into folders by common extension or any other criteria
- Batch processing can be applied to specific folders, or the project as a whole
- A DTD / Schema can be assigned to specific folder, allowing immediate validation
- XSL transformations can be assigned to specific folders, allowing immediate transformations
- The destination folders of XSL transformation files can be specified

  These settings can all be defined by using the menu option **Project | Project Properties**.

- XML files can be placed unter Souce control using the menu option **Project | Source control | Add to source control** (Please see the Reference manual or online help for more information).
- Personal, network and web folders can be added to projects, allowing batch validation.

Adding files to a project

Creating and adding files to a Project:
There are now many different files open in the main window. You can access these files as an unit by grouping them into an XML Spy project.

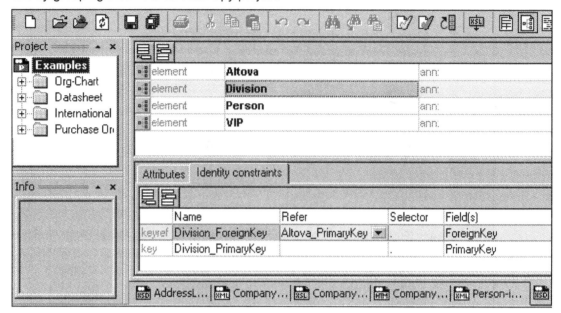

1. Select the menu option **Project | New Project**.

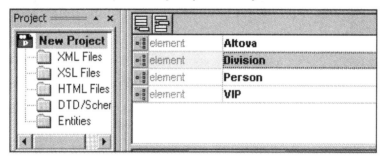

The project window now contains several folders under the New Project folder.
2. Click the **CompanyLast.xml** tab, to make it the active file in the main window.
3. Select the menu option **Project | Add active and related files to project.**

Three files have been added to the New Project folder: CompanyLast.xml, Company.xsl and AddressLast.xsd.
4. Click the **Person-import.xml** tab, and then select the menu option **Project | Add active file to project**.

5. Use the same method to add the **Company.html** and **DB2schema.xsd** files to the project. The project should now look like the diagram below.

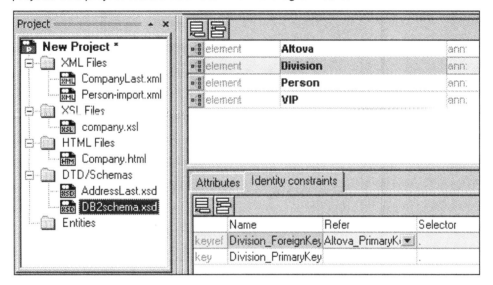

6. Select the menu option **Project | Save Project** and enter "**Tutorial**" as the project name.

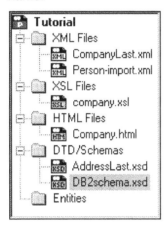

To delete files from a project:
1. Click on the file you want to delete in the project window, and hit the **Delete** key.

To add new folders to a project:
1. Select the menu option **Project | Add folder to Project**, and fill in the Properties dialog.

To add a file to a specific folder:
1. Click the file to make it active in the main window.
2. **Right click** the **folder** you want to place the active file into (in the Project window), and select the menu option "**Add active file**".
   This method allows you to add a file to any folder in the current project.

That's it !

If you have come this far congratulations, and thank you!

We hope that this tutorial has been helpful in introducing you to the basics of XML Spy. If you need more information please use the context-sensitive online help system, or print out the Tutorial.PDF file that accompanied your version of XML Spy.

If you have any comments regarding the tutorial, please feel free to contact us at support@xmlspy.com.

Part III

3   User Reference

The reference section contains a complete description of all XML Spy windows and menu commands and explains their use in general.

We've tried to make this user manual as comprehensive as possible. If you have questions which are not covered by this documentation and you are a registered user, please don't hesitate to contact us through the Support Center on the XML Spy web site.

Windows

The XML Spy user interface provides several windows that show both your document, project and intelligent editing "entry-helper" windows, that can be freely arranged to suit your personal working style.

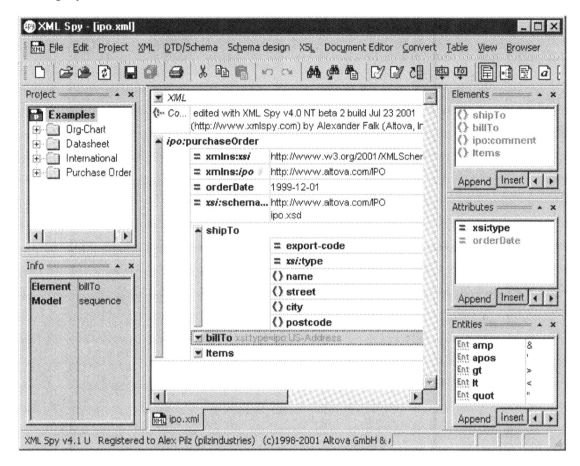

The central area shows the main window, where you edit (and view) your XML, XML Schema, or XSL documents in the Enhanced Grid view, Schema view, Text view, Document Editor view, embedded Database/table view, or Browser view.

The left area contains the project and info windows; the right area contains the entry helpers for intelligent editing of elements, attributes, and entities.

Main Window

The Main Window is where you view and edit all documents in XML Spy. XML Spy allows you to open any number of XML documents simultaneously. To switch between them click on the any part of the window you wish to bring to the front.

You can also use the commands on the Window menu to organize your windows. If your windows are maximized, XML Spy also provides tabs, letting you switch between all open windows. Keyboard equivalents are: CTRL+TAB and CTRL+F6.

Right click on a tab, opens the context-menu enabling you to perform various functions on that XML document. (e.g. print, close, mail etc.).

XML Spy provides advanced views on your documents:
- An Enhanced Grid View for structured editing
- An embedded Database/Table view, available from within the Enhanced Grid view, that shows repeated elements in a tabular fashion
- A Schema Design View for viewing and editing XML Schemas
- A Text View with syntax-coloring for source-level work,
- A Document Editor view allowing you to edit XML documents based on templates created in XSLT Designer, and
- An integrated Browser View that supports both CSS and XSL style-sheets.

To switch any main window between the different views, use the commands on the View menu or the corresponding toolbar buttons.

Please note:
You can set your personal default viewing preferences on a per-file-type basis in the File Types tab on the Tools | Options dialog. Select the menu option **Tools | Options** to open this dialog box.

Enhanced Grid View

Click the Enhanced Grid View icon to open this view.

The Enhanced Grid View is the core presentation and editing view of XML Spy. It shows the hierarchical structure of any XML-compliant document through a set of nested containers, that can be easily expanded and collapsed to get a clear picture of the document's structure.

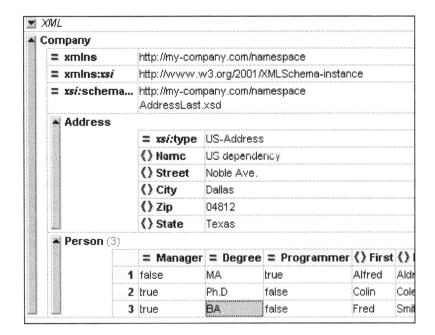

All items contained in an XML document are displayed in a structured way that allows for easy manipulation of contents and structure at the same time.

An hierarchical item (such as the XML declaration, document type declaration, or any element that contains child elements) is represented with a gray side bar and a tiny arrow. Clicking the side bar expands or collapses the item.

Please note:

An element is denoted with the () icon, eg. () **header**

An attribute is denoted with the ≡ icon, eg. ≡ style

Display & Navigating
The contents of an hierarchical item depend on its kind and – in the case of elements – mostly consists of attributes, character data, comments and child elements.

Element and Attribute order
To emphasize the strong coupling between attributes and the respective parent element, **attributes are always listed first** and cannot be preceded by comments, character data or child elements. The order of the individual attributes is, however, preserved from the input file and can be modified if necessary.

Following the attributes, the remaining items within an element appear exactly in the order found in the source file, and can be rearranged without restriction using drag & drop.

Elements and character data
If an element contains only character data, the data will be shown in the same line as the element and the element will not be considered hierarchical by nature. The character data for any other element will be shown indented with the attributes and potential child elements and will be labeled as "Text".

If an element is collapsed, its attributes can be shown in the same line in a different color. This attribute preview is especially helpful, when editing XML documents that contain a huge number of elements of the same kind that only differ by their contents and attributes (e.g. database-like applications).

Customizing the grid view
The grid view can easily be customized using the mouse to adjust column widths.

To resize a column to the width of its largest entry:
1.   Double-click on the grid line to the right of that column.

To adjust the column widths to display all content:
1.   Select the menu item View | Optimal widths command, or click on the Optimal widths icon .

The heights of the cells are generally determined by their contents and can only be adjusted by the user using the menu option **Tools | Options| View** tab **| Enhanced Grid view,** "Limit cell height to xx lines".

You can also use the keyboard to navigate an XML document in the Enhanced Grid View.
•   The arrow keys move the selection bar in the tree and grid views
•   the + and – keys on the numeric keypad allow you to expand and collapse items.

Please note:
You can activate the Text view icon at any time, to see marked data in the source file for example.

Embedded Database/Table view
XML Spy allows you to display recurring elements in a Database/Table view. This function is available wherever the Enhanced Grid view can be activated, and can be used when editing any type of XML file - XML, XSD, XSL etc.

Intelligent editing
When editing an XML document based on a DTD or Schema, the Enhanced Grid View provides many Intelligent Editing features based on the information gathered from the Schema or DTD.

Whenever editing the **name** of an element or attribute, a popup menu opens. The options available depend on the position of the element and the content model defined by the Schema or DTD. A similar popup is displayed, if the contents of an element or attribute are restricted by an enumeration or choice of some sort.

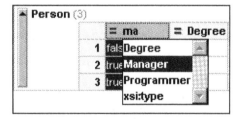

To edit an element or attribute name:
1.   Double click on the element name.
2.   Edit the name (XML Spy chooses the best match from the menu).
3.   Accept the selection by hitting the Return key (Esc. abandons the change).

To insert or append elements or attribute names:
1.   Click on the respective icon in the Attr. & Element toolbar, or

2. Double click on an element or attribute name in one of the Entry Helpers.

You will notice that the various Entry Helpers are constantly updated depending on the current selection in the Enhanced Grid View. The Info Window constantly shows important information regarding the selected element or attribute.

Enhanced Grid View context menu
In addition to the commands available through menus and toolbars, the Enhanced Grid View also provides a context-menu, activated by the right mouse-button. It contains the most useful commands in one convenient place.

Enhanced Grid View context menu:

Database/Table View

Having clicked the Enhanced Grid View icon, click on the "Display as Table" icon.

The Database/Table View is integrated into the Enhanced Grid View, and allows you to view recurring elements in grid or compressed into table form. The Database /Table view is available wherever the Enhanced Grid view can be activated, and can be used when editing any type of XML file - XML, XSD, XSL etc.

You can switch between both views, grid and table, by clicking the "Display as Table" icon or pressing the **F9** hotkey.

Editing in the table view supports drag&drop and intelligent editing functions. You can also use table-specific commands to sort elements or insert new rows.

XML documents often contain sequences of repeating elements of the same kind. XML Spy automatically detects such sequences and rearranges the presentation to show these elements in a tabular fashion - common to database- or spreadsheet-like applications.

XML Spy achieves this database/table view by taking the respective attributes and sub-elements of the repeating element, and showing them as columns of the table.

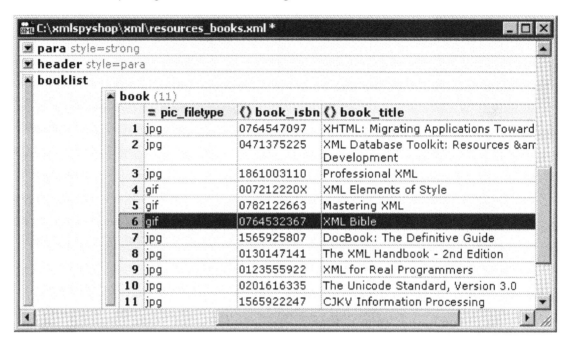

To display recurring elements in a table view:
1. Click on the recurring element in the Enhanced Grid View (flag, in this example). The "Display as table" icon is now active.

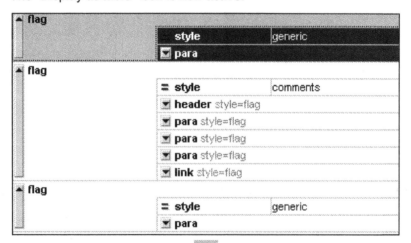

2. Click the "Display as table" icon ⊞ to activate the Table View, or select the menu

option **XML | Table | Display as Table**. The keyboard shortcut for this function is **F9**.

flag (9)			
	= style	**() header**	**() para**
1	comments	**header** style=flag	**para** align=center
			para
2	generic		**para**
3	comments	**header** style=flag	
4	generic		**para**
5	comments	**header** style=flag	**para** style=flag
			para style=flag
			para style=flag
6	generic		**para**
7	comments	**header** style=flag	**para** style=flag
8	generic		**para**
9	generic		**para** align=center

The nine "flag" elements are displayed in table form. Click in a cell to demark the table.

To return to the grid view, from the table view:
1. Click on the table "name" (flag (9) in this eg.). This selects the whole table.
2. Click the "Display as Table" icon, to deactivate the Table view and return to the Grid view.

Manipulating table data:
- Drag and drop column headers to move columns
- Sort column data using the menu command **XML | Table | Ascending Sort**
- Append (or insert) rows using the menu command **XML | Table | Insert Row**.

Exchanging data from the Database/Table view
To exchange with other applications, select elements in this table and use the copy as structured text option to copy/paste them directly into Excel for example. Data exchange works in both ways. You can therefore copy data from any spreadsheet-like application and insert it directly into XML Spy.

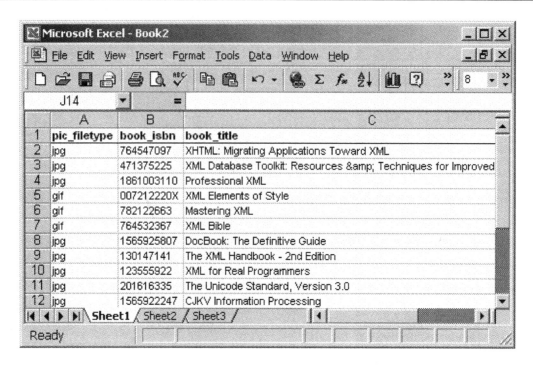

For more complex data exchange tasks, XML Spy also offers a set of unique conversion functions that let you directly import or export XML data from any text file, Word document or database.

Schema Design View

This is the default view when you double click an .XSD file.

Click the Schema Design view icon, [icon] to display W3C conformant schemas.

A Schema is a model describing the structure of information. A Schema in XML, describes the possible arrangement of tags and text in a valid document. The purpose of a schema is to allow machine validation of document structure, to enable large volume XML transactions over the web.

Schemas are defined in terms of constraints:
- The **content model** constraint, describes order and sequence of elements
- The **datatype** constraint, defines the valid units of data in the content model

Instead of using the syntax of XML 1.0 DTD declarations, schema definitions use XML element syntax. A correct XML schema definition is, therefore, a well-formed XML document.

XML Spy features:
- Supports the Final XML Schema Recommendation of May 2nd 2001, and the ability to convert schemas from the April 7th 2000 Working Draft, or Oct. 24th Candidate Recommendation to the Final Recommendation.
- Generation of DTD/Schema from an XML document
- Conversion of DTD/Schema to different Schema flavors (DTD, DCD, XML-Data, BizTalk, W3C-Schema)
- Generation of XML Schema documentation in Word or HTML format

Viewing and editing XML Schema documents
XML Spy Schema editor allows you to view and edit schemas in two different ways:

- As a Schema overview, in list form
- In a graphical view of specific schema components

Schema overview

Open a XSD document in the DTD/Schemas folder of the project window, or double click on an XSD document in Explorer. The main window then displays the Schema overview.

The top window displays all Global "definitions" (elements, complex types etc.) in list form. The bottom window displays the corresponding attributes of the currently selected component (eg. Mgr. Prg etc.).

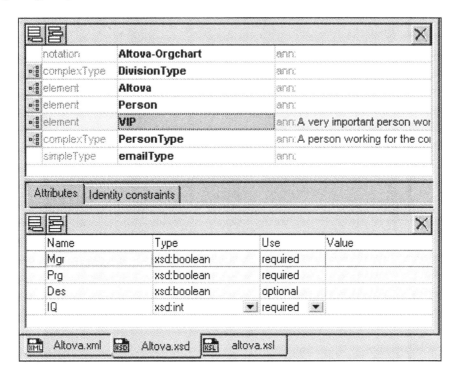

Content model

The content model is a graphical representation of a component. The tree structure as well as annotations etc. are shown for each element. This view supports drag and drop. Configure this view by selecting the menu option **Schema design | View config**.

To see graphical representation (Content model) of a component:

- Click on the 📇 icon next to the component you want to display, or
- Select the menu option **Schema design | Display Diagram,** or
- Double click on a component name in the "Component Navigator" (Top right entry helper).

The *content model* for that component, appears in a tree view.

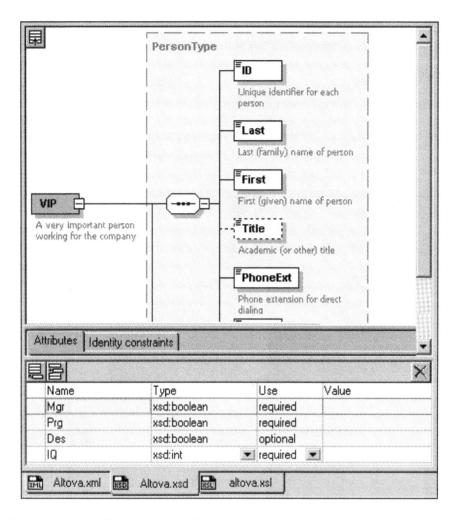

To return to the Schema overview:

- Click the "Show Globals" icon ![icon] to return to the Schema Overview.
- Select the menu option **Schema design | Display All Globals**.

To append or insert Components:

1. Click the Append ![icon] or Insert ![icon] icon at the top left of the component window.
2. Select the component you want to append from the popup.

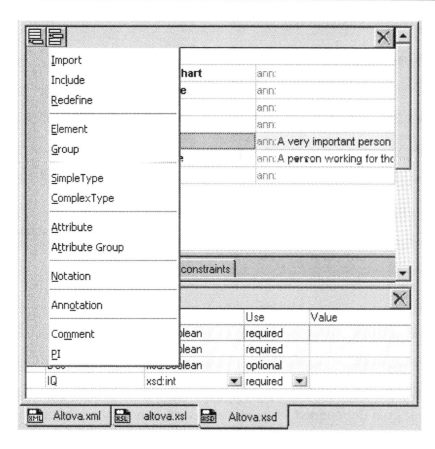

To append or insert Attributes to a component:

1. Click the Append 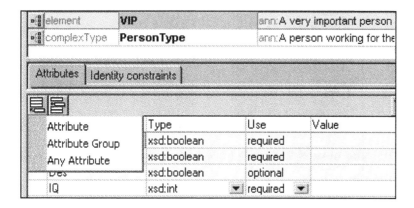 or Insert icon at the top left of the attribute window.
2. Select the attribute you want to append/insert from the popup.

Schema design content model

The content model view, enables you to directly manipulate the symbols depicting your schema. You can insert or append elements, as well as change their parameters directly.

Element Symbols

Mandatory single element. Details: MinOcc=1, MaxOcc=1

Name

Mandatory single element, containing Parsed Character Data (#PC-Data).
The content may be simple content or mixed complex content.
Details: MinOcc=1, MaxOcc=1, type=xsd:string, content=simple.

Location

Single optional element. Details: MinOcc=0, MaxOcc=1
The context menu option **Optional,** converts a mandatory element into an optional one.

Alias
1..5

Mandatory multiple element. Details MinOcc=1, MaxOcc=5.

Division
1..∞

Mandatory multiple element containing child elements.
Details: MinOcc=1, MaxOcc=unbounded, type=DivisionType, content=complex.
The context menu option **Unbounded,** changes the max. occurrence of an element to
unbounded.

Clicking on the + character of the element expands the tree view and shows the child
elements.

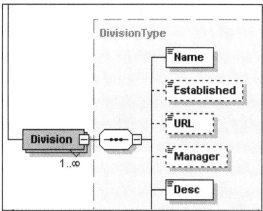

Group element. Details: name=Subsidiaries.
A named collection of elements to allow reuse in the construction of different complex types.

"Any" can be a placeholder for any element from a certain namespace.

Please note:
To display the definition of any element, hold down the CTRL key, and double click on the
element you want to see the definition of.

To add / insert / append, elements or child elements:
1. Click right on the element (or "model type" symbol), to open the context menu.
2. Select the operation you want to carry out from the menu.

Please note:
Only those operations that are possible with the element, appear in the context menu.
Invalid operations are grayed out in the context menu and cannot be selected.

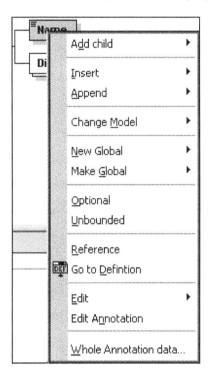

Simple types:
A "simple type" element, is defined as a datatype that only contains values and no element or
attributes. The element type is usually prefixed by the namespace prefix **xsd: string**,
indicating that it is a predefined XML Schema datatype.

Details: name=Name, type=xsd:string, content=simple.

Complex types:
"Complex type" is a datatype which may contain attributes, elements and text.
Adding sub elements to an element, automatically defines the element with the content model
as complex (Details entry helper content=complex.). Click on the "Com" tab of the component
navigator, to see the complex types.

XML Spy displays references to "external" complex types with a yellow background. In the
example below, the Person element references the PersonType complex element.

To view the referenced complex type element:
1. Double click the complex type name in the yellow box (here, PersonType), or
2. Click on the "Com" tab of the Component Navigator, and double click on the

PersonType entry.

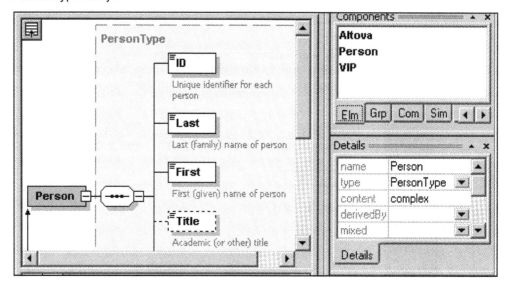

The PersonType element definition, appears in the main window.

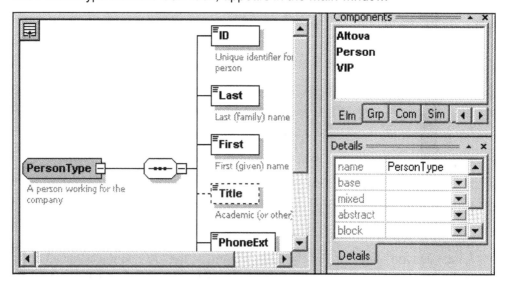

Schema, Content model

XML Spy enables you to define your content model with a few mouse clicks. All element types and methods of combining them can be defined in the content model.

Compositors
A "Compositor" defines an ordered sequence of sub elements (child elements).

To insert a compositor:
1. Click right on the element you want to add sub elements to.
2. Select **Add Child | Sequence** (Choice or All).
3. Click right on the compositor symbol and select **Add Child | Element**, to add further sub elements.

Sequence:

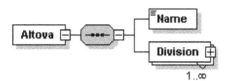

Choice:

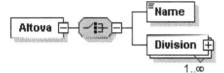

All:

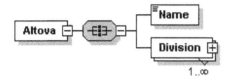

To change the compositor (model)
1. Click right on the compositor.
2. Select **Change Model | Sequence** (Choice or All).

Global components
There are two methods of defining global components: creating a new component from scratch, or changing an existing element into global component.

To create a global component from scratch:
1. Click the Insert / Append icon in the **Schema Overview**, and select the type of component you want (Element, Group, SimpleType, ComplexType etc.)
2. Enter the name of the component in the global list, and confirm with OK.

The global component appears in the respective tab (Elm, Grp, Com, Sim etc.) of the Component navigator. Double clicking on the component, displays the tree view of that component in the main window.

> Please note:
> You can create a global element while viewing a component in the content model. Click right in the main window, and select the option **New Global | Element**.

To delete a global component:
1. Switch to the Schema global overview, select the component and hit the delete key, or
2. Click the Delete icon ![X icon] of the component window.

To change an element into a global component:
1. Click right on the element and select **Make Global | Element.**

If the element is a complex type, then the option **Make Global | Complex type** becomes available.

References to global components
A reference to a global component can be created in two ways:
- You add a component to a schema which has the same name as an existing global

---

component. This causes a dialog box to appear, prompting you if you want to reference the element to it. Confirming with OK, references the component to the component definition.

- You right click an element and select the option **Reference** from the context menu.

In both cases, a link icon appears at the bottom left of the element symbol 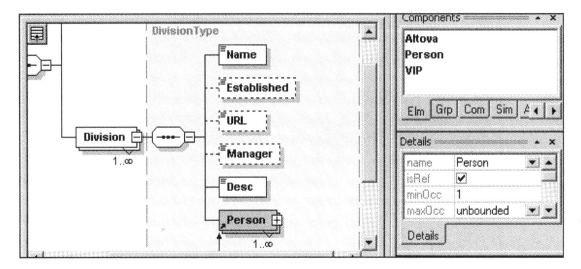 and check box "**isRef**" is set active in the Details entry helper.

Please note:
> If you create a reference to a component that does not exist, the element name appears in red as a warning that there is no definition to refer to.

To view the definition of an element:
- Use the Hotkey **CTRL+Double click** on an element.
  The element definition appears, along with the corresponding info in the details window, or
- Right click the element and select **Go to Definition** from the context menu.

To edit the name of an element:
1. Right click the element
2. Select the context menu option **Edit | Name** and edit the name. (Double clicking the element name, also enables you to edit the name.)

To edit the annotation of an element:
1. Right click the element.
2. Select the context menu option **Edit Annotation**. (Double clicking the element annotation, also enables you to edit the annotation.)

To edit (or create) appinfo for an element:
1. Right click the element.
2. Select the context menu option Whole Annotation Data.
   This opens the Annotation dialog box. If an element contains annotation text, then a row is visible when the dialog box is opened. The annotation type "doc", is displayed in the Kind column and the annotation text is visible in the Content text box.

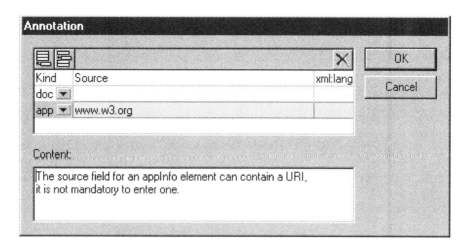

3. Click the append 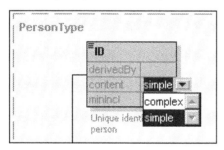or insert icon at the top left, to insert a new line. This automatically inserts a new "doc" line.
4. Click the drop down arrow next to the new doc line, and select "app".
5. Double click in the Source column to enter a URI, it is not mandatory that you enter one however.
6. Enter the appinfo content text, in the Content text box.

Configuring the content model view
- Select the menu command **Schema design | View config**.

This command allows you to **configure** the content model view. The dialog box opens at the bottom right of the XML Spy window, giving you room to see changes reflected in the content model immediately. The settings you define here, apply to the schema documentation output as well the printer output.

Changing element parameters/values directly in the content model
- Double click the cell of the element (table) you want to edit and start entering data. If a selection is possible, a drop down list appears if not, enter the parameter or value and confirm the entry with the Return key.

The entry helpers will be updated at this point, reflecting the data you entered.

Documenting the content model
- Select the menu command **Schema design | Generate documentation**.

This command **generates** detailed documentation about your schema. Documentation is generated for each element using the settings you define in the dialog box. Related elements (child elements, complex types etc.) are hyperlinked, enabling you to navigate from element to element.

Text View

Click the Text view icon,  to open this view.

When it comes down to low-level work, the text view of XML Spy is ideally suited for XML editing in its textual or source form.

The text view can be used to edit any kind of text file (even non-XML conforming documents) and offers customizable syntax-coloring (including the ability to highlight server-side VBScript or JScript code in ASP pages) as well as an automatic display of the current line and character position in the status bar.

You can use the Find and Replace commands to quickly locate or change any information, and XML Spy offers unlimited levels of Undo and Redo for all your editing operations.

Intelligent Editing
If you are working with an XML document based on a DTD or XML Schema, XML Spy provides you with various intelligent editing capabilities.

1. Type the "<" less-than character at the position you want to insert an XML element, attribute, or attribute value.
   This opens a popup list.
2. Enter the first few characters of the item you want to insert.
   An item containing those characters is highlighted.

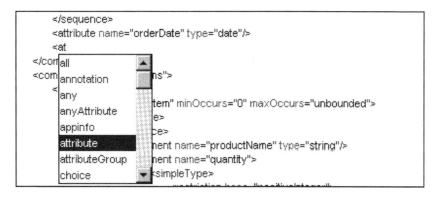

3. Click on the entry with the mouse pointer, or
    Use the arrow keys to highlight your selection and
4. Hit the Return or Space key to accept the selected choice and close the popup window.

Please note:
    The popup window also appears when you edit elements or attributes in Text view. If a
    specific attribute is defined to follow an element, a popup window containing all valid
    attributes will also appear.

Eg.

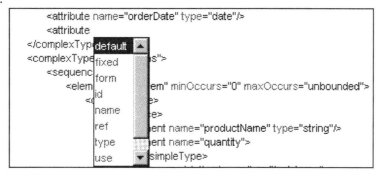

Auto-completion
Editing in the text view can easily result in unbalanced brackets, elements that are not closed
properly, or other violations of the well-formedness principle.

XML Spy automatically completes elements as well as inserting all required attributes as soon
as you finish entering the element name on your keyboard. The cursor is automatically
positioned between the start and end tags of the element, so that you can immediately
continue to add child elements or contents:

```
<img src="" alt="">|</img>
```

Use the Check well-formedness command at any time to ensure that the document meets the
XML 1.0 Specification criteria for well-formedness. This check is also automatically performed
every time you open or save a document.

Mouse & Context-Menu
You can also use the mouse during editing in the Text View. If you select text, you can either
use drag&drop to move the text block to a new location, or you can use the context-menu on
the right mouse button, to directly access frequently used editing commands - such as Cut,
Copy, Paste, Delete, Send by Mail, and Go to line/char:

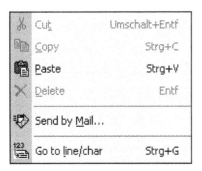

While most customers prefer the Enhanced Grid or Database/Table view for every-day work on XML data files, the text view can occasionally be very handy when editing XSL files or if you are using Active Server Pages (ASP) or any other non-XML files for your web application.

Document Editor view

Click the Document Editor icon, [icon] to open this view.

XML Spy Document Editor enables you to edit XML documents **based on templates created in XSLT Designer!** The templates in XSLT Designer are saved as ***.sps** files, and supply all the necessary information needed by Document Editor.

Templates are **opened** by Selecting the **File | New** command and then clicking the "Select a Document Editor template..." button. Please see the Document Editor documentation for further information.

Document Editor features:
- Free-flow WYSIWYG text editing
- Form-based data input
- Presentation and editing of repeating XML elements as tables
- Real-time validation, and consistency checking using XML Schema

XML Spy Document Editor is available in three versions: As a stand-alone application, integrated as a separate view within the XML Spy IDE user-interface (if you purchase the XML Spy Suite product), or as a Browser Plug-In for Internet Explorer.

Document Editor has two main areas: the main window, and the entry helpers at right. The graphic below shows the OrgChart template with all the markup info hidden.

- The **main window** allows you to display the document in several different views: the Document Editor view which is the default view for this type of document template, the Enhanced Grid view or Text view. The Enhanced Grid view incorporates a special view, called the Database/Table view, which collapses recurring XML data into table form.

- The **right area** contains three Entry helper windows, which allow you to insert specific elements (or attributes) depending on the current cursor position in the document.

Example of a partially filled in **Orgchart** template document.

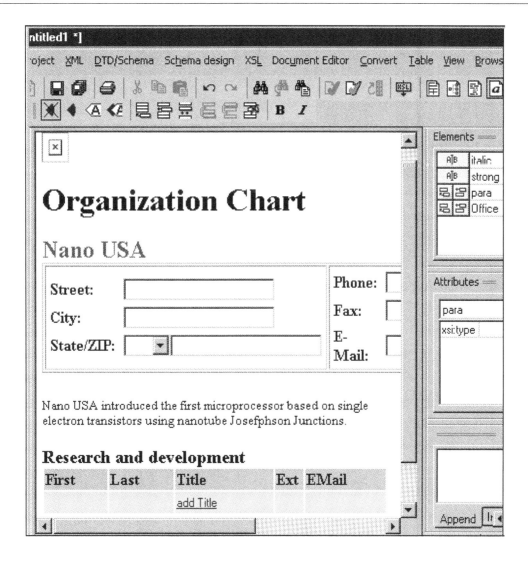

Browser View

Click the Browser View icon, 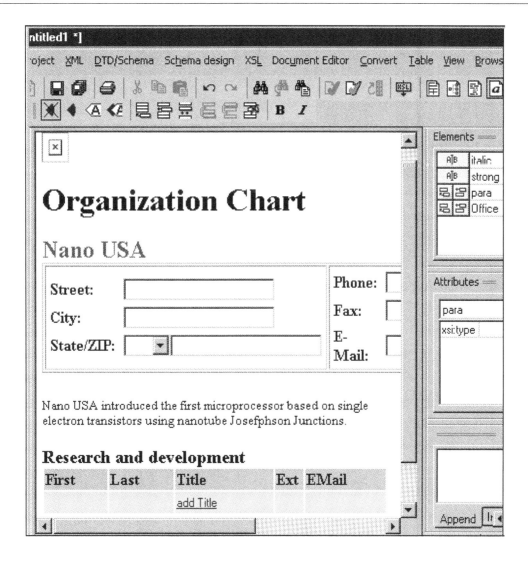 to open this view.

The Browser view requires Microsoft Internet Explorer 5, and we highly recommend you to also download the MSXML4 if you intend to work with XSLT in XML Spy, as MSXML4 already supports most of the W3C XSLT Recommendation. Please see our Download Center for more details.

Use the integrated browser view of XML Spy to preview any XML file with an XSL stylesheet, or view the output from an XSLT transformation to HTML.

```
┌─────────────────────────────────────────────────────────────────────────┐
│ ▓▓ Default.html                                                           │
├─────────────────────────────────────────────────────────────────────────┤
│                                                                           │
│    ■ 2001-10-19    Altova releases ■ XML Spy 4.1, which now includes      │
│                    support for XSL:FO (Formatting Objects).               │
│                                                                           │
│    ■ 2001-09-21    Altova   releases  ■ XML  Spy  4.0.1  -  a  maintenance │
│                    update  that  addesses several issues with the         │
│                    original 4.0 release                                   │
│                                                                           │
│    ■ 2001-09-10    The new ■ XML Spy 4.0 Product Line is released         │
│                                                                           │
│    ■ 2001-06-12    Altova becomes a sponsor of OASIS.                     │
│                                                                           │
│    ■ 2001-04-17    XML Spy 3.5 Tutorial available now. Experience how     │
│                    easy XML schema design can be. Download free from      │
│                    our ■ Download Center.                                 │
│                                                                           │
│    ■ 2001-04-11    XML Spy wins SD Magazines ■ Jolt Productivity Award.   │
│  ◄░░░░░░░░░░░░░░░░░░░░░░░░░░░░░░░░░░░░░░░░░░░░░░░░░░░░░░░░░░░░░░░░░░░░░░░    │
└─────────────────────────────────────────────────────────────────────────┘
```

Displaying source code and Browser views:
If you are using XML Spy for XHTML editing or if you have an XSL stylesheet associated with your XML document, you can display the browser view in a separate window.

This allows you to take a look at the document source in the Enhanced Grid or Text views and have the browser preview side-by-side, so that it can easily be refreshed directly from the editing view (just hit F5 in the editing view and the browser view is automatically updated).

The browser view also supports find and printing functions for when you want to document XML files that use CSS or XSL style-sheets, and offers the typical browser commands from both the Browser menu and toolbar: Back, Forward, Stop, Refresh.

Project Window

XML Spy uses the familiar tree view to manage multiple files or URLs in XML projects. Files and URLs can be grouped into folders by common extension or any arbitrary criteria to allow easy structuring and batch manipulation.

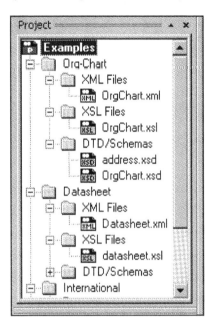

Folders can correspond to physical directories on your file system, or you can define file-type extensions for each folder to keep common files in one convenient place.

Project folders are "semantic" folders, that represent a logical grouping of files and do **not** necessarily need to correspond to any hierarchical organization of the files on your hard disk into several directories.

Assigning XSL transformations to project folders

You can assign different XSL transformation parameters to each folder and even have the same physical file present in more than one project folder - this is especially useful when you want to keep your data in one XML file and use different XSL stylesheets to produce different output (e.g. separate HTML and WML presentations).

The menu option **XSL | Assign XSL**, can only be selected when you are in the Enhanced Grid view.

Assigning DTDs / Schemas to project folders

You can assign different DTDs or Schemas to different folders. This allows you to validate a file against both a DTD and an XML Schema without changing the file itself, which is useful when you are in the process of making the transition from DTDs to Schemas.

The menu option **DTD/Schema | Assign DTD (Assign Schema)**, can only be selected when you are in the Enhanced Grid view.

Use the commands on the Project menu to manage your projects.

Entry Helper Windows

XML Spy helps you create valid XML documents by providing three palette-like windows that we call "entry helpers".

When you are working on an XML document based on a DTD or Schema, the built-in Intelligent Editing module constantly displays information on elements, attributes, and entities that can be inserted at the current cursor position, based on the information gathered from the Schema or DTD content model.

Element Entry-Helper

The **element** entry helper, allows you to insert a new element into your document by showing what elements are permissible at the current location.

You can choose to **append** an element, **insert** it before the selected element or **add** a **child**-element to the currently selected element. Depending on this context, the entry helper will automatically adjust its list of available choices.

Mandatory elements are automatically highlighted by an exclamation mark "!"

Elements that are allowed within the current parent element, but not at the position of the current selection, are shown in **gray**.

To insert an element:
- Double-click on the desired item.
  The corresponding element is inserted into the XML document, and the entry helper is automatically updated to reflect your new options.

Should you create a sequence of elements that violate the content model specified by your schema or DTD, the built-in incremental validating parser automatically detects this violation and displays its error message directly in the entry helper window.

In the **Schema Design View**, this window is called the **Component Navigator**, and displays information on **Global Components**: elements, groups, complex types, simple types, attributes and attribute groups.

To display the content model of a component:
- Click the component type tab (Elm, Grp. etc.), and
- Double click on the desired component, in the respective tab.

The content model appears in the main window as a graphic.

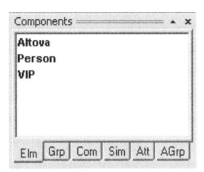

Attribute Entry-Helper

A list of available attributes for the element you are currently editing, are shown in the second palette-window and offer the same functionality as the element entry helper.

Mandatory attributes are automatically highlighted by an exclamation mark "!"

Existing attributes that cannot be added to the current element a second time - are shown in **gray**.

In the **Schema Design View**, this window is called **Details**, and displays information on the currently selected element of the content model.

To change content model parameters:
1. Use the combo boxes to select different parameters, or
2. Double click into the respective row, and edit/enter text directly.

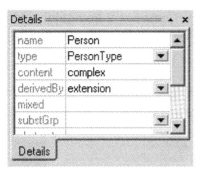

Entity Entry-Helper

The **entity entry helper** presents a list of defined entities or parameter entities that you can insert within your document.

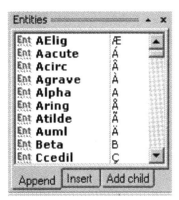

In the **Schema Design View**, this window displays further information on the currently selected element of the content model.

To change these content model parameters:
1. Use the combo boxes to select different parameters, or
2. Double click into the respective row, and edit/enter text directly

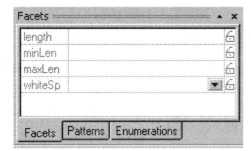

Info Window

In addition to the entry helper windows, XML Spy provides a handy information window that shows the detailed information about the attribute or element that you are working on.

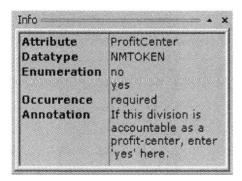

This information is available in all three editing views and can be a tremendous help in conjunction with the xsd:annotation feature of the new XML Schema draft, which allows a schema author to include comments or documentation on the use of each individual element or attribute into the schema itself.

Menus

XML Spy supports all standard Windows commands on the File and Edit menus to enable the user to quickly exploit all capabilities of the program.

Wherever appropriate, additional commands have been added to support special XML- or Internet-related features (e.g. such as opening documents directly from an URL).

In addition to the standard menus, XML Spy contains many XML-specific menus that cover the different aspects of XML editing tasks.

File Menu

The File menu contains all commands relevant to manipulating files with XML Spy, in the order common to most Windows software products.

In addition to the standard New, Open, Save, Print, Print Setup, and Exit commands, XML Spy offers special commands:

- open a document directly from a URL
- reload a file that may have changed
- switch the character-set encoding used by a file, and
- send a file by e-mail (only available, if a MAPI-compliant mail system, such as Microsoft Outlook, is installed).
- save file to URL

New...

The "New..." command is used to create a new document with XML Spy. You are presented a list of predefined document types that you can create:

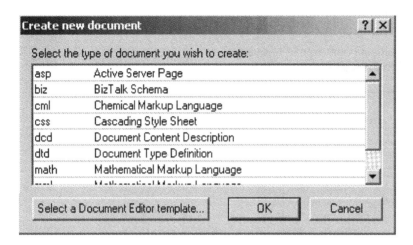

Since XML is such a versatile and universal concept, there are many different kinds of XML documents that you can create and edit with XML Spy.

Creating files not available in the "Create new document" dialog box
If the document you want to create is not listed, simply select ".xml" and change the file extension when you save the file. You can also add new file types to this list using the Tools | Options | File types tab.

Creating new templates
You can create your own templates which will then appear in the "Create new document" dialog box when you select the **File | New** command.

1. Use MS Explorer or any other text editor to open one of the **new.xxx** template files in the **..\Altova\XML SPY Suite\Template folder**. This file will act as the basis for your new XML template.
2. Make the necessary changes, declarations etc., to new template file.
3. Use **Save as...** option to save the file using the convention, **Anyname.XXX**
   Anyname is the name of your personal template (e.g **my-xml**).
   .XXX is the extension it should appear under in the dialog box (e.g. **.XML**). You can enter any type of XML extension here (.vml, .math etc.!)
4. Select **File | New** to select your new XML template.

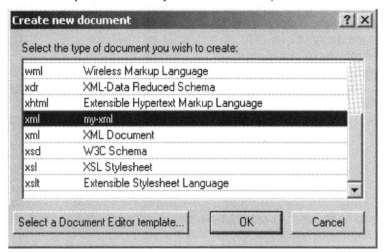

Please note:
   To delete a template, delete the template file you created.

Assigning a DTD / Schema to a new XML document

XML Spy contains built-in templates for most XML-based document types and automatically provides you with a meaningful starting point instead of a totally empty file (e.g. a ".xhtml" file automatically includes the correct DOCTYPE reference to the XHTML DTD as well as an empty <html> element to start with).

The predefined templates are placed in the \Template directory, automatically created one level below the XML Spy installation directory. You can only assign a DTC/Schema to a document from within the Enhanced Grid view.

If you select the ".xml XML Document" entry, (typically a new XML instance document) in the above dialog box, XML Spy prompts you for a DTD or Schema for the new file to be based upon:

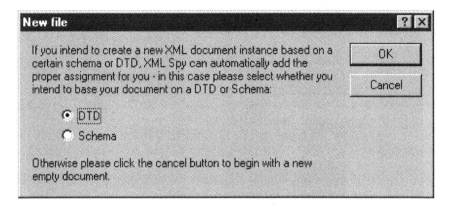

To create an empty XML document:
- Select the **File | New** menu entry, and
- Click the "**Cancel**" button in the New file dialog box, which prompts for a DTD/Schema.

Defining the root element

If you want to assign a DTD / Schema and the content model of the Schema or DTD contains more than one potential root element candidate, XML Spy asks you to select a root element from the list of possible candidates:

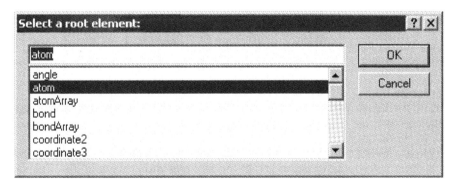

The new document is created with this element as its document root.

Open...

The "Open..." command opens any XML-related document or text file from your PC. The familiar Windows "Open" dialog box appears and allows you to select **one or more** files.

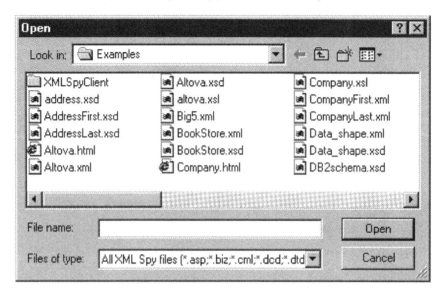

Use the "Files of type" combo box to select which kind of files you want to be displayed in the dialog box (the list of available file types can be configured through the File Types tab on the Tools | Options dialog).

After the file has been read into memory, the character-set encoding used within the file will be auto-detected by XML Spy and the file decoded accordingly.
If the character-set used to encode the file, differs from the encoding-specification in the XML-declaration in the prolog, an error message is displayed and the file is automatically opened using the correct encoding.

Auto-checks on opening
You may get an error message if your file is either not well-formed or invalid, and you have selected to perform automatic validation upon opening.

In this case the document will be opened in the appropriate view, an error message popup will be displayed with the details about the error detected, and the offending item will be highlighted in the window.

In such a case simply fix the error and click on the ⬚ Recheck ⬚ or ⬚ Revalidate ⬚ button to continue opening the file.

Opening Unicode files
If you are using the Windows 95/98 version of XML Spy and have chosen to open a Unicode file, XML Spy converts the file to a Windows 98 code-page to be used for viewing and editing, as Windows 95/98 do not support Unicode on the operating system layer (for further information please see the Unicode chapter in the background information section). The conversion is done automatically according to the settings you provide in the "Encoding" tab of the Tools | Options dialog.

Open URL...

The "Open URL..." command allows you to open non-local files from a URL (uniform resource locator) using http and WebDAV.

To open an URL address:
1.   Enter the URL you want to access, in the "Server URL" field.
2.   Enter your User-ID in the User and Password fields, if the server is password protected.
3.   Click the **Browse** button to view and navigate the directory structure of the server.

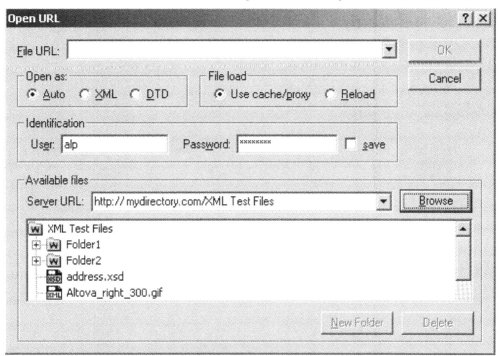

4.   Click the file you want to load into XML Spy.

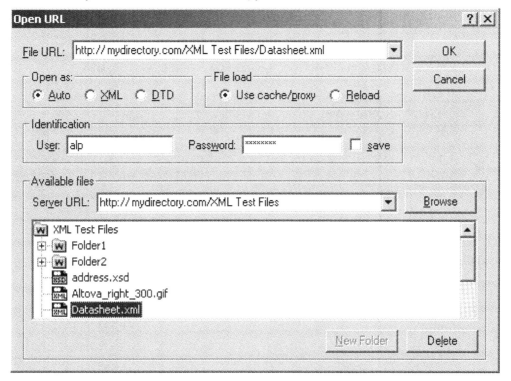

The file URL appears in the "File URL" field. The OK button only becomes active at

this point.
5. Click the OK button to load the file into XML Spy.
    The file you open appears in the main window.

The **Browse** function is only available on servers which support the following protocols:
*   FTP
*   HTTP and HTTPS, if the server supports WebDAV
*   or servers supporting WebDAV

File load:
To give you more control over the loading process, you can choose to load the file through the **local cache** or a **proxy** server (which considerably speeds up the process, if the file has been loaded before).

To reload the file anew in every case, select the **Reload** radio button - when you are working with an electronic publishing or database system for example, and wish to view the live output using XML Spy.

Repositories
Repositories supported by XML Spy come in three flavors:
*   Generic version control systems, such as Microsoft Visual Source-Safe (or compatible products)
*   Generic web servers, such as FTP or WebDAV servers; and
*   Specialized XML or schema repositories, such as Tamino, TEXTML Server, Virtuoso, or XML Canon.

XML Spy currently supports Source-Safe, FTP and WebDAV servers, as well as Virtuoso through WebDAV. Other repository interfaces will be available in future versions.

Reload

The Reload command allows you to reload documents from the URL.

XML Spy automatically monitors all open files (on the local network) for changes made by other programs (or people), and automatically prompts you to reload such a file, if you have checked the corresponding box on the File tab of the Tools | Options dialog.

This option is useful for documents that you open through a URL, which are dynamically created. This command is rarely used when working on documents that are accessed as files on your local hard disk or through a network file server.

Encoding...

The "Encoding..." command lets you view the current encoding of a file and select a different encoding when saving the current document the next time.

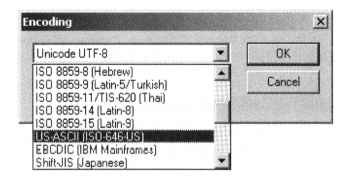

If you select a different encoding than the one in use before, the encoding-specification in the XML-declaration in the prolog will be adjusted accordingly. For 16-bit and 32-bit per character encodings (UTF-16, UCS-2, and UCS-4) you can also specify the byte-order to be used for the file.

You can also enter the new encoding into the encoding-specification of the XML-declaration. When saving a document, XML Spy automatically checks the encoding-specification and opens a dialog box if it cannot recognize the encoding name entered by the user.

If your document contains characters that cannot be represented in the selected encoding, you will get a warning message as soon as you save your file.

Close

The "Close" command closes the active document window. If the file was modified (the file name is appended with an asterisk "*" in the title bar), you will be asked if you wish to save the file first.

Close All

The "Close All" command closes all open document windows. If any document has been modified (asterisk "*" appended to the file name in the title bar), you will be asked if you wish to save the file first.

Save

The "Save" command saves the contents of the active document to the file it has been opened from.

When saving a document in XML Spy, the file is automatically checked for well-formedness. All XML documents must be well-formed – otherwise they could not be interpreted by any other XML application. The XML-Declaration is also checked for an encoding specification and it is applied to the document when the file is saved.

You can optionally have XML Spy automatically validate a document upon saving (this can be defined in the File tab on the Tools | Options dialog).

If a validation error occurs, XML Spy will bring up a popup message with a detailed error explanation and will highlight the offending item. You can then choose to fix the problem or save the document as is. In the latter case, you will be prompted to correct the error the next time you open the file with XML Spy.

Save As...

The "Save As..." command shows the familiar Windows "Save as..." dialog box to prompt for the name and location of the file that is to be saved. The same checks and validations occur as for the "Save" command.

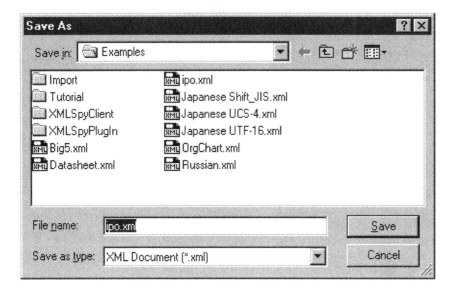

Save to URL...

The "Save to URL..." command allows you to save non-local files to a specified URL (uniform resource locator) address.

To save an XML document to a URL address:
1. Make sure the file you want to save is active in the XML Spy main window.
2. Select the menü option **File | Save to URL**
3. Click the **Browse** button to see and navigate the directory structure of the server.
4. Enter the file name in the URL field, or mark the file in the "Available files" list box, if you want to overwrite it.

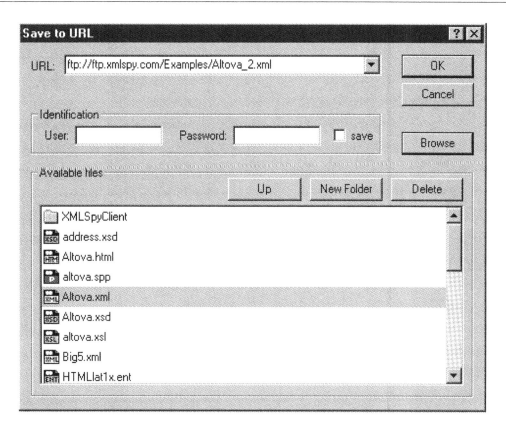

The **Browse** function is only available on servers which support the following protocols:
- FTP
- HTTP and HTTPS, if the server supports WebDAV
- or servers supporting WebDAV

Password protected servers
If the server you connect to is password protected, enter the required data and click the OK button to connect. You can also enter these data in the User and Password fields. The Save check box, supplies the password data for the logon attempt.

Repositories
Repositories supported by XML Spy come in three flavors:
- Generic version control systems, such as Microsoft Visual Source-Safe (or compatible products)
- Generic web servers, such as FTP or WebDAV servers; and
- Specialized XML or schema repositories, such as Tamino, TEXTML Server, Virtuoso, or XML Canon.

XML Spy currently supports Source-Safe, FTP and WebDAV servers, as well as Virtuoso through WebDAV. Other repository interfaces will be available in future versions.

Save All

The "Save All" command saves all modifications that have been made to any open documents. The command is useful if you edit multiple documentations simultaneously.

If a document has never been saved (e.g. after using the New command), the Save as... dialog box is presented for that document.

Send by Mail...

The "Send by Mail" command lets you create mail messages from any XML file, group of files (in the Project window), or selection within a file. To use this function you must be using a MAPI compliant e-mail system.

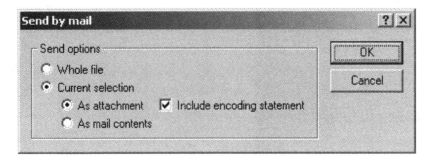

If you choose to send an entire file or group of files, they are always included as an attachment to the mail message:

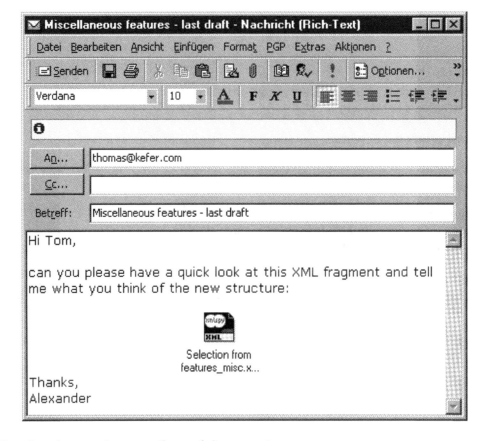

Sending fragments or portions of documents
When you want to send a fragment of an XML file, select the elements you wish to send in either Enhanced Grid View or Text View.

XML Spy gives you the choice of either creating an attachment file that contains only your current selection or simply sending the selection as XML text in the contents of the mail message.

Sending URLs by mail

When you send an URL (from the project window) you are prompted if you want to first retrieve the document referred to by the URL and then send the file as an attachment, or if you wish to just include the URL so that the recipient of your message can access the document through the URL:

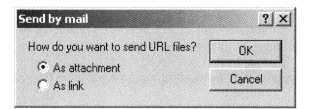

Print...

The "Print..." command opens the "Print" dialog box where you can control what appears on the printout. This dialog box contains different items, depending on the current view mode.

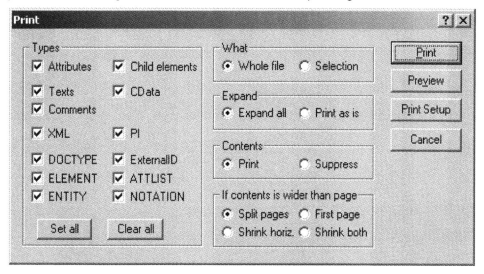

Enhanced Grid View options:

- The "**Types**" group box allows you to select the items you wish to appear in the output. You can hide comments as well as processing instructions or DTD items. For an explanation of the item types, please refer to the XML specification.
- The "**What**" group box allows you to print the entire file or just the current selection.
- The "**Expand**" group box allows you to print the document as is, or as a document with all child elements expanded fully.
- The "**Contents**" group box you can decide to print the contents of all elements in a document, or you may also print only those elements that form the hierarchical "tree" structure of the document.
  This should, however, not be confused with the optional tree view on the left side of each document window, which is only used as a navigation aid on the screen and cannot be printed.
- In the "**If contents are wider than page**" group box you can decide what to do if the

document is larger than one page of paper.

- The "*Split pages*" option, prints the entire document in its regular size and splits the contents on as many pages (both horizontally and vertically) as are required. These pages can later be glued together to form a poster.
- The "*First page*" option, is useful if your page is slightly narrow and most of the important information is contained on the left side, anyway. This will result in output that is split into vertical pages (as necessary). Only the first page is printed horizontally - the document is printed as one huge vertical strip.
- The "*Shrink horizontally*" option, reduces the size of the output, until it fits horizontally on the page. The output may, however, still span several pages vertically and is split accordingly.
- The "*Shrink both*" option, shrinks the document in both directions until it fits exactly on one sheet, thus making it useful for overviews.
- The "Print" button prints the document with the selected options.
- The "Preview" button opens a print preview window that lets you view the final output before committing it to paper.
- The "Print Setup" button opens the "Print Setup" dialog box and allows you to adjust the paper format, orientation, and other printer options for this print job only.

If you choose the Preview button, XML Spy will show a miniature image of the pages to be printed:

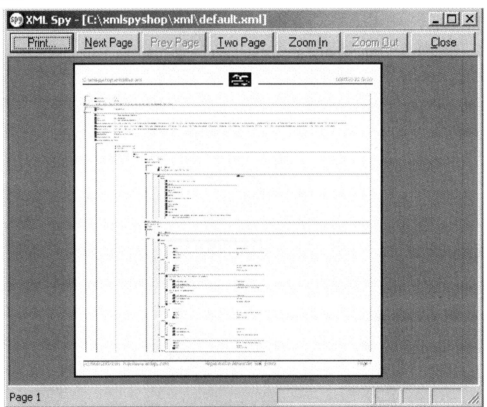

You can navigate within the preview mode using the "Next Page" and "Prev Page" buttons or "Zoom In" to take a close look at some details.

The "Print..." button lets you print the pages, whereas the "Close" button allows you to return to the previous dialog box without starting the print process.

Print Setup...

The "Print Setup..." command, displays the printer-specific "Print Setup" dialog box, enabling you to set the paper format, orientation, and other printer options for all **successive print jobs**.

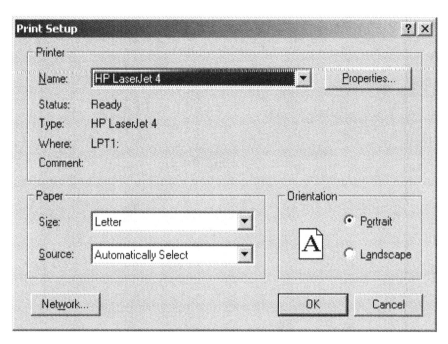

This is an example using an HP LaserJet 4 printer attached to the parallel port (LPT1:).

Most Recently Used Files

The list of most recently used files, shows the file name and path information for the nine most recently used files, which you can select with the mouse.

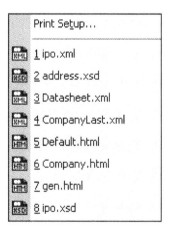

To access these files using the keyboard, press:
ALT+F,1 to open the File menu, and select the first file in the list.

Exit

The exit command is used to quit XML Spy when you are finished working with your documents. If you have any open files with unsaved changes, XML Spy will automatically prompt you to save these changes.

XML Spy also saves modifications you have made to program settings, as well as information about the most recently used files and projects to the Registry, a message box appears during this process.

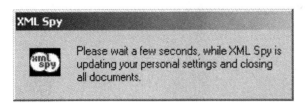

Edit Menu

The Edit menu contains all commands relevant to editing operations within XML Spy in the order common to most Windows software products.

In addition to the standard Undo, Redo, Cut, Copy, Paste, Delete, Select All, Find, Find next and Replace commands, XML Spy offers special commands to:

- copy the selection to the clipboard as XML-Text,
- Copy as structured text, or
- copy an XPath selector to the selected item to the clipboard.

All commands can be applied while editing text, as well as while operating on whole items or even discontinuous selections of more than one item.

Undo

      Hotkey: **CTRL + Z**

The "Undo" command contains support for unlimited levels of Undo! Every action in XML Spy can be undone and it is possible to undo one command after another. The Undo history is retained after using the "Save" command, enabling you go back to a state the document was in before you saved your changes.

> Please note:
> when you have turned on dynamic syntax coloring updates in the Text View and your operating system is using RichEdit 2.0 (i.e. earlier versions of Windows 95/98 and Windows NT 4.0), syntax coloring changes appear as undoable operations. If you want to avoid this, please update to RichEdit 3.0 or disable the dynamic syntax coloring

update feature (for further information please see the background information on the RichEdit Component).

Redo

  Hotkey: **CTRL + Y**

The "Redo" command allows you to redo previously undone commands – thereby giving you a complete history of the work you have completed. You can step back and forward through this history using the Undo and Redo commands.

Cut

  Hotkey: **Shift + Delete**, or **CTRL + X**

The Cut command copies the selected text or items to the clipboard and deletes them from their present location.

Copy

  Hotkey: **CTRL + C**

The Copy command copies the selected text or items to the clipboard. This can be used to duplicate data within XML Spy or to move data to another application.

> Please note:
> XML Spy provides two different commands for copying elements to the clipboard in a textual form: Copy as XML-Text and Copy as Structured Text.

You can use the Editing tab on the Tools | Options dialog, to choose which operation should be performed when you use the copy command on the Edit menu or the Ctrl-C shortcut.

Paste

  Hotkey: **CTRL + V**

The Paste command inserts the contents of the clipboard at the current cursor position.

Delete

  Keyboard: **Del.**

The Delete command deletes the currently selected text or items without placing them in the clipboard.

Copy as XML-Text

The "Copy as XML-Text command lets you exchange data easily with other products that allow data manipulation on the XML source layer.

While editing your document in Enhanced Grid View, you may occasionally want to copy some elements to the clipboard in their XML-Text representation:

```
<row>
```

```
<para align="left">
        <bold>Check the FAQ</bold>
    </para>
    <para>
        <link mode="internal">
            <link_section>support</link_section>
            <link_subsection>faq30</link_subsection>
            <link_text>XML Spy 4.0 FAQ</link_text>
        </link>
        <link mode="internal">
            <link_section>support</link_section>
            <link_subsection>faq25</link_subsection>
            <link_text>XML Spy 3.5 FAQ</link_text>
        </link>
    </para>
</row>
```

This command automatically formats text using the currently active settings for saving a file. These settings can be modified in the "Save File" section of the File tab of the Tools | Options dialog).

Copy as Structured Text

The " Copy as Structured Text" command copies elements to the clipboard as they appear on screen. This command is useful for copying table-like data from the Enhanced Grid View as well as the integrated Database/Table View.

The copied data can be used within XML Spy as well as third-party products, enabling you to transfer XML data to spreadsheet-like applications (e.g. Microsoft Excel).

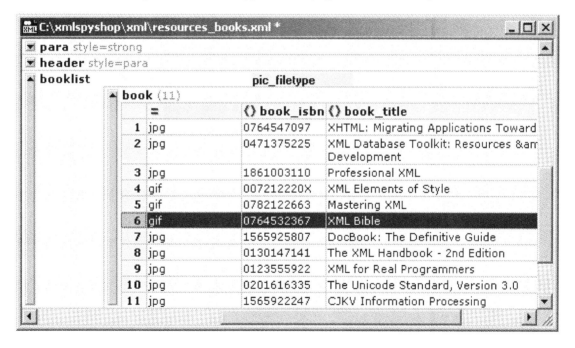

If you copy this table and paste it into Excel, the data will appear in the following way:

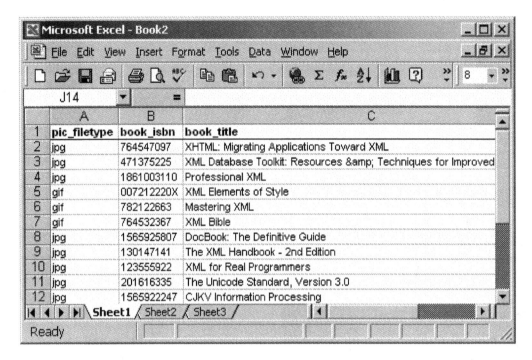

Please note:
> The results of this command depend on the way the information is currently laid out on screen. Using the same XML data (that served as an example for the Copy as XML-Text command) in the Enhanced Grid view with the **Table view active**, would result in the following:

```
row
    para
        align     bold      link
        left      Check the FAQ
            link
                mode            link_section    link_subsection    link_text
                internal        support         faq30              XML Spy 3.5
FAQ
                internal        support         faq25              XML Spy 2.5
FAQ
```

The same data would be copied to the clipboard in the following format, with the **Table view deactivated** in the Enhanced Grid View.

```
row
    para
        align     left
        bold      Check the FAQ
    para
        link
            mode                internal
            link_section        support
            link_subsection     faq30
            link_text           XML Spy 3.5 FAQ
        link
            mode                internal
            link_section        support
            link_subsection     faq25
            link_text           XML Spy 2.5 FAQ
```

Copy XPath

The "Copy XPATH" command copies the corresponding XPath Selector to the clipboard enabling you to paste it into XSLT documents or any other file that uses XPath.

When using XSLT it is very often necessary to enter so-called Selector strings that help in selecting an element or attribute from within another XML document. Selector strings are built according to the XPath definition, and XML Spy helps you to create XPath Selectors, by selecting the item you wish to address and choosing Copy XPATH from the Edit menu.

```
/main/content/list/header/clipart/@style
```

Pretty-Print XML Text

The "Pretty-Print XML Text command reformats your XML document in the text view, giving you a structured display. Note that the XML document must be well formed for this command to work.

Select All

Hotkey: **CTRL + A**

The "Select All" command selects all the text of an item or all the items in an XML document, enabling successive commands to operate on the entire text or document at once.

Find...

      Hotkey: **CTRL + F**

The "Find" command allows you to search for any occurrence of a text string in your XML document. Depending on the view you are using, the Find command will have different options.

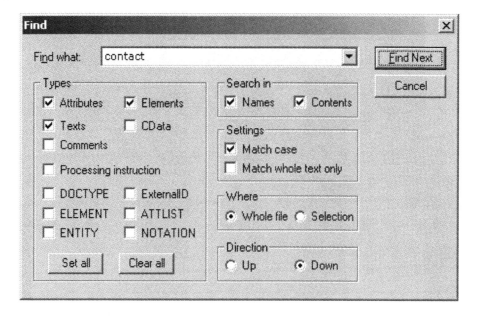

Enhanced Grid View find options:

- Enter the text string to be searched for in the "Find what" field, or use the combo box to select from one of the last 10 search criteria. The Find what field can be left empty, to search for elements, attributes etc.
- The "Types" group box, allows you to select what kind of items you wish to include in the search. This allows you to e.g. skip comments as well as processing instructions or DTD items. For an explanation of the item types, please refer to the XML specification.
- The "Search in" group box, allows you to define if you want to search for the specified text in the (element or attribute) names of items, in their contents, or in both.
- The "Settings" group box, allows you to define a case-sensitive and/or match string search.
- The "Where" group box, allows you to define your the scope of the search.
- The "Direction" group box, allows you to specify the search direction.
- The "Set all" button, activates all the check boxes in the Types group box, the "Clear all" deactivates them.

Find next

 Hotkey: **F3**

The "Find next" command repeats the last Find command to search for the next occurrence of the requested text.

Replace...

 Hotkey: **CTRL + H**

The "Replace" command is only available in the Text and Enhanced Grid View, it features the same options as the Find... command and allows you to replace the target text by any other text string of your choice.

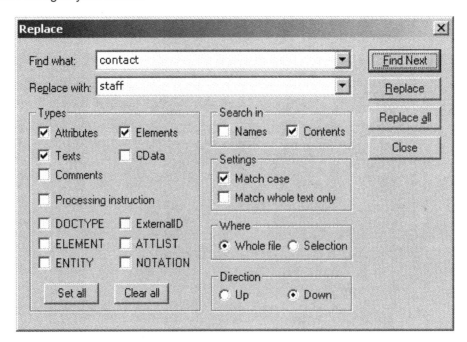

You can replace each item individually, or you can use the "Replace All" button to perform a global search and replace operation.

Please note:
As a security precaution, the "Replace all" command shows each individual replacement operation in the Enhanced Grid view. You can interrupt the operation by pressing the <ESC> key. Each replacement, is recorded as a single operation that can be undone individually.

Project Menu

XML Spy uses the familiar tree view to manage multiple files or URLs in XML projects. Files and URLs can be grouped into folders by common extension or any arbitrary criteria, allowing for easy structuring and batch manipulation.

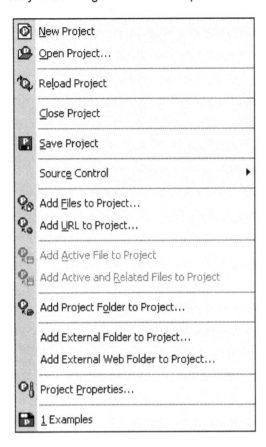

Please see the description of the Project Window for a general introduction to the XML Spy project management.

Please note:
most project-related commands are also available on the **context-menu**, when you **right-click** on any item in the project window.

New Project

This command creates a **new** project in XML Spy.

If you are currently working with another project, a prompt appears asking if you want to close all documents belonging to the current project.

Open Project...

This command **opens** an existing project in XML Spy.

If you are currently working with another project, the previous project is closed first.

Reload Project

This command **reloads** the current project from disk.

If you are working in a multi-user environment, it can sometimes become necessary to reload the project from disk, as other users might have made changes to the project.

Please note:
XML Spy project (.spp) files are actually XML documents that you can edit like any regular XML File. This should only be attempted by advanced users!

Close Project

This command **closes** the active project.

If the project has been modified, you will be asked if you want to save the project first.

When a project, or XML file is modified, an asterisk "*" is automatically appended to the file name in the title bar.

Save Project

This command **saves** the current project.

Source control

XML Spy supports Microsoft Source-Safe and other compatible repositories.

A source control project is, however, not the same as a XML Spy project. Source control projects are extremely directory dependent, whereas XML Spy projects are logical constructions without direct directory dependence.

The following text uses Microsoft Source-Safe as the Source Control provider.

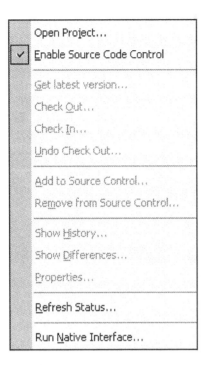

Open project

The Open Project command mirrors (or creates) an existing source control project locally. This command can only take effect if an XML Spy project has previously been added to source control provider using the menu option Add to Source Control.

1. Select a source control provider from the list of those installed on your PC, and confirm with the OK button.

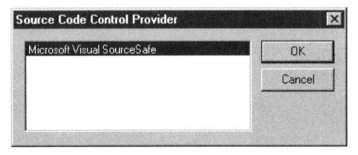

2. Enter your login data in the Source Control Login dialog box, and confirm with OK.

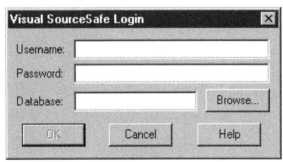

3. Define the directory to contain the local project.
4. Select the Source control project you want to download.
    If the folder you define does not exist at the location, a dialog box opens prompting you

to create it there. Click Yes to confirm the new directory.
5. Click the OK button to download the source control project.

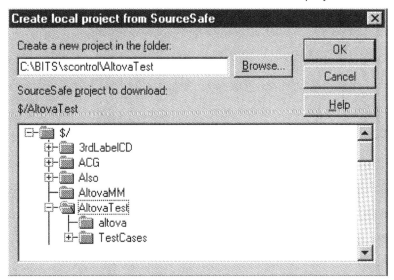

6. **XML Spy** now displays the Open dialog box, and attempts to find the XML Spy project file (*.spp) in the local directory. Click the project file you want to create, if there are several to choose from.

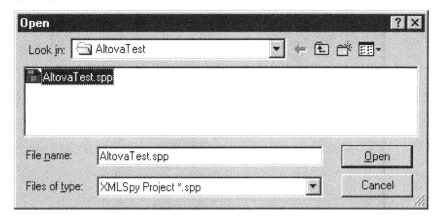

A message box might appear at this point stating that the directory is under source control, offering you the option of checking it out or not.
7. Click the OK, if you want source control to be enabled.
    The Check out dialog box opens, allowing you to check out the *.spp file.
8. Add any comments to the file in the Comment text box and Click OK, to check out the XML Spy project file. Depending on your source control provider, the dialog box might contain extra command buttons. In this case the Advanced... button opens the Advanced Check Out Options dialog box.

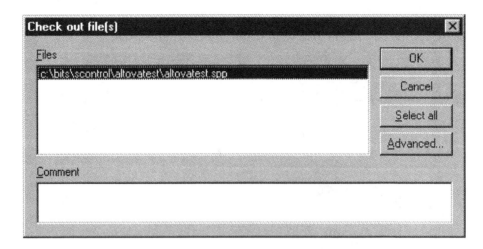

The *.spp file is checked out, and all the XML files contained in the XML Spy project, are copied to the local directory.

Result in XML Spy:
The AltovaTest directory has been created locally, and all files included in the XML Spy project are made available in the project window. You can now work with these files as you normally do.

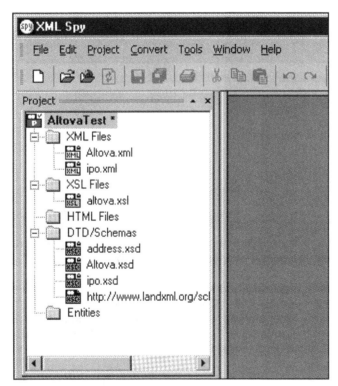

Source control symbols in XML Spy

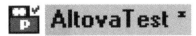

The **red check mark** denotes **checked out**, i.e. the AltovaTest project file has been checked out.
The asterisk denotes that changes have been made to the file, and you will be prompted to

save it when you exit.

 Altova.xml

The lock symbol, at the top right corner the XML symbol, denotes that the file is **under source control**, but is currently not checked out.

 http://www.landxml.org.

This URL document is part of the AltovaTest project but is **not under source control**. Documents opened via URL, cannot be placed under source control.

Enable Source code control

This command allows you to enable or disable source control for a project.

To disable source control for a project:
1.   Click on the project file or any other file in the project window.
2.   Select the menu option **Project | Source control** and deactivate the **Enable Source Code Control** check box.

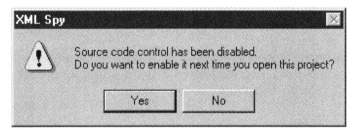

To **provisionally** disable source control for the project select YES.

To **permanently** disable source control for the project select NO.

Get Latest Version

This command **gets** the latest source control version of file you select.

The file is a copy of the source control file and is placed in your local working directory.

Check Out

This command **checks out** the latest source control version of file(s) you select, and flags it as "checked out" for all other users.

Shortcut: Right click an item in the project window, and select "Check out" from the context menu.

The following items can be checked out:
- Single files, click on the respective files (CTRL + click, for several)
- XML Spy project folders, click on the folders (CTRL + click, for several)
- XML Spy project, click on the project file icon.

![AltovaTest icon]

The red check mark denotes that the file has been checked out.

Check In

This command **checks in** the previously checked out files, i.e. your locally updated files, and places them in the source control project.

Shortcut: Right click a checked out item in the project window, and select "Check in" from the Context menu.

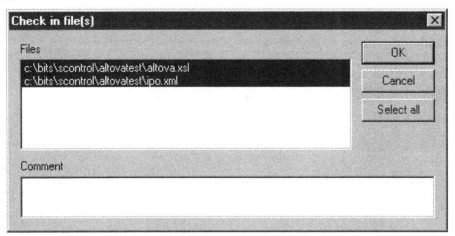

The following items can be checked in:
- Single files, click on the respective files (CTRL + click, for several)
- XML Spy project folders, click on the folders (CTRL + click, for several)
- A complete XML Spy project, click on the project file icon.

 Altova.xml

The lock symbol denotes that the file is **under source control**, but is currently not checked out.

Undo Check Out...

This command **rejects changes** made to previously checked out files, i.e. your locally updated files, and retains the old files in the source control project.

Shortcut: Right click a checked out item in the project window, and select "Undo Check out" from the Context menu.

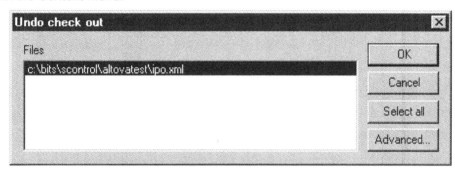

The Undo check out option can apply to the following items:
- Single files, click on the respective files (CTRL + click, for several)
- XML Spy project folders, click on the folders (CTRL + click, for several)
- XML Spy project, click on the project file icon.

Add to Source Control

This command **adds** an XML Spy project to your Source Control provider.

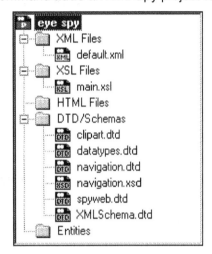

To add an XML project to the source control provider:
1. Click the XML Spy project icon and select the menu option **Project | Source control | Add to Source control.**
2. Select your source control provider from the list box.
3. Enter the source control login data.
4. Select the source control project (directory) to which your XML project should be added, and confirm with the OK button.

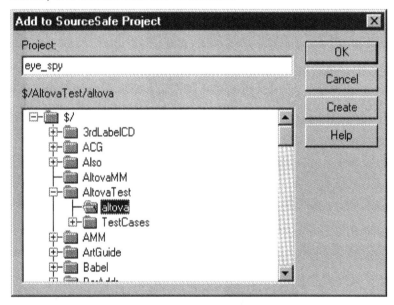

If the project does not exist, the following dialog box opens, prompting for more information.

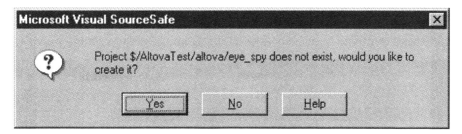

5. Select Yes to create the new project and NO to cancel.

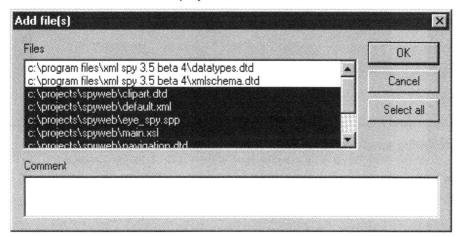

6. Select the XML Spy project files that you want to be placed under control of the source control provider, and confirm with OK.

The files are transferred to the source control provider and are now under source control. These files are marked with the "lock symbol" in the project window. The files you did not transfer do not have the lock symbol (datatypes.dtd and XMLschema.dtd in this example).

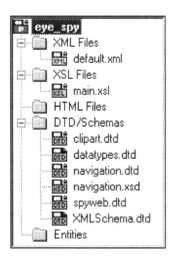

Remove from Source Control

This command **removes** previously added files, from the source control provider.

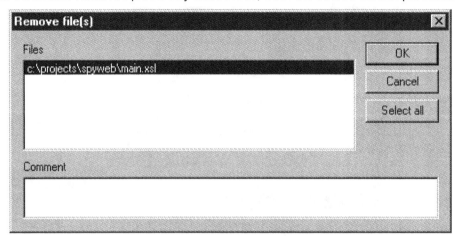

The following items can be removed from source control:
- Single files, click on the respective files (CTRL + click, for several)
- XML Spy project folders, click on the folders (CTRL + click, for several)
- A complete XML Spy project, click on the project file icon.

Show History

This command **displays** the history of a file, it can only be used on single files.

To show the history of a file:
1. Click on the file in the project window
2. Select the menu option **Project | Source control | Show history**.

   A dialog box prompting for more information may appear at this time (this example uses MS Source-Safe).

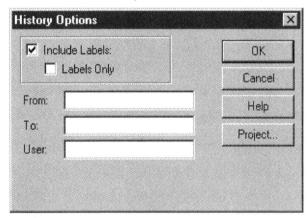

3. Select the appropriate entries and confirm with OK.

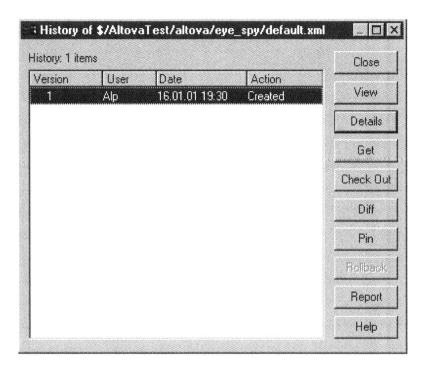

Show Differences

This command **displays** the differences between the file currently in the source control repository, and the file of the same name that you have checked out.

This command can only be used on single files.

To show the differences between two files:
Having checked out a file from your project,
1. Click on the file in the project window.
2. Select the menu option **Project | Source control | Show Differences**.
   A dialog box prompting for more information may appear at this time.

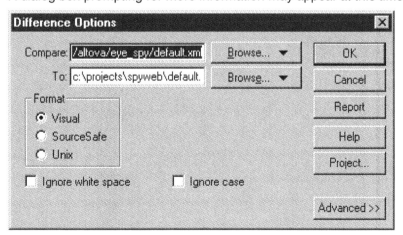

3. Select the appropriate entries and confirm with OK.

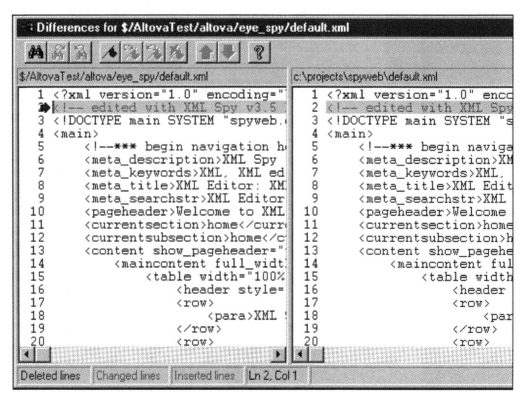

The differences between the two files are highlighted in both windows (this example uses MS Source-Safe).

Properties

This command **displays** the properties of the currently selected file, and is dependent on the source control provider you use.

This command can only be used on single files.

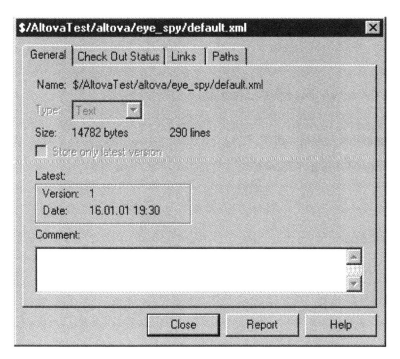

Refresh Status

This command **refreshes** the status of all project files independent of their current status.

Run Native Interface

This command **starts** your source control software with its usual user interface.

Add Files to Project...

This command **adds** files to the current project.

Use this command to add files to any folder in your project. You can either select a single file or any group of files (using CTRL + click) in the Open dialog box.

If you are adding files to the project, they will be distributed among the respective folders based on the File Type Extensions defined in the Project Properties dialog box.

Add URL to Project...

This command **adds** an URL to the current project.

XML Spy also allows you to add URLs to a project. Whenever a batch operation is performed on a URL or on a folder that contains a URL item, XML Spy will retrieve the document from the URL , and perform the requested operation.

Add Active File to Project

This command **adds** the active file to the current project.

If you have just opened a file from your hard disk or through an URL, you can add the file to the current project using this command.

Add Active And Related Files to Project

This command **adds** the currently active XML document and all related files to the project.

When working on an XML document that is based on a DTD or Schema, XML Spy also lets you add both the XML document and all related files (e.g. the DTD and all external parsed entities it refers to) to the current project.

Add Project Folder to Project...

This command **adds** a new folder to the current project.

Use this command to add a new folder to the current project. You can also access this command from the context-menu when you right-click on a folder in the project window.

Add External Folder to Project...

This command **adds** a new **external folder** to the current project.

Use this command to add a **local** or **network** folder to the current project. You can also access this command from the context-menu when you right-click a folder in the project window.

To add an external folder to the project
1. Select the menu option **Project | Add External Folder to project**.
2. Select the folder you want to include from the "Browse for Folder" dialog box, and click OK to confirm.

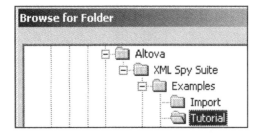

The selected folder now appears in the project window.

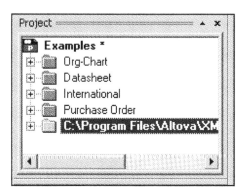

3. Click the plus icon to view the folder contents.

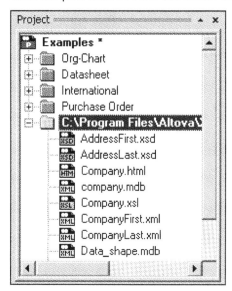

To filter the folder contents:

1. **Right click** the local folder, and select the popup menu option **Properties**.
    This opens the Properties dialog box.

2. Click in the **File extensions** field and enter the file extensions of the file types you
    want to see. You can separate each file type with a **semicolon** to define multiple types
    (XML and Schema XSDs in this example).
3. Click OK to confirm the selection.

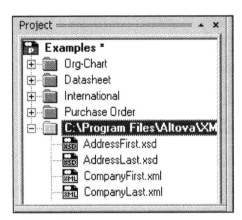

The Project window now only shows the XML and XSD files of the tutorial folder.

Validating and checking a folder for well-formedness:
Having selected the file types you want to see or check, from the external folder,

1. Click the folder and click the "Check well-formedness" or "Validate" icon, (hotkeys F7 or F8).
    All the files visible under the folder are checked.

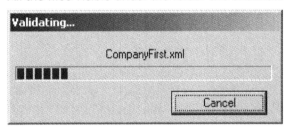

If a file is mal-formed or invalid, then this file is opened in the main window, allowing you to edit it. In this case the CompanyLast file is opened because the PhoneExt value does not match the facet defined in the underlying schema file. This schema only allows only two digit numbers.

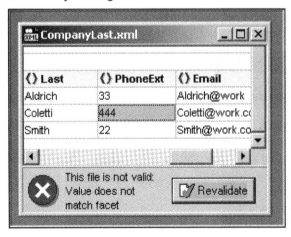

2. Correct the error and restart the process to recheck the rest of the folder.

Please note
    You can select discontinuous files in the folder, by holding down CTRL and clicking the files singly. Only these files are then checked when you click F7 or F8.

To update the project folder contents:

You might add or delete files in the local or network directory at any time. To update the folder view,
- Right click the external folder, and select the popup menu option **Refresh external folder**.

Deleting files or folders:
- Right click a **folder** and hit the **Del.** key, to delete the folder from the Project window. This only deletes the folder from the Project view, and does not delete anything on your hard disk or network.
- Right clicking a **single file** and hitting Del. **does not delete** a file from the Project window. You have to delete it physically and then Refresh the external folder contents.

Add External Web Folder to Project...

This command **adds** a new **external web folder** to the current project.

Use this command to add a web folder to the current project. You can also access this command from the context-menu when you right-click a folder in the project window.

To add an external web folder to the project
1. Select the menu option **Project | Add External Web Folder to project**. This opens the "Add Web folder to project" dialog box.

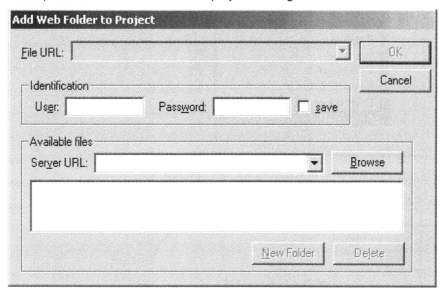

2. Click in the Server URL field to enter the server URL, and enter the login ID in the User and Password fields.
3. Click the Browse button to connect to the server and view the files available there.

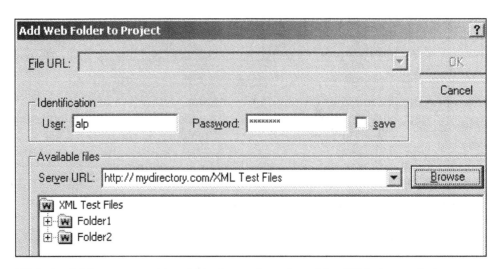

4. Click the **folder** you want to add to the project view. The OK button only becomes active once you do this. The Folder name and http: server address now appear in the File URL field.
5. Click OK to add the folder to the project.

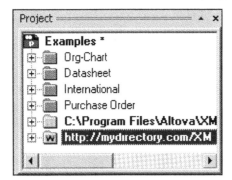

6. Click the plus icon to view the folder contents.

To filter the folder contents:
1. **Right click** the web folder, and select the popup menu option **Properties**.
    This opens the Properties dialog box.
2. Click in the **File extensions** field and enter the file extensions of the file types you want to see. You can separate each file type with a **semicolon** to define multiple types

(XML and Schema XSDs for example).
3. Click OK to confirm the selection.
    The Project window now only shows the XML and XSD files of the web folder.

Validating and checking a folder for well-formedness:
1. Click the folder and click the "Check well-formedness" or "Validate" icon, (hotkeys F7 or F8).
    All the files visible under the folder are checked.

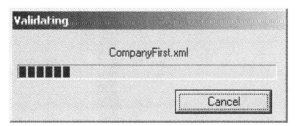

If a file is mal-formed or invalid, then this file is opened in the main window, allowing you to edit it.
2. Correct the error and restart the process to recheck the rest of the folder.

Please note
    You can select discontinuous files in the folder, by holding down CTRL and clicking the files singly. Only these files are then checked when you click F7 or F8.

To update the project folder contents:
Files may be added or deleted from the web folder at any time. To update the folder view,
*   Right click the external folder, and select the popup menu option **Refresh external folder**.

Deleting files or folders:
*   Right click a **folder** and hit the **Del.** key, to delete the **folder** from the Project window. This only deletes the folder from the Project view, and does not delete anything on the web server.
*   Right clicking a **single file** and hitting Del. **does not delete** a file from the Project window. You have to delete it physically and then Refresh the external folder contents.

Project Properties...

The Properties command lets you define important settings for any of the specific folders in your project.

To define the Project Properties for a folder:
1. Right click on the folder you want to define the properties for, and
2. Select the **Properties...** command from the context menu.

Please note:
    if your project file is under source control, a prompt appears asking if you want to check out the project file (*.spp). Click OK, if you want to edit settings and be able to save them.

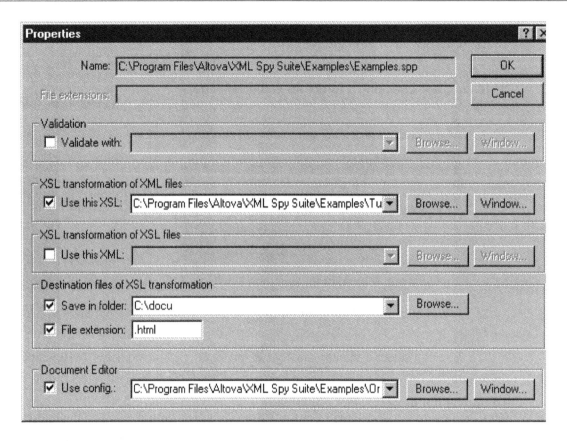

File extensions
The File extensions help to determine the automatic file-to-folder distribution that occurs when you add new files to the project (as opposed as to one particular folder).

Validate
Define the DTD or Schema document that should be used to validate all files in the current folder (Main Pages in this example).

XSL transformation of XML files
You can define the XSL Stylesheet to be used for XSL Transformation of all files in the folder.

If you are developing XSL Stylesheets yourself, you can also assign an example XML document to be used to preview the XSL Stylesheet in response to an XSL Transformation command issued from the stylesheet document, instead of the XML instance document.

Destination files of XSL transformation
For batch XSL Transformations, you can define the destination directory the transformed files should be placed in.

If you have added one file or URL to more than one folder in your project, you can use the properties command to set the default folder, whose settings should be used when you choose to validate or transform the file in non-batch mode.

Document Editor

The "Use config." option allows you to select an SPS file when editing XML files using Document Editor, in the current folder. Please see the Document Editor manual for more information.

Most Recently Used Projects

This command displays the file name and path for the nine most recently used projects, allowing quick access to these files.

Also note, that XML Spy can automatically open the last project that you used, whenever you start XML Spy. (**Tools | Options| File** tab, Project | Open last project on program start)

XML Menu

The XML menu contains all commands necessary for manipulating XML documents with XML Spy. You will find commands to insert or append elements, modify the element hierarchy, and set a namespace prefix for items.

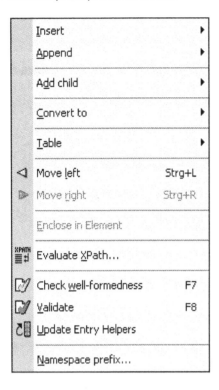

You can also check documents for well-formedness or validate them against any Schema or DTD.

Insert

The Insert command inserts a new item directly before the currently selected one. In case of an attribute, it may appear a few lines before the current item, as all attributes must immediately follow their parent element.

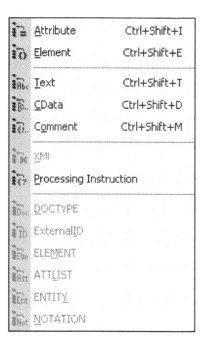

Insert Attribute

        Hotkey: **CTRL+SHIFT+I**

This command **inserts** a new **attribute** before the selected item.

If the current selection is any element other than the first element, the attribute is inserted before the first element to satisfy the well-formedness constraints of XML.

Insert Element

        Hotkey: **CTRL+SHIFT+E**

This command **inserts** a new **element** before the selected item.

If the current selection is an attribute, the new element is inserted before the first element to satisfy the well-formedness constraints of XML.

Insert Text

        Hotkey: **CTRL+SHIFT+T**

This command **inserts** new **text content** before the selected item.

If the current selection is an attribute, the text is inserted before the first element to satisfy the well-formedness constraints of XML.

Insert CDATA

        Hotkey: **CTRL+SHIFT+D**

This command **inserts** a new **CDATA block** before the selected item.

If the current selection is an attribute, the CDATA is inserted before the first element to satisfy the well-formedness constraints of XML.

Insert Comment

     Hotkey: **CTRL+SHIFT+M**

This command **inserts** a new **comment** before the selected item.

If the current selection is an attribute, the Comment is inserted before the first element to satisfy the well-formedness constraints of XML.

Insert XML

This command **inserts** new **XML declaration**
`<?xml version="1.0" encoding="UTF-8"?>` before the selected item.

> Please note:
> Each XML document may only contain one XML declaration and it must appear at the very top of the file.

Insert Processing Instruction

This command **inserts** a new **Processing Instruction** (PI) before the selected item.

If the current selection is an attribute, the PI is inserted before the first element to satisfy the well-formedness constraints of XML.

Insert DOCTYPE

This command **inserts** a Document Type Declaration - or more precisely, the **DOCTYPE block** for the internal subset of a Document Type Declaration (DTD) - before the selected item.

> Please note:
> The DOCTYPE block may only appear at the top of an XML instance document between the XML Declaration and the root element of the XML document.

You could also use the Assign DTD command instead, which lets you create a DOCTYPE statement that refers to an external DTD document.

Insert ExternalID

This command **inserts** an **external ID** (SYSTEM or PUBLIC) into a DOCTYPE declaration, before the selected item.

Insert ELEMENT

This command **inserts** an **element declaration** into a DOCTYPE declaration or into an external Document Type Definition (DTD), before the selected item.

Insert ATTLIST

This command **inserts** an **attribute list declaration** into a DOCTYPE declaration or into an external Document Type Definition (DTD), before the selected item.

Insert ENTITY

This command **inserts** an **entity declaration** into a DOCTYPE declaration or into an external Document Type Definition (DTD) before the selected item.

Insert NOTATION

This command inserts a **notation declaration** into a DOCTYPE declaration or into an external Document Type Definition (DTD) before the selected item.

Append

The Append command appends an item as the last item **inside the parent** of the currently selected item. This is useful whenever you want to add more than one item in sequence.

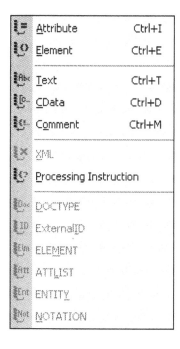

Append Attribute

        Hotkey: **CTRL+I**

This command **appends** a **new attribute** after the last element within the same parent.

Append Element

 Hotkey: **CTRL+E**

This command **appends** a **new element** after the last element within the same parent.

Append Text

 Hotkey: **CTRL+T**

This command **appends** a new **text content block** after the last element within the same parent.

Append CDATA

 Hotkey: **CTRL+D**

This command **appends** a new **CDATA block** after the last element within the same parent.

Append Comment

 hotkey: **CTRL+M**

This command appends a **new comment** after the last element within the same parent.

Append XML

This command **inserts** a new **XML declaration**
`<?xml version="1.0" encoding="UTF-8"?>` as the first item in a document.

> Please note:
> Each XML document may only contain one XML declaration and it must appear at the very top of the file.

Append Processing Instruction

This command **appends** a new **Processing Instruction** (PI) after the last element within the same
parent.

Append DOCTYPE

This command **appends** a new Document Type Declaration - or more precisely, the **DOCTYPE block** for the internal subset of a Document Type Declaration (DTD) - after the last element within the same parent.

> Please note:
> A DOCTYPE block may only appear at the top of an XML instance document between the XML Declaration and the root element of the XML document.

Append ExternalID

This command **appends** an **external ID** (SYSTEM or PUBLIC) in a DOCTYPE declaration after the last element of the same parent.

Append ELEMENT

This command **appends** an **element declaration** in a DOCTYPE declaration or in an external Document Type Definition (DTD).

Append ATTLIST

This command **appends** an **attribute list declaration** in a DOCTYPE declaration or in an external Document Type Definition (DTD).

Append ENTITY

This command **appends** an **entity declaration** in a DOCTYPE declaration or in an external Document Type Definition (DTD).

Append NOTATION

This command **appends** a **notation declaration** in a DOCTYPE declaration or in an external Document Type Definition (DTD).

Add Child

The Add Child command adds a child item to the currently selected element. This is useful for adding attributes to an item, or creating child elements.

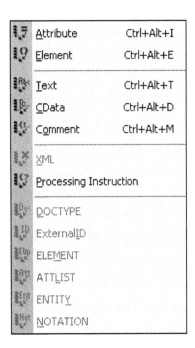

Add Child Attribute

        Hotkey: **CTRL+ALT+I**

This command **inserts** a **new attribute** as a child of the selected item.

Add Child Element

        Hotkey: **CTRL+ALT+E**

This command **inserts** a **new element** as a child of the selected item.

Add Child Text

        Hotkey: **CTRL+ALT+T**

This command **inserts** new **text content** as a child of the selected item.

Add Child CDATA

        Hotkey: **CTRL+ALT+D**

This command **inserts** a new **CDATA block** as a child of the selected item.

Add Child Comment

        Hotkey: **CTRL+ALT+M**

This command **inserts** new **Comment** as a child of the selected item.

Add Child XML

This command is only available, when you are looking at a totally empty file...

This command **inserts** a new **XML declaration**
`<?xml version="1.0" encoding="UTF-8"?>` as a child of the selected item.

Add Child Processing Instruction

This command **inserts** a new **Processing Instruction** (PI) as a child of the selected item.

Add Child DOCTYPE

This command is only available, if you are looking at a total empty file.

This command **inserts** a **Document Type Declaration** - or more precisely, the DOCTYPE block for the internal subset of a Document Type Declaration (DTD) - as a child of the selected item.

Please note:
A DOCTYPE block may only appear at the top of an XML instance document between the XML Declaration and the root element of the XML document.

Add Child ExternalID

This command **inserts** an **external ID** (SYSTEM or PUBLIC) into a DOCTYPE **declaration** as a child of the selected item.

Add Child ELEMENT

This command **inserts** an **element declaration** into a DOCTYPE declaration or into an external Document Type Definition (DTD) as a child of the selected item.

Add Child ATTLIST

This command **inserts** an **attribute list declaration** into a DOCTYPE declaration or into an external Document Type Definition (DTD) as a child of the selected item.

Add Child ENTITY

This command **inserts** an **entity declaration** into a DOCTYPE declaration or into an external Document Type Definition (DTD) as a child of the selected item.

Add Child NOTATION

This command **inserts** a **notation declaration** into a DOCTYPE declaration or into an external Document Type Definition (DTD) as a child of the selected item.

Convert To

The convert to command converts an item to a different item type. Depending on the location of the item (not on its current kind), some or all options on the item type submenu may or may not be available. This operation can only be performed on one individual item, not on an element that contains any child elements.

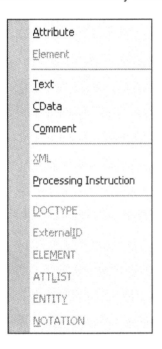

If the operation would result in the loss of data (e.g. converting an attribute to a comment looses the attribute name), a brief warning dialog box will appear.

Convert To Attribute

This command **converts** the selected item into a new **attribute**.

Convert To Element

This command **converts** the selected item into an **element**.

Convert To Text

This command **converts** the selected item into **text content**.

Convert To CDATA

This command **converts** the selected item into a **CDATA block**.

Convert To Comment

This command **converts** the selected item into a **comment**.

Convert To XML

This command **converts** the selected item to an XML declaration
`<?xml version="1.0" encoding="UTF-8"?>`.

> Please note:
> Each XML document may only contain one XML declaration and it must appear at the very top of the file.

Convert To Processing Instruction

This command **converts** the selected item to a new **Processing Instruction** (PI)

Convert To DOCTYPE

This command **converts** the selected item to a Document Type **Declaration** - or more precisely, the **DOCTYPE block** for the internal subset of a Document Type Declaration (DTD).

Please note:
A DOCTYPE block may only appear at the top of an XML instance document between the XML Declaration and the root element of the XML document.

Convert To ExternalID

This command **converts** the selected item to an **external ID** (SYSTEM or PUBLIC) in a DOCTYPE **declaration**.

Convert To ELEMENT

This command **converts** the selected item to an **element declaration** in a DOCTYPE declaration or in an external Document Type **Definition** (DTD).

Convert To ATTLIST

This command **converts** the selected item to an **attribute list** declaration in a DOCTYPE declaration or in an external Document Type **Definition** (DTD).

Convert To ENTITY

This command **converts** the selected item to an **entity declaration** in a DOCTYPE declaration or in an external Document Type **Definition** (DTD).

Convert To NOTATION

This command **converts** the selected item to a **notation declaration** in a DOCTYPE declaration or in an external Document Type **Definition** (DTD).

Table

The Table menu command contains all commands relevant to the Database/Table View in XML Spy.

The **Database/Table** commands can only be selected if the **Enhanced Grid view** is active!

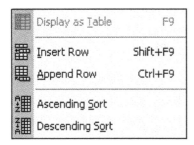

Display as Table

          Hotkey: **F9**

This command allows you **switch** between two views of repeated elements in the **Enhanced Grid view**. The Grid view (default view, in the Enhanced Grid view) and the Database/Table view.

1. Select one of the repeated elements in the grid view.
    The Displays as Table icon is only made active when you make the correct selection.

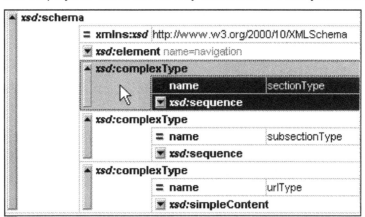

2. Click the icon or press the F9 Hotkey.

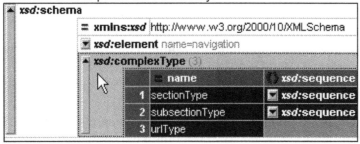

This effectively breaks out all attributes and sub-elements, and show them as columns similar to any spreadsheet- or database-like application.

Insert Row

     Hotkey: **SHIFT+F9**

This command **inserts** new **rows** to the table in the Database/Table View:

1. Click a row number in the table (or one of the cells), and
2. Select the menu option **XML | Table | Insert row** (or Shift+F9).

This inserts a new row (i.e. a new element) before the currently selected row.

Append Row

     Hotkey: **CTRL+F9**

This command **appends** new rows to the table in the Database/Table View

1. Click a row number in the table (or one of the cells), and
2. Select the menu option **XML | Table | Insert row** (or Ctrl+F9)

This appends a new row (i.e. a new element) to the end of the table.

Ascending Sort

This command **sorts** column elements in ascending order (in the table) in the Database/Table View:

1. Click a column header in the table, and
2. Select the menu option **XML | Table | Ascending sort** (or clicking on the A-Z icon)

XML Spy will automatically try to determine what kind of data you are using in the selected column, and choose an alphabetic or numeric sort method accordingly.

If XML Spy is not sure which sort order to use, it opens this dialog box to prompt for help:

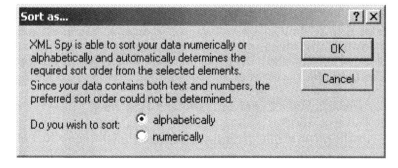

Descending Sort

This command **sorts** column elements in descending order (in the table) in the Database/Table View

1. Click a column header in the table, and
2. Select the menu option **XML | Table | Descending sort** (or clicking on the Z-A icon)

XML Spy will automatically try to determine what kind of data you are using in the selected column, and choose an alphabetic or numeric sort method accordingly.

If XML Spy is not sure which sort order to use, it opens a dialog box to prompt for help.

Move Left

   Hotkey: **CTRL+L**

This command **moves** the current element to the left by one level, thereby changing a child element into a sibling of its parent. This is also often referred to as the "**Promote**" command.

Move Right

   Hotkey: **CTRL+R**

This command **moves** the current element to the right by one level, thereby turning it into a child element of the element directly above. This is also often referred to as the "**Demote**" command.

Enclose in Element

When editing textual data, it is often convenient to insert a new sub-element that contains some text, which is already present in the document.

The Enclose in Element command lets you accomplish this with any text selection within another element. Once you select this command from the menu or toolbar, the **currently selected text** is cut from its parent element and **inserted** into a newly created **child element**.

If you are editing a document based on a Schema or DTD, you will automatically be presented with a list of valid choices for the kind of element you are allowed to insert in this position.

Evaluate XPath

XML Spy includes an **XPath Visualizer** that allows you to define/check XPath expressions in your XML documents and display the results immediately.

XPath provides a method to find elements, attributes, and other specific items in any type of XML document. The XML Spy XPath Visualizer allows you to enter an XPath into a field and have it evaluated immediately, with the resultant (node set) displayed in a window. Clicking one of these nodes, displays that specific node in the currently active XML Document. The XPath expression is also automatically checked to see if it is valid when you enter it.

The XPath Visualizer is available in the **Enhanced Grid** and **Text view**.

Please see the XPath specifications at http://www.w3.org/TR/xpath for more information.

XPath uses in XML Spy
- When creating Identity Constraints
- Setting breakpoints using the SOAP debugger
- Checking XSLT code

To evaluate an XPath expression:

1. Open an XML document in XML Spy (e.g. CompanyLast).

2. Select the menu option **XML | Evaluate XPath** or click the Evaluate XPath 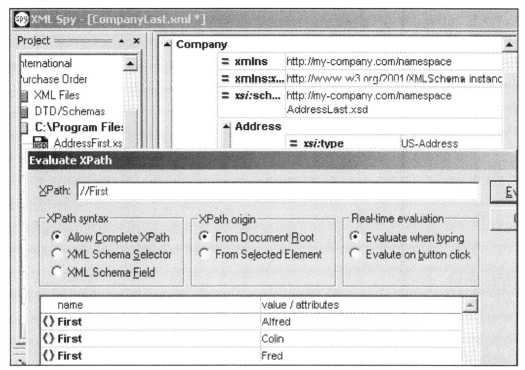 icon.
3. Type an XPath expression in the XPath field (e.g. //First).

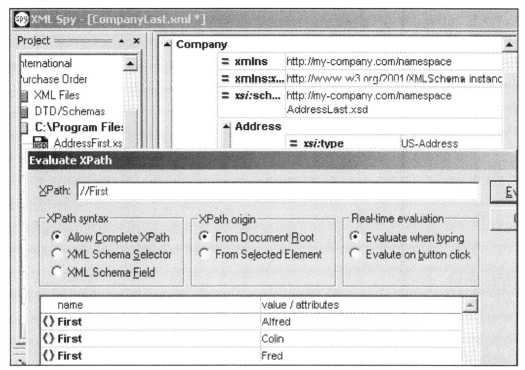

The resultant node set, all "First" elements under the Document Root, appears in the node set window.
4. Click one of the "First" elements in the node set window.
5. The corresponding element appears in the currently active XML document.

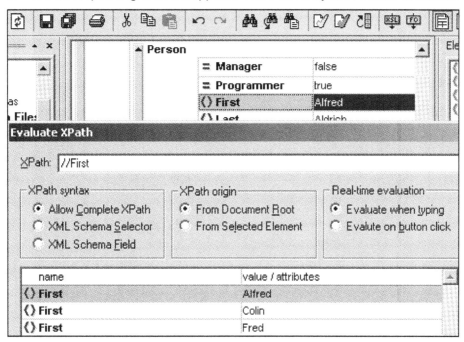

XPath Visualizer options

XPath syntax

This option group allows you to select which syntax you want to use when evaluating an XPath. When entering an XPath, the expression is constantly monitored for adherence to these syntax rules. An invalid expression automatically appears in red. As soon as the expression becomes valid the expression changes from red into black.

Allow Complete XPath:
This is the default option and checks against the complete XPath syntax.

XML Schema Selector:
This option checks the XPath against the XML Schema Selector syntax.

XML Schema Field:
This option checks the XPath against the XML Schema Field syntax.

XPath origin

This option group lets you define **from where** in the XML document you want to start your search. The option you select here remains active the next time you search for an XPath.

From Document Root:
This is the default option, and starts the search from the beginning of the XML document.

From Selected Element:
Select this option if you want to start your search from the currently selected element, attribute etc. in the XML document. Note that the current element position does not change if you click one of the node set results in the node set window.

Real-time evaluation

Evaluate when typing:
This is the default option, and presents results in the node set window while you are typing in the expression.

Evaluate on button click:
This option defers the XPath evaluation until you click the Evaluate button.

Node set window

This window displays the results of the evaluated XPath expression. The XPath results in this window can appear as nodes, numbers, boolean expressions, or error messages.

XPath examples

A few examples of XPath expressions and their results are shown below. These examples use the **CompanyLast.xml** file available in the **..\Examples\Tutorial** folder supplied with XML Spy.

Find all the elements in the first occurence of the person child element.

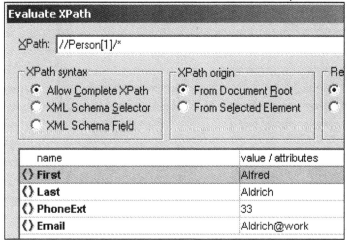

Find all the person elements, where the Manager attribute value is true.

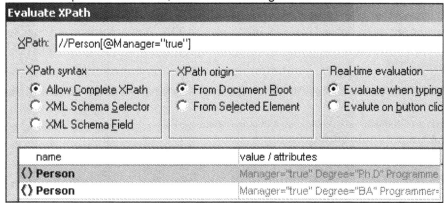

Find the total value of all the PhoneExt elements.

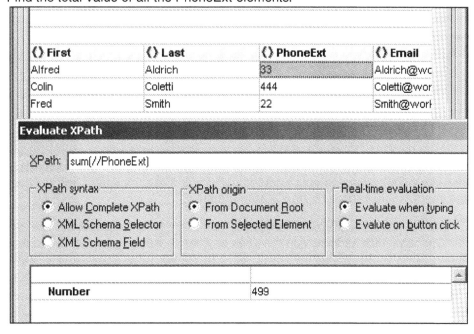

Entering the SUM-Function in CAPS displays an error message in the node set window. All XPath expressions are case sensitive, this includes function names as well as node names.

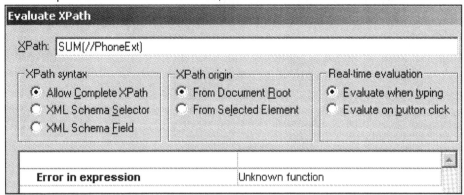

Check Well-Formedness

This command **checks** the document for well-formedness by the definitions of the XML 1.0 specification.

Every XML document must be well-formed and therefore XML Spy automatically checks for well-formedness whenever a document is opened, saved, or the view mode is switched from Text to any other view.

If the well-formedness check succeeds, a brief message is displayed at the bottom of the main window:

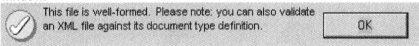

If any error is encountered during the well-formedness check, the source of the problem is highlighted and a corresponding error message is shown:

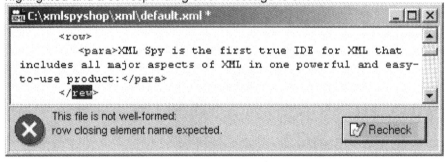

It is generally not permitted to save a mal-formed XML document, but XML Spy gives you a "Save anyway" option when the automatic well-formedness check upon saving fails. This is useful, when you want to suspend your work temporarily and resume it later, without being able to make the intermediate version of the file well-formed.

The Check well-formedness command normally operates on the active main window. You can also use the Check well-formedness command on any file, folder, or group of files in the active project window. Click on the respective folder, and then on the "Check well-formedness" icon.

Validate

This command validates an XML document against the rules set forth in its Schema or Document Type Definition (DTD) or it can validate any XML Schema or DTD against the rules set forth in the corresponding specification.

XML Spy uses its built-in incremental validating parser that supports all major Schema dialects, such as DTD, DCD, XDR, XML-Data, BizTalk, and the new W3C XML Schema Definition Language (XSD) .

If the validation succeeds, a brief message is displayed at the bottom of the main window:

If an error is encountered during the validation, the source of the problem is highlighted and a corresponding error message is shown:

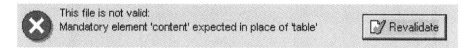

The Validate command also automatically includes a well-formedness check, so there is no need to first use the Check well-formedness command manually before validating a file.

Please note that you can use this command to validate XML instance documents and for validating XML schemas or DTDs.

This command normally operates on the active main window, but you can also use the Validate command on any file, folder, or group of files in the active project window, where you can also define the Schema or DTD to validate with on a per-folder basis in the project properties. Click on the respective folder, and then on the "Validate" icon.

Validate XML

When you validate an XML document, XML Spy first tries to locate any reference to a supported schema dialect within the document. It then loads the corresponding schema or DTD into memory, and uses its definitions to validate your XML instance document.

Once the Schema or DTD has been loaded into memory, XML Spy also provides you with intelligent editing functions in the Info Window and Entry-Helpers.

As long as the XML instance document is open, XML Spy will also keep the Schema or DTD in memory (see the Flush Memory Cache command on the DTD/Schema menu).

Validate Schema

XML Spy supports all major Schema dialects, such as DTD, DCD, XDR, XML-Data, BizTalk, and the new W3C XML Schema Definition Language (XSDL)

Validate these **schemas** against their specification by clicking on the Validate button. You can then be sure that they can be used to create, edit, and validate XML instance documents that are based on these schemata.

Update Entry-Helpers

This command **updates** the Entry-Helper windows, by reloading the underlying DTD or Schema.

If you have modified the Schema or DTD that an open XML document is based upon, it is advisable to reload that Schema or DTD to update the intelligent editing information (such as the Entry-Helper and Info windows) presented in the XML document, to reflect your changes.

Namespace Prefix...

This command lets you set the namespace prefix (identifier) for a group of selected elements (including their child elements).

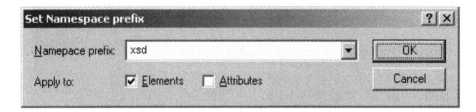

You can choose to set the namespace prefix on either elements, attributes, or both.

Please note:
Attributes don't need to have the same prefix as their parent elements, since attributes always inherit the element's namespace, if no prefix is given.

DTD/Schema Menu

XML Spy contains many commands that let you operate with Schemas and Document Type Definitions (DTDs) efficiently.

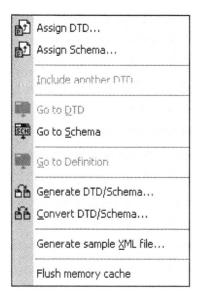

You can:
- Assign DTDs or Schemas to be used for validation with any XML instance document
- Generate a Schema from an example XML document (or from a group of files in the project window)
- Convert between all major schema dialects, and
- Locate the definition of any element or attribute in the corresponding schema while editing your XML documents.
- Generate a sample XML file based on an existing schema.

Assign DTD...

This command **assigns** a Document Type Definition (**DTD**) to an XML document to enable Validation and Intelligent editing.

The command opens the Assign File dialog to let you specify the DTD file you wish to assign, and inserts the required DOCTYPE statement into your XML document:

```
<!DOCTYPE main SYSTEM "http://link.xmlspy.com/spyweb.dtd">
```

Assign Schema...

This command **assigns** a Schema to an XML document to enable Validation and Intelligent editing.

The command opens the Assign File dialog to let you specify the XSD, XDR, or BizTalk schema file you wish to assign, inserts the required namespace declaration attributes into your XML document:

```
xmlns="http://www.xmlspy.com/schemas/icon/orgchart"
xmlns:xsi="http://www.w3.org/1999/XMLSchema-instance"
xsi:schemaLocation="http://www.xmlspy.com/schemas/icon/orgchart
                    http://schema.xmlspy.com/schemas/icon/orgchart.xsd"
```

The declarations generated by XML Spy depend on the Schema kind and - in case of the new W3C XML Schemas - also on the potential use of a targetNamespace in the Schema document.

Include another DTD...

This command allows you to include another Document Type Definition (DTD) or external parsed entity into the internal subset of a document type definition, or in any DTD document. This is done by defining a corresponding external parsed entity declaration and using that entity in the following line:

```
<!ENTITY % navigation.dtd SYSTEM "S:\xml\navigation.dtd">
%navigation.dtd;
```

The command opens the Assign File dialog to let you specify the DTD file you want to include in your DTD.

Go to DTD

This command **opens** the Document Type Definition document (**DTD**) on which the current XML document is based.

Go to Schema

This command **opens** the Schema document (**XSD**) on which the current XML document is based.

Go to Definition

This command **displays** the exact definition of an element or attribute in the corresponding Document Type Definition or Schema document.

To see the item definition in Enhanced Grid view:
1. Click left on the item.
2. Select the menu item **DTD/Schema | Go to Definition,** or click on the icon.

To see the item definition in Schema design view:
1. Use CTRL + Double click on the item you want to see the definition of, or
2. Click the item and select menu option **DTD/Schema | Go to Definition,** or click on the icon.

In both cases, the corresponding DTD or Schema file is opened, and the item definition is highlighted.

Generate DTD/Schema...

This command **generates** a new **DTD** or **Schema** from an XML document (or from a set of documents in the project window).

Use this function when you are defining a new schema or DTD, as it is often helpful to use an example XML document as a starting point.

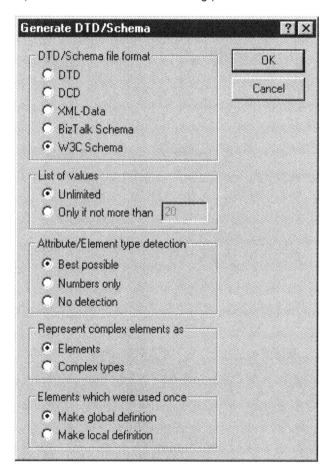

If you are targeting one of the modern schema kinds (e.g. XSD or BizTalk), XML Spy can automatically detect datatypes (such as date, time, number, uri, etc.) being used in your XML documents and create the corresponding restrictions in the schema.

XML Spy will also optionally detect typical enumeration scenarios, where an element or attribute can only contain items from a predefined list of values. You can also decide how to represent complex elements and how elements that only appear only once should be treated.

This command normally operates on the active main window, but you can also use the Generate DTD/Schema command on any file, folder, or group of files in the active project window.

Convert DTD/Schema...

This command **converts** an existing **DTD** (or Schema) into an **XML Schema** compliant with the May 2nd 2001 Recommendation, or any of the other available schema dialects.

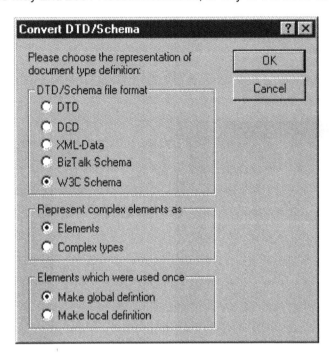

Generate sample XML file

This command **generates** an XML file based on the currently active **schema** in the main window.

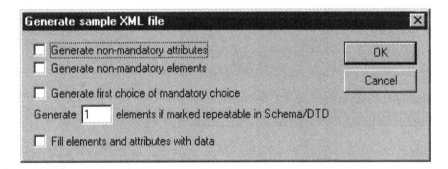

Generate non-mandatory attributes
Activating this option generates all mandatory and non-mandatory attributes defined in the schema.

Generate non-mandatory elements
Activating this option generates all mandatory and non-mandatory elements defined in the schema.

Generate first choice of mandatory choice

Activating this option generates/inserts the first choice of a mandatory choice.

Generate "1" elements if marked repeatable in Schema/DTD
Activating this option generates the number of repeatable elements you enter in the text box.

Fill elements and attributes with data
Activating this option inserts the data type descriptors/values for the respective elements/attributes. Eg. Boolean = 1, xsd:string = string, Max/Min inclusive = the value defined in the schema.

Flush Memory Cache

This command **flushes** all cached Schema and DTD documents from memory.

To speed up validation and intelligent editing, XML Spy caches all recently used DTD, external parsed entity, and Schema documents in memory. Information from these documents is also displayed, when you are using the Go to Definition command.

Use this command if memory is tight on your system, or if you have been using many different documents based on different schemas recently.

Schema design Menu

The Schema design menu allows you to:
- Define your schema settings
- Save a component diagram
- Generate Schema documentation in as much detail as you wish, and
- Define how much element information you want to display during editing.

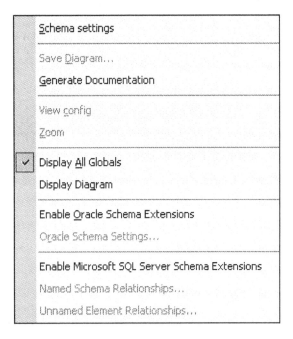

Schema settings

This command lets you define the **global schema settings**.

You set the **Default Element Form** to Qualified or Unqualified. The same can be defined for the Default Attribute form. These defaults can be changed for each element or form in the Details entry helper.

Enter the Block and Final defaults in the respective text boxes, and enter the schema version number in the Version field.

Click on the "Target namespace" radio button, and enter the namespace if you want to include it.

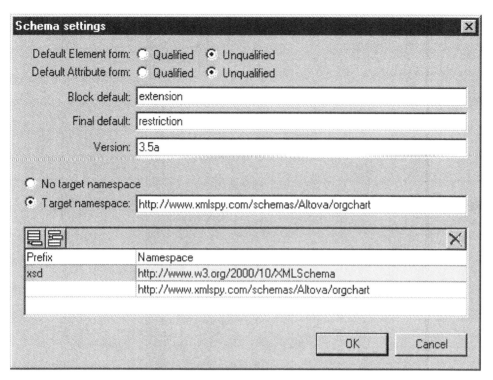

You can see these settings if you switch to the Text view of XML Spy.

```
<?xml version="1.0" encoding="UTF-8"?>
<xsd:schema
targetNamespace="http://www.xmlspy.com/schemas/Altova/orgc
hart" xmlns="http://www.xmlspy.com/schemas/Altova/orgchart"
xmlns:xsd="http://www.w3.org/2000/10/XMLSchema"
elementFormDefault="unqualified"
attributeFormDefault="unqualified" blockDefault="extension"
finalDefault="restriction" version="3.5a">
     <xsd:notation name="Altova-Orgchart"
public="http://www.xmlspy.com/schemas/Altova/orgchart"/>
     <xsd:complexType name="DivisionType">
        <xsd:sequence>
           <xsd:element name="Name" type="xsd:string">
              <xsd:annotation>
                 <xsd:documentation>Division Name
```

Save Diagram...

This command **saves** the component graphic (content model in the main window) in PNG format.

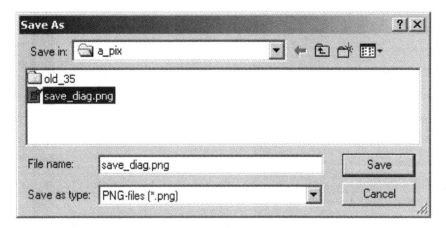

Generate Documentation

This command **generates** detailed documentation about your schema.

Documentation is generated for each element using the settings you define in the dialog box. Related elements (child elements, complex types etc.) are hyperlinked, enabling you to navigate from element to element. The element symbols in the content model diagrams are also hyperlinked, enabling you to see their definitions by clicking on them.

Schema documentation is also generated for **schema components included** in a schema document.

Output format:
You can output your schema documentation in HTML or Word format.

Include:
Select which items you want to include in the documentation: index (if you include other schemas components) global elements, groups, complex types etc.

Details:
Select the details you want to include in the documentation: diagram, attributes, facets, source code etc. The Diagram option includes the graphical representation of each schema item in the document.

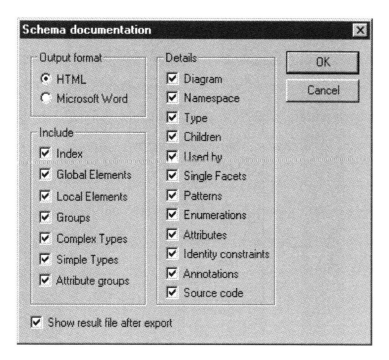

Show result after export:
Activating this option generates the documentation and displays it immediately after the export
process is complete. If you select HTML, the HTML document appears in the Browser view of
XML Spy. Selecting Word creates and displays the Word document.

element **Person**

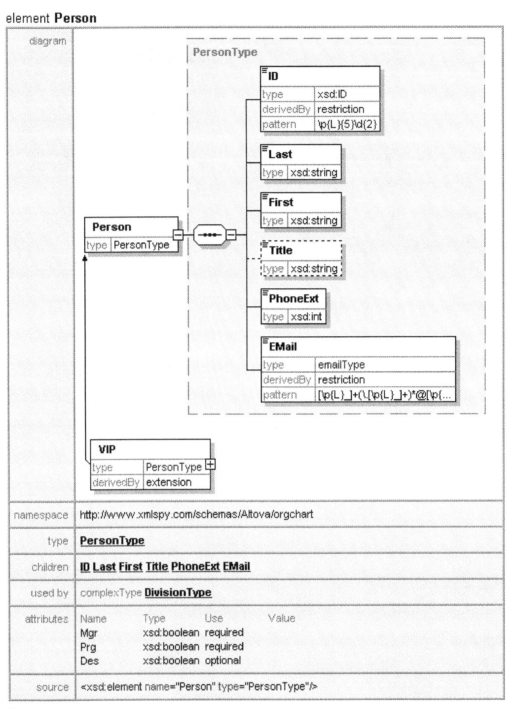

namespace	http://www.xmlspy.com/schemas/Altova/orgchart
type	**PersonType**
children	**ID Last First Title PhoneExt EMail**
used by	complexType **DivisionType**
attributes	Name Type Use Value Mgr xsd:boolean required Prg xsd:boolean required Des xsd:boolean optional
source	<xsd:element name="Person" type="PersonType"/>

Example 1:

Example 2:
Schema documentation showing the index and the included schema components from the address.xsd schema.

View config

This command allows you to configure the **content model view**.

The dialog box opens at the bottom right of the XML Spy window, giving you room to see changes reflected in the content model immediately.

The settings you define here, apply to the schema documentation output as well the printer output.

To define the data to appear in the content model:

1. Click the Append 🗔 or Insert 🗔 icon to add a line.
2. Select the parameter you want to display from the combo box.

The content model view is updated, showing the parameter(s) you selected.

To delete a line/parameter from the content model:

1. Select the line you want to delete.
2. Click the Delete icon ⊠.

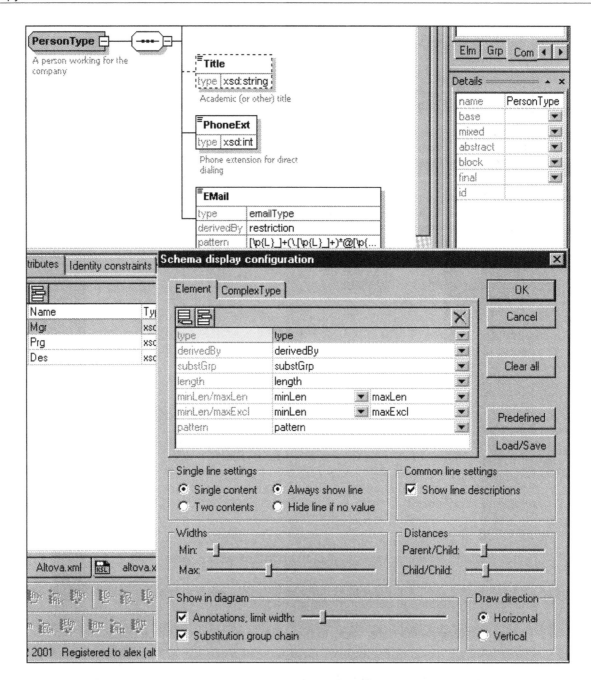

Single line settings:
You can define if the lines are to contain single or double content, and the parameters to be displayed in each case. You can also define if the line is mandatory or only visible if it contains data.

Please note:
You can define the single/double setting for **each** line. Select the line you want to configure and click the single or double content radio button.

Common line settings
This option toggles the line descriptions on and off.

Widths

These sliders enable you to set the min. and max. size of the element rectangles in the content model view. Change the sizes if parameter text is not fully visible, or you want to standardize your display.

Distances

These sliders let you define the horizontal and vertical distances between various elements on screen.

Show in diagram

The Annotations check box toggles the display of annotation text on or off, as well as the annotation text width with the slider. You can also toggle the display of the substitution groups on or off.

Draw direction

These options define the orientation of the element tree on screen, horizontal or vertical.

The **Load/Save** button allows you to load and retrieve the settings you make here.
The **Predefined** button, resets the display configuration to default values.
The **Clear all** button empties the list box of all entries.

Content model editing

You can change element parameters/values directly in the content model.

- Double click the cell of the element (table) you want to edit and start entering data. If a selection is possible, a drop down list appears if not, enter the parameter or value and confirm the entry with the Return key.

The entry helpers will be updated at this point, reflecting the data you entered.

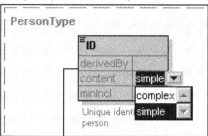

Zoom

This command controls the zoom factor of the content model view.

Drag the slider to see to change the zoom factor directly, or click in the entry box and enter the numeric value.

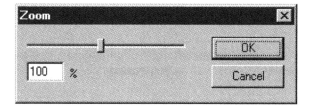

Display all Globals

This command displays the global components in the Schema overview, and is only available when you are viewing the content model of a component.

Alternatively:

- Click the "Show Globals" icon ▦ to return to the Schema Overview.

Display Diagram

This command **displays** the **content model** of the currently selected **component**.

To see the content model of a component:
- Click on the ▦ icon next to the component you want to display, or
- Select the menu option **Schema design | Display Diagram,** or
- Double click on a component name in the "Component Navigator" (Top right entry helper).

Enable Oracle Schema extensions

XML Spy provides preliminary support for Oracle schema extensions for use with "Project XDB".

Using these extensions will allow you to configure and customize how the Project XDB version of Oracle 9i, will store XML documents internally. These XML documents are then accessible from an XML perspective as well as through SQL queries and legacy tools.

Please see the Oracle.com website for more information.

Selecting this menu option inserts an Oracle.com/xdb namespace into the schema file

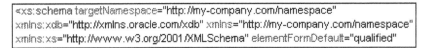

```
<xs:schema targetNamespace="http://my-company.com/namespace"
xmlns:xdb="http://xmlns.oracle.com/xdb" xmlns="http://my-company.com/namespace"
xmlns:xs="http://www.w3.org/2001/XMLSchema" elementFormDefault="qualified"
```

and makes an Oracle tab available in the Details entry helper.

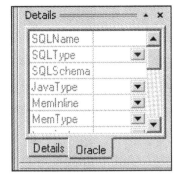

Oracle extensions can be defined for elements, attributes and complex types. Use the entry helpers to define the schema settings in the same was as you normally would with XML Spy.

Please note:
> **Disabling** this menu option **deletes** all the Oracle schema extension information from your schema file. A warning message appears, allowing you to reconsider. Confirming

this action with OK, deletes all the info. This action cannot be undone!

Oracle Schema settings

This command allows you to define the global settings for Oracle schema extensions.

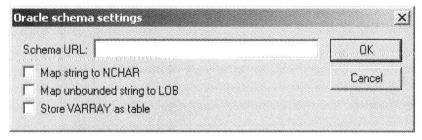

You have to have previously enabled the Oracle schema extensions, using the menu option "Enable Oracle schema extensions", to be able to access this menu option.

Enable Microsoft SQL Server Schema Extensions

XML Spy provides support for Microsoft SQL Server 2000 Schema Extensions.

Using these extensions will allow you to configure and customize how SQL Server stores XML documents internally. These XML documents are then accessible from an XML perspective as well as through SQL queries and legacy tools.

Please see the microsoft.com website for more information on SQL Schema Extensions.

Selecting this menu option inserts a SQL namespace into the schema file

and makes a SQL Server tab available in the Details entry helper.

SQL extensions can be defined for elements, attributes and complex types. Use the entry helpers to define the schema settings in the same was as you normally would with XML Spy.

> Please note:
> **Disabling** this menu option **deletes** all the SQL Server schema extension information from your schema file. A warning message appears, allowing you to reconsider. Confirming this action with OK, deletes all the info. This action cannot be undone!

Named Schema Relationships...

This command allows the definition of **named** relationships to provide the information needed to create the document hierarchy. You have to have previously enabled the SQL Server schema extensions, using the menu option "Enable SQL Server Schema Extensions", to be able to access this menu option.

To create a named schema relationship:

1. Click the insert 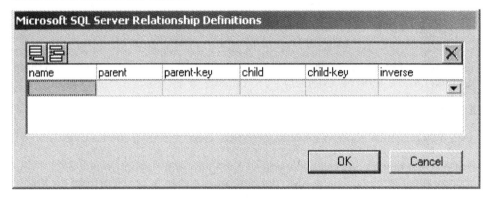 or append icon ![icon], to add a new row to the dialog box.
2. Click the field and enter the corresponding relationship name.
3. Click OK to confirm the entries.

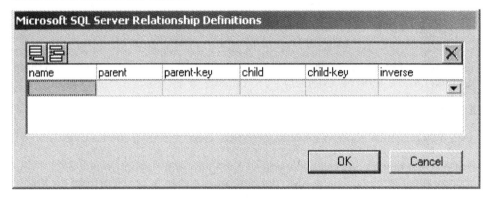

This generates a SQL relationship element, placing it just after the namespace declaration.

Please note:

Click the delete icon ![icon], to delete a row from the dialog box.

Unnamed Element Relationships...

This command allows the definition of **unnamed** relationships to provide the information needed to create the document hierarchy. You have to have previously enabled the SQL Server schema extensions, using the menu option "Enable SQL Server Schema Extensions", to be able to access this menu option.

To create an unnamed schema relationship:

1. Click the insert ![icon] or append icon ![icon], to add a new row to the dialog box.
2. Click the field and enter the corresponding relationship name.
3. Click OK to confirm the entries.

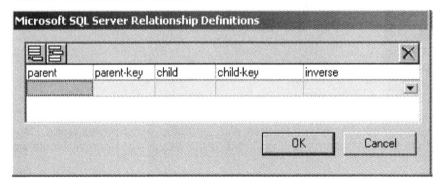

This generates a SQL relationship element for the currently selected schema element.

Please note:

Click the delete icon , to delete a row from the dialog box.

XSL Menu

The eXtensible Stylesheet Language (XSL) and in particular the XSL Transformation (XSLT), lets you specify let you specify how an XML document should be converted into other XML documents or text files, such a HTML, XHTML, or WML pages.

XML Spy supports XSL and XSLT through both its Intelligent editing features in the Text and Enhanced Grid Views, as well as through a set of commands that lets you perform common XSL-related operations.

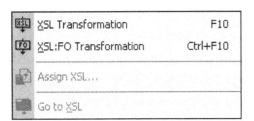

Please see the technical background information on XSLT Processors for further details.

XSL Transformation

    Hotkey: **F10**

This command performs an **XSL Transformation** of any XML document.

XML Spy can either use the Microsoft-supplied MSXML module or you can specify an external XSLT processor in the XSL tab on the Tools | Options dialog. You can also download other XSLT processors using the **Help | Components Download** menu option.

If your XML document contains a reference to an XSL stylesheet, which can be assigned using the Assign XSL command, the it is automatically used by the XSLT transformation command. Alternatively, you can also define the XSLT stylesheet to transform from, on a per-folder basis in the project properties (Select **Project | Project Properties** to open this dialog).

This command generally operates on the currently active main window, but you can also use the XSL Transformation command in batch-processing mode on any file, folder, or group of files in the active project window.

Please see the technical background information ons XSLT Processors for further details.

XSL:FO Transformation

    Hotkey: **CTRL+F10**

This command performs an **XSL: FO Transformation** of an XML document containing XSL Formatting Object markup. XSL Formatting Objects let you specify document layout: margins, text direction, pagination etc. of your XML documents.

XML Spy uses Apache Software Foundation's FOP tool to transform the FO file.

You can output the FO file:
- Directly onto screen using the built-in FOP viewer
- or generate an **output file** enabling you to create a PDF file, a TXT file, an Area tree (XML), a MIF file, a PCL or PS (postscript) file.

You can download the Apache FOP processor using the **Help | Components Download** menu option.

The FOP batch file path needed to start the FOP processor can be edited in the XSL tab on the Tools | Options dialog.

This XSL:FO command generally operates on the currently active main window, but you can also right click any file, folder, or group of files in the active project window and select the XSL:FO Transformation command to transform and display or output the document.

Transforming with XSL:FO

As an XSL FO file is an XML document, it must begin with the standard XML processing instruction and the FO root element.

To create a new FO document:
 1. Select the Menu option **File | New.**
 2. Click the **.fo Formatting Objects** entry, and confirm with OK.

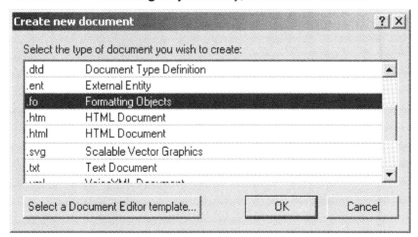

This creates an empty FO document containing the XSL FO declaration.

```
<?xml version="1.0" encoding="UTF-8"?>
<fo:root xmlns:fo="http://www.w3.org/1999/XSL/Format">
</fo:root>
```

 3. Enter the FO markup between the <fo:root> start and </fo:root> end tag.

To transform an existing FO document:
 1. Open a FO document in XML Spy. This example uses the **tiger.fo** document in the tutorial folder:
 2. Select the menu option **XSL | XSL:FO** or click the FO icon in the title bar.
      This opens the "Choose XSL:FO output" dialog box.

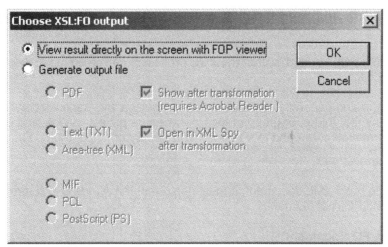

3. Clicking **OK**, causes the FO document to be transformed and displayed in the FOP viewer. Click the Next icon in the viewer, to see the next page of this document.
4. Close the window viewer window when you want to return to XML Spy. Click the print icon to print icon if you want to print the document.

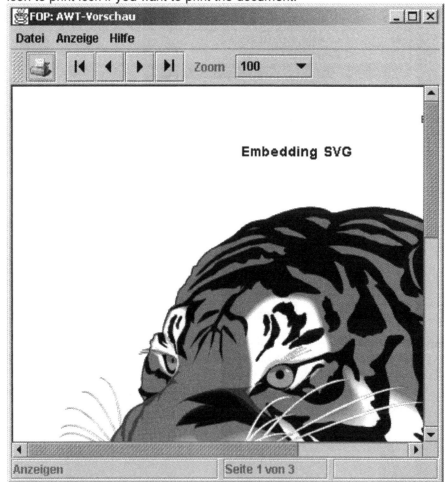

5. Clicking the "Generate output file" radio button enables you to select the specific type of output you want to create. Confirming with OK creates the output you choose.

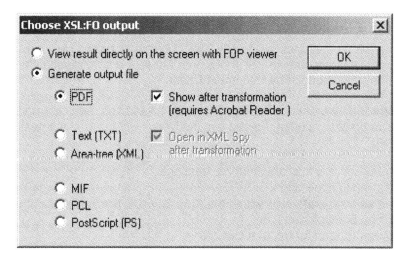

Assign XSL...

This command **assigns** an **XSL stylesheet** to an XML document, enabling XSL Transformation or rendering by an XML-compatible browser.

The command opens the Assign File dialog to let you specify the XSL or XSLT file you want to assign, and inserts the required processing instruction into your XML document:

```
<?xml-stylesheet type="text/xsl" href="http://link.xmlspy.com/main.xsl"?>
```

Go to XSL

This command **opens** the corresponding XSL or **XSLT document**, if your XML document contains a reference to an XSL stylesheet.

Document Editor Menu

XML Spy Document Editor enables you to edit XML documents **based on templates created in XSLT Designer!** The templates in XSLT Designer are saved as ***.sps** files, and supply all the necessary information needed by Document Editor.

Templates are **opened** by Selecting the **File | New** command and then clicking the "Select a Document Editor template..." button. Please see the Document Editor documentation for further information.

XML Spy Document Editor is available in three versions:
- As a stand-alone application,
- Integrated as a separate view within the XML Spy IDE user-interface (if you purchase the XML Spy Suite product), or
- As a Browser Plug-In for Internet Explorer.

Assign configuration file...

This command assigns a Spy Structure file (SPS) to an **XML document** to enable viewing and editing in the Document Editor view.

The command opens a dialog box enabling you to specify the SPS file you wish to assign, and inserts the required SPS statement into your XML document.

Hide markup

This command hides markup symbols in the Document Editor view.

Show small markup

This command shows small markup symbols in the Document Editor view.

Show large markup

This command shows large markup symbols in the Document Editor view.

Show mixed markup

This command shows mixed markup symbols in the Document Editor view.

Append row

This command appends a row to the current table in the Document Editor view.

Insert row

This command inserts a row into the current table in the Document Editor view.

Duplicate row

This command duplicates the current table row in the Document Editor view.

Move row up

This command moves current row up by one row in the Document Editor view.

Move row down

This command moves the current row down by one row in the Document Editor view.

Delete row

This command deletes the currently active row in the Document Editor view.

Convert Menu

XML Spy provides powerful data exchange functions that allow you to convert back and forth between text, word processor, database, and XML files. You can also create a schema **from** an existing database as well as create a database, based on an existing schema.

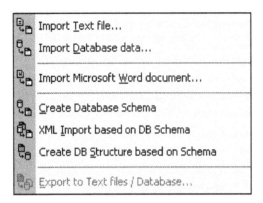

Import Text file...

This command lets you **import** any **structured text** file into XML Spy and convert it to XML format immediately. This is useful when you want to import legacy data from older systems, as most software products support a text export interface of some kind.

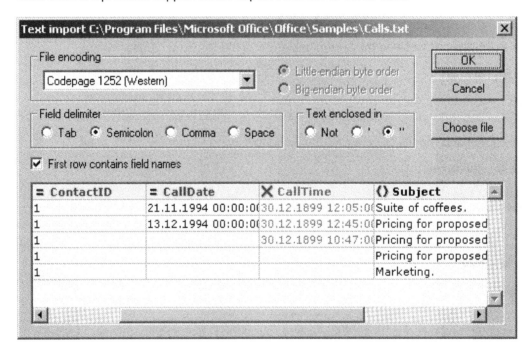

Unicode conversion

In order to convert the data into Unicode (the basis of all XML documents), you need to specify which character-set the file is currently encoded in.

For US or Western European Windows systems this will most likely be Codepage 1252, also referred to as the ANSI encoding. If you are importing 16-bit or 32-bit Unicode (UCS-2, UTF-

16, or UCS-4) files, you can also switch between little-endian and big-endian byte order.

Field Delimiter
To successfully import a text file, you need to specify the field delimiter that is used to separate columns or fields within the file. XML Spy will auto-detect common row separators (CR, LF, or CR+LF).

Text enclosed in
Text files exported from legacy systems sometimes enclose textual values in quotes to better distinguish them from numeric values. If this is the case, XML Spy lets you specify what kind of quotes are being used in your file, and removes them automatically when the data is imported.

First row contains field names
It is also very common for text files to contain the field names in the first row within the file. XML Spy allows you to define your XML element or attribute names according to this information.

Choose file
Click on the "Choose file" button to select the specific file to be imported, after having defined the import parameters. The file name will be retained the next time you use this dialog box, allowing you to change settings and re-import the same file if the resulting XML file does not match your expectations.

Having selected the file to be imported, XML Spy provides a preview of the data import. Any changes in the above options will be reflected in the preview immediately.

Renaming field or column names
Rename a field or column name by clicking on its title and editing the name.

Attribute, Element, or no columns
XML Spy lets you choose if you want to import a column as an attribute, element, or if you'd rather skip the column entirely.

Click on the icons to the left of the column titles to, toggle between these three options. In the example above,
ContactID and CallDate - are imported as attributes
CallTime - is not imported
Subject - is imported as an element.

Import Database data...

This command lets you **import database data** from many sources.

You can select:
- an existing database: such as Microsoft Access (i.e. Jet Engine), SQL Server, Oracle, or any other ODBC or ADO-conformant database).

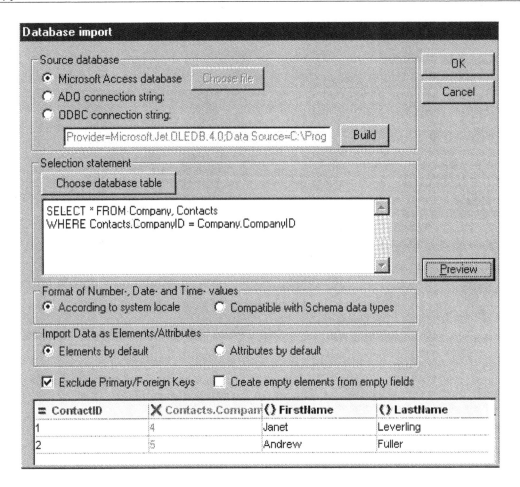

Source database
Once you have selected your data source, you can choose the database table to be imported from a list. If you need help in entering an ADO connection string, click the Build button, which opens the ADO Data Link properties dialog box.
To define the ODBC connection string, please see: Setting up the ADO or ODBC connection string using the Data Source Administrator.

Selection statement
Click on the "Choose database table" button, to select the database, or enter an arbitrary SELECT statement to create the record-set you intend to import. You can also enter a ADO shape string (selection statement) if you selected the ADO connection string radio button.

Having configured the data source, click the **Preview** button to verify that this is indeed the correct data that you wish to import. For security reasons, the OK button is only enabled after you have previewed the data.

> Please note:
> If you used the menu option **Convert | XML Import based on DB Schema** prior to opening this dialog box, the automatically generated select statement (used in that process) will appear in Select statement text box. You can now reuse or edit the select statement and start a new import.

Format of Number, Date and Time values
XML Spy lets you choose different representations for date and number formats - depending on whether you intend to use the resultant XML file in conjunction with the new unified

datatypes proposed by the most recent XML Schema draft, or if you want to keep those formats corresponding to the locale in use in your country.

Import data as Elements/Attributes
These options let you specify how you want the parent and child elements to be imported: as elements or attributes. The preview is updated when you select one of these options.

Exclude Primary/Foreign keys
This option enables you to exclude the primary or foreign keys for all the tables you are importing.

Please note:
This option **only** affects the keys of database tables that have been **exported** using the XML Spy Conversion option "**Export to Text files / Database...**", with the "Create Primary/Foreign keys" being active. The key names are PrimaryKey and ForeignKey respectively.

Create empty elements from empty fields
This option lets you create empty elements for all the empty fields that exist in the tables you import.

Attribute, Element, or no columns
XML Spy lets you choose if you want to import a parent column as an attribute, element, or if you'd rather skip the column entirely.

Click on the icons to the left of the column titles, to toggle between these three options. In the example above,
>   ContactID - is imported as an attribute
>   Contacts.Company - is not imported
>   FirstName, LastName - are imported as elements.

>   Please note:
>   The selections you make here initially apply to the parent items as well. Changing parent items directly, takes precedence over these settings, but only applies to the parent elements and not to any child elements.
>   Clicking the Preview button, resets any changes made to the parent elements in the Preview view.

ADO connection string

If you need help in entering an ADO connection string, click the Build button, which opens the ADO Data Link properties dialog box.

ADO Data Link properties dialog box:

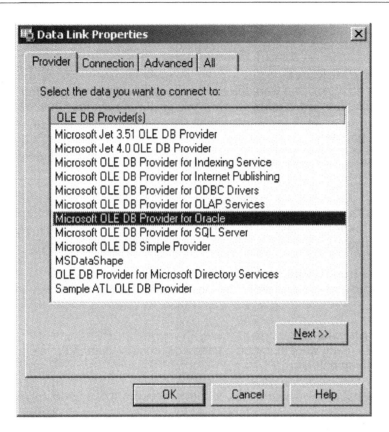

Select the corresponding OLE DB Provider from the list and click on the Next button to enter the connection properties:

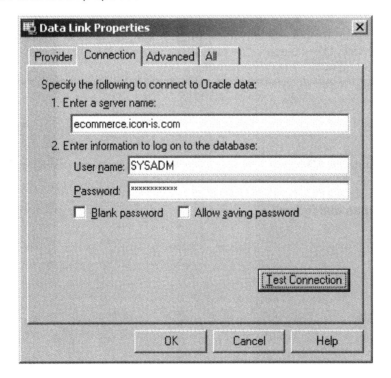

XML Spy relies on the ActiveX Data Object (ADO) interface for much of the basic database connectivity. ADO is included with Windows 2000 and Microsoft Office 2000, but you may need to install it if you are using an older version of Windows or Office.

Please see the Setting up the ADO or ODBC connection... for an alternative method of doing the same thing.

> Please note:
> Activate the "Allow saving password" check box, to enter your password info into the connection string, and avoid an error message when the connection takes place.

Please refer to our FAQ for more information on ADO and to download the Microsoft Data Access Components (MDAC) which allow you to upgrade to the latest ADO version. We also recommend that you visit the Microsoft Universal Data Access site on the Internet.

After you have imported your data and converted it to XML format, you may also want to use the Generate DTD/Schema function to get all the datatype information you need from your database into your XML documents.

XML Spy now makes it possible for you to convert a database into a schema. MS Access and several other databases are able to automatically provide the key and keyref information for the ADO driver, used to create the database hierarchy.

Please see the section under the **Convert menu | Create Database Schema** for more information.

Import Microsoft Word document...

This command enables the direct **import** of any **Word document** and conversion into XML format, if you have been using paragraph styles in Microsoft Word. This option requires Microsoft Word or Microsoft Office (Version 97 or 2000).

When you select this command, the Open dialog box appears. Select the Word document you want to import.

XML Spy automatically generates an XML document with included CSS stylesheet. Each Word paragraph generates an XML element, whose name is defined as the name of the corresponding paragraph style in Microsoft Word.

Create Database Schema

XML Spy enables you to create a schema based upon an external database file. Microsoft Access databases, as well as ADO and ODBC compatible databases, are supported.

To create a schema from a database file:
1. Select the menu option **Convert | Create Database Schema.**

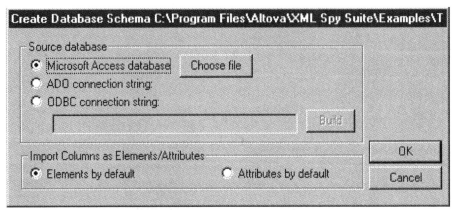

2. Select **Microsoft Access database**, and click the Choose file button.
3. Select the **DB2schema.mdb** file supplied with XML Spy, and click the **Open** button.
4. Click the **OK** button of the Create Database Schema dialog box, to start the conversion process.

   The generated schema appears in the Schema Design View. Click the "Identity constraints" tab, to see the keyref and key fields of the respective elements.

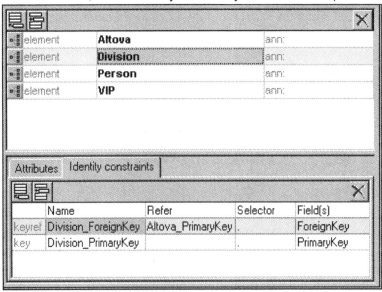

5. Click the component icon next to the **Altova** global element, to see the content model.

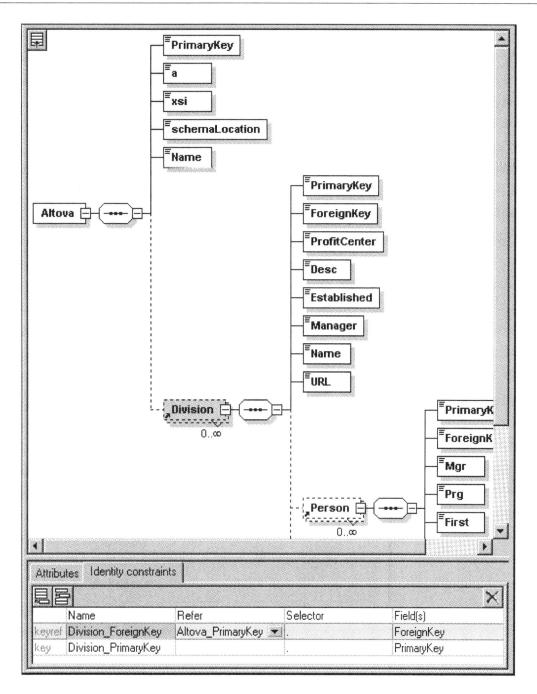

6. Select the menu option **File | Save as**, and save the new schema e.g.
    DB2schema.xsd.

7. Click the Display all globals icon ![icon], to return to the schema overview.

Please note:
    When generating the schema, all namespace prefix colons are automatically
    converted into underscore characters.

Databases currently supporting the key and keyref fields:
MS Access and several other databases are able to automatically provide the key and keyref
information for the ADO driver, used to create the database hierarchy.

To create relationships for NON MS Access databases:
1. Click the "**ADO connection string**" radio button in the Create Database Schema dialog box box.

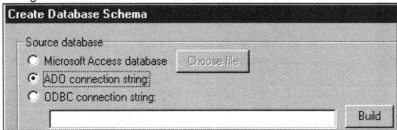

2. Click the **Build** button that has now become active.
    This opens the Data Link Properties dialog box.
3. Select the corresponding **Microsoft OLE DB Provider** (or vendor specific provider) for the database you use, do not select one of the generic drivers.

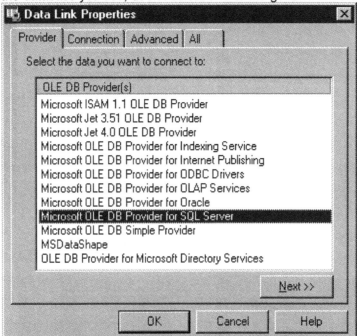

4. Click the **Next** button to switch to the Connection tab and fill in the required information: the data source, the user name and password, and activate the **Allow saving password** check box.
5. Click the Test Connection button to test the connection, and Click OK to confirm the settings.

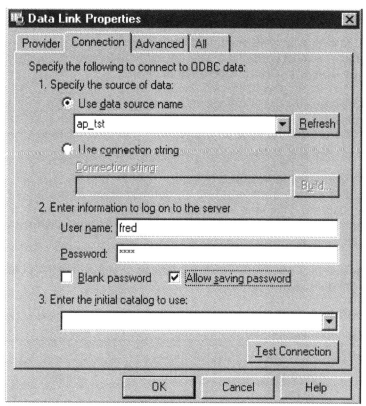

6. Click OK in the Create Database Schema dialog box, to create the schema.

To convert from... SQL server databases:
*   Select the **Microsoft OLE DB provider for SQL server** provider.

To convert from Oracle... databases:
*   Select the **Microsoft OLE DB provider for Oracle** provider.

To convert from... MS Access:
*   Click the **Microsoft Access Database** radio button in the Create Database Schema dialog box. This selects the correct provider, there is no need to use the ADO connection string and Data Link Properties dialog box.
*   If however, you want to build the connection string yourself, please use the **MicrosoftJet 4.0 OLE DB** provider.

To convert from... Other databases:
*   Select the corresponding Microsoft OLE DB, or vendor specific provider, from the Data Link Properties dialog box.

To convert from... databases without a specific provider:
Other databases will create a flat structured schema, including all tables and their corresponding datatypes.

*   Use drag and drop in the schema overview, to create the necessary relations between the imported elements.

*   To create an element hierarchy you have to directly edit the key and keyref fields, visible in the Identity constraints tab. Please see "Creating Identity Constraints" in the Reference manual for more information.

XML Import based on DB Schema

XML Spy allows you to create an XML document containing database data based on an existing XML Schema. You must currently create the schema (on which the import is based) using the menu option **Convert | Create Database schema.**

In the case of an MS Access database the Identity constraints, which define the database hierarchy, are automatically created in the generated schema. For other databases you have to define the identity constraints in the schema file yourself, please see Creating identity constraints.

Specifying the data you want to import

You can specify the data set you want to import, by defining which table is to act as the root table of the imported data set. This then **automatically** creates a shape string which is placed in the Selection statement text box. The database data is then imported into XML Spy with all hierarchical relationships intact.

The source database can be a Microsoft Access database or you can build an ADO connection string to connect to the database of your choice.

To import XML data from a Microsoft Access database:

1. Open the **DBschema2xml.xsd** schema file supplied with XML Spy (Tutorial folder).

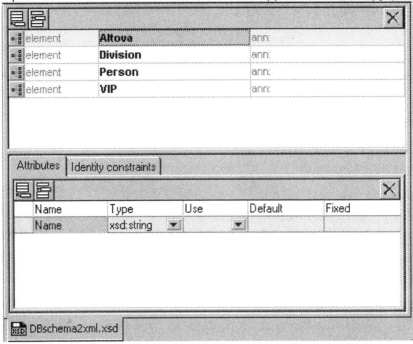

2. Select the menu option **Convert | XML Import based on DB Schema**.
   This opens the "Select root table from database schema" dialog box. This is where you define which tables you want to import. The root table becomes the top level table in the table hierarchy you import.

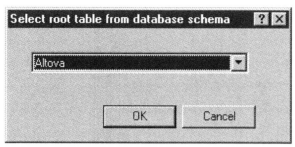

3. Click the **OK** button when you have selected the root table.
    The "Database import based on Schema" dialog box opens. The select statement,
    based on your root element choice, is automatically generated and placed in the Select
    statement text box.

Please note:
    You cannot edit the select statement here! You can however, start a new import using
    the **Convert | Import database data...** command. The same shape string will then
    appear in the Select statement text box, where it can be edited.
4. Click the Microsoft Access database radio button.

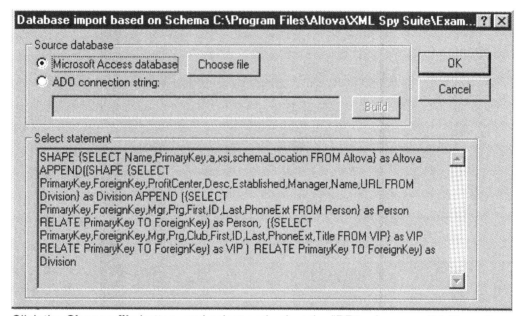

5. Click the **Choose file** button, and select and select the "**DB2schema.mdb**" file as the
    source of the database data (in the Tutorial folder).
6. Click the **OK** button to import the database data.
    The XML document appears as an "Untitledx.xml" file in the main window.

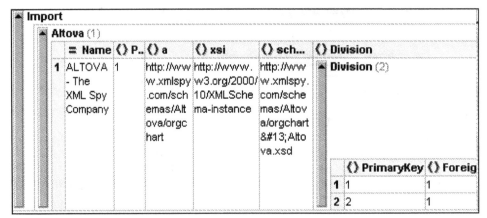

7. Click the Altova element and select the menu option **XML | Table | Display as table**, or press the **F9** function key, to remove the table formatting and display the data vertically. The Division elements were treated the same way to produce the screen shot below.

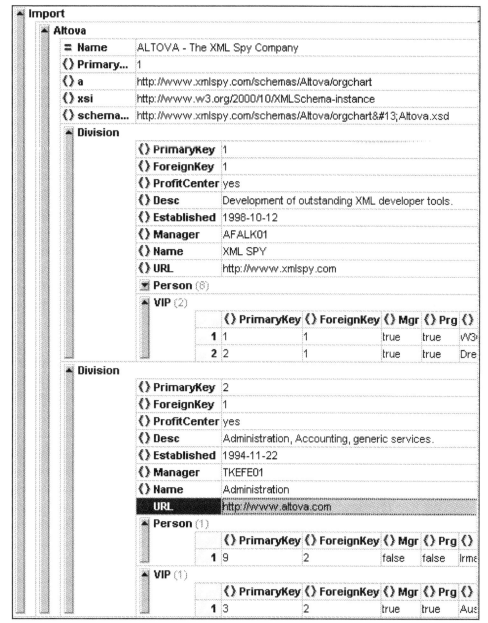

In this case the complete database was imported, the root table being Altova. The item Altova Name, was imported as an attribute in keeping with the schema definition DBschema2xml.xsd (visible in the attribute tab of the schema at the beginning of this section).

Importing a partial data set:
1. Repeat the above sequence and select **Division** as the root table.
2. Use the **DB2schema.mdb** file as the data source.
   The screen shot shows the resulting XML document. The Person table is expanded and the Division table formatting is disabled for a better overview.

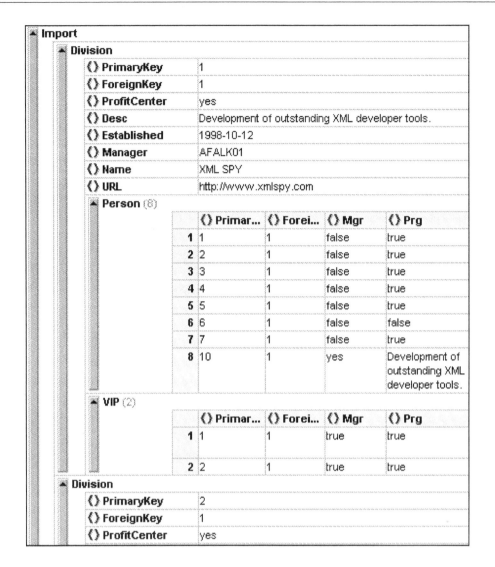

Create DB Structure based on Schema

XML Spy allows you to create an empty database (or skeleton database) based on an existing schema file. The schema structure, defined by the identity constraints, is mirrored in the resulting database.

To create a Database based on a schema:
1. Open the schema file **DB2Schema.xsd** in the Tutorial folder.
2. Select the menu option **Convert | Create DB Structure based on Schema**.
3. Click the "Create a new MS Access database" radio button and confirm with OK.

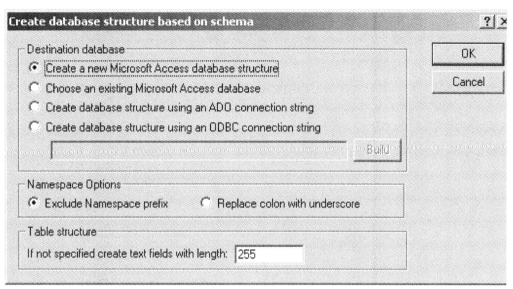

4. Enter the database name in the **Save as...** dialog box (eg. DB-based-xsd.mdb).
    The message "Export has been successfully completed" appears when the export has
    been completed successfully, confirm with OK.

Viewing the generated Database:

1. Double click the **DB-based-xsd.mdb** file in Explorer, or open the file in MS Access.

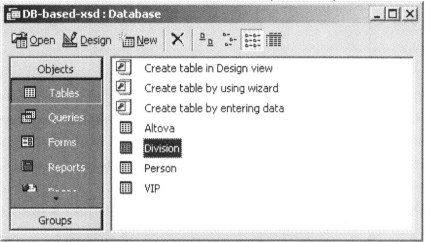

2. Double click the **Division** entry to see the Division Table.

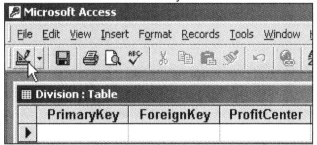

3. Select the menu option **View | Design view**, or click the "View" icon to change into the
    Design view.

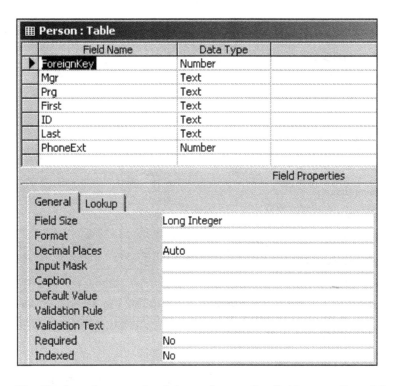

The Design view supplies information on the field properties of the database table: the field names, data types, etc. The parameter settings you see here have been transferred from the schema definition.

Export to Text files / Database...

This command **exports XML data** into other formats for exchange with databases or legacy systems.

Depending on the output data format required, you may want to use either XSLT Transformations or this Export command to export your XML data.

You first need to define the structure of the data to be exported. Since XML is structured hierarchically and most database and legacy systems use the relational model, XML Spy will help you in producing output that can be interpreted in a relational context.

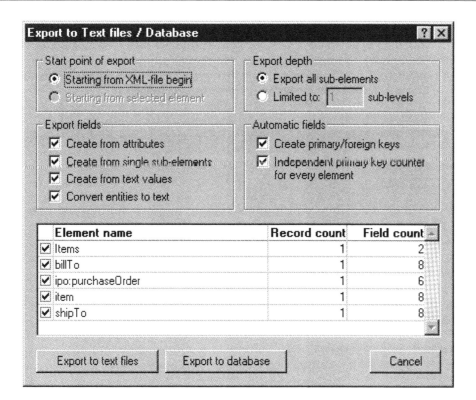

Start point of export
You can choose to export the entire XML document or restrict your export to the data starting from the currently selected element (and its child items).

Export fields
Depending on your XML data, you may want to export only elements, attributes, or the textual content of your elements into the fields common to structured text files or databases.

The list of available element types, in the preview window, lets you choose which elements you want to export, and also displays you how many records and fields this will produce once the export operation is started.

Export depth
You can choose to export all sub-elements, or limit the number of sub-element levels.

Automatic fields
XML Spy will produce one output file or table for each element type selected. You can choose to automatically create primary/foreign key pairs to link your data in the relational model, or define a primary key for each element.

When you are finished defining the scope of your export operation, click one of the two "Export" buttons, to export your data to a set of text files or to a database.

Export Database

This command button allows you to specify the type of database you want to export your data to.

You can select the destination database and the action to be performed:
• Create a new Microsoft Access (Jet Engine) database file

- Add the data to the tables in an existing Access file, or
- Export the data to any other ODBC or ADO-compliant database system (such as SQL Server or Oracle).
- The Namespace options allow you to either exclude the namespace prefix, or replace the namespace prefix colon with an underscore character.

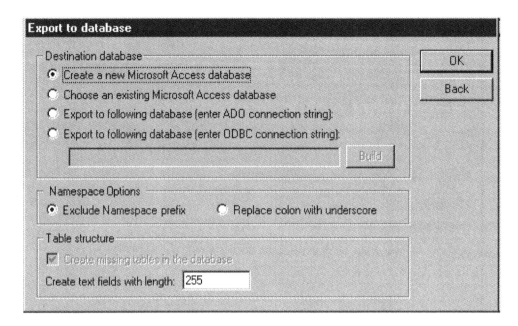

The Build button lets you create the necessary ADO connection string - for more information see the Import Database command and ADO connection string.

Export Text File

This command button allows you to **specify** the formatting of the text files to be exported.

If you are exporting XML data to text files, you must specify the desired character-set encoding to be used. The same options are also available in the Import text file dialog box.

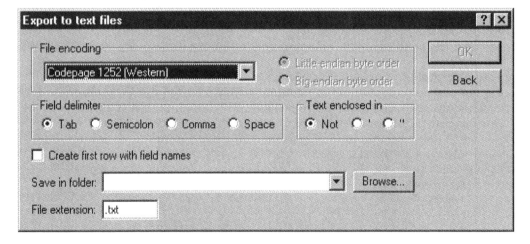

The set of text files will be generated in the folder you specify, and each file name will be generated from the corresponding element name. You can also specify the file extension to be used.

Convert - How to...

The How to... sections in this manual go into more detail about a specific subject in a task oriented way, and are generally sequential in nature. Tasks may build upon previous ones and may also use their data (or files) further on in the section.

In this section you will learn how to:

- **Export hierarchical XML data**, using the **Data_shape.xml** file supplied with XML Spy, and **orcate** a MS Access database called "Data_shape.mdb".

- Define an **ODBC (and ADO) connection** to the "Data_shape.mdb" database.

- **Import a single table** using the ODBC connection.

- **Import specific (hierarchical) portions** of the database data, using ADO data shape commands.
- Create **Identity constraints** in a schema, enabling you to import database data hierarchically - or create an XML document based on a database schema.

Files used in this How to... section:

- **Data_shape.xml** file, from which you will create a MS Access database
- **Shapes.txt** file, a file containing all the shape strings used in this section to import data using the ADO shape string function
- **No-constraints.xsd** file, for which you will create Identity constraints, enabling you to import specific data sets hierarchically.

Exporting hierarchical data

To export hierarchical data:
1. Open the **Data_shape.xml** file supplied with XML Spy.

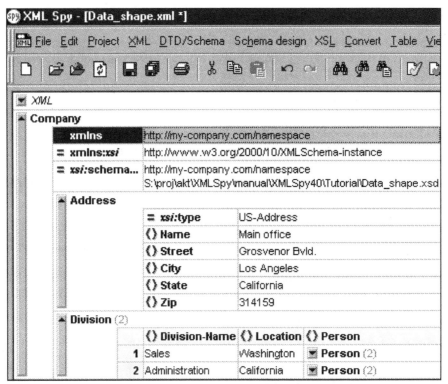

2. Select the menu option **Convert | Export to Text files / Database**.

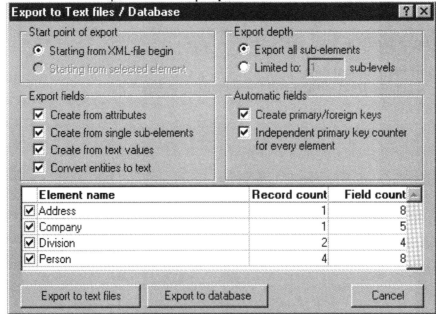

Retain the default settings as they are, all check boxes are active.
3. Click the "Export to database" button, and select the **Create a new Microsoft Access Database** radio button. Confirm with OK.

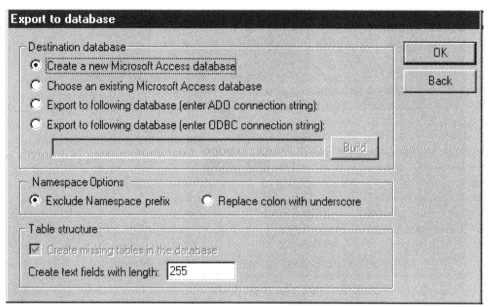

4. Enter the name of the new database in the "**Save as...**" dialog box (eg.
    Data_shape.mdb), and confirm by clicking on the Save button.
5. Once the export process has been successfully completed, click OK to confirm.

•   Double clicking the Data_shape.mdb file, opens it in MS Access. The exported
    database appears in this form:

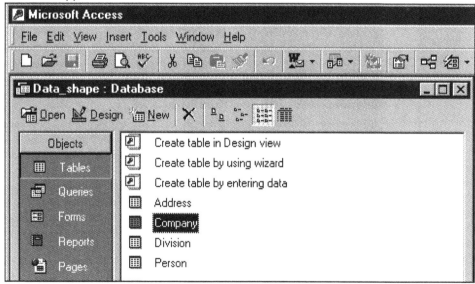

Setting up the ADO or ODBC connection using the ODBC Data Source Administrator

This example uses Microsoft Access as the target database. The exported data can be
imported using either an ODBC or an ADO data connection.

To set up a Database connection:
1. Click the **Start** button and select **Settings | Control Panel**. Then double click the
    Administrative tools folder.

2. Double click the **Data Sources (ODBC)** icon, to open the ODBC Data Source Administrator dialog box.

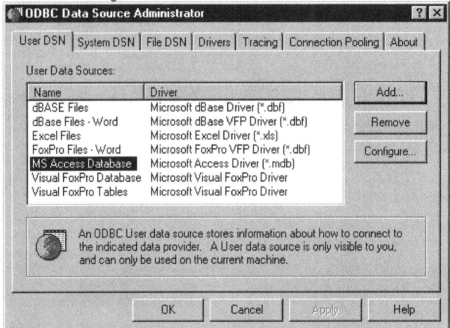

3. Click the **Add...** button to define a new data source.

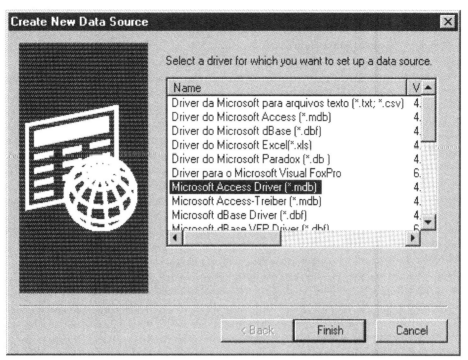

4. Select the **Microsoft Access Driver (*.mdb)** driver for the data source, and click the Finish button.

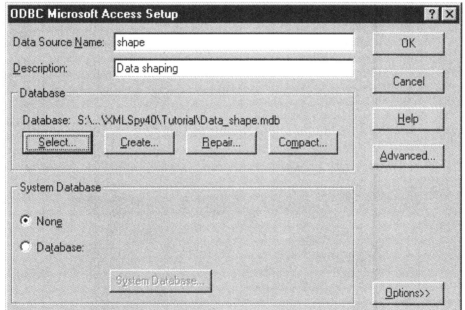

5. Enter "**shape**" as the Data Source Name, and enter a description in the Description field.
6. Click the **Select** button and select the previously exported database (Data_shape.mdb). Confirm the selection with OK.
   The file name and path appear above the Select button.
7. Click the **OK** button to confirm these settings. The Data Source Name "shape" appears in the User Data Sources list.

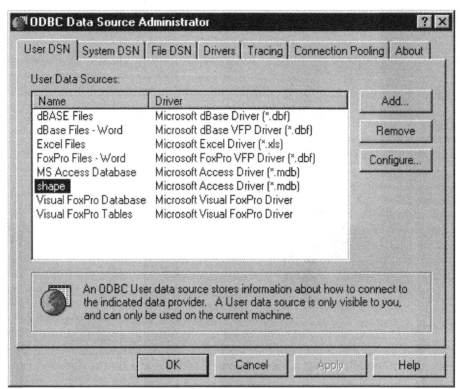

8. Click the **OK** button to complete the connection setup, and close or minimize the Administrative Tools folder.
    You are now ready to import MS Access table data hierarchically into XML Spy.
9. Switch back to XML Spy to start the import process.

Importing a table using ODBC

ODBC currently only supports the importing of a single database table, hierarchical data cannot be imported using this method.

To import a table using ODBC:
1. Select the menu option **Convert | Import Database data...**

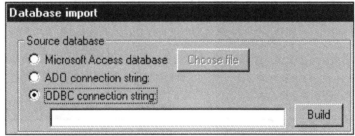

2. Click the **ODBC connection string** radio button, and then the **Build** button.

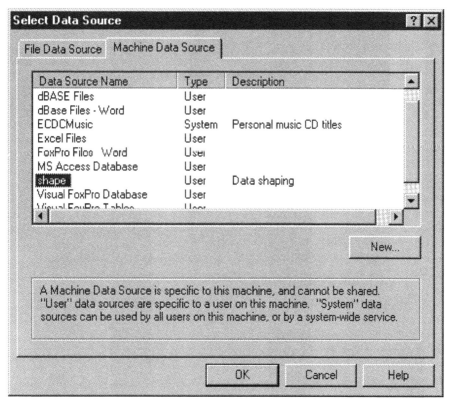

3. Click the **Machine Data Source** tab, select the previously defined "shape" data source, and click the OK button. The ODBC connection string now appears in the text box.
   If a User name and Password dialog box is opened at this point, enter the information as requested.

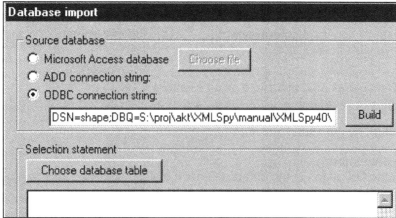

4. Click the **Choose database table** button and select the database table you want to import (in this case Person). The select statement SELECT * FROM "Person", appears in the Selection statement text box.
5. Click the **Preview** button to see the database data.
6. Activate the **Exclude Primary/Foreign Keys** check box, to avoid importing the key fields (this only applies to key fields that were created by XML Spy during the export process).

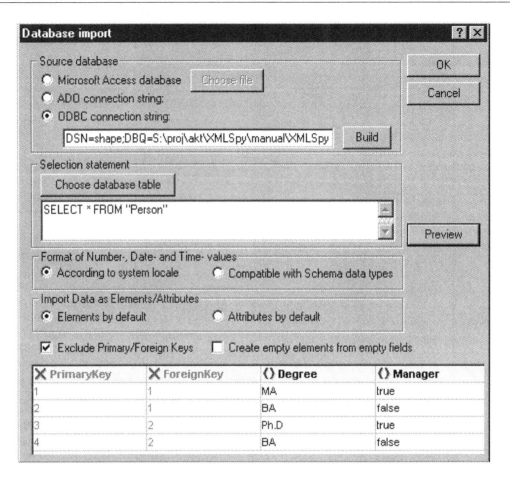

Defining which fields to import:

The preview window allows you to directly select and define the field data you want to import.

Clicking repeatedly on the **element symbol** <> to the left of the element name, cycles through the available possibilities:

<>	Define and import this field as an **Element**.
=	Define and import this field as an **Attribute**.
×	**Skip**, do not import this field.

Starting the data import:

1. Click the **OK** button of the database import dialog box, when you have decided which fields you want to import (no changes in this example).

XML Spy creates an **untitled XML file** containing the Person table data. The **root element** is called Import, and each Person element is a table row.

Importing hierarchical data - Data shaping (ADO)

XML Spy allows you to import hierarchical database data using the ADO data shaping function. This allows you to re-import specific parts of external databases.

You can either write your own selection strings or have XML Spy automatically create them using the **Create Database schema** and then the **XML Import based on DB Schema** commands.

To be able to use **data shaping** you have to use:
- The MSDataShape provider
- The special Data shape language, which is a subset of SQL

Both these modules are available if you have installed Microsoft Data Access Components Version 2.6 or later.

To import hierarchical data into XML Spy:

1. Select the menu option **Convert | Import Database data...**

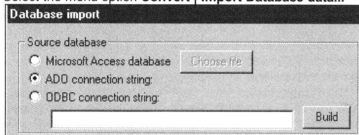

2. Click the **ADO connection string** radio button, and then the **Build** button.

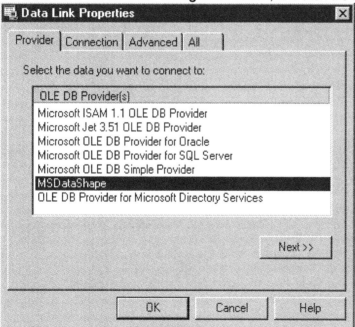

3. Double click the **MSDataShape** entry in the list box.
   This automatically switches you to the Connection tab.

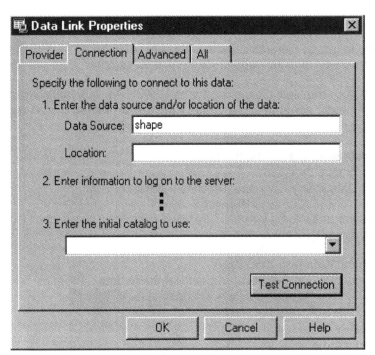

4. Enter "**shape**" in the Data Source field.
5. Click on the "**Test Connection**" button (at the bottom of the dialog box), if you want to make sure you can connect to the database - and then click OK to close the Test connection message box.
6. Click **OK** to close the Data Link Properties dialog box.

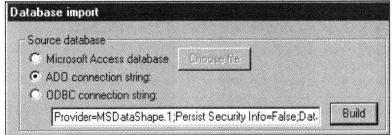

The ADO connection string now appears in the text box.
7. Open the **shape.txt** file supplied with the tutorial; copy the first Shape select statement, and paste it into the Selection statement text box.

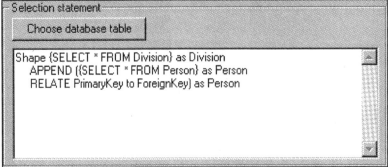

8. Click the "**Preview**" button to see a portion of the database data.

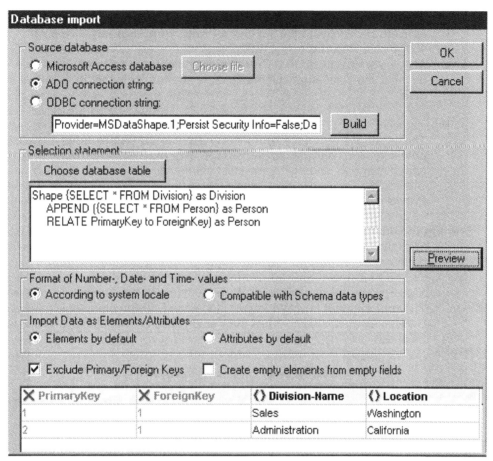

- Only the top level (parent) of the database data, defined by the shape command, is visible in the preview window.

Defining how the parent elements will be imported

The preview window allows you to directly select and define the field data you want to import.

Clicking repeatedly on the **element symbol** () to the left of the element name, cycles through the available possibilities:

()	Define and import this field as an **Element**.
=	Define and import this field as an **Attribute**.
X	**Skip**, do not import this field.

Please note:
> You can only directly influence the parent elements that you see here. You cannot change or choose to skip any elements below these ones (i.e. child elements).

Defining how the child elements will be imported

While the shape string allows you to import child objects, you can only define that all child items are to be imported as Elements or Attributes.

- Select either the **Elements by default** or **Attributes by default** option, to define how you want to import the child elements. The preview is updated when you select one of these options.

- Activate or deactivate the "**Exclude Primary/Foreign keys**" check box, to define if you want to import the data with or without primary or foreign keys.
- Activate or deactivate the "**Create empty elements from empty fields**" check box, to define if you want empty elements to be created for those fields that do not contain any data.

Please note:
The selections you make here initially apply to the parent items as well. Changing parent items directly, takes precedence over these settings, but only applies to the parent elements and not to any child elements.
Clicking the Preview button, resets any changes made to the parent elements in the Preview view.

Starting the data import

1. Click the **OK** button of the Database import dialog box, when you have completed your definition of the data you want to import.

   XML Spy creates an **untitled XML file** containing the Division and Person table data. The **root element** is called Import, and each Division element is a table row. Each Division element also contains the Person child elements, displayed in table form.

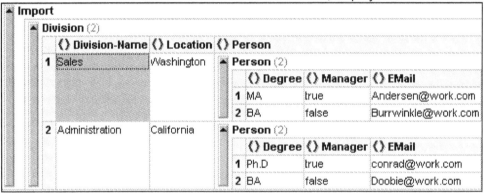

Click the Row element and press **F9** (or click the Display as Table icon ![table icon]) to remove the table formatting. Each Division element is now displayed separately.

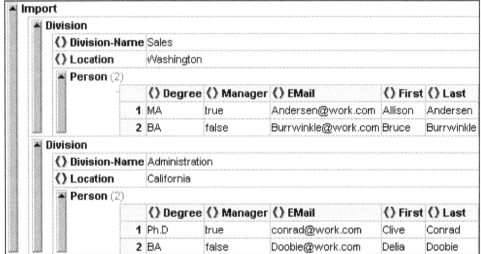

Shape strings

Data shaping is one of the new features of ADO 2.6. The basic idea behind data shaping, is the **hierarchical record set**. Data shaping allows a column of a master record set to itself contain another record set - a child record set.

It is important to distinguish between **hierarchical record sets** and **hierarchical databases**.
- Hierarchical record sets are standard record sets, where the data is represented hierarchically by parent, child or even grandchild tables.
- Hierarchical databases actually store data in an hierarchical format.

Please note:
  To be able to use the Shape language, you must have Microsoft Data Access Components Version 2.1 or later, installed on your computer. Please contact your IT-department for help if this is not the case.

Please see: the link http://support.microsoft.com/support/kb/articles/Q189/6/57.ASP for more information on Shape commands in general.

Importing hierarchical data
To import hierarchical data you can construct you own shape commands manually and enter them into the Selection statement text box, or have XML Spy automatically create them using the **Create Database schema** and then the **XML Import based on DB Schema** commands. The Shape commands are included in the Shapes.txt file, and on the following pages.

Please note:
- The **Data_shape.mdb** file was created by exporting to an Access database from the Data_shape.xml file (this XML file is included with XML Spy)
- All these examples are imported **without** external primary and foreign **key values**
- All the imported data are defined as **Elements by default**
- The "Create empty elements from empty fields" check box is inactive
- The preview window of the Database import dialog box of the data is included
- The resulting import file is displayed vertically, allowing you to see the data structure more clearly (the **Display as table** function is deactivated for the respective row element)
- Child elements (eg. Persons) are expanded

Shape string to import Division and Persons
Shape {SELECT * FROM Division} as Division
    APPEND ({SELECT * FROM Person} as Person
    RELATE PrimaryKey to ForeignKey) as Person

Preview window:

X PrimaryKey	X ForeignKey	() Division-Name	() Location
1	1	Sales	Washington
2	1	Administration	California

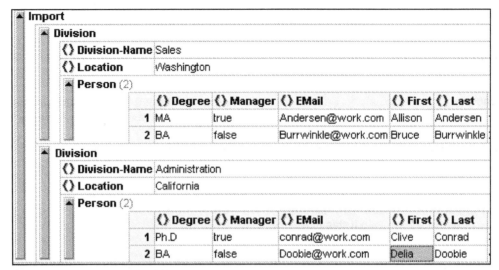

Result on import into XML Spy

Shape String to import Company, Division and Persons
SHAPE {SELECT * FROM Company} as Company
   APPEND((Shape {SELECT * FROM Division} as Division
    APPEND ({SELECT * FROM Person} as Person
   RELATE PrimaryKey to ForeignKey) as Person) as Division
   RELATE PrimaryKey to ForeignKey) as Division

Preview window:

✗ PrimaryKey	✗ ForeignKey	() xmlns	() xsi
1	0	http://my-company.com/	http://www.w3.org/200

Please note:
> The **name space prefix** has been suppressed in these examples because the option "Exclude Namespace" was activated during the export process. Thus xmlns:xsi becomes xsi, and xsi:SchemaLocation becomes SchemaLocation.

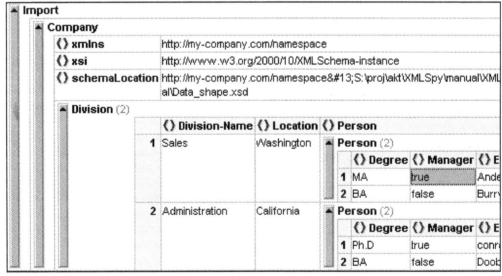

Result on import into XML Spy

Shape string to import Company, Address and Division
SHAPE {SELECT * FROM Company} as Company
   APPEND ({SELECT * FROM Address} as Address
   RELATE PrimaryKey to ForeignKey) as Address,
       ({SELECT * FROM Division} as Division
   RELATE PrimaryKey to ForeignKey) as Division

Preview window:

X PrimaryKey	X ForeignKey	() xmlns	() xsi
1	0	http://my-company.com/	http://www.w3.org/200

Result on import into XML Spy

Shape string to import Company, Address, Division and Persons
SHAPE {SELECT * FROM Company} as Company
APPEND({SELECT * FROM Address} as Address
  RELATE PrimaryKey to ForeignKey) as Address,
   ((SHAPE{SELECT * FROM Division} as Division
     APPEND ({SELECT * FROM Person} as Person
     RELATE PrimaryKey to ForeignKey) as Person) as Division
   RELATE PrimaryKey to ForeignKey) as Division

Preview window:

X PrimaryKey	X ForeignKey	() xmlns	() xsi
1	0	http://my-company.com/	http://www.w3.org/200

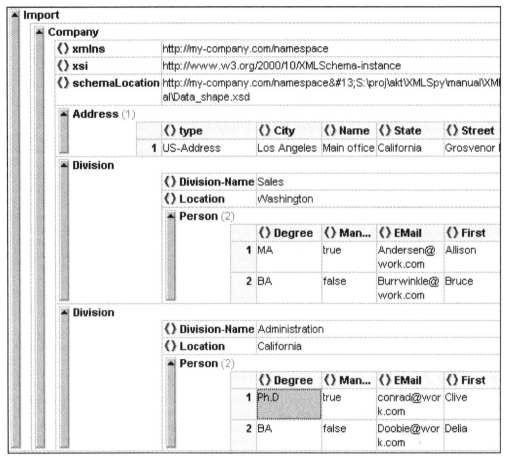

Result on import into XML Spy

Creating Identity constraints

MS Access databases automatically generate Identity constraints when you use the **Convert | Create Database Schema** command to create a schema.

Defining identity constraints:
The aim of this section is to be able to import XML data based upon a schema, using the **Convert | XML Data Import based on DB Schema**. This command uses the active schema file as a base for importing data from an external database. The schema file delivers some of the necessary information needed to automatically generate a select statement string.

1. Open the **No-constraints.xsd** file in the Tutorial folder of XML Spy.
2. Click the **Altova** element to select it and click the **Identity constraints** tab.
3. Click the **Append** icon and select the Key entry.

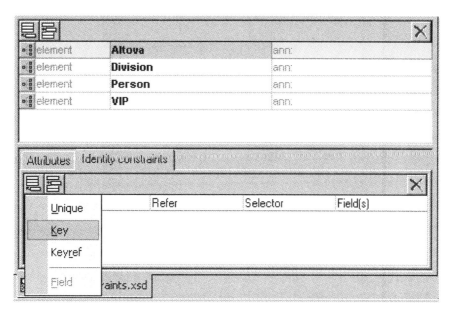

4. Enter **Altova-Primary** in the Name field and hit the Tab key.
5. Enter a period character "." in the Selector field and hit the Tab key again.
6. Enter PrimaryKey in the Field(s) cell and hit Return to confirm.

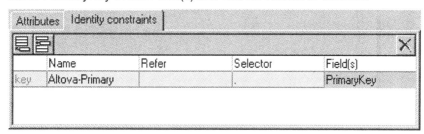

This has defined the Altova element as the top-level table.

7. Click the **Division** element in the schema overview, click the **Append** icon and select the **Keyref** entry.
8. Enter **Division-Foreign** in the Name field, hit the Tab key and select **Altova-Primary** from the combo box and hit the Tab key.

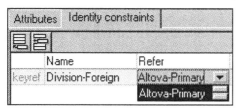

9. Enter a period character "." in the Selector field and hit the Tab key again.
10. Enter **ForeignKey** in the Field(s) cell and hit Return to confirm.
11. Click the Append icon and select the Key entry. Use the same method to enter the following data: Name=Division-Primary, Selector=".", and Field(s)=PrimaryKey.

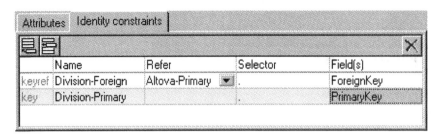

You have now created a relationship between the Altova and Division tables/elements, where the Division table is linked to the Altova table.

Checking the relationship
1. Select the menu option **Convert | XML import based on DB Schema**.
2. Select **Altova** as the root table in the dialog box that opens.
    This opens the "Database import based on Schema" dialog box. The automatically generated shape string appears in the Select statement text box. The select string shows that the Altova table is related to the Division table.

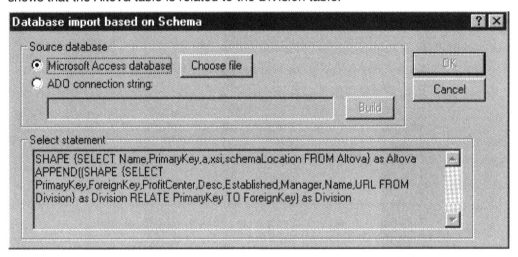

3. Click the Cancel button to close the dialog box for the moment.

Completing the identity constraints
We now have to define the rest the remaining identity constraints for the Person and VIP tables (elements in the schema). Use the method outlined above to add Key and Keyref fields to the Person and VIP elements.

Person element:

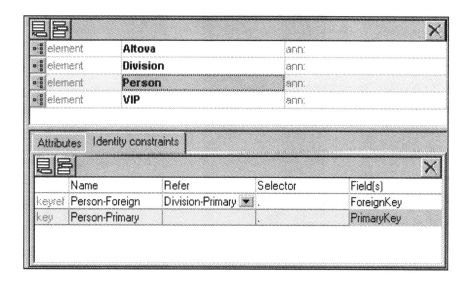

VIP element:

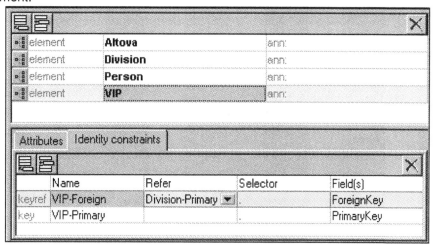

Importing data using a schema (with identity constraints)
1. Select the menu option **Convert | XML import based on DB Schema**.
2. Select **Altova** as the root table in the dialog box that opens. (You can choose any one of the entries as the root table, Division, Person or VIP.)
    This opens the "Database import based on Schema" dialog box. The automatically generated shape string appears in the Select statement text box.

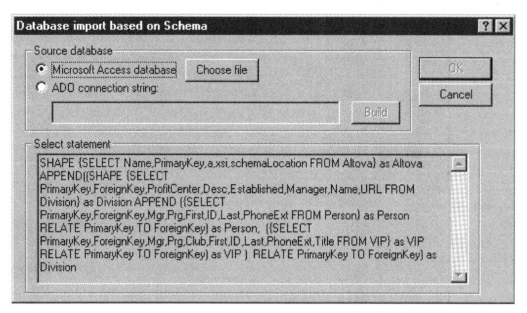

3. Click the "**Choose file**" button, select the DB2schema.mdb file in the Tutorial folder, and click the Open button. This enables the OK button in the Database import... dialog box.
4. Click the OK button to start the data import.
   The XML document appears as an "Untitledx.xml" file in the main window. Scroll right to see the complete structure.

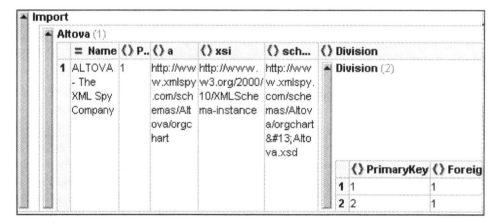

Please note:
   If you want to edit the select statement, start a new data import using the menu option **Convert | Import database data**. The select statement is automatically made available to Select statement text box after having used the **Convert | XML Import based on DB Schema**. You can now edit the select statement and import the data from here.

View Menu

The View menu controls the display of the active Main window and allows you to change the way XML Spy displays your XML documents.

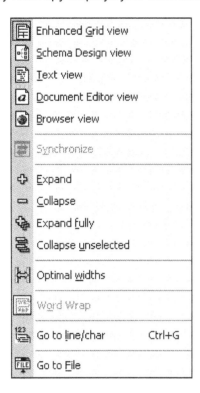

Enhanced Grid View

This command **switches** the current document into Enhanced Grid View.

This view includes an (optional) tree and structured grid display and is the preferred view for editing XML documents. If the previous view was the Text View, the document is automatically checked for well-formedness.

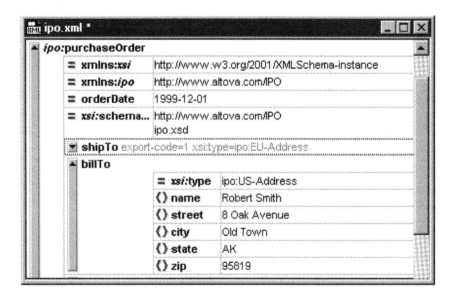

Embedded Database/Table view

XML Spy allows you to display recurring elements in a Database/Table view from within the Enhanced Grid view. This function is available wherever the Enhanced Grid view can be activated, and can be used when editing any type of XML file - XML, XSD, XSL etc.

For further information on this view, please see the detailed description of the various views in the Main Window section in the XML Spy Reference.

Schema Design View

This command **switches** the current document into Schema Design view.

XML Spy Schema editor allows you to view and edit schemas in two different ways:
- As a Schema overview, in list form
- In a graphical view of specific schema components

Schema overview

Open a XSD document in the DTD/Schemas folder of the project window, or double click on an XSD document in Explorer. The main window then displays the Schema overview.

The **top window** displays **all Global** "components" (elements, complex types etc.) in list form. The bottom window displays the corresponding attributes of the currently selected component (eg. VIP Mgr. Prg etc.).

Schema overview:

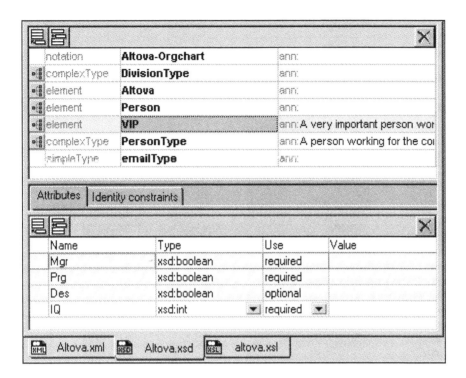

To see graphical representation (Content model) of a component:
- Click on the ⊞ icon next to the component you want to display, or
- Select the menu option **Schema design | Display Diagram,** or
- Double click on a component name in the "Component Navigator" (Top right entry helper).

The *content model* for that component, appears in a tree view.

Graphical content model view

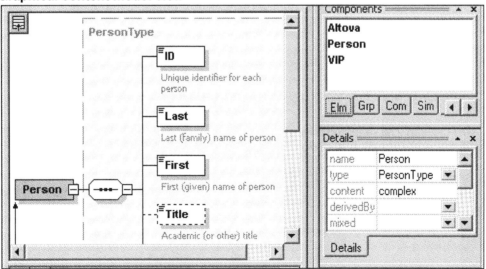

Text View

This command **switches** the current document into Text View.

This view allows you to edit the XML source in a source-code fashion and includes syntax-coloring.

If the previous view was the Enhanced Grid View, the document is automatically formatted according to the settings defined when saving a file (these can be modified in the "Save File" section of the File tab of the Options dialog). Use the menu command **Tools | Options** to open this dialog.

For further information on this view, see the detailed description of the various views in the Main Window section in the XML Spy Reference.

Browser View

This command **switches** the current document into Browser View.

This view uses an XML-enabled browser (preferably Internet Explorer 5) to render the XML document using information from potential CSS or XSL style-sheets.

When switching to browser view, the document is first checked for validity, if you have selected Validate upon saving in the File tab of the I Options dialog. Use the menu command **Tools | Options** to open this dialog.

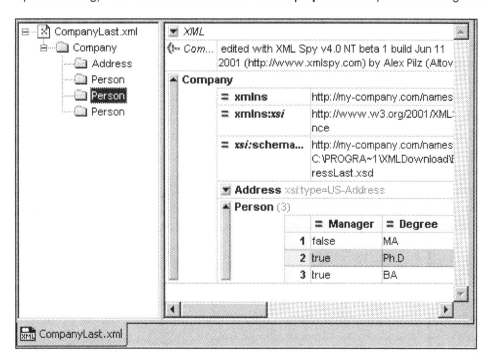

Default.html

2001-10-19	Altova releases **XML Spy 4.1**, which now includes support for XSL:FO (Formatting Objects).
2001-09-21	Altova releases **XML Spy 4.0.1** - a maintenance update that addesses several issues with the original 4.0 release
2001-09-10	The new **XML Spy 4.0 Product Line** is released
2001-08-12	Altova becomes a sponsor of **OASIS**.
2001-04-17	XML Spy 3.5 Tutorial available now. Experience how easy XML schema design can be. Download free from our **Download Center**.
2001-04-11	XML Spy wins SD Magazines **Jolt Productivity Award**.

For further information on this view, please see the detailed description of the various views in the Main Window section in the XML Spy Reference.

Synchronize

This command **synchronizes** the **Enhanced Grid view** and **Tree view** in the main window.

To see the Tree view, you must activate the "Show Tree" check box in the File tab of the Options dialog). Use the menu command **Tools | Options** to open this dialog box.

Click an item in the Tree or Grid view, and select the menu option **View | Synchronize.** The view in the other window is opened to the same level, and the item is highlighted.

You can also double-click on an element in the tree view, to navigate to that item in the grid.

Expand

     Hotkey: **Num +**

This command **expands** the selected element by one level.

The command can be used in the Tree and Enhanced Grid views. The keyboard shortcut is the + key on the **numeric keypad**.

In the Enhanced Grid view, the element and all its children remain selected after expansion. This allows you to expand a large element by pressing the + key repeatedly.

You can expand and collapse any element by clicking on the gray bar to the left of each element.

Collapse

     Hotkey: **Num -**

This command **collapses** the selected element by one level.

The command can be used in the Tree and Enhanced Grid views. The keyboard shortcut is the - key on the **numeric keypad**.

You can expand and collapse any element by clicking on the gray bar to the left of each element.

Expand fully

     Hotkey: **Num ***

This command **expands** all child items of the **selected element**, down to the last level of nesting.

The command can be used in the Tree and Enhanced Grid views. The keyboard shortcut is the * key on the **numeric keypad**.

Collapse unselected

Hotkey: **CTRL Num -**

This command allows you to focus on one element and its children, and ignore all the other surrounding elements.

The command can be used in the Tree and Enhanced Grid views. The keyboard shortcut is the **CTRL** and - key on the **numeric keypad**.

Simply select the item that you want to work with and choose this command to collapse all other (unselected) elements.

Optimal widths

This command **adjusts** the widths of all columns so that the text of the entire document fit into the designated columns.

If you expand and collapse several elements, select the "Optimal widths" command, as only visible items are taken into account when calculating the optimum column widths.

Word wrap

This command enables or disables word wrapping in the **Text view**.

Go to line/char...

    Hotkey: **CTRL+G**

This command goes to a **specific line number** and/or character position in an XML document in the Text view.

If you are working with an external XSLT processor (see the XSL page on the Tools | Options dialog for details) you may often get error messages by line number and character position. XML Spy lets you quickly navigate to that spot, using this command:

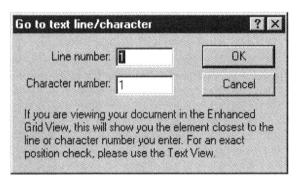

This command works in both the Text View and Enhanced Grid View, but will only be able to show an approximate position in the grid view by highlighting the element closest to the character position specified.

Go to File

This command **opens** a document that is being **referred** to, from within the file you are currently editing.

Select the file name, path name, or URL you are interested in, and choose this command from the View menu.

You can select:
- An entire element or attribute in the Enhanced Grid View
- Some characters from within any item in the Text or Enhanced Grid Views.
- An enclosed string. If you text cursor is between quotes, XML Spy will automatically use the entire string that is enclosed in the quotes.

Browser Menu

This menu contains commands that are only available when the Browser View has been activated.

Back

      Hotkey: **Backspace**

This command displays a previously viewed page. You can also use the keyboard Backspace key to achieve the same effect.

This can be useful if you click a link in your XML document and want to return to it.

Forward

This command is only available once you have used the Back command, and moves you forward through previously viewed pages.

Stop

This command instructs the browser to stop loading your document.

This is useful if large external files or graphics would be loaded over a slow Internet connection.

Refresh

      Hotkey: **F5**

This command updates the Browser View by reloading the XML document and potential external CSS or XSL style-sheets as well as DTDs. You can also use the F5 key to trigger this command.

Fonts

This command allows you to select the default font site for rendering the text of your XML document. It is similar to the Font-Size command in most browsers.

Separate Window

This command opens the browser view in a separate window, so that side-by-side viewing is possible. (eg. text or enhanced grid) view.

If you have separated the browser view, press F5 in the editing view to automatically refresh the corresponding browser view.

Soap Menu

XML Spy supports SOAP Version 1.1 and WSDL Version 1.1.

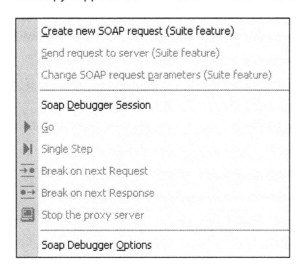

Please note that the SOAP interface and Soap debugger are only available in the XML Spy Suite version!

The **Soap - How to...** section that follows the menu descriptions, shows you how to use the SOAP debugger using the **nanonull.com timeservice** server supplied by Altova. Please use this service to test the SOAP debugger. The AirportWeather webservice, described on the following pages, might not always be available to you.

Use the SOAP functionality:
- To test your webservices without having to implement client applications
- For quick testing of third party webservices

For more info on these specifications please see:
SOAP   http://www.w3.org/TR/SOAP/
WSDL   http://www.w3.org/TR/wsdl

Create new SOAP request

This command creates a new SOAP request document in XML Spy.

Creating a new SOAP request:
1. Select the menu option **Soap | Create new SOAP request**.
    This opens a dialog box where you have to enter the local path or URL of a WSDL file describing the webservice. In this example the capescience.com AirportWeather websevice. The URL for this webservice is:
    http://www.capescience.com/webservices/airportweather/AirportWeather.wsdl

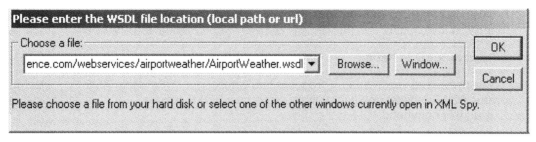

2. Cliok OK to confirm the selection and connect to the capescience.com server.
    This opens a dialog box from which you select a specific SOAP operation.

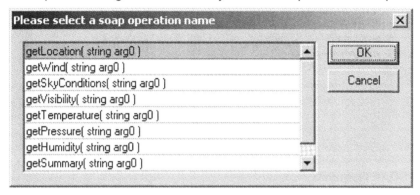

Please note:
    If the connection fails or the URL is incorrect, an error message will appear at this
    point.

3. Click the **getSummary (string arg0)** entry, and confirm with OK.
    This creates an Untitled.xml document in XML Spy containing the SOAP request data.

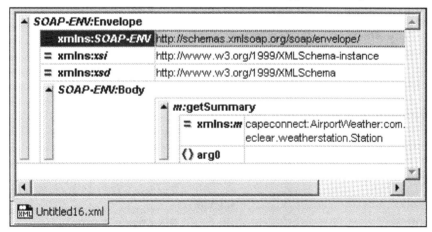

4. Click one of the fields to deselect the table highlighting.
    Before the request can be sent, we have to specify the airfield for which we want the
    weather summary.
5. Click the **arg0** field, and enter **KJFK** for the JFK weather report.

This completes the **definition** of this SOAP request, all we have to do now is send the request and see if we receive an answer. Please see "Send request to server".

Send request to server

This command sends a SOAP request to a webservice from within XML Spy. Having defined your SOAP request document, see Create new SOAP request, the request can be sent off using this command.

Previously defined SOAP request document:

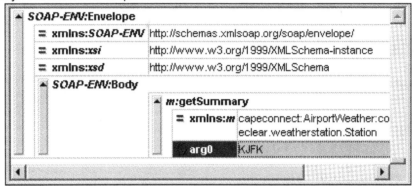

Sending a SOAP Request:

1. Making sure that the SOAP request document is active, select the menu option **Soap | Send request to server**.

    After a few seconds wait, a new XML document is automatically created in XML Spy containing the SOAP Response from the respective server. In this example, the location and weather status of JFK are displayed in the new document.

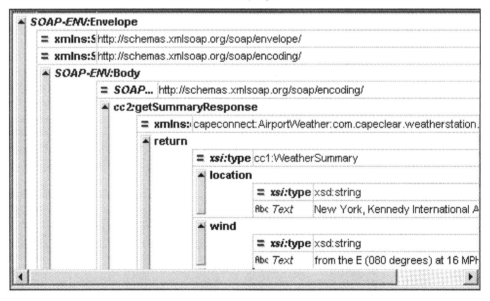

To change the SOAP request parameters not displayed in the request document (owing to the fact that they are transferred in the HTTP header) please see "Edit SOAP request parameters".

Change SOAP request parameters

This command allows you to change the currently defined SOAP parameters of the SOAP request document. This example uses the previously defined SOAP request document.

To change the SOAP request parameters:

1. Making sure that the SOAP request document is active, select the menu option **Soap | Change SOAP request parameters**.
   This opens the SOAP request settings dialog box. You can now either change the Connection end point or SOAP action settings. Confirm the changes with OK.

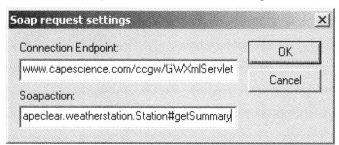

2. You can now resend the SOAP request using the menu option **Soap | Send request to server.**
   A SOAP response document will be generated and displayed in the main window in a few seconds.

Please note:

Only change the SOAP action settings if a full list of the SOAP methods and their corresponding SOAP actions are available to, and accessable by you.

Soap Debugger Session

This command starts a SOAP debugger session.

- A dialog box is immediately opened after you select this command. You then have to select a WSDL file location, generally a URL.
- Select the source and target ports needed for the debugger proxy server and the webservice, in the following dialog box.

   This opens the SOAP debuggers proxy server in its **inactive** state. Clicking one of the SOAP toolbar icons, starts the SOAP debugger and waits for the client requests.

   Please see the SOAP - How to... section for a more detailed description.

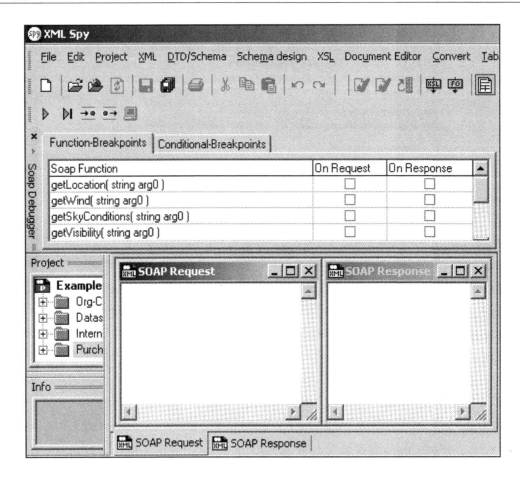

Go

This command activates the SOAP proxy server and processes the WSDL file until a breakpoint is encountered. The respective SOAP document then appears in one of the SOAP document windows.

Single Step

This command allows you to single-step through the incoming and outgoing SOAP requests and responses. The SOAP debugger stops for each request and response. The proxy server is also started if it was inactive.

Break on next Request

This command causes the debugger to stop on the next SOAP request, and display the data in the SOAP Request document window. You can directly edit the data in this window before sending it on to the webservice.

Break on next Response

This command causes the debugger to stop on the next SOAP Response, and display the data in the SOAP Response document window. You can directly edit the data in this window before sending it on to the client.

Stop the proxy server

This command stops the debugger proxy server.

Soap debugger options

This command allows you to define the SOAP debugger options. Please define these settings **before** you start the SOAP debugger.

Hide:
You can hide the entry helpers as well as the project or info windows, enabling you to see more of the data in the SOAP documents.

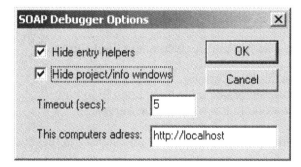

Timeout (secs)
Most clients have timeout setting in the data receiving function. The time the debugger remains in a breakpoint is per default 5 seconds. A data packet (http1.1 100 Continue") message is sent to the client once every timeout period you define.

Setting the timeout period to zero suppresses the data packet, you remain in the breakpoint for as long as you want.

This computers address:
Address of the computer on which the SOAP debugger is running. This computer must be accessable to the Client computer.

Enter the address in the form **http://computer name**, where "computer name" is the web address or IP address of the computer on which the SOAP debugger is running. Do not enter a port number in the address. The "localhost" entry always points to your local computer.

Soap - How to...

The How to... sections in this manual go into more detail about a specific subject in a task oriented way, and are generally sequential in nature. Tasks may build upon previous ones and may also use their data (or files) further on in the section.

In this SOAP - How to... section you will learn how to:

- Send and receive SOAP requests using the SOAP debugger
- Set breakpoints for sending and receiving SOAP requests
- Edit an incorrect SOAP request before sending it on to the webservice

When developing an application that accesses data from a webservice and does further data processing, something might happen that you don't expect. Wouldn't it be great to be able to see and edit the data that is actually transmitted?

This is where XML Spy SOAP debugger comes in. It works as a **proxy server** between your client and the webservice. The debugger functionality goes a lot deeper than a normal trace utility that only stores every call's Request and Response.

XML Spy SOAP debugger allows you to set breakpoints for every Request and Response message and even define Conditional breakpoints via XPath expressions.

SOAP debugger supports:
- Stepping through SOAP requests and responses
- Modification of the SOAP requests and responses and
- Forwarding of modified requests to the client or server.

SOAP communication process

Once the proxy server has been started, the SOAP communication process is as follows:

- Proxy server listens continually to a socket/port for incoming **client requests**

1. Client application **sends** a request to **proxy server**
2. Client requests can be modified if/when breakpoints have been triggered
3. Proxy server **request data** is forwarded to the **webservice server**

   - The **websevice server responds** to the proxy request, and sends the response data back to the proxy server

1. Server responses can be modified if/when breakpoints have been triggered
2. Proxy server **response data** is forwarded to the **client application**

- Client application receives response data from proxy server

How to... example client and server applications:
- The **Client** application, which sends and receives SOAP messages is the Browser window
- The "Nanonull Time Service" service will act as the **webservice server**.
  The URL for this webservice is:
  http://www.nanonull.com/TimeService/TimeService.asmx?WSDL

Port settings
The SOAP debugger uses the 8080 port to monitor the clients' requests. The port can only be altered when a new SOAP debugging session is started. Note that this port may be disabled by personal firewalls, or advertising filters. You would therefore have to disable these programs, or select a different port address.

Using SOAP debugger

Having started XML Spy,
1. Select the menu option **Project | Open Project**.
2. Select the "**Webservice debugger example.spp**" file in the **..\Altova\XML Spy Suite\Examples** folder.
3. Click the + sign of the HTML folder to see the folder contents.

4. Double click the **DebuggerClient.htm** file to start the SOAP Client and connect to the webservice.

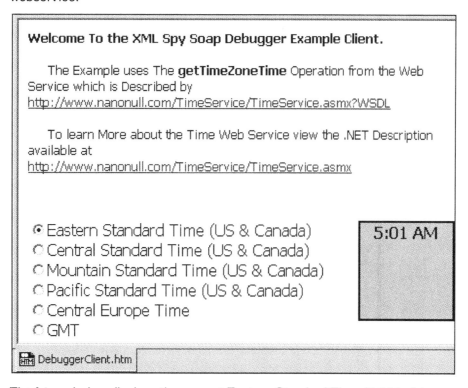

The **htm** window displays the current Eastern Standard Time (5:01 in this example).
5. Click the GMT radio button to see the current Greenwich Mean Time.

An error has obviously occured at this point. We should have a correct time in the clock display. We will have to activate the SOAP debugger to analyze the SOAP messages, see if we can locate the error and perhaps fix it.

Configuring the SOAP debugger
1.   Select the menu option **SOAP | SOAP debugger options**.
2.   Activate the "Hide project/info windows" check box, and click OK to confirm.

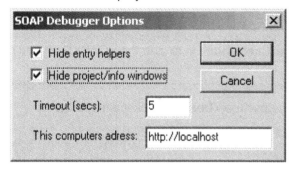

This allows more room for the SOAP request and response windows. Make sure you define these settings **before** you start the SOAP debugger.

To start the XML Spy SOAP debugger:
1.   Select the menu option **SOAP | SOAP Debugger Session**.
     This opens the "Enter the WSDL file location..." dialog box.

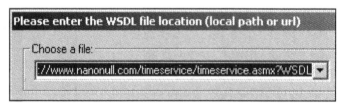

2.   Enter the WSDL file location into the text box
     http://www.nanonull.com/TimeService/TimeService.asmx?WSDL and click OK.
     The following dialog box displays the source and target port settings. The **source port** setting (8080) is a default setting and is automatically entered. This setting can be changed every time the debugger is started.
     The **target** settings are supplied by the WSDL file, and also appear automatically.

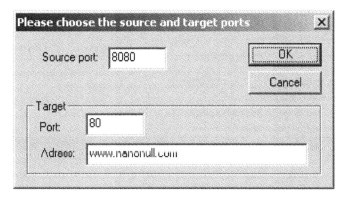

3. Click the **OK** button to start the SOAP debugger session.

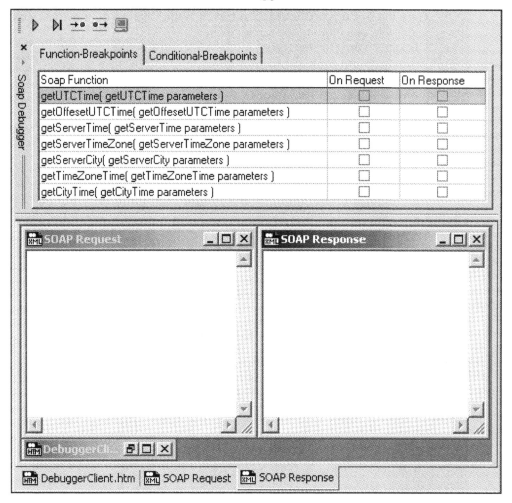

This opens the SOAP debugger proxy server in its **inactive** state. You can see this by noting that the proxy server icon is disabled.

Setting debugger breakpoints:
This webservice uses the method **getTimeZoneTime** to find the time zone time.
1. Activate the **On Request** and **On Response** check boxes for this method. This enables you to analyze both SOAP requests and responses for errors.

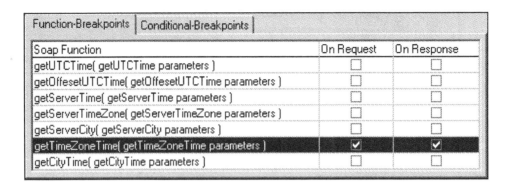

2. Click the **GO** icon ▷ (or use the menu command **SOAP | GO**).
3. Click the **DebuggerClient tab** to switch to the Client. You may have to maximize the window to see more of the contents.
4. Click the "Turn On Debugging Mode" button in the client window.

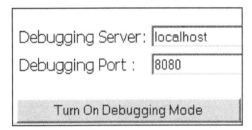

This displays a "Debugging is on" message, and sends off the SOAP request to the debugger.

Viewing and editing the SOAP request
The SOAP request automatically appears in the SOAP request window of the debugger. We can now look at the request and edit any errors it might contain.

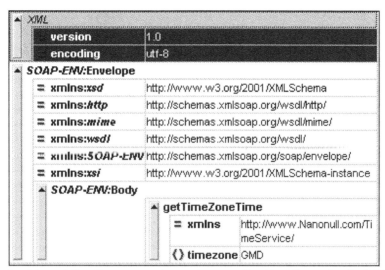

Looking at the **timezone** element, we notice that the value is **GMD**. This cannot be correct, so we will change it to GMT and see what happens.

1. Double click in the **timezone** field, change the entry to **GMT** and hit Enter.

2. Click the **GO** icon ▷ (or use the menu command **SOAP | GO**) to send the **corrected request** to the webservice.
    After a few seconds, the **webservice response** to the SOAP request appears in the SOAP response window.

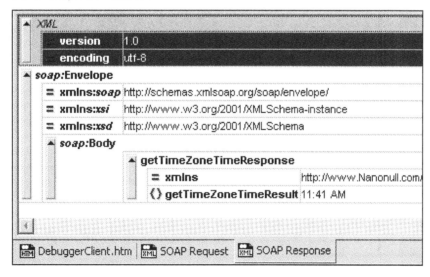

We did not receive an error message in the response, so we can assume that this is the correct time.

3. Click the debugger **GO** icon ▷ to send this response to the **client** (the Browser window in this case).
4. Click the **DebuggerClient.htm** tab to switch back to the client, and see the new result.

The error message has disappeared, and the correct GMT time is displayed.

5. Select the menu option **SOAP | SOAP debugger session** to close the debugger session.

Fixing the error

Now that we know that the **client** is actually sending the illegal value "GMD" instead of "GMT" in it's request and the server would correctly respond to "GMT", we have successfully identified the SOAP Client as being the component that causes the error, so we can go about fixing it.

In the **DebuggerClient.html** file click on the Text View button, open the Find dialog, and enter "GMT". XML Spy will display this code fragment:

```
else if(timezone[5].checked)
        msCurrentTimeZone='GMD';
```

Change the value from "GMD" to "GMT" and switch back to the Browser View. The SOAP Client now works correctly. Problem solved!

Setting breakpoints in SOAP debugger

The SOAP debugger window is where you set and delete breakpoints. It is separated into two tabs.

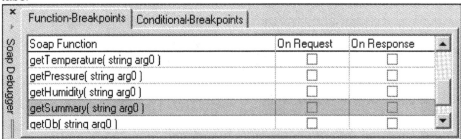

Functional-Breakpoints tab

The "Functional breakpoints" tab, allows you to set a breakpoint on either Requests and/or Responses to SOAP methods. The debugger highlights the line of the function which triggered a breakpoint.

Data packets to and from the client are analyzed and matched to the corresponding functions from the WSDL file. If a breakpoint is set for a specific method, then this is where the SOAP debugger stops. The toolbar buttons are enabled at this point.

The data is displayed in the "Soap Request" or "Soap Response" document window. The SOAP documents displayed in the SOAP windows can be modified at this point. The data is sent the moment you click one of the toolbar icons (except for the "stop server" icon).

Conditional-Breakpoints

The "Conditional Breakpoints" tab, allows you to use Xpath expressions to define breakpoints.

If a SOAP **request** causes an error, the SOAP **response** must contain a "faultcode" element. We therefore want to have a breakpoint triggered whenever a faultcode element appears.

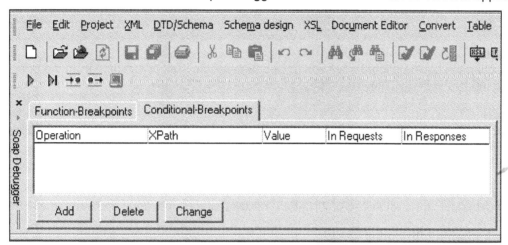

To add a conditional breakpoint:
1. Click the Conditional Breakpoints tab, and then the Add button.

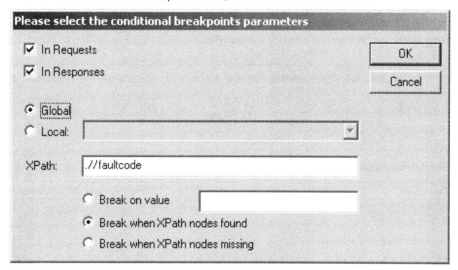

2. Enter the XPath expression (e.g. **.//faultcode**) in the XPath field.
3. Click the "Break when XPath nodes found" radio button.
4. Click the OK button to confirm the settings.
   The SOAP debugger will stop whenever a **.//faultcode** element appears in a SOAP request or response.

In Requests
This option lets you define the specific action to be taken if a breakpoint occurs in a SOAP Request. The rest of the dialog box options relate to the SOAP Request. You can of course use the same settings for the SOAP Responses, if you also activate the "In Responses" check box.

In Responses
This option lets you define the specific action to be taken if a breakpoint occurs in a SOAP Response. The rest of the dialog box options relate to the SOAP Response. You can of course

use the same settings for the SOAP Responses, if you also activate the "In Requests" check box.

Global
Selecting the Global option, defines that every method/function is scanned for the condition you define.

Local
Selecting the Local option, forces you to select a specific method/function from the ones supplied by the WSDL file. This method/function is then scanned for the condition you define.

XPath
Enter the specific XPath expression/node here. An XPath has to be entered here, to be able to use any one of the specific radio button options.
Please see the XPATH section for more information.

Break on value
The debugger stops when one of the XPath nodes matches the value you enter in this field.

Break when XPath nodes found
The debugger stops when the specific XPath node, **.//faultcode** entered in the XPath field, **exists** in the SOAP Request or Response.

Break when XPath nodes missing
The debugger stops when the specific XPath node , **.//faultcode** entered in the XPath field, is **missing** from the SOAP Request or Response.

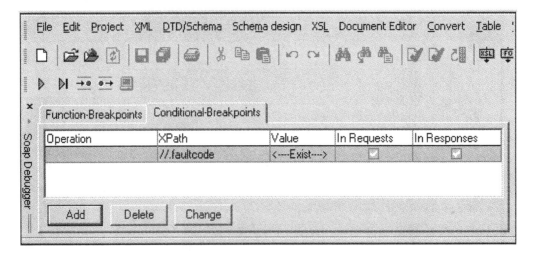

Operation
The Operation column contains the method the being searched for. If you selected the **Global** radio button then this field remains empty. If you selected **Local**, then the method you selected is displayed here.

XPath
This column contains the XPath expression you defined.

Value
This column contains the XPath value against which the XPaths nodes are checked for a match. If you selected "Break on value" the specific string you entered is displayed here. If you selected "Break when XPath nodes found", then <--Exist--> is displayed. If you selected "Break

when XPath nodes missing", then <--Missing--> is displayed.

In Requests
The check box displays if the XPath expression is checked in the SOAP request.
You can change the settings by directly clicking the check box in the column.

In Responses
The check box displays if the XPath expression is checked in the SOAP response.
You can change the settings by directly clicking the check box in the column.

To edit the Conditional Breakpoints:
- Double click the respective line in the tab, or
- Click the Change button.

To delete a conditional Breakpoint
- Click the line you want to delete, and click the Delete button.

Tools

The tools menu allows you to:
- Access the scripting environment of XML Spy. You can create, manage and store your own forms, macros and event handlers.
- View the currently assigned macros
- Assign (or deassign) scripts to a project
- Customize your version of XML Spy: define your own toolbars, keyboard shortcuts, menus, and macros
- Define the global XML Spy program settings

Switch to scripting environment

The scripting environment is currently available as a downloadable component. If you have not downloaded and installed the scripting component, you will be prompted to do so when you select the "Switch to Scripting environment" menu item.

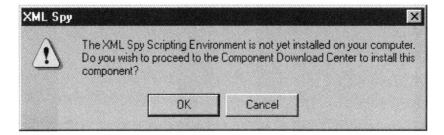

Clicking OK, connects you with the Altova Component Download Center from where you can choose to download the "XML Spy Scripting Environment".

Having downloaded the component, double click on the **Spyscripting.exe** to install it.

This command switches to the scripting environment, a predefined global scripting project is active the first time you start the form editor. Please see the Scripting section in this manual for more information.

Show macros

This command opens a dialog box which displays a list of all macros defined in the global scripting project and in the scripting project associated with the current project opened in XMLSpy.

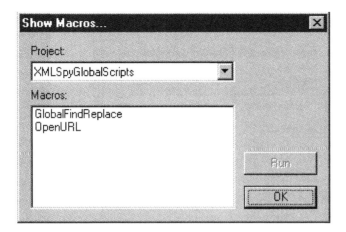

The "Run" button in the dialog box, calls the selected macro.

Project

This command opens a further submenu from where you can assign (or deassign) scripts to a project.

Please note:
  You have to have a XML Spy project open for these menu items to become active.

Assign script to Project

This command enables you to assign scripts to an scripting project.

Unassign Scripts from Project

This command enables you to de-assign scripts from a scripting project.

Project Scripts active

This command allows you to activate or temporarily deactivate project scripts.

Customize...

The customize command lets you customize XML Spy to suit your personal needs.

Commands

The Commands tab allows you customize your menus or toolbars.

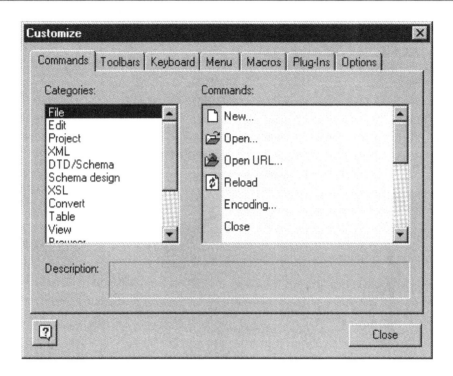

To add a command to a toolbar or menu:
1. Open this dialog box using **Tools | Customize.**
2. Select the command category in the Categories list box. The commands available appear in the Commands list box.
3. Click on a command in the commands list box and drag "it" to an to an existing menu or toolbar.
4. An I-beam appears when you place the cursor over a valid position to drop the command.
5. Release the mouse button at the position you want to insert the command.

- A small button appears at the tip of mouse pointer when you drag a command. The check mark below the pointer means that the command cannot be dropped at the current cursor position.
- The check mark disappears whenever you can drop the command (over a tool bar or menu).
- Placing the cursor over a menu when dragging, opens it, allowing you to insert the command anywhere in the menu.
- Commands can be placed in menus or tool bars. If you created you own toolbar you can populate it with your own commands/icons.

Please note:
   You can also edit the commands in the **context menus** (right click anywhere opens the context menu), using the same method. Click the Menu tab and then select the specific context menu available in the Context Menus combo box.

To delete a command or menu:
1. Open this dialog box using **Tools | Customize.**
2. Click on the menu entry or icon you want to delete, and drag with the mouse.
3. Release the mouse button whenever the check mark icon appears below the mouse pointer.
   The command, or menu item is deleted from the menu or tool bar.

Toolbars

The Toolbars tab allows you to activate or deactive specific toolbars, as well as create your own specialized ones.

XML Spy toolbars contain symbols for the most frequently used menu commands.
For each symbol you get a brief "tool tip" explanation when the mouse cursor is directly over the item and the status bar shows a more detailed description of the command.

You can drag the toolbars from their standard position to any location on the screen, where they appear as a floating window. Alternatively you can also dock them to the left or right edge of the main XML Spy window.

- Toolbar settings defined in the Grid, Schema design and Text view are valid in those views. The Browser view toolbars are independent of all the other views.

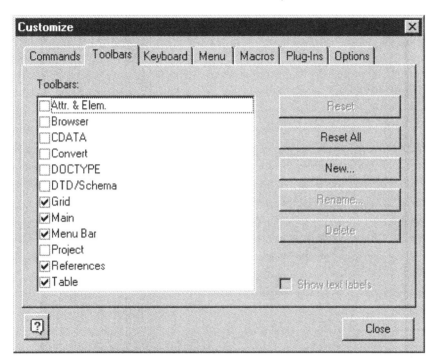

To activate or deactivate a toolbar:
1. Click the check box to activate (or deactivate) the specific toolbar.

To create a new toolbar:
1. Click the **New...** button, and give the toolbar a name in the Toolbar name dialog box.
2. Add commands to the toolbar using the Commands tab of the Customize dialog box.

To reset the Menu Bar
- Click the Menu Bar entry and
- Click the **Reset** button, to reset the menu commands to the state they were in when XML Spy was installed.

To reset all toolbar and menu commands
- Click the **Reset All** button, to reset all the toolbar commands to the state they were when XML Spy was installed. A prompt appears stating that all toolbars and menus will be reset.

- Click Yes to confirm the reset.

To change a toolbar name:
- Click the **Rename**... button to edit the name of the toolbar.

To delete a toolbar:
- Click the **Delete** button to delete the currently highlighted toolbar in the Toolbars list box.
- A prompt appears, asking if you really want to delete the toolbar. Click Yes to confirm the deletion.
- or, click right on the menu or icon bar, and select the Delete entry in the popup menu.

Show text labels:
This option places explanatory text below toolbar icons when activated.

Keyboard

The Keyboard tab allows you to define (or change) keyboard shortcuts for any XML Spy command.

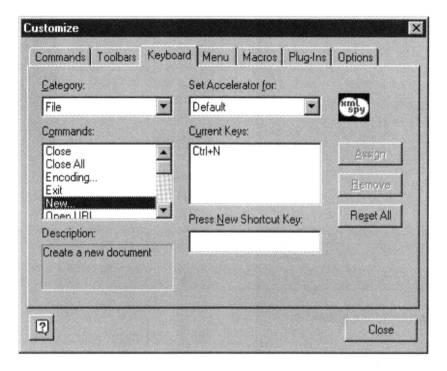

To assign a new Shortcut to a command:
1. Select the commands category using the **Category** combo box.
2. Select the **command** you want to assign a new shortcut to, in the Commands list box
3. Click in the "**Press New Shortcut Key**:" text box, and press the shortcut keys that are to activate the command.
   The shortcuts appear immediately in the text box. If the shortcut was assigned previously, then that function is displayed below the text box.
4. Click the **Assign** button to permanently assign the shortcut.
   The shortcut now appears in the Current Keys list box.
   (To **clear** this text box, press any of the control keys, CTRL, ALT or SHIFT).

To deassign (or delete a shortcut):

1. Click the shortcut you want to delete in the Current Keys list box, and
2. Click the **Remove** button (which has now become active).
3. Click the Close button to confirm all the changes made in the Customize dialog box.

Set accelerator for:
Currently no function.

Currently assigned keyboard shortcuts:
Hotkeys by key

F1   Help Menu
F3   Find Next
F5   Refresh
F7   Check well-formedness
F8   Validate

F9   Database/Table view
SHIFT + F9   Insert table row
CTRL + F9   Append row

F10   XSL Transformation
CTRL + F10 XSL:FO Transformation

Num +   Expand
Num -   Collapse
Num *   Expand fully
CTRL + Num-   Collapse unselected
CTRL + G   Goto line/char

CTRL+TAB and CTRL+F6   Cycle through open windows
Arrow keys (up / down)   Move selection bar
Esc.   Abandon edits/close dialog box

Return /Space bar   confirms a selection

Alt + F4   Closes XML Spy
CTRL + F4   Closes active window
Alt + F, 1   Open last file

CTRL + Double click an element (Schema view)
                        Display element definition

CTRL + N   File New
CTRL + O   File Open
CTRL + S   File Save
CTRL + P   File Print

CTRL + A   Select All
Shift + Del   Cut (or CTRL + X)
CTRL + C   Copy
CTRL + V   Paste

CTRL + Z   Undo
CTRL + Y   Redo

Del			Delete (Delete item in Schema/Enhanced Grid view)

CTRL + F		Find
F3			Find Next
CTRL + H		Replace

CTRL + I			Append Attribute
CTRL + E			Append Element
CTRL + T			Append Text
CTRL + D			Append CDATA
CTRL + M			Append Comment

CTRL + SHIFT + I		Insert Attribute
CTRL + SHIFT + E		Insert Element
CTRL + SHIFT + T		Insert Text content
CTRL + SHIFT + D		Insert CDATA
CTRL + SHIFT + M	Insert Comment

CTRL + ALT + I		Add Child Attribute
CTRL + ALT + E		Add Child Element
CTRL + ALT + T		Add Child Text
CTRL + ALT + D		Add Child CDATA
CTRL + ALT + M		Add Child Comment

Hotkeys by function
Abandon edits		Esc.
Add Child Attribute	CTRL + ALT + I
Add Child CDATA		CTRL + ALT + D
Add Child Comment	CTRL + ALT + M
Add Child Element	CTRL + ALT + E
Add Child Text		CTRL + ALT + T
Append Attribute		CTRL + I
Append CDATA		CTRL + D
Append Comment		CTRL + M
Append Element		CTRL + E
Append row		CTRL + F9
Append Text		CTRL + T
Check well-formedness F7
Closes active windowCTRL + F4
Closes XML Spy		Alt + F4
Collapse			Num -
Collapse unselected	CTRL + Num-
Confirms a selection	Return / Space bar
Copy			CTRL + C
Cut			SHIFT + Del (or CTRL + X)
Cycle through windows CTRL + TAB and CTRL + F6
Database/Table view F9
Delete item		Del
Expand			Num +
Expand fully		Num *
File New			CTRL + N
File Open			CTRL + O
File Print			CTRL + P
File Save			CTRL + S
Find			CTRL + F
Find Next		F3
Goto line/char		CTRL + G

Help Menu	F1
Insert Attribute	CTRL + SHIFT + I
Insert CDATA	CTRL + SHIFT + D
Insert Comment	CTRL + SHIFT + M
Insert Element	CTRL + SHIFT + E
Insert table row	SHIFT + F9
Insert Text content	CTRL + SHIFT + T
Move selection bar	Arrow keys (up / down)
Open last file	Alt + F, 1
Paste	CTRL + V
Redo	CTRL + Y
Refresh	F5
Replace	CTRL + H
Select All	CTRL + A
To view an element definition	CTRL + Double click on an element.
Undo	CTRL + Z
Validate	F8
XSL Transformation	F10
XSL:FO Transformation	CTRL + F10

Menu

The Menu tab allows you to customize the main menu bars as well as the (popup - right click) context menus.

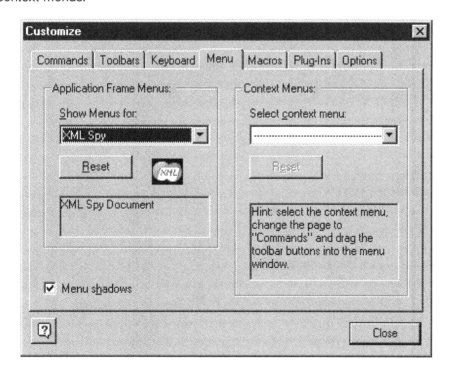

You can customize both the Default and XML Spy menu bars.

The **Default** menu is the one visible when no XML documents of any type are open in XML Spy.

File   Edit   Project   Convert   Tools   Window   Help

The **XML Spy** menu is the menu bar visible when at least one XML document has been opened.

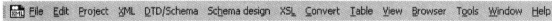

To customize a menu:
1. Select the menu bar you want to customize from the "Show Menus for:" combo box
2. Click the **Commands** tab, and drag the commands to the menu bar of your choice.

To delete commands from a menu:
1. Click right on the command, or icon representing the command, and
2. Select the **Delete** option from the popup menu,

   or,
1. Select **Tools | Customize** to open the Customize dialog box, and
2. Drag the command away from the menu, and drop it as soon as the check mark icon appears below the mouse pointer.

To reset either of the menu bars:
1. Select either the Default or XML Spy entry in the combo box, and
2. Click the **Reset** button just below the menu name.
   A prompt appears asking if you are sure you want to reset the menu bar.

To customize any of the Context menus (right click menus):
1. Select the context menu from the combo box.
2. Click the **Commands** tab, and drag the commands to context menu that is now open.

To delete commands from a context menu:
1. Click right on the command, or icon representing the command, and
2. Select the **Delete** option from the popup menu

   or,
1. Select **Tools | Customize** to open the Customize dialog box, and
2. Drag the command away from the context menu, and drop it as soon as the check mark icon appears below the mouse pointer.

To reset any of the context menus:
1. Select the context menu from the combo box, and
2. Click the **Reset** button just below the context menu name.
   A prompt appears asking if you are sure you want to reset the context menu.

To close an context menu window:
1.   Click on the **Close icon** at the top right of the title bar, or
2.   Click the Close button of the Customize dialog box.

Menu animations
•   Select one of the menu animations from the combo box, if you want animated menus.

Menu shadows
•   Click the Menu shadows check box, if you want all your menus to have shadows.

Macros

The Macros tab allows you to place macros (created using the XML scripting environment) in a toolbar or menu.

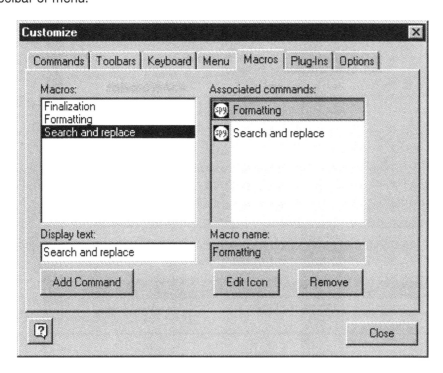

To place a macro (icon) into a toolbar or menu:
1.   Start the scripting environment using **Tools | Switch to Scripting environment**.
2.   Double click the XMLSpyMacros entry in the Modules folder of the **XMLSpyGlobalScripts** project.
     Previously defined macros are then be visible in the right hand window.
3.   Switch back to XML Spy, and select **Tools | Customize** and click on the Macros tab. The macros defined in the scripting environment are now visible in the Macros list box at left.
4.   Click the macro name and then the **Add Command** button. This places the macro name in the Associated commands list box.
5.   Click the macro name in the Associated commands list box, and drag it to any tool bar or menu.

•   To edit a macro icon, click the Edit Icon button.

•   To delete a macro from the Associated commands list box, click the Delete button.

Plug-Ins

The Plug-Ins tab allows you to place plug-ins in a toolbar or menu.

To place a plug-in icon into a toolbar or menu:
1. Click the "**Add Plug-In...**" button.

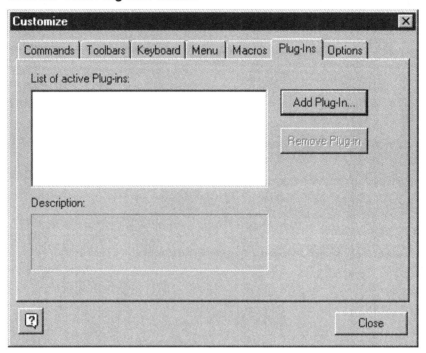

2. Select the folder and then click the plug-in file to mark it (XMLSpyPlugIn.dll in this case).

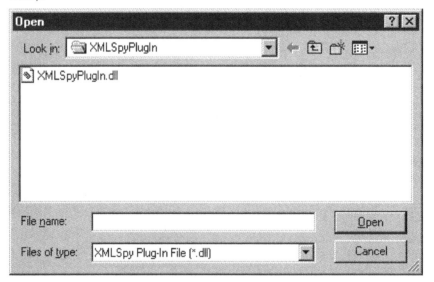

3. Click the **Open** button to install the plug-in.
   The plug-in name appears in the "list of active plug-ins" list, and the plug-in icon(s) appears in a new toolbar.

To remove a plug-in:
1. Click the plug-in name in the "List of active plug-ins" list and click the "Remove Plug-

in" button.

Options

The Options tab allows you to set general environment settings.

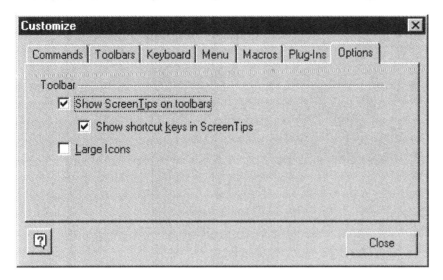

Toolbar
When active, the **Show Tooltips on toolbars** check box displays a popup when the mouse pointer is placed over an icon in any of the icon bars. The popup contains a short description of the icon function, as well as the associated keyboard shortcut, if one has been assigned.

The **Show shortcut keys in Tooltips** check box, allows you to decide if you want to have the shortcut displayed in the tooltip.

When active, the **Large icons** check box switches between the standard size icons, and larger versions of the icons.

Customize context menu

The Customize context menu allows you to further customize icons and menu items.

To open the customize context menu:
1. First open the Customize menu by selecting **Tools | Customize**.
2. Then place the mouse pointer over an icon (or menu) and **click right** to open the context menu.

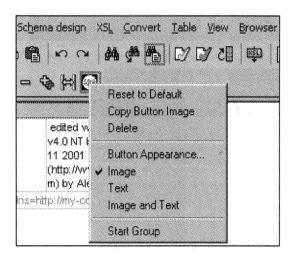

Reset to default
Currently no function.

Copy Button image
This option copies the icon you right click, to the clipboard.

Delete
This option deletes the icon or menu you right click. Deleting a menu, deletes all menu options contained in it!

To restore a deleted menu:
- Select the Menu tab
- Select the menu you want to restore (XML Spy or Default).
- Click the Reset button below the menu selection combo box.

Button Appearance...
This option allows you to edit the button image as well as the button text. Currently only the macro icons can be edited (default XML Spy icon).

The Image only, Text only and Image and text radio buttons, let you define what you want to edit. Click the Select User-defined Image radio button and click one of the icons.

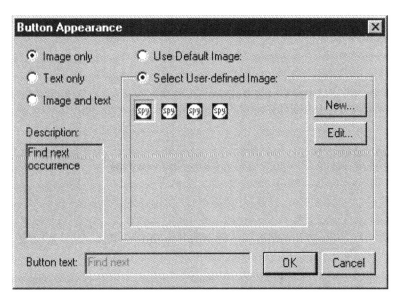

Click the Edit... button, to open the Edit button image dialog box. The Button text can be edited if you select either Text only or Image and text options.

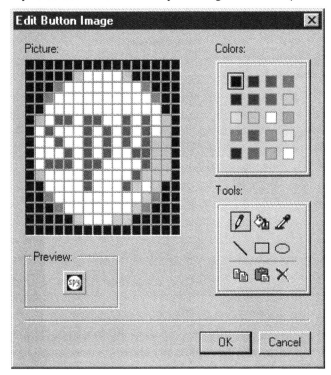

Image
This option changes the graphical display of an icon to the text representing it.

Text
This option changes the textual description of a function to the graphical image (icon) representing that function.

Image and Text
This option enables the simultaneous display of an icon and its text.

Start group
This option inserts a vertical divider to the left of the icon you right clicked.

Options

The "Options" command allows you to define the global program settings in a tabbed dialog box. These settings are saved in the registry, and apply to all current and future document windows.

The Apply button displays the changes in the currently open documents, and fixes the current settings. The changes are seen immediately in the background windows.

File

The "File" tab defines the way XML Spy opens and saves XML documents. You can also find related settings in the Encoding tab.

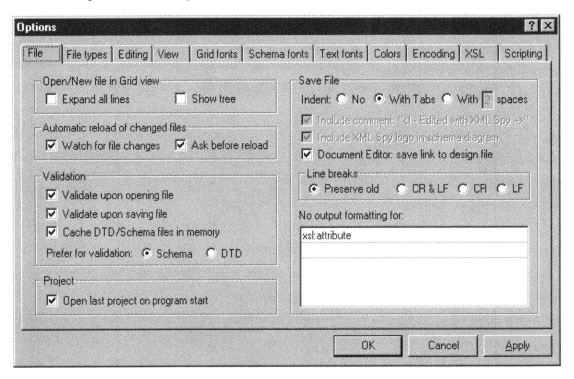

Open/New file in Grid view
You can choose to open an existing file or create a new file either in the Enhanced Grid View or in the text view. If you select the grid view, you can optionally show the tree structure, and automatically expand all lines at the same time.

Automatic reload of changed files
If you are working in a multi-user environment, or if you are working on files that are dynamically generated on a server, you can instruct XML Spy to watch for changes to the files that you are currently editing. XML Spy will then prompt you to reload the file, whenever a change is detected.

Validation
If you are using document type definitions (DTDs) or schemas to define the structure of your XML documents, you can automatically check the document for validity whenever it is opened or saved.

XML Spy can also cache these files in memory to save any unnecessary reloading (e.g. when the Schema being referred to, is accessed through a URL).

Project
When you start XML Spy, you can open the last-used project automatically.

Save File
XML Spy uses TAB-characters (0x09) to indent the individual elements forming the structure of the XML document. In certain situations this may be undesirable. Deactivate the "Indent elements using tabs" check box, If this is the case.

No formatting output for
You can selectively turn off output formatting for certain elements, by entering them in the list box (e.g. necessary for xsl:attribute when you are editing XSL Stylesheets).

When saving an XML document, XML Spy includes a short comment <!-- Edited with XML Spy 4.x http://www.xmlspy.com --> near the top of the file. This option can only be deactivated by licensed users.

When saving a content model diagram (using the menu option Schema design | Generate Documentation), XML Spy includes a comment <!-- Generated with XML Spy 4.x Schema Editor - http://www.xmlspy.com -->) at the bottom of the diagram. This option can only be deactivated by licensed users.

Line breaks
Line-breaks in the document file can be preserved so that the same characters will be used that were found when opening the file. You can choose to encode line breaks in any of the three possible forms (CR&LF for PCs, CR for the MacOS, or LF for Unix).

File types

The "File types" tab allows you to customize the behavior of XML Spy on a per-file-type basis.

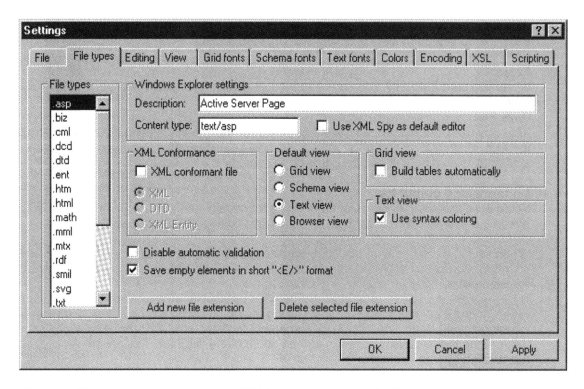

Choose a file type from the "File types" list box, to customize the functions for that particular file type:

Windows Explorer settings
You can modify the file type description and MIME-compliant content type used by Windows Explorer, and you can define if XML Spy is to be the default editor for this file type.

XML Conformance
XML Spy lets you edit XML files as well as non-XML files. You must define the XML-Conformance settings for each new file type you add. Since XML allows for special grammar rules when dealing with external Document Type Definitions (DTDs) and external parsed entities, the exact grammar to be used can also be set here.

Do not modify these settings unless you are adding a new file type and are sure of what you are doing.

Default view
This group lets you define the default XML Spy view to be used for each file type.

Grid view
This check box lets you define if the Enhanced Grid View should automatically build tables.

Text view
This text box lets you set syntax-coloring for particular file types.

Disable automatic validation
If you are using partial XML-documents that are included in another file and cannot be validated individually, you can turn off automatic validation per file type.

Save empty elements in short <E/> format
Some XML tools may have problems understanding the short <Element/> form for empty elements defined in the XML 1.0 Specification. You can instruct XML Spy to save elements in

the longer (but nonetheless also valid) <Element></Element> form.

Add new file extension button
Adds a new file type to the File types list. Define the settings for this new file type using the options in this dialog box.

Delete selected file extension button
Deletes the currently selected file type and all associated settings.

Editing

The "Editing" tab defines the behavior of the Enhanced Grid View, when exchanging data using the clipboard and moving items with drag & drop.

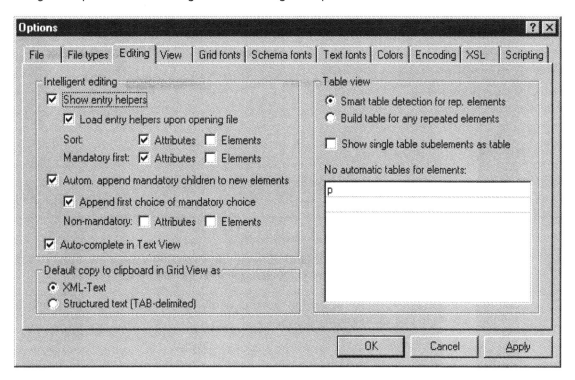

Intelligent editing
While editing documents, XML Spy provides Intelligent Editing based on these settings. You can also customize various aspects of the behavior of these Entry helpers here.

Default copy to clipboard in grid view as
You can choose the format in which data will be exported to foreign applications using the clipboard. If you select XML-Text, the contents of the clipboard will be formatted and tagged just like the resulting XML file itself.

The structured text mode attempts to format the clipboard contents as a table, for use in a spreadsheet or database application. This option does not affect the internal clipboard format that XML Spy uses for copying and pasting.

Table view
You can also control, how XML Spy decides when to display repeating elements in the Table View.

View

The "View" tab allows you customize the XML documents presentation.

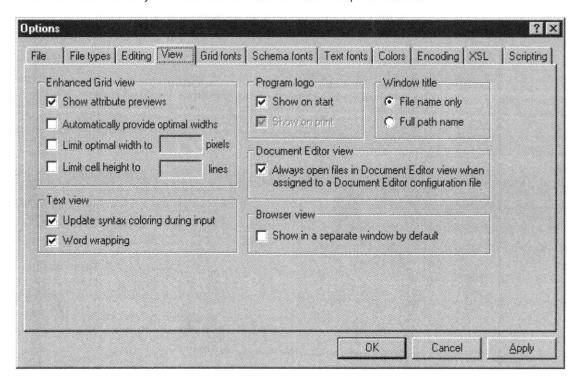

Enhanced Grid view
Collapsed elements in the Enhanced Grid View can be displayed in preview form. This displays the attributes and their values in gray in the same line as the element.

XML Spy lets you automatically apply the Optimal Widths command while editing, and lets you limit the maximum cell width and height.

Text view
The Text View supports syntax-coloring, which can be updated dynamically while typing or be disabled entirely.

Program logo
You can turn off the splash screen upon program startup, to speed up XML Spy.

Window title
The window title for each document window can contain only file name, or the full path name.

Document Editor view
XML files based on a document template (*.sps), are automatically opened in the Document Editor view when this option is active.

Browser view
You can choose to see the browser view in a separate window, enabling side-by-side placement of the edit and browser views.

Grid fonts

The "Grid fonts" tab allows you to customize the appearance of text in the Enhanced Grid view.

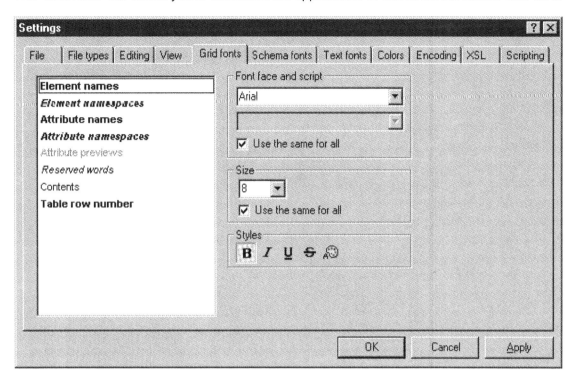

Font face and script
You can select the font face and size to be used for displaying the various items in the Enhanced Grid View. The same fonts are also used for printing and consequently only TrueType fonts can be selected.

Size
If you want to use the same font size for all items, click on the "Use same for all" check box.

Styles
The style and color can be set using the combo boxes. The current settings are immediately reflected in the list, so that you can preview the way your document is going to look.

In the Windows 95/98 version of XML Spy, it is possible to select a "Script" for some fonts. This is especially necessary when editing documents with a non-Roman writing systems. The script selected in the font settings dialog box, needs to match the character set code-page selected when opening a document (i.e. when editing a Cyrillic ISO-8859-5 document, the code-page being used to edit the file should be set to 1251 and the font script needs to be set to "Cyrillic").

Schema fonts

The "Schema fonts" tab allows you to customize the appearance of text in the Text view.

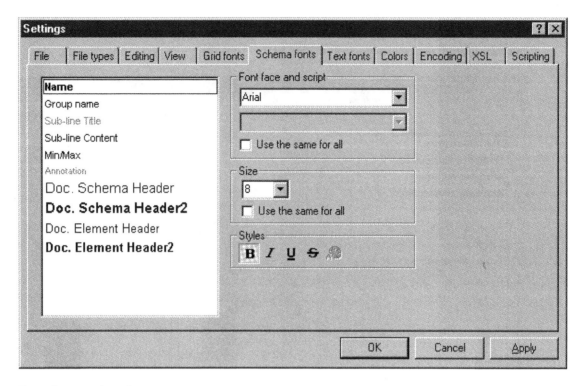

Font face and script
You can select the font face and size to be used for displaying the various items in the Schema Design view. The same fonts are used when printing and creating schema documentation, consequently only TrueType fonts can be selected.

The "Doc." Schema and Element headers, are the fonts that are used when creating schema documentation.

Size
If you want to use the same font size for all items, click on the "Use same for all" check box.

Styles
The style and color can be set using the combo boxes. The current settings are immediately reflected in the list, so that you can preview the way your document is going to look.

In the Windows 95/98 version of XML Spy, it is possible to select a "Script" for some fonts. This is especially necessary when editing documents with a non-Roman writing systems. The script selected in the font settings dialog box, needs to match the character set code-page selected when opening a document (i.e. when editing a Cyrillic ISO-8859-5 document, the code-page being used to edit the file should be set to 1251 and the font script needs to be set to "Cyrillic").

Text fonts

The "Text fonts" tab allows you to customize the appearance of text in the Text view.

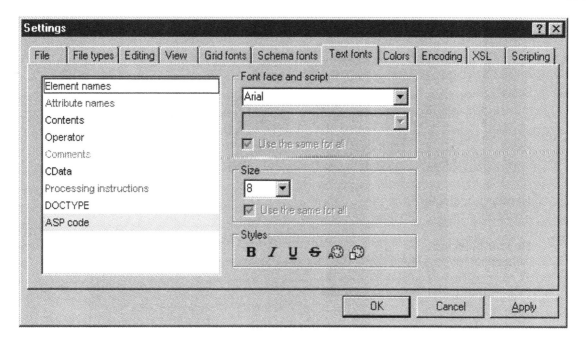

Again you can choose the font face, style and size, but this time the same font, style and size is always being used for all elements. Only the color can be adjusted individually to provide full customization of the syntax coloring option.

Setting the background color is only supported when RichEdit 3.0 is available on your system.

Colors

The "Colors" tab allows you to customize the colors used in the **Enhanced Grid view**, when viewing elements in the Database/Table view.

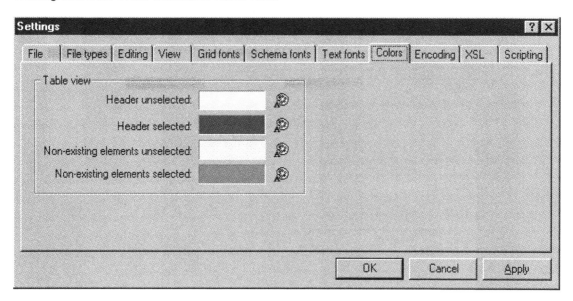

Example:

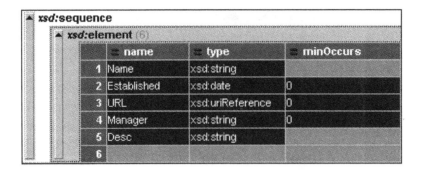

Header unselected
This option defines the color of the table header when deselected.

Header selected
This option defines the color of the table header when selected.

Non-existing elements unselected
This option defines the color of the empty elements when deselected.

Non-existing elements selected
This option defines the color of the empty elements when selected.

In addition to the colors you define here, XML Spy uses the regular selection and menu color preferences set in the Display Settings on the Control Panel of your Windows installation.

Encoding

The "Encoding" tab specifies the kind of character-set encoding to be used when creating new files, as well as the encoding to be assumed, when opening files that lack an encoding declaration.

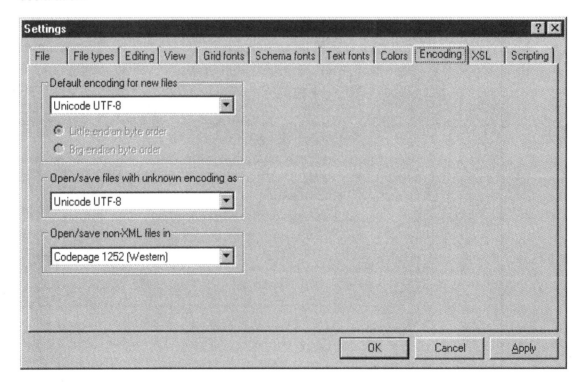

Default encoding for new files
The default encoding for new files can be pre-determined in the Settings dialog box so that each new document is automatically created with a proper XML-declaration and includes the encoding-specification that you most commonly need.

The encoding for existing files will, of course, always be remembered independently of this setting and can only be changed by the "Encoding" command on the "File" menu.
If a two- or four-byte encoding is selected as the default encoding (i.e. UTF-16, UCS-2, or UCS-4) you can also choose between little-endian and big-endian byte-ordering for the XML filoc.

Open/save files with unknown encoding as
You can choose how an XML file is to be interpreted if the encoding-specification is missing, and the encoding cannot be auto-detected. In most cases this will very likely be UTF-8 or ISO-8895-1, even though the XML specification theoretically only allows UTF-8 files to lack an encoding-specification.

Open/save non-XML files in
Sometimes is can be convenient to also use XML Spy for editing non-XML files (such as Active Server Pages (ASP) or similar web-related documents. Since these files do not contain any encoding statements, you must specify a default Windows Code Page to be used for access these files.

XSL

The "XSL" tab allows you to define which program to use for XSL Transformations.

XML Spy includes full support for XSL Transformations, and can either use the MSXML 3.0 or 4.0 parser (which is pre-installed) or any external XSLT processor for this purpose. The "Choose version automatically" option is active per default. XML Spy first tries to use version 4.0 and if not available version 3.0. You can however, manually choose either version by clicking the respective radio button.

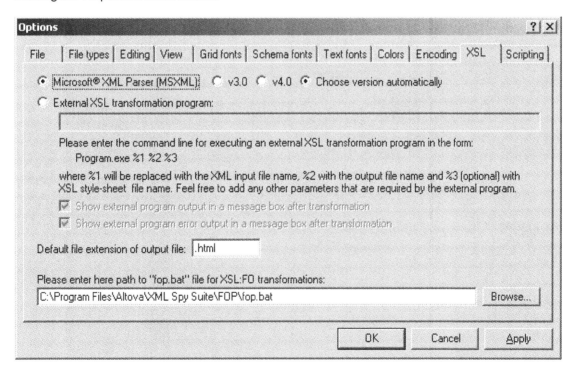

Use Microsoft XML Parser (MSXML) 3.0 or 4.0

If you are using Internet Explorer 5 or above (i.e. the MSXML module) for XSLT processing, you must specify if the resulting output is to be transformed as an XML-compliant document (such as XHTML or WML), or non-XML compliant text files.

Installing other XML Parsers

The Component Download Center, accessible through the menu option **Help | Components Download**, allows you to download and use different XSL processors. The XSL tab below, shows that Infoteria iXSLT 2.0c has been installed.

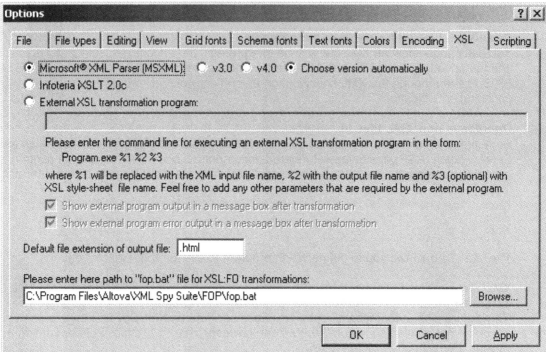

External XSL transformation program

If you are using an external XSL processor, you must specify a command-line string that is to be executed by XML Spy in order to initiate the XSL Transformation. In this case, use the following variables to build your command-line string:

%1   the XML instance document that is to be processed
%2   the output file that is to be generated
%3   the XSL Stylesheet to be used (optional, if the document contains an <?xsl-stylesheet ...?> reference

You can also choose to show the result of the external XSLT processor directly within XML Spy in a message box.

Please see the technical background information ons XSLT Processors for further details.

Scripting

The "Scripting" tab allows you to select the scripting environment and other scripting specific parameters.

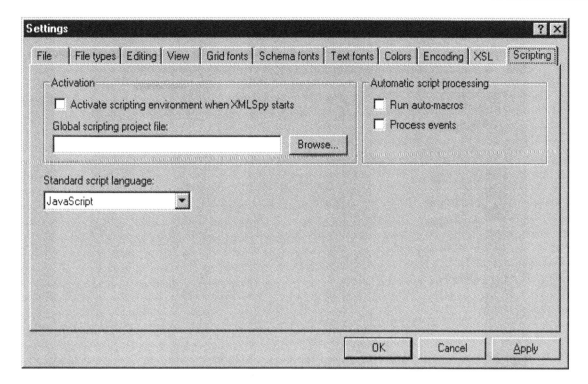

Activation:
Define if the scripting environment is to be active when XML Spy starts. Click the Browse... button to select the scripting project file.

Standard script language:
Select the scripting language you want to use, JavaScript or VBscript.

Automatic script processing:
This section defines if auto-macros have the right to run, and if event processing is to be enabled.

Window Menu

To organize the individual document windows in an XML Spy session, the Window menu contains standard commands common to most Windows applications.

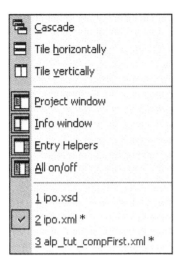

You can cascade the open document windows, tile them, or arrange document icons once you have minimized them. You can also switch the various Entry Helper windows on or off (such as Project, Info, or Entry-Helpers) or switch to each open document window directly from the menu.

Cascade

This command rearranges all open document windows so that they are all cascaded (i.e. staggered) on top of each other.

Tile horizontally

This command rearranges all open document windows as **horizontal tiles**, making them all visible at the same time.

Tile vertically

This command rearranges all open document windows as **vertical tiles**, making them all visible at the same time.

Project Window

This command lets you switch the Project Window on or off.

This is a dockable window. Dragging on its title bar detaches it from its current position and makes it a floating window. Click right on the title bar, to allow docking or hide the window.

Info Window

This command lets you switch the Info Window on or off.

This is a dockable window. Dragging on its title bar detaches it from its current position and makes it a floating window. Click right on the title bar, to allow docking or hide the window.

Entry Helpers

This command lets you switch all three Entry-Helper Windows on or off.

All three Entry helpers are dockable windows. Dragging on a title bar detaches it from its current position and makes it a floating window. Click right on the title bar, to allow docking or hide the window.

All on/off

This command lets you switch all dockable windows on, or off:

- the Project Window
- the Info Window
- the three Entry-Helper Windows

This is useful if you want to hide all non-document windows quickly, to get the maximum viewing area for the document you are working on.

Currently open window list

This list shows all currently open windows, and lets you quickly switch between them.

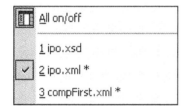

You can also use the Ctrl-TAB or CTRL F6 keyboard shortcuts to cycle through the open windows.

Help Menu

The Help menu contains all commands required to get help or more information on XML Spy, as well as links to information and support pages on our web server.

The Help menu also contains the Registration dialog, which lets you enter your license key-code, once you have purchased the product.

XML Spy Quick Help

XML Spy includes a **context-sensitive online help** system that is based on the Microsoft HTML Help Viewer and lets you directly access information on each menu command, dialog box and window from within XML Spy.

Press the "F1" button on your keyboard to access the context-sensitive help for the currently open dialog box, or press "F1" while you are browsing through the menus with your mouse.

All dialogs include a small question mark symbol (?) in their window title bar. Click on this symbol to access the context-sensitive help topic for that dialog box.

If you would like to learn more about any topic, you can also use the Table of contents and Index commands on the Help menu or search through the entire text of the electronic documentation using the Search command.

Table of contents...

This command displays a **hierarchical representation** of all chapters and topics contained in the online help system. Use this command to jump to the table of contents directly from within XML Spy.

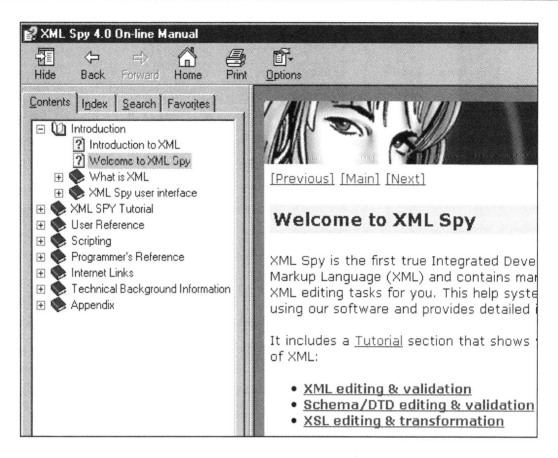

Once the help window is open, use the three tabs to toggle between the table of contents, index, and search panes. The Favorites tab lets you bookmark certain pages within the help system.

Index...

This command accesses the **keyword index** of XML Spy Online Help. You can also use the Index tab in the left pane of the online help system.

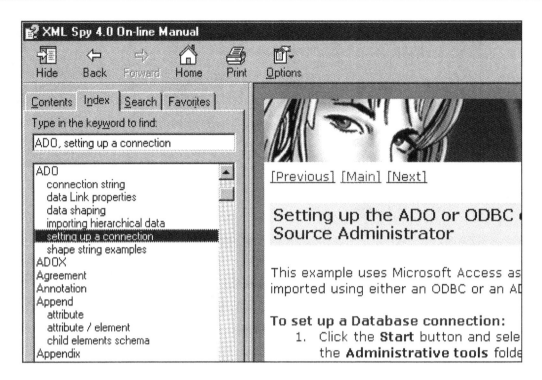

The index, lists all relevant keywords and lets you navigate to a topic by double-clicking the respective keyword. If more than one topic matches the selected keyword, you are presented a list of available topics to choose from:

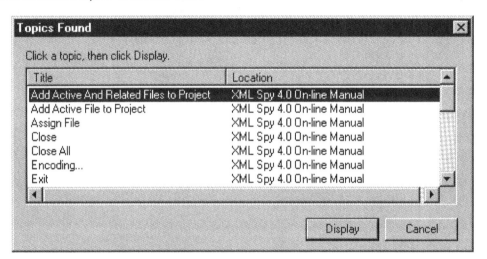

Search...

The Search command performs a **full-text search** in the entire online help system.

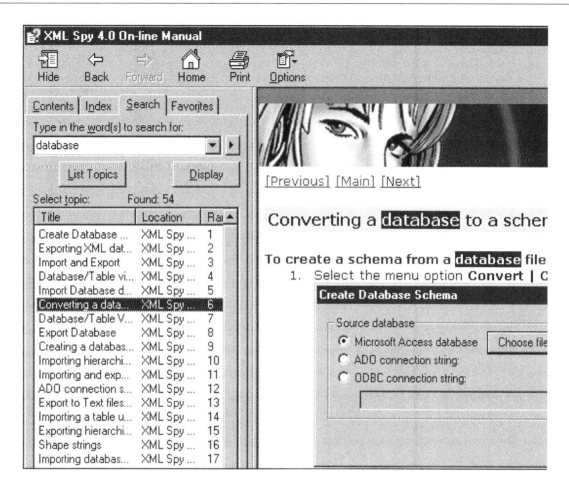

- Once you enter your search term into the query field and hit the Return key.
  The online help system displays a list of available topics that contain the search term you've entered.
- Double-click on any item in the list to display the corresponding topic.

Registration...

When you start XML Spy for the first time, you are automatically presented with the Registration dialog box, which lets you register your software product in order to be eligible for technical support and activate your license, which is done by entering a unique key-code to unlock the software.

FREE Evaluation Version

If you have downloaded the XML Spy from our web server and would like to activate your **FREE** 30-day evaluation version, please enter your name, company, and e-mail address and click on the "Request FREE evaluation key..." button. XML Spy then uses your Internet connection to transmit the information you have just entered to our web server, where a personal unique evaluation license will be generated for you. The license key-code, which is necessary to unlock your software, will then be sent to the e-mail address you have entered - it is therefore important, that you enter your **real e-mail address** in the registration dialog box!

Once you have clicked the request button, please go to your favorite mail software and retrieve the license key-code from our e-mail message, which you should be receiving in a matter of a few minutes (depending on transient Internet conditions).

If you requested a key-code and it didn't arrive in a short space of time, the process may have failed due to Firewall restrictions in your network. If this is the case, please send a short message with your information via e-mail to evaluate@xmlspy.com and our support staff will generate a key-code for you manually.

When you have received your evaluation key-code, please enter it into the key-code field in the registration dialog box and click on OK to start working with XML Spy.

Whenever you want to place an order for a licensed version of XML Spy, you can also use the "Order license key..." button in the registration dialog box or the Order form menu command to proceed to the Secure XML Spy Online Shop on the Internet.

Licensed Version

If you have purchased a *single-user* license for XML Spy, you will receive an e-mail message from us that contains your license-data and includes your name, company and key-code. Please make sure that you enter **all fields** from your license e-mail into the registration dialog box. The key-code will only be able to unlock your software installation, if the entries in the name and company fields match the name and company entered into our order form.

If your company has purchased a *multi-user* license for XML Spy, you will receive an e-mail message from us that contains your license-data and includes your company name and key-code.

Please make sure that you enter the company name and key-code from your license e-mail into the registration dialog box and also enter your personal name into the name field. The key-code will only be able to unlock your software installation, if the value in the company field match the company name entered into our order form.

Please note that the XML Spy License-Agreement does not allow you to install more than the licensed number of copies of XML Spy on the computers in your organization (per-seat license).

Order form...

When you want to place an order for a licensed version of XML Spy, use this command or the "Order license key..." button in the registration dialog to proceed to the Secure XML Spy Online Shop on the Internet, where you can choose between different single- and multi-user license packs.

Once you have placed your order, you can choose to pay by credit card, send a check by mail, or use a bank wire transfer.

Support Center...

If you have any questions regarding our product, please feel free to use this command to query to our support center on the Internet at any time. This is the place where you'll find links to the FAQ, support form, and e-mail addresses for contacting our support staff directly.

FAQ on the web

To help you in getting the best support possible, we are providing a list of Frequently Asked Questions (FAQ) on the Internet, that is constantly updated as our support staff encounters new issues that are raised by our customers.

Please make sure to check the FAQ before contacting our technical support team. This will allow you to get help more quickly.

We regret that we are not able to offer technical support by phone at this time, but our support staff will typically answer your e-mail incidents within one business day.

If you would like to make a feature suggestion for a future version of XML Spy or if you wish to send us any other general feedback, please use the questionnaire form.

Components download

The Components download option, currently lets you to download the latest Microsoft XML Parser, as well as an alternate XSLT Transformation System, and will be expanded in the future.

XML Spy on the Internet...

This command takes you directly to the XML Spy web-server http://www.xmlspy.com where you can find out about news, product updates and additional offers from the XML Spy team.

XML Spy Training

This command takes you directly to the XML Spy web-server http://www.xmlspy.com where you can find out about our authorized XML Spy Training Partners who provide courses on using XML Spy and Advanced XML Application Development (AXAD).

Japanese distributor...

If you are located in Japan, you may prefer to contact our Japanese distributor on the Internet by using this menu command.

About XML Spy...

This command shows the XML Spy splash screen and copyright information dialog box, which includes the XML Spy logo.

Please note that this dialog box shows the version number - to find the number of the actual build you are using, please look at the status bar, which always includes the full version and build number.

Dialogs

Most dialog boxes in XML Spy are shown in response to a certain menu command or click on a toolbar button and are, therefore, explained in the individual chapters that describe the respective commands.

This section describes standard dialog boxes, that are used by more than one command.

Assign File

The Assign File dialog box is opened by the Assign DTD, Assign Schema, or Assign XSL commands and prompts you for a file or path name to be used for the requested process:

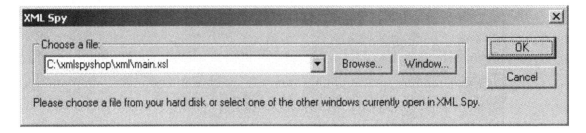

You can either:
- enter a path name into the text box
- select from a list of most recently used filenames using the drop-down list
- browse for a file on your computer (using the common Open dialog box), or
- use the Window button to select any currently open window or any file that is part of the current project.

Select file

The Select File dialog box lets you choose any currently open window or any file from your current project, as a convenient way to locate a file to be used for the various Assign commands.

Double clicking an entry in either window, places the file name in the Assign File dialog box.

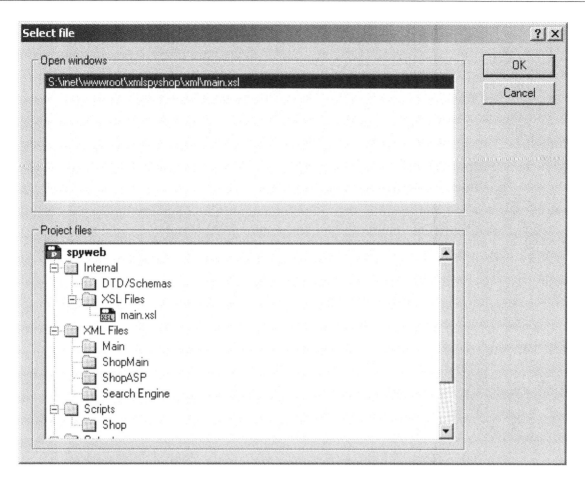

Both windows show the available files based on their extensions depending on which command was selected: Assign DTD, Assign Schema, or Assign XSL.

Part IV

4   Scripting

The XMLSpyFormEditor

XMLSpyFormEditor is the scripting environment of XMLSpy. It gives you the ability to create, manage and store your own forms, macros and event handlers.

Before you can start using the scripting environment, you must download it from the Component Download Center on our web site http://www.xmlspy.com. Afterwards you can start the installation.

To invoke the scripting environment select "Switch to scripting environment" from the "Scripting" menu of XMLSpy. There is a predefined global scripting project active the first time you start the form editor. This project is installed with the scripting component of XMLSpy and contains a sample that interacts with the Altova.xml file.

The screen shot below shows the "FormDate" form and the implementation of the On_BeforeStartEditing event handler. Both are part of the provided Altova sample.

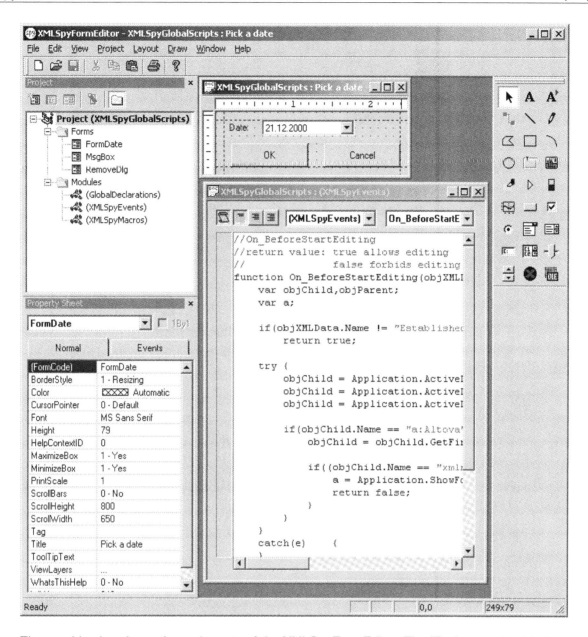

The graphic also shows the main parts of the XMLSpyFormEditor. The "Project window" (left), the "Property Sheet" (left), the client area with any open forms or modules (in the middle) and the "Tool Bar" on the right.

To test the sample, switch back to XMLSpy and open the file Altova.xml. Activate the Enhanced Grid View and try to start editing the "/a:Altova/Division/Established" (XPath) element.

Project Window
The Project window gives you access to the forms and modules of a all open scripting projects. There is always one active scripting project. The title of the active project is printed in bold. Several commands of the File and Project menus refer to the currently active project only.

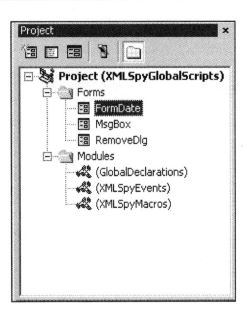

Two context-sensitive popup menus are available within the Project Bar. The first appears if you right-click the title of a project, and the second if you click a form or module. These popup menus gives you access to functions also available in the "File" and "Project" menus in the menu bar.

The Property Sheet

The Property Sheet lists all properties and events of the selected user interface element (buttons, list-boxes, ActiveX controls, etc.) of the active form.

It gives you the ability to modify these properties and to add code to the empty event handlers. The combo-box at the top lists all controls of the form.

The pictures below shows the three pages of the Microsoft DatePicker ActiveX control. Please note that different controls have different properties, and not all controls have three tabs in the Property Sheet.

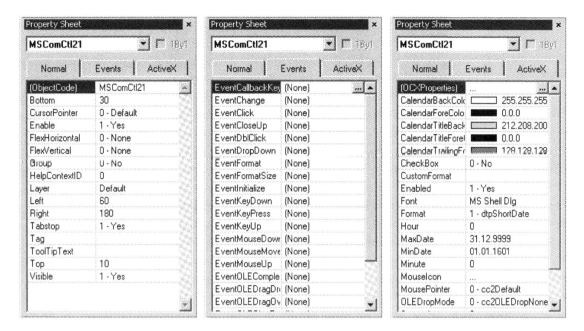

The name of a control is specified by the (ObjectCode) property (here MScomCtl21). If you write some scripting code and need access to methods or properties of the control, you must use this name. Example:

```
var strTmp;
strTmp = "";
strTmp = MSComCtl21.Year + '-' + MSComCtl21.Month + '-' +
MSComCtl21.Day;
```

The "How to create a form" page gives you an example on adding some code to the click-event of a control.

The Tool Bar

Use the Tool Bar to add controls to your forms. Select a control from the bar and draw a rectangle in your form, to set its place and size.

The most common controls from the Tool Bar are:

A   Static Text - Adds text fields like captions or field descriptions.

    Button   - Adds a button to your form. It is possible to assign bitmaps to these buttons.

    CheckBox - Enables Yes-No style elements

    ComboBox - Gives the user the ability to enter text or to select an entry from the drop-down list.

    ListBox   - Displays a list of items for selection.

    EditBox   - Defines a single line of text.

    MultiEditBox   - Defines multiple lines of text.

    ActiveX   - Allows the integration of an ActiveX control in the form.

All of these controls have their own properties and events. Select a control in your form and use the Property Sheet to modify the properties and add some scripting code to the provided events.

Main scripting features

With the introduction of the COM API, the possibilities of XMLSpy became substantially expanded. It is the combination of common programming techniques using functions, recursions, global variables, error handling and so on, that gives the user the ability to deal with complex problems, to automate repetitive jobs or to realize completely new tasks. The scripting environment is the tool for creating and organizing these scripts.

Macros

Macros are used to implement complex or repetitive tasks and for direct user input via forms (dialogs). Macros don't have parameters and return values. It is possible to access all variables and functions which are declared in the global declarations and to display forms. Please see "How to write a macro" for a simple example. See also "Calling macros from XMLSpy".

Events

Events are a powerful way to react to user input and modify the behaviour of XMLSpy. All scripting code of an event is executed immediately, and gives you the ability to directly influence on the users handling of XMLSpy.

Most events have parameters which inform the script about the currently modified data. The return value informs the application how to continue its own processing (eg. forbid editing). See How to handle an event to learn more about the implementation of events.

Forms

Dialog boxes enable your scripts and XMLSpy to interact with the user. You are free to add any type of control to your forms. These controls use their own event handlers for the implementation of their functionality. A list of supported events for the selected control appears in the Property Sheet on the "Events" page. See "How to create a form" for a description of creating forms.

Programming details

1. Because macros don't have parameters or return values, a function header should not exist in the macro implementation.

2. Event handlers need function headers with the correct spelling of the event name, or the event handler won't get called.

3. It is possible to declare local variables and helper functions within macros and event handlers.
   Example:

```
//return value: true allows editing
//              false forbids editing

var txtLocal;

function Helper()
{
     txtMessage = txtLocal;
     Application.ShowForm("MsgBox");
}

function On_BeforeStartEditing(objXMLData)
{
     txtLocal = "On_BeforeStartEditing()";
     Helper();
}
```

4. Recursive functions are supported. The function DeleteXMLElements() from "How to create a Form" calls itself recursively.

5. A form can display another form with the function Application.ShowForm().

6. Out-parameters from methods of the XMLSpy API require special variables in JavaScript.
   Example:

   ```
   // use JavaScript method to access out-parameters
   var strError = new Array(1);
   var nErrorPos = new Array(1);
   var objBadData = new Array(1);

   bOK = objDoc.IsValid(strError,nErrorPos,objBadData);
   ```

7. While a macro is executed, event handlers from XMLSpy are not processed.

Calling macros from XMLSpy

Once you have written your own macros (see also "How to write a macro"), you will want to execute them from XMLSpy. There are two ways to run macros.

Calling macros from the "Show macros..." dialog
To show this dialog select "Show macros..." from the "Scripting" menu.

The dialog displays a list of all macros defined in the global scripting project and in the scripting project associated with the current project opened in XMLSpy.

Additionally, there is a "Run" button to call any selected macro. Before the macro is executed, the "Show macros..." dialog is closed.

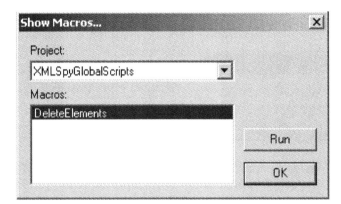

The "Project" - list box lets you switch between the global scripting project and the project scripts.

Calling macros from the "Scripting" menu
The XMLSpy API includes a function to add menu items with associated macros to the "Scripting" menu.

To **add** a menu item call the XMLSpy API function AddMacroMenuItem().

To **reset** the "Scripting" menu call ClearMacroMenu(). This removes all previously added menu items. These commands will generally be called from the "Autorun" macro of the global scripting project, or during the "On_OpenProject" event.

Example:

```
Application.AddMacroMenuItem("DeleteElements","Delete Elements
Dialog");
```

The first parameter is the name of the macro. If you run the macro and there is an open project with scripts associated to it, XMLSpy searches for the macro in the project scripts first. If there are no project scripts, or XMLSpy can't find the macro, it tries to find the macro in the global scripts.

The second parameter is the display text for the menu item.

Projects and Scripts

It is possible to assign scripts to a normal XMLSpy project.

The assigned scripts will be loaded each time XMLSpy opens the project. The scripting project is closed when XMLSpy closes its project.

To assign and unassign scripts to a project, use the menu items from the "Project" submenu of the "Scripting" menu. These menu items are not active if there is no currently active XMLSpy project.

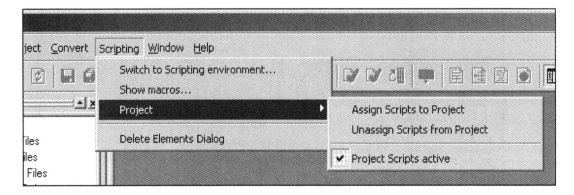

To **assign a script**, select the "Assign Scripts to Project" menu item. A standard file dialog appears enabling you to choose the scripting project file. The scripts are loaded and you are able to edit them if you switch to the scripting environment.

If you want to **see the path** of a scripting project after you have assigned it, select "Project Information" from the "Project" menu of the XMLSpyFormEditor.

To **unassign the current scripts** from the project select "Unassign Scripts from Project". XMLSpyFormEditor closes the scripting project immediately.

It is possible to **temporarily deactivate** the project scripts with the "Project Scripts active" menu item. The associated scripting project file will not be unassigned.

Any forms, macros and events which are defined in the project scripts, "override" any existing definitions from the global scripts.

Example:
If the event handler for On_BeginEditing() exists in the project and global scripts, and XMLSpy raises this event, the event handler from the project scripts will be called.

You have to remove the predefined (but empty) event handlers from the project scripts manually, if you want the event handlers from the global scripts to get called. This is also true for the ShowForm() method of the Application object, to show a form and the AddMacroMenuItem() method to add a macro to the "Scripting" menu.

Scripting Settings

The graphic below shows the settings page for the scripting environment of XMLSpy:

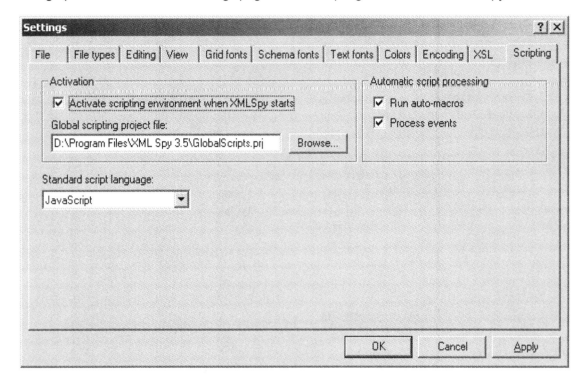

Activate scripting environment when XMLSpy starts
If this checkbox is not selected, the scripting environment is not activated until the user selects "Switch to scripting environment" from the Scripting menu of XML Spy, for the first time.

Global scripting project file
This property sets the global scripting project file. If this file does not exist when the scripting environment starts, a new project will be created.

Run auto-macros
Enables or disables the execution of auto-macros. Currently "Autorun" from the global scripts is the only supported automatic macro. "Autorun" executes when the scripting environment starts.

Process events
Enables or disables the execution of event handlers.

Standard script language
A new global scripting project created from XMLSpy will use this scripting language.

How To

How to write a macro

The goal of this tutorial is to write a macro that removes all namespace prefixes from the active document. To add a macro you have to switch to the XMLSpyFormEditor. Use "Switch to scripting environment" from the scripting menu to show the main window of the form editor. If the scripting environment was not installed before, you have to do it now.

Open the **XMLSpyMacros** module with a double-click on the tree item in the project window. Use the "Add Function" command either from the "Project" menu, or from the popup menu which appears if you right-click the module in the project bar:

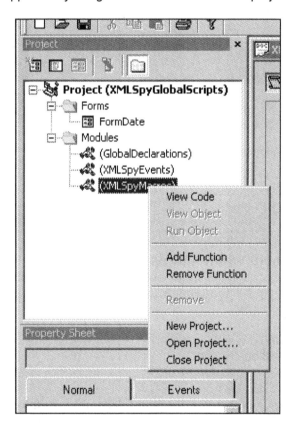

Type in "RemoveNamespaces" for the macro name in the following dialog. XMLSpyFormEditor creates a new macro and adds it to the (XMLSpyMacros) module.

Note that macros don't support parameters or return values. There is therefore no function header. Enter the code below in the macros window:

```
if(Application.ActiveDocument != null) {
        RemoveAllNamespaces(Application.ActiveDocument.RootElement);
        Application.ActiveDocument.UpdateViews();
}
```

We now have to write the RemoveNamespaces function. Place this function into the global declarations module, so that it is accessible from our macros, events and forms.

Activate the (GlobalDeclarations) module and add the RemoveNamespaces() function to any previously defined global variables and functions as follows:

```
function RemoveAllNamespaces(objXMLData)
{
        if(objXMLData == null)
                return;

        if(objXMLData.HasChildren){
                var objChild;

                // spyXMLDataElement := 4
                objChild = objXMLData.GetFirstChild(4);

                while(objChild)      {
                        RemoveAllNamespaces(objChild);

                        try     {
                                var nPos,txtName;
                                txtName = objChild.Name;

                                if((nPos = txtName.indexOf(":")) >= 0) {
                                        objChild.Name =
txtName.substring(nPos+1);
                                }

                                objChild = objXMLData.GetNextChild();
                        }
                        catch(Err)    {
                                objChild = null;
                        }
                }
        }
}
```

This completes the creation of the new macro. You can run it from the "Show macros..." dialog in the "Scripting" menu of XMLSpy.

The sample can be easily extended to perform renaming instead of removing of the namespaces. Design a form (see also "How to create a form") where the user can specify the old and the new namespace names. Then change the try-catch-block of the RemoveAllNamespaces() function to something like this:

```
try    {
        var nPos,txtName;
        txtName = objChild.Name;

        if((nPos = txtName.indexOf(":")) >= 0) {
                var txtOld;
                txtOld = txtName.substring(0,nPos);

                if(txtOld == txtOldNamespace)
                        objChild.Name = txtNewNamespace + ":" +
                        txtName.substring(nPos+1);
        }

        objChild = objXMLData.GetNextChild();
}
catch(Err)    {
        objChild = null;
}
```

This code assumes that txtOldNamespace and txtNewNamespace are declared as globals and are set with the proper values.

How to handle an event

To handle an event you have to switch to the XMLSpyFormEditor. Use "Switch to scripting environment" from the scripting menu, to show the main window of the form editor.

Open the (XMLSpyEvents) module with a double-click at the tree item in the project bar.

Normally all events should be predefined in this module. If the event you want to write code for does not have an entry in the event list box, use the "Add Function" command either from the "Project" menu, or from the popup menu which appears if you right-click the module in the project bar to create it again.

Note that you must use the exact same spelling as was used when XMLSpyFormEditor created the new project and inserted the predefined event handlers for you. You must also fill in possible parameters into the function header. The best way to recreate a deleted event handler is to create a new scripting project and copy name and function definition from there.

The screen shot shows you the (XMLSpyEvents) module and the list of predefined events. Choose On_OpenProject to add some scripting code which will be executed each time XMLSpy opens a project.

```
MyScripts : (XMLSpyEvents)                                    _ □ ✕

[XMLSpyEvents]        ▼     On_BeforeDrag              ▼

//On_BeforeDrag                    On_BeforeDrag
//return value: true allows draggi  On_BeforeDrop
//                 false forbids drag  On_BeforeStartEditing
function On_BeforeDrag() {          On_EditingFinished
                                    On_FocusChanged
}                                   On_OpenProject


//End of On_BeforeDrag
```

The script sequentially opens all XML files located in the XML folder of the project and validates them. If the validation fails the scripts stops and shows the validation error. If the file passes the validation it will be closed.

We now need to add some code to the On_OpenProject event handler:

```
function On_OpenProject()
{
        var     bOK;
        var     nIndex,nCount;
        var     objItems,objXMLFolder = null;

        objItems = Application.CurrentProject.RootItems;
        nCount = objItems.Count;
```

```
            // search for XML folder
            for(nIndex = 0;nIndex < nCount;nIndex++)        {
                    var txtExtensions;
                    txtExtensions = objItems.Item(nIndex).FileExtensions;

                    if(txtExtensions.indexOf("xml") >= 0)   {
                            objXMLFolder = objItems.Item(nIndex);
                            break;
                    }
            }

            // does XML folder exist?
            if(objXMLFolder)     {
                    var objChild,objDoc;

                    nCount = objXMLFolder.ChildItems.Count;

                    // step through associated xml files
                    for(nIndex = 0;nIndex < nCount;nIndex++)        {
                            objChild = objXMLFolder.ChildItems.Item(nIndex);

                            try     {
                                    objDoc = objChild.Open();

                                    // use JScript method to access out-parameters
                                    var strError = new Array(1);
                                    var nErrorPos = new Array(1);
                                    var objBadData = new Array(1);

                                    bOK =
objDoc.IsValid(strError,nErrorPos,objBadData);

                                    if(!bOK)        {
                                            // if the validation fails, we should
display the
                                            // message from XMLSpy
                                            // of course we have to create the form
"MsgBox" and
                                            // define the global txtMessage variable
                                            //
                                            // txtMessage = Position:" + nErrorPos[0] +
"\n" +                                  //                     strError[0];
                                            // txtMessage +=     "\n\nXML:\n" +
objBadData[0].Name + ", " +
                                            //                     objBadData[0].TextValue;
                                            //
                                            // Application.ShowForm("MsgBox");

                                            break;
                                    }

                                    objDoc.Close(true);
                                    objDoc = null;
                            }
                            catch(Err)     {
                                    // displaying the error description here is a good
idea

                                    // txtMessage = Err.Description;
                                    // Application.ShowForm("MsgBox");

                                    break;
                            }
                    }
            }
    }
```

That's all. Switch to XMLSpy, open a project and see what happens.

How to create a Form

This section explains how to create a new Form in the XMLSpyFormEditor and how to display it in XMLSpy. The sample builds a dialog where the user can type in the name of elements that are to be deleted from the active XML file in XMLSpy.

To create a form, switch to the XMLSpyFormEditor. Use "Switch to scripting environment" from the scripting menu, to show the main window of the form editor. There is at least one project open, the global project.

There are two ways for adding a new form to a project. You can use the "Add Form" command from the "Project" menu, or click the "New Form" Button in the project window. In both cases, the new form is added immediately and appears as a separate window.

The screen shot shows the XMLSpyFormEditor right after the creation of a new form:

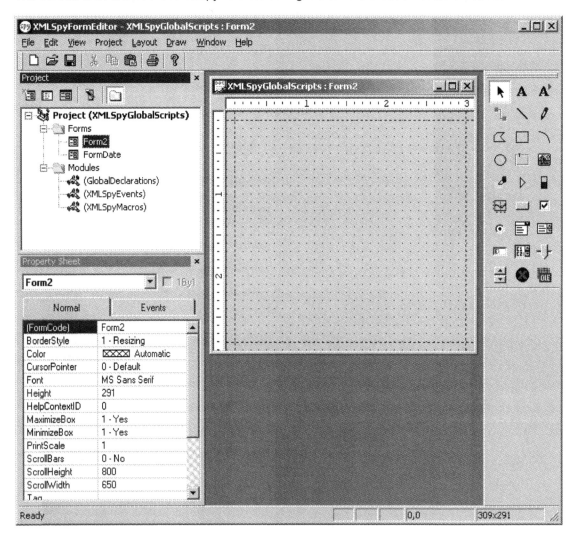

You could change the name of the new form now. To do so, enter a new name in the Property Sheet in the line (FormCode). For our example type in "RemoveDlg". Type in the form-title you like in the "Title" line of the Property Sheet.

We then insert an edit box where the user can type in the name of the elements to remove from the XML file. Select the edit box icon 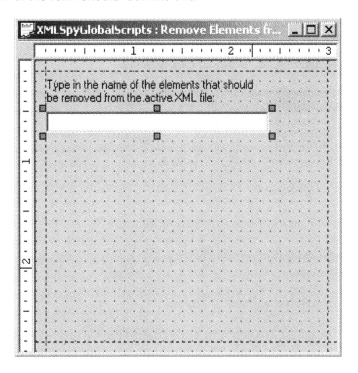 from the tool bar on the right side of the main window. Define a rectangle with the mouse for the edit box in the display area of our RemoveDlg form.

In the (ObjectCode) line of the Property Sheet, type in "EditElements" as the name of the new edit box. Add a caption for the edit box with the static text icon **A** from the tool bar. The edit window of the form should look like this:

We now need two buttons in our form, "Delete" and "Cancel". Use the button icon to draw them in our form window. Type in "BtnDelete" and "BtnCancel" as names in the (ObjectCode) lines of the button properties.

Set the button text in the Text fields to "Delete" and "Cancel". Additionally set the type of the Cancel - Button to "0 - OK" in the ButtonType field of the properties.

After we have designed our form we need some scripting code to make it useful.

We need a function that recursively steps through the XML file, and deletes all XMLData objects with a given name. We declare this in the (GlobalDeclarations) module of the project. If the module is not visible, double-click it in the project bar. Type in the following code:

```
var txtElementName;

function DeleteXMLElements(objXMLData)
{
        if(objXMLData == null)
                return;

        if(objXMLData.HasChildren){
                var objChild;
                objChild = objXMLData.GetFirstChild(-1);

                while(objChild)     {
                        DeleteXMLElements(objChild);
```

```
try     {
        if(objChild.Name == txtElementName)
                objXMLData.EraseCurrentChild();

        objChild = objXMLData.GetNextChild();
}
catch(Err)    {
        objChild = null;
}
        }
    }
}
```

After this your global declarations module should look like this:

```
//(GlobalDeclarations)

var txtElementName;

function DeleteXMLElements(objXMLData)
{
    if(objXMLData == null)
        return;

    if(objXMLData.HasChildren)   {
        var objChild;
        objChild = objXMLData.GetFirstChild(-1);

        while(objChild) {
            DeleteXMLElements(objChild);

            try {
                if(objChild.Name == txtElementName)
                    objXMLData.EraseCurrentChild();

                objChild = objXMLData.GetNextChild();
            }
            catch(Err)   {
                objChild = null;
            }
        }
    }
}
//End of (GlobalDeclarations)
```

Select the BtnDelete button and choose the "Events" tab from the property sheet. Click on the edit code icon ▦ in the "EventClick" line of the tab. The Mini-Editor window pops up with the predefined function header of the click-event. This function will be executed every time the user clicks the "Delete" button. Add the following code to the event:

```
if(EditElements.Text != "")        {
     txtElementName = EditElements.Text;
     DeleteXMLElements(Application.ActiveDocument.RootElement);
}
```

The Delete - Button sets the global variable txtElementName to the string from the edit box and calls DeleteXMLElements() with the root element of the active document.

There is not much left to do.
Select the (XMLSpyMacros) module, create a new macro (see also "How to write a macro") called "DeleteElements" and enter this code:

```
var a;

if(Application.ActiveDocument != null)
     a = Application.ShowForm("RemoveDlg");
```

Run the macro from the "Show macros..." dialog of the "Scripting" menu within XMLSpy.

Part V

5 Programmer's Reference

Basic concepts

The introduction of the COM based API makes the functionality of XMLSpy available to other applications. It is now possible to automate a wide range of tasks from simple file validations to complex XML content modifications using the XMLData interface. The API is also the main requirement for the built-in scripting environment of XMLSpy. See the chapter "Scripting" in this manual for further documentation.

XMLSpy and the XMLSpyAPI, follow the common specifications for automation servers from Microsoft. It is possible to access the methods and properties from most development environments such as C, C++, VisualBasic, Delphi and from scripting languages like VBScript and JavaScript.

To support scripting, concessions had to be made to make all parameters compatible to the VARIANT structure and allow special handling of JavaScript out-parameters (see "How to handle an event" for an example).

The following limitations have to be considered in your client code:

1. Don't hold references to objects in memory longer than you need them, especially those from the XMLData interface. If the user interacts between two calls of your client, then there is no guarantee that these references are still valid.

2. Free references explicitly.

3. Be aware that if your client code crashes instances of XMLSpy may still remain in the system.

4. Don't forget to disable dialogs if the user interface is not visible.

5. See "Error handling" to avoid annoying error messages.

6. Terminate XMLSpy with the "Application.Quit" method.

Object model

The starting point for every application which uses the XMLSpy API is the "Application" object. This object contains general methods like import/export support and references to the open documents and any open project.

To create an instance of the Application object, call CreateObject("XMLSpy.Application") from VisualBasic or a similar function from your preferred development environment to create a COM object. There is no need to create any other objects, to use the complete XMLSpy API (It is in fact not even possible). All other interfaces are accessed through other objects with the Application object as the starting point.

The picture below shows you the links between the main objects of the XMLSpy API:

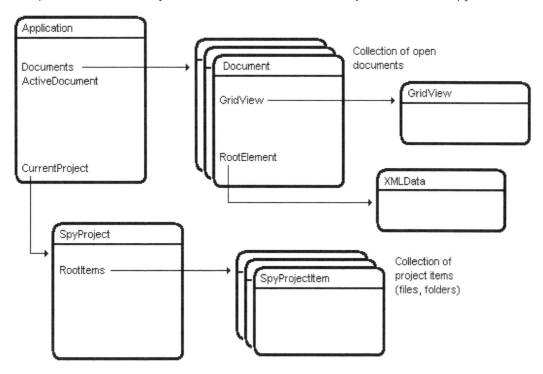

The application object consists of the following parts:

1. Document collection and reference to the active document.

2. Reference to current project and methods for creating and opening of projects.

3. Methods to support the export to and import from databases, text files and Word documents.

4. URL management.

5. Methods for macro menu items.

Once you have created an Application object you can start using the functionality of XMLSpy. Most of the times you either open a project and access the documents from there or you directly open a document via the "Documents" interface.

Simple document access

Create and open files

Use the methods of the "Documents" interface to create and open documents. This interface is accessible via the "Application.Documents" property.

Example:

```
Dim objDoc As Document
Set objDoc = objSpy.Documents.OpenFile("C:\xmlfiles\myfile.xml",
False)
```

Sometimes it is necessary to show a file dialog to the user to select a file. This usually happens in the scripting environment and you only need to pass True as the second parameter to OpenFile().

To create a new file use "Documents.NewFile()". Any existing file with the same path will be overwritten during the next Document.Save() call.

Documents collection

All open documents are accessible via the "Documents" collection. All collection objects in the XMLSpy API conform to the Microsoft specifications. So it is possible to use the For-Each loop in VisualBasic to iterate through the open documents.

Example:

```
Dim objDocs As Documents
Dim objDoc As Document

Set objDocs = objSpy.Documents

For Each objDoc In objDocs
        'do something useful with your document
        objDoc.AssignXSL "C:\myXSL.xsl", False
Next
```

Another way to access a document is the "Documents.Item" method. The method takes an index as a parameter and gets the corresponding document object from the collection. Please note that 0 (zero) is the first index value. "Documents.Count" retrieves the total number of documents.

Example:

```
Dim objDocs As Documents
Dim objDoc As Document

Set objDoc = objDocs.Item(1)          'gets the first document
```

Validation

One common task on documents is to validate them against an assigned schema or DTD. If the XML file has no schema or DTD already assigned, use "Document.AssignSchema" or "Document.AssignDTD" to add the necessary references to the document.

Examples:

```
objSpy.ActiveDocument.AssignSchema "C:\mySchema.xsd", False
```

or

```
objSpy.ActiveDocument.AssignDTD "C:\myDTD.dtd", False
```

If you want the user to select a schema or DTD, pass True as the second parameter to these functions to display a file-dialog. These methods only put the reference into the document and do not check the existence of the specified file. If the file path is not valid, the validation will fail.

After you have assigned a valid schema or DTD reference to your file, you are able to validate it with "Document.IsValid". IsValid needs some out-parameters that must be declared as VARIANTs to be accessible from script languages like VBScript and JavaScript.

Example:

```
Dim bValid        As Boolean
Dim strMsg        As Variant
Dim nPos          As Variant
Dim objBadXMLData As Variant

bValid = objSpy.ActiveDocument.IsValid(strMsg, nPos,
objBadXMLData)

If bValid = False Then
        a = MsgBox("The document is not valid:" & Chr(13) &
                   strMsg & Chr(13) & "position: " & nPos &
                   Chr(13) & "XMLData name: " &
objBadXMLData.Name)
Else
        a = MsgBox("The document is valid")
End If
```

Import and Export

Before you implement your import and export tasks with the XMLSpy API, it is a good practice to test the connections, parameters, SLQ queries and so on in XML Spy. This way, you are able to verify the results and to make quick adjustments to all import or export parameters.

Most of the methods for importing and exporting data are placed in the "Application" object, the remaining functions are accessible via the "Document" interface.

There is some preparatory work necessary, before the actual import or export can be started. Every import/export job consists of two parts. You need to define a connection to your data and the specific behaviour for the import/export process.

In case of an import, the connection is either a database, a text-file or a Word document. The behaviour is basically which data (columns) should be imported in XMLSpy.

In case of an export, the connection is either a database or a text file. Specify which data (elements of the XML file) and additional parameters (e.g. automatic key generation or number of sub-levels) to use from the XML-structure for the behaviour.

The properties in the DatabaseConnection, TextImportExportSettings and ExportSettings interfaces have default values. See the corresponding descriptions in the "Interfaces" chapter for further information.

Import from database

These are the steps to establish a connection to an existing database for import:

1. Use a "DatabaseConnection" object and set the properties:
    The method "Application.GetDatabaseSettings" returns a new object for a database connection:

    Dim objImpSettings As DatabaseConnection
    Set objImpSettings = objSpy.GetDatabaseSettings

You have to set either a ADO connection string,

    objImpSettings.ADOConnection = strADOConnection

or the path to an existing database file:

    objImpSettings.File = "C:\myDatabase.mdb"

To complete the settings you create a SQL select statement to define the data to be queried:

    objImpSettings.SQLSelect = "SELECT * FROM myTable"

2. Call "Application.GetDatabaseImportElementList" to get a collection of the resulting columns of the SQL query:

    ```
    Dim objElementList As ElementList
    Set objElementList =
    objSpy.GetDatabaseImportElementList(objImpSettings)
    ```

    This collection gives you the opportunity to control which columns should be imported and what type the new elements will become. Each item of the collection represents one column to import. If you remove an item, the corresponding column will not be

imported. You can additionally modify the "ElementListItem.ElementKind" property, to
set the type of the created XML elements for each column.

Please consider that GetDatabaseImportElementList() executes the SQL query and
could initiate a time consuming call. To avoid this, it is possible to pass a null-pointer
(Nothing in VisualBasic) as the second parameter to ImportFromDatabase() to import
all columns as plain XML elements.

3. Start the import with "Application.ImportFromDatabase":

```
        Dim objImpDoc As Document
        Set objImpDoc =
objSpy.ImportFromDatabase(objImpSettings,objElementList)
```

Import from Text
Importing data from a text file is similar to the import from a database. You must use other
interfaces (described in steps 1-3 below) with different methods and properties:

1. Use a "TextImportExportSettings" object and set the properties:
    The method "Application.GetTextImportExportSettings" returns a new object to specify
    a text file for import.

```
        Dim objImpSettings As TextImportExportSettings
        Set objImpSettings = objSpy.GetTextImportExportSettings
```

You have to set at least the ImportFile property to the path of the file for the import.
Another important property is HeaderRow. Set it to False, if the text file does not
contain a leading line as a header row.

```
        objImpSettings.ImportFile = "C:\myFile.txt"
        objImpSettings.HeaderRow = False
```

2. Call "Application.GetTextImportElementList" to get a collection of all columns inside
    the text file:

```
        Dim objElementList As ElementList
        Set objElementList =
objSpy.GetTextImportElementList(objImpSettings)
```

3. Start the import with "Application.ImportFromText":

```
        Dim objImpDoc As Document
        Set objImpDoc =
objSpy.ImportFromText(objImpSettings,objElementList)
```

Export to database

1.   Use a "DatabaseConnection" object and set the necessary properties.
     All properties except "SQLSelect" are important for the export. "ADOConnection" or
     "File" defines the target for the output. You need to set only one of them.

2. Fill an "ExportSettings" object with the required values.
    These properties are the same options as those available in the export dialog of
    XMLSpy. Select the menu option Convert | Export to Text files/Database to see the
    options and try a combination of export settings. After that it is easy to transfer these
    settings to the properties of the interface.

Call "Application.GetExportSettings" to get a ExportSettings object:

```
Dim objExpSettings As ExportSettings
Set objExpSettings = objSpy.GetExportSettings

objExpSettings.CreateKeys = False
objExpSettings.ExportAllElements = False
objExpSettings.SubLevelLimit = 2
```

3. Build an element list with "Document.GetExportElementList".
    The element list enables you to eliminate XML elements from the export process. It also gives you information about the record and field count in the "RecordCount" and "FieldCount" properties. Set the "ExportSettings.ElementList" property to this collection. It is possible to set the element list to null/Nothing (default) to export all elements.

4. Call "Document.ExportToDatabase" to execute the export.
    The description of the ExportToDatabase method contains also a code example for a database export.

Export to text

1. Use a "TextImportExportSettings" object and set the necessary properties.

2. Fill an "ExportSettings" object with the required values.
    See item number 2 from "Export to database" earlier on this page.

3. Build an element list with "Document.GetExportElementList".
    See item number 3 from "Export to database" earlier on this page.

4. Call "Document.ExportToText" to execute the export.
    The description of the ExportToText method contains also a code example for a database export.

Using XMLData

XMLData gives you access to the elements of an currently open XML file. It enables you to perform all necessary modifications to the elements of the XML structure. The main functionality of XMLData is:

1. Access to the names and values of all kinds of elements (e.g. elements, attributes)

2. Creation of new elements of all kinds,

3. Insertion and appending of new elements.

4. Erasing of existing child elements.

Structure of XMLData

Before you can use the XMLData interface, you have to know how an existing XML file is mapped into a XMLData structure. One major thing you must be aware of is, that XMLData has no seperate branch of objects for attributes.

The attributes of an element are also children of the element. The "XMLData.Kind" property, gives you the opportunity to distinguish between the different types of children of an element.

Example:

This XML code,

```
<ParentElement>
      <FirstChild attr1="Red" attr2="Black">
            This is the value of FirstChild
      </FirstChild>
      <SecondChild>
            <!--Your Comment-->
            </DeepChild>
      </SecondChild>
      This is Text
</ParentElement>
```

is mapped to the following XMLData object structure:

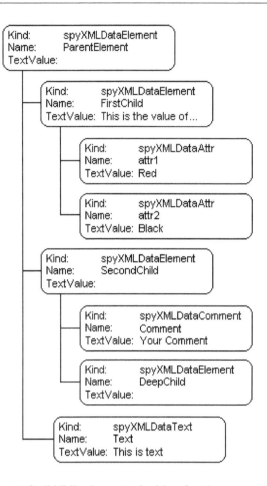

The parent of all XML elements inside of a document is the property "Document.RootElement". Use this XMLData object to get references to all other XML elements in the structure.

Name and value of elements

To get and to modify the name and value of all types of XML elements use the "XMLData.Name" and "XMLData.TextValue" properties. It is possible that several kinds of XMLData objects and empty elements do not have a text value associated.

Creation and insertion of new XMLData objects

The creation of a new XML language entity requires the following steps:

1. Create the new XMLData object:
    Use the "Document.CreateChild" method to create a new XMLData object. Set name and value after you have inserted the new XML entity (see point 3).

2. Find the correct location for the new XMLData object:
    To insert a new XMLData object you have to get a reference to the parent first. If the new child is to become the last child of the parent, use the "XMLData.AppendChild" method to insert the XMLData object.
    If the new child should be located elsewhere in the sequence of child objects, use the "XMLData.GetFirstChild" and "XMLData.GetNextChild" to move the iterator to the child before which the new child should be inserted.

3. Insert the new child with "XMLData.InsertChild"

The new child will be inserted immediately before the current child.

The following example adds a third child between <FirstChild> and the <SecondChild> element:

```
Dim objParent As XMLData
Dim objChild As XMLData
Dim objNewChild As XMLData

Set objNewChild =
objSpy.ActiveDocument.CreateChild(spyXMLDataElement)

'objParent is set to <ParentElement>
'GetFirstChild(-1) gets all children of the parent element
'and move to <SecondChild>
Set objChild = objParent.GetFirstChild(-1)
Set objChild = objParent.GetNextChild

objParent.InsertChild objNewChild
objNewChild.Name = "OneAndAHalf"
Set objNewChild = Nothing
```

Copying of existing XMLData objects

If you want to insert existing XMLData objects at a different place in the same document or into another document you can't use the XMLData.InsertChild and XMLData.AppendChild methods. These methods only work for new XMLData objects.

Instead of using InsertChild or AppendChild you have to copy the object hierarchy manually. The following function written in JavaScript is an example for recursively copying XMLData:

```
// this function returns a complete copy of the XMLData object
function GetCopy(objXMLData)
{
        var objNew;
        objNew =
Application.ActiveDocument.CreateChild(objXMLData.Kind);

        objNew.Name = objXMLData.Name;
        objNew.TextValue = objXMLData.TextValue;

        if(objXMLData.HasChildren)     {
              var objChild;
              objChild = objXMLData.GetFirstChild(-1);

              while(objChild)    {
                    try {
                          objNew.AppendChild(GetCopy(objChild));
                          objChild = objXMLData.GetNextChild();
                    }
                    catch(e) {
                          objChild = null;
                    }
              }
        }

        return objNew;
}
```

Erasing of XMLData objects

XMLData provides two methods for the deletion of child objects, "XMLData.EraseAllChildren" and "XMLData.EraseCurrentChild".

To erase XMLData objects you need access to the parent of the elements you want to remove. Use "XMLData.GetFirstChild" and "XMLData.GetNextChild" to get a reference to the parent XMLData object.

See the method descriptions of "EraseAllChildren" and "EraseCurrentChild" for examples how to erase XML elements.

Error handling

The XMLSpy API returns errors in two different ways. Every API method returns a HRESULT. This return value informs the caller about any malfunctions during the execution of the method. If the call was successful, the return value is equal to S_OK. C/C++ programmers generally use HRESULT to detect any errors.

VisualBasic, scripting languages and other high-level development environments, don't give the programmer access to the returning HRESULT of a COM call. They use the cooond error raising mechanism also supported by the XMLSpy API, the IErrorInfo interface. If an error occurs the API creates a new object that implements the IErrorInfo interface. The development environment takes this interface, and fills its own error handling mechansim with the provided informations.

The next paragraphs describes how to deal with errors raised from the XMLSpy API in different development environments.

VisualBasic

A common way to handle errors in VisualBasic is to define an error handler. This error handler can be set with the On Error statement. Usually the handler displays a error message and does some cleanup to avoid spare references and any kind of resource leaks. VisualBasic fills its own Err object with the information from the IErrorInfo interface.

Example:

```
Sub Validate()
      'place variable declarations here

      'set error handler
      On Error GoTo ErrorHandler

      'if IsValid() fails, program execution continues
      'at ErrorHandler:
      bValid =
objSpy.ActiveDocument.IsValid(strMsg,nPos,objBadXMLData)

      'additional code comes here

      'exit
      Exit Sub

      ErrorHandler:
      Set objBadXMLData = Nothing

      MsgBox("Error: " & (Err.Number - vbObjectError) & Chr(13)
&
             "Description: " & Err.Description)
   End Sub
```

JavaScript

The Microsoft implementation of JavaScript (JScript) provides a try - catch mechanism to deal with errors raised from COM calls. It is very similar to the VisualBasic approach, because you also declare an error object containing the necessary informations.

Example:

```
function Validate()
{
```

```
                // please insert variable declarations here

        try    {
                bValid =
objSpy.ActiveDocument.IsValid(sMsg,nPos,objBad);
                }
        catch(Error)        {
                objBad = null;
                sError = Error.description;
                nErrorCode = Error.number;
                return false;
        }

        return bValid;
   }
```

C/C++

C/C++ gives you easy access to the HRESULT of the COM call and to the IErrorInterface.

```
        HRESULT      hr;

        // call IsValid() from the XMLSpy API
        if(FAILED(hr = ipDoc-
>IsValid(&varMsg,&varPos,&varBadData)))    {
                IErrorInfo  *ipErrorInfo = NULL;

                if(SUCCEEDED(::GetErrorInfo(0,&ipErrorInfo)))    {
                        BSTR   bstrDescr;
                        ipErrorInfo->GetDescription(&bstrDescr);

                        // handle error information
                        wprintf(L"Error message:\t%s\n",bstrDescr);
                        ::SysFreeString(bstrDescr);

                        // release error info
                        ipErrorInfo->Release();
                }
        }
```

DOM and XMLData

The XMLData interface gives you full access to the XML structure behind the current document with less methods than DOM and is much simpler. The XMLData interface is a minimalist approach to reading and modifying existing, or newly created XML data. You might however, want to use a DOM tree because you can access one from an external source or you just prefer the MSXML DOM implementation.

The **ProcessDOMNode()** and **ProcessXMLDataNode()** functions provided below convert any segments of an XML structure between XMLData and DOM.

To use the **ProcessDOMNode()** function:
- pass the root element of the DOM segment you want to convert in **objNode** and
- pass the plugin object with the CreateChild() method in **objCreator**

To use the **ProcessXMLDataNode()** function:
- pass the root element of the XMLData segment in **objXMLData** and
- pass the DOMDocument object created with MSXML in **xmlDoc**

```
/////////////////////////////////////////////////////////////////
// DOM to XMLData conversion
function ProcessDOMNode(objNode,objCreator)
{
    var objRoot;
    objRoot = CreateXMLDataFromDOMNode(objNode,objCreator);

    if(objRoot) {
        if((objNode.nodeValue != null) &&
(objNode.nodeValue.length > 0))
            objRoot.TextValue = objNode.nodeValue;
            // add attributes
        if(objNode.attributes) {
            var Attribute;
            var oNodeList = objNode.attributes;

            for(var i = 0;i < oNodeList.length; i++) {
                Attribute = oNodeList.item(i);

                var newNode;
                newNode =
ProcessDOMNode(Attribute,objCreator);

                objRoot.AppendChild(newNode);
            }
        }
        if(objNode.hasChildNodes)       {
            try {
                // add children
                var Item;
                oNodeList = objNode.childNodes;

                for(var i = 0;i < oNodeList.length; i++) {
                    Item = oNodeList.item(i);

                    var newNode;
                    newNode =
ProcessDOMNode(Item,objCreator);
```

```
                                        objRoot.AppendChild(newNode);
                        }
                }
                catch(err) {
                }
            }
        }
    }
    return objRoot;
}

function CreateXMLDataFromDOMNode(objNode,objCreator)
{
    var bSetName = true;
    var bSetValue = true;

    var nKind = 4;

    switch(objNode.nodeType)         {
        case 2:nKind = 5;break;
        case 3:nKind = 6;bSetName = false;break;
        case 4:nKind = 7;bSetName = false;break;
        case 8:nKind = 8;bSetName = false;break;
        case 7:nKind = 9;break;
    }
    var objNew = null;
    objNew = objCreator.CreateChild(nKind);

    if(bSetName)
        objNew.Name = objNode.nodeName;

    if(bSetValue && (objNode.nodeValue != null))
        objNew.TextValue = objNode.nodeValue;

    return objNew;
}
////////////////////////////////////////////////////////////////////
// XMLData to DOM conversion

function ProcessXMLDataNode(objXMLData,xmlDoc)
{
    var objRoot;
    objRoot = CreateDOMNodeFromXMLData(objXMLData,xmlDoc);

    if(objRoot) {
        if(IsTextNodeEnabled(objRoot) &&
(objXMLData.TextValue.length > 0))
            objRoot.appendChild(xmlDoc.createTextNode(objXMLData
.TextValue));

        if(objXMLData.HasChildren)      {
            try {
                var objChild;
                objChild = objXMLData.GetFirstChild(-1);

                while(true) {
                    if(objChild)        {
                        var newNode;
                        newNode =
```

```
        ProcessXMLDataNode(objChild,xmlDoc);

                                        if(newNode.nodeType == 2)        {
                                                // child node is an
attribute
                                                objRoot.attributes.setNamedI
tem(newNode);
                                        }
                                        else
                                                objRoot.appendChild(newNode)
;
                                }
                                objChild = objXMLData.GetNextChild();
                        }
                }
                catch(err) {
                }
            }
        }
        return objRoot;
}

function CreateDOMNodeFromXMLData(objXMLData,xmlDoc)
{
        switch(objXMLData.Kind) {
                case 4:return xmlDoc.createElement(objXMLData.Name);
                case 5:return xmlDoc.createAttribute(objXMLData.Name);
                case 6:return xmlDoc.createTextNode(objXMLData.TextValue);
                case 7:return
xmlDoc.createCDATASection(objXMLData.TextValue);
                case 8:return xmlDoc.createComment(objXMLData.TextValue);
                case 9:return
xmlDoc.createProcessingInstruction(objXMLData.Name,objXMLData.TextValu
e);
        }

        return xmlDoc.createElement(objXMLData.Name);
}
function IsTextNodeEnabled(objNode)
{
        switch(objNode.nodeType) {
                case 1:
                case 2:
                case 5:             '
                case 6:
                case 11:return true;
        }
        return false;
}
```

Document Editor View

Row operations

Repeatable elements can be created within an XML Document. This is made possible by the specific schema file to which the XML file is assigned. The WYSIWIG environment allows you to manipulate rows and their data, individually.

An XML row may be implemented by an HTML table, but this need not always be the case. The XSLT Designer *.SPS file defines the HTML page layout. While editing XML data, an external script performs the row operations (on each row individually).

If an external script is to perform row operations then two steps must occur:
- The first step checks whether the cursor is currently in a row using a property. E.g. **IsRowInsertEnabled**, which returns a TRUE or FALSE value.
- If the return value is TRUE then the row method can be called. E.g. **RowAppend**, which has no parameters and returns no value.

The following is a list of properties and methods available that perform table operations. Each of the properties return a BOOL and each of the methods have no parameters.

IsRowInsertEnabled, RowInsert:	Row insertion operation.
IsRowAppendEnabled, RowAppend:	Append row operation.
IsRowDeleteEnabled, RowDelete:	Delete row operation.
IsRowMoveUpEnabled, RowMoveUp:	Move the XML data up one row location.
IsRowMoveDownEnabled, RowMoveDown:	Move the XML data down one row location.
IsRowDuplicateEnabled, RowDuplicate:	Duplicate the currently selected XML row.

Editing operations

When XML data is displayed as HTML data, it is possible to manipulate individual elements using standard editing operations cut, copy and paste.

Not all XML data elements can be edited however, and it is therefore necessary first to test if editing is possible. This is achieved in the same way as row operations, starting with a property to test editing capabilities and then calling the method to perform the editing operation.

The only method that does not have a test is the method **EditSelectAll**, which automatically selects all elements displayed in the document. The following is a list of properties and methods available that perform editing operations. Each of the properties returns a BOOL and each of the methods have no parameters.

IsEditUndoEnabled, **EditUndo**	Undo an editing operation
IsEditRedoEnabled, **EditRedo**:	Redo an editing operation
IsEditCopyEnabled, **EditCopy**	Copy the selected text to the Windows clipboard
IsEditCutEnabled, **EditCut**	Cut the selected text to the Windows clipboard
IsEditPasteEnabled, **EditPaste**	Paste the Windows clipboard text to the current cursor position
IsEditClearEnabled, **EditClear**	Clear the selected text from the XML document

Events

The Document Editor View provides events which can be handled using the XMLSpy scripting environment. All event handlers take no parameters and any returned value will be ignored. To retrieve information when a specific event is raised you have to read the according properties of the event object.

List of currently available events:

    On_DocEditDragOver
    On_DocEditDrop
    On_DocEditKeyDown
    On_DocEditKeyUp
    On_DocEditKeyPressed
    On_DocEditMouseMove
    On_DocEditButtonUp
    On_DocEditButtonDown
    On_DocEditContextMenu
    On_DocEditPaste
    On_DocEditCut
    On_DocEditCopy
    On_DocEditClear
    On_DocEditSelectionChanged

To add an event handler please see "How to handle an event".

Interfaces

Objects

Application
DatabaseConnection
Document
Documents
ElementList
ElementListItem
ExportSettings
GridView
SpyProject
SpyProjectItem
SpyProjectItems
TextImportExportSettings
XMLData

Enumerations

Description

This chapter contains the reference of the XMLSpy 1.2 Type Library.

Most of the given examples are written in VisualBasic. These code snippets assume that there is a variable defined and set called objSpy of type Application. There are also some code samples written in JavaScript.

Application
See also

Methods
GetDatabaseImportElementList
GetDatabaseSettings
GetDatabaseTables
ImportFromDatabase

GetTextImportElementList
GetTextImportExportSettings
ImportFromText

ImportFromWord

ImportFromSchema

GetExportSettings

NewProject
OpenProject

AddMacroMenuItem
ClearMacroMenu

ShowForm

ShowApplication

URLDelete
URLMakeDirectory

Quit

Properties
ActiveDocument
Documents

CurrentProject

WarningNumber
WarningText

Description
Application is the root for all other objects. It is the only object you can create by CreateObject (VisualBasic) or other similar COM related functions.

Example

```
Dim objSpy As Application
Set objSpy = CreateObject("XMLSpy.Application")
```

XMLSpyApplication.GetDatabaseImportElementList

See also

Declaration: GetDatabaseImportElementList(*pImportSettings* as DatabaseConnection) as ElementList

Return Value
The function returns a collection of ElementListItems.

Description
GetDatabaseImportElementList retrieves information about the database as specified in pImportSettings to create the list of elements ppElementList. This list is used to exclude elements from import and to set the kind of the imported elements. See also ImportFromDatabase. The items of the collection are described in ElementListItem.

Example
See example at ImportFromDatabase.

XMLSpyApplication.GetDatabaseSettings

See also

Declaration: GetDatabaseSettings as DatabaseConnection

Return Value
Returns a DatabaseConnection object.

Description
GetDatabaseSettings creates a new object of database settings. The object is used to define a connection to a database. See also ImportFromDatabase.

Example
See example of ImportFromDatabase.

XMLSpyApplication.GetDatabaseTables

See also

Declaration: GetDatabaseTables(*pImportSettings* as DatabaseConnection) as ElementList

Return Value
The function returns a collection of ElementListItems.

Description
GetDatabaseTables reads the table names from the database.

Example

```
Dim objImpSettings As DatabaseConnection
Set objImpSettings = objSpy.GetDatabaseSettings
objImpSettings.ADOConnection = TxtADO.Text

'store table names in list box
ListTables.Clear

Dim objList As ElementList
Dim objItem As ElementListItem
On Error GoTo ErrorHandler
Set objList = objSpy.GetDatabaseTables(objImpSettings)

For Each objItem In objList
      ListTables.AddItem objItem.Name
Next
```

XMLSpyApplication.ImportFromDatabase

See also

Declaration: ImportFromDatabase(_pImportSettings_ as
DatabaseConnection,_pElementList_ as ElementList) as Document

Return Value
Creates a new document.

Description
ImportFromDatabase imports the database as specified in pImportSettings. pElementList
declares the tables to import. See Application.GetDatabaseImportElementList for more
information about the list of elements.

Example

```
Dim objImpSettings As DatabaseConnection
Set objImpSettings = objSpy.GetDatabaseSettings

objImpSettings.ADOConnection = strADOConnection
objImpSettings.SQLSelect = "SELECT * FROM MyTable"

Dim objDoc As Document
On Error Resume Next
Set objDoc = objSpy.ImportFromDatabase(
                            objImpSettings,
                            objSpy.GetDatabaseImportElementLis
t(objImpSettings))
      CheckForError
```

XMLSpyApplication.GetTextImportElementList

See also

Declaration: GetTextImportElementList(_pImportSettings_ as
TextImportExportSettings) as
ElementList

Return Value
The method returns a collection of ElementListItems.

Description
GetTextImportElementList gets information about the text-file as specified in pImportSettings.
See also ImportFromText.

Example

```
Dim objImpSettings As TextImportExportSettings
Set objImpSettings = objSpy.GetTextImportExportSettings

objImpSettings.ImportFile = "C:\ImportMe.txt"
objImpSettings.HeaderRow = False

Dim objList As ElementList
Set objList = objSpy.GetTextImportElementList(objImpSettings)

'exclude first column
objList.RemoveItem 1

Dim objImpDoc As Document
On Error Resume Next
Set objImpDoc = objSpy.ImportFromText(objImpSettings, objList)
CheckForError
```

XMLSpyApplication.GetTextImportExportSettings

See also

Declaration: GetTextImportExportSettings as TextImportExportSettings

Return Value

Description
GetTextImportExportSettings creates a new object of common import and export settings for
text-files. See also the example for Application.GetTextImportElementList and Import and
Export.

XMLSpyApplication.ImportFromText

See also

Declaration: ImportFromText(*pImportSettings* as
TextImportExportSettings,*pElementList* as ElementList) as Document

Return Value
Creates a new document.

Description
ImportFromText imports the text-file as specified in pImportSettings. pElementList declares the
tables to import.

Example

```
        Dim objImpSettings As TextImportExportSettings
        Set objImpSettings = objSpy.GetTextImportExportSettings

        objImpSettings.ImportFile = strFileName
        objImpSettings.HeaderRow = False

        Dim objImpDoc As Document
        On Error Resume Next
        Set objImpDoc = objSpy.ImportFromText(objImpSettings,
                                    objSpy.GetTextImportElementList(ob
jImpSettings))

        CheckForError
```

XMLSpyApplication.ImportFromWord

See also

Declaration: ImportFromWord(*strFile* as String) as Document

Return Value
The method creates a new document.

Description
ImportFromWord imports the Word-Document strFile.

Application.ImportFromSchema

See also

Declaration: ImportFromSchema(*pImportSettings* as DatabaseConnection,*strTable* as String,*pSchemaDoc* as Document) as Document

Parameters

pImportSettings
Used to specify the database connection. See also Import and Export.

strTable
Sets the root table from the schema for import.

pSchemaDoc
Schema document for import.

Return Value
Creates a new document.

Description
ImportFromSchema imports the database as specified in pImportSettings.

XMLSpyApplication.GetExportSettings

See also

Declaration: GetExportSettings as ExportSettings

Return Value

The method returns a ExportSettings object.

Description

GetExportSettings creates a new object of common export settings. This object is used to pass the parameters to the export functions and defines the behaviour of the export calls. See also the export functions from Document and the examples at Import and Export.

XMLSpyApplication.NewProject

See also

Declaration: NewProject(*strPath* as String,*bDiscardCurrent* as Boolean)

Return Value

Description

NewProject creates a new project.

If there is already a project open that has been modified and bDiscardCurrent is false, NewProject() fails.

XMLSpyApplication.OpenProject

See also

Declaration: OpenProject(*strPath* as String,*bDiscardCurrent* as Boolean,*bDialog* as Boolean)

Parameters

strPath
Path and file name of the project to open. Can be empty if bDialog is true.

bDiscardCurrent
Discard currently open project and possible lose changes.

bDialog
Show dialogs for user input.

Return Value
none

Description

OpenProject opens an existing project.

If there is already a project open that has been modified and bDiscardCurrent is false, OpenProject() fails.

Application.AddMacroMenuItem

See also

Declaration: AddMacroMenuItem(*strMacro* as String, *strDisplayText* as String)

Return Value

Description

Adds an menu item to the scripting menu. This new menu item invokes the macro defined by strMacro. See also "Calling macros from XMLSpy".

Application.ClearMacroMenu

See also

Declaration: ClearMacroMenu

Return Value

Description

Removes all menu items from the scripting menu. See also "Calling macros from XMLSpy".

Application.ShowForm

See also

Declaration: ShowForm(*strFormName* as String) As Long

Return Value

Returns zero if the user pressed a cancel-button or the form calls TheView.Cancel().

Description

Displays the form strFormName.

Forms, event handlers and macros can be created with the XMLSpyFormEditor. Select "Switch to scripting environment" from the "Scripting" menu to invoke the scripting environment.

Application.ShowApplication

See also

Declaration: ShowApplication(*bShow* as Boolean)

Return Value

Description

The method shows (bShow = True) or hides (bShow = False) XMLSpy.

Application.URLDelete

See also

Declaration: URLDelete(*strURL* as String,*strUser* as String,*strPassword* as String)

Return Value
none

Description
The method deletes the file at the URL strURL.

Application.URLMakeDirectory

See also

Declaration: URLMakeDirectory(*strURL* as String,*strUser* as String,*strPassword* as String)

Return Value
none

Description
The method creates a new directory at the URL strURL.

Application.Quit

See also

Declaration: Quit

Return Value
none

Description
This method terminates XMLSpy. All modified documents will be closed without saving the changes. This is also true for an open project.

XMLSpyApplication.ActiveDocument

See also

Declaration: ActiveDocument as Document

Description
Reference to the active document. If no document is open, ActiveDocument is null (Nothing).

XMLSpyApplication.Documents

See also

Declaration: Documents as Documents

Description
Collection of all open documents. See also "Simple document access".

Application.CurrentProject

See also

Declaration: CurrentProject as SpyProject

Description
Reference to the active document. If no project is open, CurrentProject is null (Nothing).

XMLSpyApplication.WarningNumber

See also

Declaration: WarningNumber as integer

Description
Some methods fill the property WarningNumber with additional information if an error occurs.

Currently just Documents.OpenFile fills this property.

XMLSpyApplication.WarningText

See also

Declaration: WarningText as String

Description
Some methods fill the property WarningText with additional information if an error occurs.

Currently just Documents.OpenFile fills this property.

Document
See also

Methods
AssignDTD
AssignSchema
AssignXSL
TransformXSL

GenerateDTDOrSchema
ConvertDTDOrSchema
CreateSchemaDiagram

CreateChild

ExportToDatabase
ExportToText
GetExportElementList

IsValid
IsWellFormed

Save
SaveToURL
SaveInString

SetActiveDocument

SetEncoding

SetPathName
GetPathName

StartChanges
EndChanges

SwitchViewMode
UpdateViews

Close

Properties

GridView
DocEditView

CurrentViewMode

RootElement

Title

IsModified

Description
Document Class

XMLSpyDocument.AssignDTD

See also

Declaration: AssignDTD(*strDTDFile* as String,*bDialog* as Boolean)

Description
The method places a reference to the DTD file "strDTDFile" into the document. Note that no error occures if the file does not exist or is not accessible.

If bDialog is true XMLSpy presents a dialog to set the file.

See also "Simple document access".

XMLSpyDocument.AssignSchema

See also

Declaration: AssignSchema(*strSchemaFile* as String,*bDialog* as Boolean)

Description
The method places a reference to the schema file "strSchemaFile" into the document. Note that no error occures if the file does not exist or is not accessible.

If bDialog is true XMLSpy presents a dialog to set the file.

See also "Simple document access".

XMLSpyDocument.AssignXSL

See also

Declaration: AssignXSL(*strXSLFile* as String,*bDialog* as Boolean)

Description
The method places a reference to the XSL file "strXSLFile" into the document. Note that no error occures if the file does not exist or is not accessible.

If bDialog is true XMLSpy presents a dialog to set the file.

XMLSpyDocument.TransformXSL

See also

Declaration: TransformXSL

Description
TransformXSL processes the XML document via the associated XSL file. See "Document.AssignXSL" to place a reference to a XSL file in the document.

XMLSpyDocument.GenerateDTDOrSchema

See also

Declaration: GenerateDTDOrSchema(*nFormat* as SPYDTDSchemaFormat,*nValuesList* as integer,*nDetection* as SPYTypeDetection, *nFrequentElements* as SPYFrequentElements)

Parameters

nFormat
Sets the schema output format to DTD, DCD, XMLData, BizTalk or W3C.

nValuesList
Set to 0 (zero) for unlimited.

nDetection
Specifies attribute/element detection.

nFrequentElements
Create complex elements as elements or complex types.

Description
To generate a DTD or schema from the current document use the GenerateDTDOrSchema method.

XMLSpyDocument.ConvertDTDOrSchema

See also

Declaration: ConvertDTDOrSchema(*nFormat* as SPYDTDSchemaFormat, *nFrequentElements* as SPYFrequentElements)

Parameters

nFormat
Sets the schema output format to DTD, DCD, XMLData, BizTalk or W3C.

nFrequentElements
Create complex elements as elements or complex types.

Description
ConvertDTDOrSchema takes an existing schema format and converts it into a different format.

Document.CreateSchemaDiagram

See also

Declaration: CreateSchemaDiagram(*nKind* as SPYSchemaDefKind,*strName* as String,*strFile* as String)

Return Value
none

Description
The method creates a diagram of the schema type strName of kind nKind and saves the output file into strFile.

XMLSpyDocument.CreateChild

See also

Declaration: CreateChild(*nKind* as SPYXMLDataKind) as XMLData

Return Value
The method returns the new XMLData object.

Description
To create a new XMLData object use the CreateChild() method. See also "Using XMLData".

XMLSpyDocument.ExportToDatabase

See also

Declaration: ExportToDatabase(*pFromChild* as XMLData, *pExportSettings* as ExportSettings, *pDatabase* as DatabaseConnection)

Description
ExportToDatabase exports the xml-document starting with the element pFromChild. pExportSettings defines the behaviour of the export (see Application.GetExportSettings), pDatabase sets the destination of the export (see Application.GetDatabaseSettings).

Example

```
Dim objDoc As Document
Set objDoc = objSpy.ActiveDocument

'set the behaviour of the export with ExportSettings
Dim objExpSettings As ExportSettings
Set objExpSettings = objSpy.GetExportSettings

'set the destination with DatabaseConnection
Dim objDB As DatabaseConnection
Set objDB = objSpy.GetDatabaseSettings

objDB.CreateMissingTables = True
objDB.CreateNew = True
objDB.File = "C:\Export.mdb"
```

```
        objDoc.ExportToDatabase objDoc.RootElement, objExpSettings,
objDB
        If Err.Number <> 0 Then
            a = MsgBox("Error: " & (Err.Number - vbObjectError) &
Chr(13) &
                        "Description: " & Err.Description)
        End If
```

XMLSpyDocument.ExportToText

See also

Declaration: ExportToText(*pFromChild* as XMLData,*pExportSettings* as ExportSettings,*pTextSettings* as TextImportExportSettings)

Description
ExportToText exports the XML data structure into a text file.

Example

```
        Dim objDoc As Document
        Set objDoc = objSpy.ActiveDocument

        Dim objExpSettings As ExportSettings
        Set objExpSettings = objSpy.GetExportSettings
        objExpSettings.ElementList = objDoc.GetExportElementList(
                                        objDoc.RootElement,
                                        objExpSettings)

        Dim objTextExp As TextImportExportSettings
        Set objTextExp = objSpy.GetTextExportSettings
        objTextExp.HeaderRow = True
        objTextExp.DestinationFolder = "C:\Exports"

        On Error Resume Next
        objDoc.ExportToText objDoc.RootElement, objExpSettings,
objTextExp

        If Err.Number <> 0 Then
            a = MsgBox("Error: " & (Err.Number - vbObjectError) &
Chr(13) & "Description: "                      & Err.Description)
        End If
```

XMLSpyDocument.GetExportElementList

See also

Declaration: GetExportElementList(*pFromChild* as XMLData,*pExportSettings* as ExportSettings) as ElementList

Return Value
Returns a collection of elements.

Description
GetExportElementList creates a collection of elements to export depending on the settings in pExportSettings and starting from the element pFromChild. See also "Import and Export".

XMLSpyDocument.IsValid

See also

Declaration: IsValid(*strError* as Variant,*nErrorPos* as Variant,*pBadData* as Variant) as Boolean

Return Value
True if the document is valid, false if not.

Description
IsValid() validates the document against its associated schema or DTD. strError and nErrorPos give you the same information as XMLSpy if you validate the file within the editor.

XMLSpyDocument.IsWellFormed

See also

Declaration: IsWellFormed(*pData* as XMLData,*bWithChildren* as Boolean,*strError* as Variant,*nErrorPos* as Variant,*pBadXMLData* as Variant) as Boolean

Return Value
True if the document is well formed.

Description
IsWellFormed checks the document for well-formedness starting at the element pData.

If the document is not well formed, strError contains a error message, nErrorPos the position in the file and pBadXMLData holds a reference to the element which breaks the well-formedness. These out-parameters are defined as VARIANTs to support scripting languages like VBScript.

XMLSpyDocument.Save

See also

Declaration: Save

Description
The method writes any modifications of the document to the associated file. See also "Document.SetPathName".

Document.SaveToURL

See also

Declaration: SaveToURL(*strURL* as String,*strUser* as String,*strPassword* as String)

Return Value

Description
SaveToURL() writes the document to the URL strURL. This method does not set the permanent file path of the document.

XMLSpyDocument.SaveInString

See also

Declaration: SaveInString(*pData* as XMLData,*bMarked* as Boolean) as String

Parameters

pData
XMLData element to start. Set pData to Document.RootElement if you want to copy the complete file.

bMarked
If bMarked is true, only the elements selected in the grid view are copied.

Return Value
Returns a string with the XML data.

Description
SaveInString starts at the element pData and converts the XMLData objects to a string representation.

XMLSpyDocument.SetActiveDocument

See also

Declaration: SetActiveDocument

Description
The method sets the document as the active and brings it to the front.

XMLSpyDocument.SetEncoding

See also

Declaration: SetEncoding(*strEncoding* as String)

Description
SetEncoding sets the encoding of the document like the menu item "File/Encoding..." in XMLSpy. Possible values for strEncoding are for example:

        8859-1,
        8859-2,
        ASCII, ISO-646,
        850,
        1252,
        1255,
        SHIFT-JIS, MS-KANJI,
        BIG5, FIVE,
        UTF-7,
        UTF-8,
        UTF-16

XMLSpyDocument.SetPathName

See also

Declaration: SetPathName(*strPath* as String)

Description
The method SetPathName sets the path of the active document. SetPathName only copies the string and does not check if the path is valid.

All succeeding save operations are done into this file.

Document.GetPathName

See also

Declaration: GetPathName as String

Description
The method GetPathName gets the path of the active document.

See also Document.SetPathName.

XMLSpyDocument.StartChanges

See also

Declaration: StartChanges

Description
After StartChanges is executed XMLSpy will not update its editor windows until "Document.EndChanges" is called. This increases performance of any complex tasks to the XML structure.

XMLSpyDocument.EndChanges

See also

Declaration: EndChanges

Description
Use the method EndChanges to display all changes since the call to "Document.StartChanges".

Document.SwitchViewMode

See also

Declaration: SwitchViewMode(*nMode* as SPYViewModes) as Boolean

Return value
Returns true if view mode is switched.

Description
The method sets the current view mode of the document in XMLSpy. See also Document.CurrentViewMode.

XMLSpyDocument.UpdateViews

See also

Declaration: UpdateViews

Description
To redraw the Enhanced Grid View and the Tree View call UpdateViews. This can be important after you changed the XMLData structure of a document.

This method does not redraw the text view of XMLSpy.

XMLSpyDocument.Close

See also

Declaration: Close(*bDiscardChanges* as Boolean)

Description
To close the document call this method. If bDiscardChanges is true and the document is modified, the document will be closed but not saved.

XMLSpyDocument.GridView

See also

Declaration: GridView as GridView

Description
This property provides access to the grid view functionality of the document.

Document.DocEditView

See also

Declaration: DocEditView as DocEditView

Description

Holds a reference to the current Document Editor view object.

XMLSpyDocument.RootElement

See also

Declaration: RootElement as XMLData

Description
The property RootElement provides access to the root element of the XML structure of the

---

document.

XMLSpyDocument.Title

See also

Declaration: Title as String

Description
Title is the file name of the document.

This property is read-only.

To get the path of the file use Document.GetPathName.

Document.CurrentViewMode

See also

Declaration: CurrentViewMode as SPYViewModes

Description
The property holds the current view mode of the document. See also
Document.SwitchViewMode.

Document.IsModified

See also

Declaration: IsModified as Boolean

Description

True if the document is modified.

Documents
See also

Methods
NewFile
OpenFile
OpenURL
OpenURLDialog
NewFileFromText

Properties
Count
Item

Description
Documents Class

XMLSpyDocuments.OpenFile

See also

Declaration: OpenFile(*strPath* as String,*bDialog* as Boolean) as Document

Parameters

strPath
Path and file name of file to open.

bDialog
Show dialogs for user input.

Return Value
Returns the opened file on success.

Description
OpenFile opens the file strPath. If bDialog is TRUE, a file-dialog will be displayed.

Example

```
Dim objDoc As Document
Set objDoc = objSpy.Documents.OpenFile(strFile, False)
```

XMLSpyDocuments.NewFile

See also

Declaration: NewFile(*strFile* as String,*strType* as String) as Document

Parameters

strFile
Full path of new file.

strType
Type of new file as string (i.e. "xml", "xsd", ...)

Return Value
Returns the new file.

Description
NewFile creates a new file of type strType (i.e. "xml").

The just now created file is also the ActiveDocument.

Documents.OpenURL

See also

Declaration: OpenURL(*strURL* as String,*nURLType* as SPYURLTypes,*nLoading* as SPYLoading,*strUser* as String,*strPassword* as String) as Document

Parameters

strURL
URL to open as document.

nURLType
Type of document to open. Set to -1 for auto detection.

nLoading
Set nLoading to 0 (zero) if you want to load it from cache or proxy. Otherwise set nLoading to 1.

strUser
Name of the user if required. Can be empty.

strPassword
Password for authentification. Can be empty.

Return Value
The method returns the opened document.

Description
OpenURL opens the URL strURL.

Documents.OpenURLDialog

See also

Declaration: OpenURLDialog(*strURL* as String,*nURLType* as SPYURLTypes,*nLoading* as SPYLoading,*strUser* as String,*strPassword* as String) as Document

Parameters

strURL
URL to open as document.

nURLType
Type of document to open. Set to -1 for auto detection.

nLoading
Set nLoading to 0 (zero) if you want to load it from cache or proxy. Otherwise set nLoading to 1.

strUser
Name of the user if required. Can be empty.

strPassword
Password for authentification. Can be empty.

Return Value
The method returns the opened document.

Description
OpenURLDialog displays the "open URL" dialog to the user and presets the input fields with the given parameters.

Documents.NewFileFromText

See also

Declaration: NewFileFromText(*strText* as String,*strType* as String) as Document

Parameters

strText:
The content of the new document in plain text.

strType:
Type of the document to create (i.e. "xml").

Return Value
The method returns the new document.

Description
NewFileFromText creates a new document with strText as its content.

XMLSpyDocuments.Count

See also

Declaration: Count as long

Description
Count of open documents.

XMLSpyDocuments.Item

See also

Declaration: Item(*n* as long) as Document

Description
Gets the document with the index n in this collection. Index is 1-based.

GridView
See also

Methods
Deselect
Select

SetFocus

Properties
CurrentFocus

IsVisible

Description
GridView Class

XMLSpyGridView.Deselect

See also

Declaration: Deselect(*pData* as XMLData)

Description
Deselects the element pData in the grid view.

XMLSpyGridView.Select

See also

Declaration: Select(*pData* as XMLData)

Description
Selects the XML element pData in the grid view.

XMLSpyGridView.SetFocus

See also

Declaration: SetFocus(*pFocusData* as XMLData)

Description
Sets the focus to the element pFocusData in the grid view.

XMLSpyGridView.CurrentFocus

See also

Declaration: CurrentFocus as XMLData

Description
Holds the XML element with the current focus.

This property is read-only.

XMLSpyGridView.IsVisible

See also

Declaration: IsVisible as Boolean

Description
True if the grid view is the active view of the document.

This property is read-only.

DocEditView

See also

Methods

LoadXML
SaveXML

EditClear
EditCopy
EditCut
EditPaste
EditRedo
EditSelectAll
EditUndo

RowAppend
RowDelete
RowDuplicate
RowInsert
RowMoveDown
RowMoveUp

ApplyTextState
IsTextStateApplied
IsTextStateEnabled

MarkUpView

SelectionSet
SelectionMoveTabOrder

GetNextVisible
GetPreviousVisible

GetAllowedElements

Properties

CurrentSelection

event

XMLRoot

IsEditClearEnabled

IsEditCopyEnabled
IsEditCutEnabled
IsEditPasteEnabled
IsEditRedoEnabled
IsEditUndoEnabled

IsRowAppendEnabled
IsRowDeleteEnabled
IsRowDuplicateEnabled
IsRowInsertEnabled
IsRowMoveDownEnabled
IsRowMoveUpEnabled

Description

Interface for Document Editor view.

ApplyTextState

See also

Declaration: ApplyTextState(*elementName* as String)

Description

Applies or removes the text state defined by the parameter elementName. Common examples for the parameter elementName would be strong and italic.

In an XML document there are segments of data, which may contain sub-elements. For example consider the following HTML:

```
<b>fragment</b>
```

The HTML tag <b> will cause the word fragment to be bolded. However, this only happens because the HTML parser knows that the tag <b> is bold. With XML there is much more flexibility. It is possible to define any XML tag to do anything you desire. The point is that it is possible to apply a Text state using XML. But the Text state that is applied must be part of the schema. For example in the OrgChart.xml OrgChart.sps, OrgChart.xsd example the tag <strong> is the same as bold. And to apply bold the method **ApplyTextState()** is called. But like the row and edit operations it is necessary to test if it is possible to apply the text state.

See also IsTextStateEnabled and IsTextStateApplied.

EditClear

See also

Declaration: EditClear

Description

Clears the current selcotion.

EditCopy

See also

Declaration: EditCopy

Description

Copies the current selection to the clipboard.

EditCut

See also

Declaration: EditCut

Description

Cuts the current selection from the document and copies it to the clipboard.

EditPaste

See also

Declaration: EditPaste

Description

Pastes the content from the clipboard into the document.

EditRedo

See also

Declaration: EditRedo

Description

Redo the last undo step.

EditSelectAll

See also

Declaration: EditSelectAll

Description

The method selects the complete document.

EditUndo

See also

Declaration: EditUndo

Description

Undo the last action.

IsTextStateApplied

See also

Declaration: IsTextStateApplied(*elementName* as String) as Boolean

Description

Checks to see if the it the text state has already been applied. Common examples for the parameter elementName would be strong and italic.

IsTextStateEnabled

See also

Declaration: IsTextStateEnabled(*elementName* as String) as Boolean

Description

Checks to see if it is possible to apply a text state. Common examples for the parameter elementName would be strong and italic.

LoadXML

See also

Declaration: LoadXML(*xmlString* as String)

Description

Loads the current XML document with the XML string applied. The new content is displayed immediately.

MarkUpView

See also

Declaration: MarkUpView(*kind* as long)

Description

By default the document displayed is using HTML techniques. But sometimes it is desirable to show the editing tags. Using this method it is possible to display three different types of markup tags:

0	hide the markup tags
2	show the large markup tags
3	show the mixed markup tags.

RowAppend

See also

Declaration: RowAppend

Description

Appends a row at the current position.

See also Row operations.

RowDelete

See also

Declaration: RowDelete

Description

Deletes the currently selected row(s).

See also Row operations.

RowDuplicate

See also

Declaration: RowDuplicate

Description

The method duplicates the currently selected rows.

See also Row operations.

RowInsert

See also

Declaration: RowInsert

Description

Inserts a new row immediately above the current selection.

See also Row operations.

RowMoveDown

See also

Declaration: RowMoveDown

Description

Moves the current row one position down.

See also Row operations.

RowMoveUp

See also

Declaration: RowMoveUp

Description

Moves the current row one position up.

See also Row operations.

SaveXML

See also

Declaration: SaveXML as String

Return Value
XML structure as string

Description

Saves the current XML data to a string that is returned to the caller.

IsEditClearEnabled

See also

Declaration: IsEditClearEnabled as Boolean

Description

True if EditClear is possible.

See also Editing operations.

IsEditCopyEnabled

See also

Declaration: IsEditCopyEnabled as Boolean

Description

True if copy to clipboard is possible.

See also EditCopy and Editing operations.

IsEditCutEnabled

See also

Declaration: IsEditCutEnabled as Boolean

Description

True if EditCut is currently possible.

See also Editing operations.

IsEditPasteEnabled

See also

Declaration: IsEditPasteEnabled as Boolean

Description

True if EditPaste is possible.

See also Editing operations.

IsEditRedoEnabled

See also

Declaration: IsEditRedoEnabled as Boolean

Description

True if EditRedo is currently possible.

See also Editing operations.

IsEditUndoEnabled

See also

Declaration: IsEditUndoEnabled as Boolean

Description

True if EditUndo is possible.

See also Editing operations.

IsRowAppendEnabled

See also

Declaration: IsRowAppendEnabled as Boolean

Description

True if RowAppend is possible.

See also Row operations.

IsRowDeleteEnabled

See also

Declaration: IsRowDeleteEnabled as Boolean

Description

True if RowDelete is possible.

See also Row operations.

IsRowDuplicateEnabled

See also

Declaration: IsRowDuplicateEnabled as Boolean

Description

True if RowDuplicate is currently possible.

See also Row operations.

IsRowInsertEnabled

See also

Declaration: IsRowInsertEnabled as Boolean

Description

True if RowInsert is possible.

See also Row operations.

IsRowMoveDownEnabled

See also

Declaration: IsRowMoveDownEnabled as Boolean

Description

True if RowMoveDown is currently possible.

See also Row operations.

IsRowMoveUpEnabled

See also

Declaration: IsRowMoveUpEnabled as Boolean

Description

True if RowMoveUp is possible.

See also Row operations.

XMLRoot

See also

Declaration: XMLRoot as XMLData

Description

XMLRoot is the parent element of the currently displayed XML structure. Using the XMLData interface you have full access to the complete content of the file.

See also Using XMLData for more informations.

DocEditView.event

See also

Declaration: event as DocEditEvent

Description

The event property holds a DocEditEvent object which contains informations about the current event.

DocEditView.GetPreviousVisible

See also

Declaration: GetPreviousVisible(*pElement* as XMLData) as XMLData

Description

The method gets the previous visible XML element in the document.

DocEditView.GetNextVisible

See also

Declaration: GetNextVisible(*pElement* as XMLData) as XMLData

Description

The method gets the next visible XML element in the document.

DocEditView.SelectionMoveTabOrder

See also

Declaration: SelectionMoveTabOrder(*bForward* as Boolean,*bTag* as Boolean)

Description

SelectionMoveTabOrder() moves the current selection forwards or backwards.

If bTag is false and the current selection is at the last cell of a table a new line will be added.

DocEditView.SelectionSet

See also

Declaration: SelectionSet(*pStartElement* as XMLData,*nStartPos* as long,*pEndElement* as XMLData,*nEndPos* as long) as Boolean

Description

Use SelectionSet() to set a new selection in the Document Editor view. Its possible to set pEndElement to null (nothing) if the selection should be just over one (pStartElement) XML element.

DocEditView.CurrentSelection

See also

Declaration: CurrentSelection as DocEditSelection

Description

The property provides access to the current selection in the Document Editor view.

DocEditView.GetAllowedElements

See also

Declaration: GetAllowedElements(*nAction* as
DOCEDElementActions,*pStartElement* as XMLData,*pEndElement* as
XMLData,*pElements* as Variant)

Description

GetAllowedElements() returns the allowed elements for the various actions specified by
nAction.

JavaScript example:

```
function GetAllowed()
{
        var objView = Application.ActiveDocument.DocEditView;

        var arrElements = new Array(1);

        var objStart = objView.CurrentSelection.Start;
        var objEnd = objView.CurrentSelection.End;

        var strText;
        strText = "valid elements at current selection:\n\n";

        for(var i = 1;i <= 4;i++)     {
                objPlugIn.GetAllowedElements(i,objStart,objEnd,arrEl
ements);
                strText = strText + ListArray(arrElements) + "------
-----------\n";
        }

        return strText;
}

function ListArray(arrIn)
{
        var strText = "";

        if(typeof(arrIn) == "object") {
                for(var i = 0;i <= (arrIn.length - 1);i++)
                        strText = strText + arrIn[i] + "\n";
        }

        return strText;
}
```

VBScript example:

```
Sub DisplayAllowed
        dim objView
        set objView = Application.ActiveDocument.DocEditView

        dim arrElements()

        dim objStart
        dim objEnd
        set objStart = objView.CurrentSelection.Start
        set objEnd = objView.CurrentSelection.End

        dim strText
        strText = "valid elements at current selection:" & chr(13)
& chr(13)

        dim i

        For i = 1 To 4
                objView.GetAllowedElements
i,objStart,objEnd,arrElements
                strText = strText & ListArray(arrElements) & "------
---------" & chr(13)
        Next

        msgbox strText
End Sub

Function ListArray(arrIn)
        dim strText

        If IsArray(arrIn) Then
                dim i

                For i = 0 To UBound(arrIn)
                        strText = strText & arrIn(i) & chr(13)
                Next
        End If

        ListArray = strText
End Function
```

DocEditDataTransfer

See also

Methods

getData

Properties

dropEffect
ownDrag
type

Description

DocEditDataTransfer interface.

DocEditDataTransfer.getData

See also

Declaration: getData as Variant

Description

getData gets the actual data associated with this dataTransfer object. See also
DocEditDataTransfer.type for more informations.

DocEditDataTransfer.dropEffect

See also

Declaration: dropEffect as long

Description

The property stores the drop effect from the default event handler. You can set the drop effect
if you change this value and set DocEditEvent.cancelBubble to TRUE.

DocEditDataTransfer.ownDrag

See also

Declaration: ownDrag as Boolean

Description

The property is TRUE if the current dragging source comes from inside of the Document Editor
view.

DocEditDataTransfer.type

See also

Declaration: type as String

Description

Holds the type of the data you get with the DocEditDataTransfer.getData method.

Currently supported data types are:

OWN	data from Document Editor view itself
TEXT	plain text
UNICODETEXT	plain text as UNICODE

DocEditEvent

See also

Properties

altKey
altLeft
ctrlKey
ctrlLeft
shiftKey
shiftLeft

keyCode
repeat

button

clientX
clientY

dataTransfer

srcElement
fromElement

propertyName

cancelBubble
returnValue

type

Description

DocEditEvent interface.

DocEditEvent.altKey

See also

Declaration: altKey as Boolean

Description

True if the right ALT key is pressed.

DocEditEvent.altLeft

See also

Declaration: altLeft as Boolean

Description

True if the left ALT key is pressed.

DocEditEvent.ctrlKey

See also

Declaration: ctrlKey as Boolean

Description

True if the right CTRL key is pressed.

DocEditEvent.ctrlLeft

See also

Declaration: ctrlLeft as Boolean

Description

True if the left CTRL key is pressed.

DocEditEvent.shiftKey

See also

Declaration: shiftKey as Boolean

Description

True if the right SHIFT key is pressed.

DocEditEvent.shiftLeft

See also

Declaration: shiftLeft as Boolean

Description

True if the left SHIFT key is pressed.

DocEditEvent.keyCode

See also

Declaration: keyCode as long

Description

Keycode of the currently pressed key.

This property is read-write.

DocEditEvent.repeat

See also

Declaration: repeat as Boolean

Description

True if the onkeydown event is repeated.

DocEditEvent.button

See also

Declaration: button as long

Description

Specifies which mouse button is pressed:

0	No button is pressed.
1	Left button is pressed.
2	Right button is pressed.
3	Left and right buttons are both pressed.
4	Middle button is pressed.
5	Left and middle buttons both are pressed.
6	Right and middle buttons are both pressed.
7	All three buttons are pressed.

DocEditEvent.clientX

See also

Declaration: clientX as long

Description

X value of the current mouse position in client coordinates.

DocEditEvent.clientY

See also

Declaration: clientY as long

Description

Y value of the current mouse position in client coordinates.

DocEditEvent.dataTransfer

See also

Declaration: dataTransfer as Variant

Description

property dataTransfer

DocEditEvent.srcElement

See also

Declaration: srcElement as Variant

Description

Element which fires the current event.

This is usually an XMLData object.

DocEditEvent.fromElement

See also

Declaration: fromElement as Variant

Description

Currently no event sets this property.

DocEditEvent.propertyName

See also

Declaration: propertyName as String

Description

Currently no event sets this property.

DocEditEvent.cancelBubble

See also

Declaration: cancelBubble as Boolean

Description

Set cancelBubble to TRUE if the default event handler should not be called.

DocEditEvent.returnValue

See also

Declaration: returnValue as Variant

Description

Use returnValue to set a return value for your event handler.

DocEditEvent.type

See also

Declaration: type as String

Description

Currently no event sets this property.

DocEditSelection

See also

Properties

Start
StartTextPosition
End
EndTextPosition

DocEditSelection.Start

See also

Declaration: Start as XMLData

Description

XML element where the current selection starts.

DocEditSelection.StartTextPosition

See also

Declaration: StartTextPosition as long

Description

Position in DocEditSelection.Start.TextValue where the selection starts.

DocEditSelection.End

See also

Declaration: End as XMLData

Description

XML element where the current selection ends.

DocEditSelection.EndTextPosition

See also

Declaration: EndTextPosition as long

Description

Position in DocEditSelection.End.TextValue where the selection ends.

SpyProject

See also

Methods
CloseProject
SaveProject
SaveProjectAs

Properties
RootItems
ProjectFile

Description
SpyProject Class

XMLSpyPrj.CloseProject

See also

Declaration: CloseProject(*bDiscardChanges* as Boolean,*bCloseFiles* as Boolean,*bDialog* as Boolean)

Parameters

bDiscardChanges:
Set bDiscardChanges to FALSE if you want to save the changes of the open project files and the project.

bCloseFiles:
Set bCloseFiles to TRUE to close all open project files.

bDialog
Show dialogs for user input.

Description
CloseProject closes the current project.

XMLSpyPrj.SaveProject

See also

Declaration: SaveProject

Description
SaveProject saves the current project

XMLSpyPrj.SaveProjectAs

See also

Declaration: SaveProjectAs(*strPath* as String,*bDialog* as Boolean)

Parameters

strPath
Full path with file name of new project file.

bDialog
If bDialog is TRUE, a file-dialog will be displayed.

Description
SaveProjectAs stores the project data into a new location.

XMLSpyPrj.RootItems

See also

Declaration: RootItems as SpyProjectItems

Description
Root level of collection of project items.

SpyProject.ProjectFile

See also

Declaration: ProjectFile as String

Description
Path and filename of the project.

SpyProjectItem
See also

Methods
Open

Properties
ChildItems
ParentItem
FileExtensions
ItemType
Name
Path
ValidateWith
XMLForXSLTransformation
XSLForXMLTransformation
XSLTransformationFileExtension
XSLTransformationFolder

Description
SpyProjectItem Class

XMLSpyPrjItem.Open

See also

Declaration: Open as Document

Return Value
The project item opened as document.

Description
Opens the project item.

XMLSpyPrjItem.ChildItems

See also

Declaration: ChildItems as SpyProjectItems

Description
If the item is a folder, ChildItems is the collection of the folder content.

SpyProjectItem.ParentItem

See also

Declaration: ParentItem as SpyProjectItem

Description

Parent item of the current project item. Can be NULL (Nothing) if the project item is a top-level item.

XMLSpyPrjItem.FileExtensions

See also

Declaration: FileExtensions as String

Description

Used to set the file extensions if the project item is a folder.

XMLSpyPrjItem.ItemType

See also

Declaration: ItemType as SPYProjectItemTypes

Description

This property is read-only.

XMLSpyPrjItem.Name

See also

Declaration: Name as String

Description

Name of the project item.

This property is read-only.

XMLSpyPrjItem.Path

See also

Declaration: Path as String

Description

Path of project item.

This property is read-only.

XMLSpyPrjItem.ValidateWith

See also

Declaration: ValidateWith as String

Description

Used to set the schema/DTD for validation.

XMLSpyPrjItem.XMLForXSLTransformation

See also

Declaration: XMLForXSLTransformation as String

Description
Used to set the XML for XSL transformation.

XMLSpyPrjItem.XSLForXMLTransformation

See also

Declaration: XSLForXMLTransformation as String

Description
Used to set the XSL for XML transformation.

XMLSpyPrjItem.XSLTransformationFileExtension

See also

Declaration: XSLTransformationFileExtension as String

Description
Used to set the file extension for XSL transformation output files.

XMLSpyPrjItem.XSLTransformationFolder

See also

Declaration: XSLTransformationFolder as String

Description
Used to set the destination folder for XSL transformation output files.

SpyProjectItems

See also

Methods
AddFile
AddFolder
AddURL
RemoveItem

Properties
Count
Item

Description
SpyProjectItems Class

XMLSpyPrjItems.AddFile

See also

Declaration: AddFile(*strPath* as String)

Parameters

strPath
Full path with file name of new project item

Description
The method adds a new file to the collection of project items.

XMLSpyPrjItems.AddFolder

See also

Declaration: AddFolder(*strName* as String)

Parameters

strName
Name of the new folder.

Description
The method AddFolder adds a folder with the name strName to the collection of project items.

XMLSpyPrjItems.AddURL

See also

Declaration: AddURL(*strURL* as String,*nURLType* as SPYURLTypes,*strUser* as String,*strPassword* as String,*bSave* as Boolean)

Description

strURL
URL to open as document.

nURLType
Type of document to open. Set to -1 for auto detection.

nLoading
Set nLoading to 0 (zero) If you want to load it from cache or proxy. Otherwise set nLoading to 1.

strUser
Name of the user if required. Can be empty.

strPassword
Password for authentification. Can be empty.

bSave
Save user and password information.

Description
The method adds an URL item to the project collection.

XMLSpyPrjItems.RemoveItem

See also

Declaration: RemoveItem(*pItem* as SpyProjectItem)

Description
RemoveItem deletes the item pItem from collection of project items.

XMLSpyPrjItems.Count

See also

Declaration: Count as long

Description
This property gets the count of project items in the collection.

The property is read-only.

XMLSpyPrjItems.Item

See also

Declaration: Item(*n* as long) as SpyProjectItem

Description
Retrieves the n-th element of the collection of project items.

XMLData
See also

Methods
InsertChild
AppendChild

EraseAllChildren
EraseCurrentChild

GetCurrentChild
GetFirstChild
GetNextChild

IsSameNode

Properties
Name
TextValue

HasChildren
MayHaveChildren

Kind
Parent

Description
XMLData Class

XMLSpyXMLData.InsertChild

See also

Declaration: InsertChild(*pNewData* as XMLData)

Description
InsertChild inserts the new child before the current child (see also XMLData.GetFirstChild, XMLData.GetNextChild to set the current child).

XMLSpyXMLData.AppendChild

See also

Declaration: AppendChild(*pNewData* as XMLData)

Description

AppendChild appends pNewData as last child to the XMLData object. See also "Using XMLData".

Example

```
Dim objCurrentParent As XMLData
Dim objNewChild As XMLData

Set objNewChild = objSpy.ActiveDocument.CreateChild(spyXMLDataElement)
Set objCurrentParent = objSpy.ActiveDocument.RootElement

objCurrentParent.AppendChild objNewChild

Set objNewChild = Nothing
```

XMLSpyXMLData.EraseAllChildren

See also

Declaration: EraseAllChildren

Description
EraseAllChildren deletes all associated children of the XMLData object.

Example

The sample erases all elements of the active document.

```
Dim objCurrentParent As XMLData

Set objCurrentParent = objSpy.ActiveDocument.RootElement
objCurrentParent.EraseAllChildren
```

XMLSpyXMLData.EraseCurrentChild

See also

Declaration: EraseCurrentChild

Description
EraseCurrentChild deletes the current XMLData child object. Before you call EraseCurrentChild you must initialize an internal iterator with XMLData.GetFirstChild.

Example

This JavaScript example deletes all elements with the name "EraseMe". The code shows you, that it is possible to call EraseCurrentChild and GetNextChild inside the same loop to continue stepping through the child elements.

```
function DeleteXMLElements(objXMLData)
{
        if(objXMLData == null)
                return;

        if(objXMLData.HasChildren){
                var objChild;
                objChild = objXMLData.GetFirstChild(-1);

                while(objChild)     {
```

```
                              DeleteXMLElements(objChild);

                              try    {
                                     if(objChild.Name == "EraseMe")
                                           objXMLData.EraseCurrentChild();

                                     objChild = objXMLData.GetNextChild();
                              }
                              catch(Err)   {
                                     objChild = null;
                              }
                       }
                }
         }
```

XMLSpyXMLData.GetCurrentChild

See also

Declaration: GetCurrentChild as XMLData

Return Value
Returns a xml element as XMLData object.

Description
GetCurrentChild gets the current child. Before you call GetCurrentChild you must initialize an internal iterator with XMLData.GetFirstChild.

XMLSpyXMLData.GetFirstChild

See also

Declaration: GetFirstChild(*nKind* as SPYXMLDataKind) as XMLData

Return Value
Returns a xml element as XMLData object.

Description
GetFirstChild initializes a new iterator and returns the first child. Set nKind = -1 to get an iterator for all kinds of children.

Example
See the example at XMLData.GetNextChild.

XMLSpyXMLData.GetNextChild

See also

Declaration: GetNextChild as XMLData

Return Value
Returns a xml element as XMLData object.

Description
GetNextChild steps to the next child of this element. Before you call GetNextChild you must initialize an internal iterator with XMLData.GetFirstChild.

Check for the last child of the element as shown in the sample below.

Example

```
On Error Resume Next
Set objParent = objSpy.ActiveDocument.RootElement

'get elements of all kinds
Set objCurrentChild = objParent.GetFirstChild(-1)

Do
        'do something useful with the child

        'step to next child
        Set objCurrentChild = objParent.GetNextChild
Loop Until (Err.Number - vbObjectError = 1503)
```

XMLSpyXMLData.Name

See also

Declaration: Name as String

Description
Used to modify and to get the name of the XMLData object.

XMLSpyXMLData.TextValue

See also

Declaration: TextValue as String

Description
Used to modify and to get the text value of this XMLData object. See also "Using XMLData".

XMLSpyXMLData.HasChildren

See also

Declaration: HasChildren as Boolean

Description
The property is true, if the object is parent of other XMLData objects.

This property is read-only.

XMLSpyXMLData.MayHaveChildren

See also

Declaration: MayHaveChildren as Boolean

Description
Tells if it is allowed to add children to this XMLData object.

This property is read-only.

XMLSpyXMLData.Kind

See also

Declaration: Kind as SPYXMLDataKind

Description
Kind of this XMLData object.

This property is read-only.

XMLData.IsSameNode

See also

Declaration: IsSameNode(*pNodeToCompare* as XMLData) as Boolean

Description

Returns true if pNodeToCompare references to the same node as the object itself.

XMLSpyXMLData.Parent

See also

Declaration: Parent as XMLData

Return value
Parent as XMLData object.
Nothing (or NULL) if there is no parent element.

Description
Parent of this element.

This property is read-only.

DatabaseConnection

See also

Properties
ADOConnection
ODBCConnection
File

CreateMissingTables
CreateNew

SQLSelect

NumberDateTimeFormat
TextFieldLen
AsAttributes
ExcludeKeys
IncludeEmptyElements

Description
DatabaseConnection specifies a database connection.

Please note that the properties of the DatabaseConnection interface are referring to the settings of the import and export dialogs of XMLSpy.

XMLSpyDatabaseConnection.ADOConnection

See also

Declaration: ADOConnection as String

Description
The property ADOConnection contains a connection string.

Example

```
Dim objSpyConn As DatabaseConnection
Set objSpyConn = objSpy.GetDatabaseSettings

Dim objADO As DataLinks
Set objADO = CreateObject("DataLinks")

If Not (objADO Is Nothing) Then
    Dim objConn As Connection
    Set objConn = objADO.PromptNew
    objSpyConn.ADOConnection = objConn.ConnectionString
End If
```

DatabaseConnection.ODBCConnection

See also

Declaration: ODBCConnection as String

Description
The property ODBCConnection contains a ODBC connection string.

XMLSpyDatabaseConnection.File

See also

Declaration: File as String

Description
The property File sets the path for the database during export or import. See also "Import and Export".

XMLSpyDatabaseConnection.CreateMissingTables

See also

Declaration: CreateMissingTables as Boolean

Description
If CreateMissingTables is true, tables which are not already defined in the export database will be created during export.

Default is true.

XMLSpyDatabaseConnection.CreateNew

See also

Declaration: CreateNew as Boolean

Description
Set CreateNew true if you want to create a new database on export. Any existing database will be overwritten. See also "DatabaseConnection.File".

Default is false.

XMLSpyDatabaseConnection.SQLSelect

See also

Declaration: SQLSelect as String

Description
The SQL query for the import is stored in the property SQLSelect. See also "Import and Export".

XMLSpyDatabaseConnection.NumberDateTimeFormat

See also

Declaration: NumberDateTimeFormat as SPYNumberDateTimeFormat

Description
The property NumberDateTimeFormat sets the format of numbers and date- and time-values.

Default is spySystemLocale.

XMLSpyDatabaseConnection.TextFieldLen

See also

Declaration: TextFieldLen as long

Description
The property TextFieldLen sets the length for created text fields during the export.

Default is 255.

DatabaseConnection.AsAttributes

See also

Declaration: AsAttributes as Boolean

Description
Set AsAttributes to true if you want to create all data as attributes.

Default is false.

DatabaseConnection.ExcludeKeys

See also

Declaration: ExcludeKeys as Boolean

Description
Set ExcludeKeys to true if you want to exclude all key rows from the import data.

Default is false.

DatabaseConnection.IncludeEmptyElements

See also

Declaration: IncludeEmptyElements as Boolean

Description
Set IncludeEmptyElements to false if you want to exclude all empty elements.

Default is true.

ExportSettings

See also

Properties

ElementList

EntitiesToText

ExportAllElements
SubLevelLimit

FromAttributes
FromSingleSubElements
FromTextValues

CreateKeys
IndependentPrimaryKey

Namespace

Description
ExportSettings Class

XMLSpyExportSettings.ElementList

See also

Declaration: ElementList as ElementList

Description
Default is empty list.

This list of elements defines the rows for the export. It is possible to remove elements from export with ElementList.RemoveElement.

XMLSpyExportSettings.EntitiesToText

See also

Declaration: EntitiesToText as Boolean

Description
Default is True.

XMLSpyExportSettings.ExportAllElements

See also

Declaration: ExportAllElements as Boolean

Description
Default is True.

If ExportAllElements is False, then ExportSettings.SubLevelLimit is used to restrict the number of sub levels to export.

XMLSpyExportSettings.SubLevelLimit

See also

Declaration: SubLevelLimit as Integer

Description
Default is 0.

Defines the number of sub levels to include for the export.
This property is ignored if ExportSettings.ExportAllElements is True.

XMLSpyExportSettings.FromAttributes

See also

Declaration: FromAttributes as Boolean

Description
Set FromAttributes to false if no export data should be created from attributes.

Default is True.

XMLSpyExportSettings.FromSingleSubElements

See also

Declaration: FromSingleSubElements as Boolean

Description
Default is True.

XMLSpyExportSettings.FromTextValues

See also

Declaration: FromTextValues as Boolean

Description
Default is True.

XMLSpyExportSettings.CreateKeys

See also

Declaration: CreateKeys as Boolean

Description
Default is True.

This property turns creation of keys on or off.

XMLSpyExportSettings.IndependentPrimaryKey

See also

Declaration: IndependentPrimaryKey as Boolean

Description
Default is True.

Turns creation of independent primary key counter for every element on or off. If ExportSettings.CreateKeys is False, this property will be ignored.

ExportSettings.Namespace

See also

Declaration: Namespace as SPYExportNamespace

Description
Default is spyNoNamespace.

The default setting removes all namespace prefixes from the element names. In some database formats the colon is not a legal character.

TextImportExportSettings

See also

Properties
HeaderRow

FieldDelimiter
EnclosingCharacter

Encoding
EncodingByteOrder

ImportFile
FileExtension
DestinationFolder

Description
TextImportExportSettings Class

XMLSpyTextImportExportSettings.HeaderRow

See also

Declaration: HeaderRow as Boolean

Description
The property HeaderRow is used during import and export.

Set HeaderRow true on import, if the first line of the text file contains the names of the columns.
Set HeaderRow true on export, if the first line in the created text files should contain the name of the columns.

Default value is true.

XMLSpyTextImportExportSettings.FieldDelimiter

See also

Declaration: FieldDelimiter as SPYTextDelimiters

Description
The property FieldDelimiter defines the delimiter between the fields during import and export.

Default is spyTabulator.

XMLSpyTextImportExportSettings.EnclosingCharacter

See also

Declaration: EnclosingCharacter as SPYTextEnclosing

Description

This property defines the character that encloses all field values for import and export.

Default is spyNoEnclosing.

XMLSpyTextImportExportSettings.Encoding

See also

Declaration: Encoding as String

Description

The property Encoding sets the character encoding for the text files for importing and exporting.

XMLSpyTextImportExportSettings.EncodingByteOrder

See also

Declaration: EncodingByteOrder as SPYEncodingByteOrder

Description

The property EncodingByteOrder sets the byte order for UNICODE characters.

Default is spyNONE.

XMLSpyTextImportExportSettings.ImportFile

See also

Declaration: ImportFile as String

Description

This property is used to set the text file for import. The string has to be a full qualified path.

See also "Import and Export".

XMLSpyTextImportExportSettings.FileExtension

See also

Declaration: FileExtension as String

Description

This property sets the file extension of the text files created on export.

XMLSpyTextImportExportSettings.DestinationFolder

See also

Declaration: DestinationFolder as String

Description
The property DestinationFolder sets the folder where the created files are saved during export.

ElementListItem

See also

Properties
ElementKind
Name

FieldCount
RecordCount

Description
ElementListItem Class

XMLSpyElementListItem.ElementKind

See also

Declaration: ElementKind as SPYXMLDataKind

Description
Kind of element.

XMLSpyElementListItem.Name

See also

Declaration: Name as String

Description
Name of the element.

XMLSpyElementListItem.FieldCount

See also

Declaration: FieldCount as long

Description
Count of fields for this element. The actual value depends on the current export settings.

XMLSpyElementListItem.RecordCount

See also

Declaration: RecordCount as long

Description
Count of records for this element. The actual value depends on the current export settings.

ElementList
See also

Methods
RemoveElement

Properties
Count
Item

Description
ElementList Class

XMLSpyElementList.RemoveElement

See also

Declaration: RemoveElement(*Index* as long)

Description
RemoveElement removes the element Index from the collection.

XMLSpyElementList.Count

See also

Declaration: Count as long

Description
Count of elements in this collection.

XMLSpyElementList.Item

See also

Declaration: Item(*n* as long) as ElementListItem

Description
Gets the element with the index n from this collection.

Enumerations

This is a list of all enumerations used by the XMLSpy API. Some API methods take them as an input parameter. If your scripting environment does not support enumerations use the number-values instead.

SPYProjectItemTypes:

spyUnknownItem	= 0
spyFileItem	= 1
spyFolderItem	= 2
spyURLItem	= 3

SPYURLTypes:

spyURLTypeAuto	= -1
spyURLTypeXML	= 0
spyURLTypeDTD	= 1

SPYXMLDataKind:

spyXMLDataXMLDocStruct	= 0
spyXMLDataXMLEntityDocStruct	= 1
spyXMLDataDTDDocStruct	= 2
spyXMLDataXML	= 3
spyXMLDataElement	= 4
spyXMLDataAttr	= 5
spyXMLDataText	= 6
spyXMLDataCData	= 7
spyXMLDataComment	= 8
spyXMLDataPI	= 9
spyXMLDataDefDoctype	= 10
spyXMLDataDefExternalID	= 11
spyXMLDataDefElement	= 12
spyXMLDataDefAttlist	= 13
spyXMLDataDefEntity	= 14
spyXMLDataDefNotation	= 15
spyXMLDataKindsCount	= 16

SPYDTDSchemaFormat:

spyDTD	= 0
spyDCD	= 1
spyXMLData	= 2
spyBizTalk	= 3
spyW3C	= 4

SPYTypeDetection:

spyBestPossible	= 0
spyNumbersOnly	= 1
spyNoDetection	= 2

SPYFrequentElements:

spyGlobalElements   = 0
spyGlobalComplexType = 1

SPYNumberDateTimeFormat:

spySystemLocale   = 0
spySchemaCompatible = 1

SPYEncodingByteOrder:

spyNONE   = 0
spyLITTLE_ENDIAN   = 1
spyBIG_ENDIAN   = 2

SPYTextDelimiters:

spyTabulator   = 0
spySemicolon   = 1
spyComma   = 2
spySpace   = 3

SPYTextEnclosing:

spyNoEnclosing = 0
spySingleQuote = 1
spyDoubleQuote = 2

SPYLoading:

spyUseCacheProxy   = 0
spyReload   = 1

SPYViewModes:

spyViewGrid   = 0
spyViewText   = 1
spyViewBrowser   = 2
spyViewSchema   = 3
spyViewContent   = 4

SPYSchemaDefKind:

spyKindElement   = 0
spyKindComplexType = 1
spyKindSimpleType   = 2
spyKindGroup   = 3
spyKindModel   = 4
spyKindAny   = 5

```
spyKindAttr              = 6
spyKindAttrGroup         = 7
spyKindAttrAny           = 8

spyKindIdentityUnique    = 9
spyKindIdentityKey       = 10
spyKindIdentityKeyRef    = 11
spyKindIdentitySelector  = 12
spyKindIdentityField     = 13

spyKindNotation                  = 14

spyKindInclude           = 15
spyKindImport            = 16
spyKindRedefine          = 17

spyKindFacet             = 18

spyKindSchema                    = 19

spyKindCount             = 20
```

SPYExportNamespace:

```
spyNoNamespace                       = 0
spyReplaceColonWithUnderscore        = 1
```

DOCEDElementActions:

```
k_ActionInsertAt         = 0
k_ActionApply            = 1
k_ActionRemoveSurr       = 2
k_ActionAppend                   = 3
k_ActionInsertBefore     = 4
```

Part **VI**

6   Document Editor

XML Spy Document Editor enables you to edit XML documents **based on templates created in XSLT Designer!**

The templates in XSLT Designer are saved as ***.sps** files, and supply all the necessary information needed by Document Editor. These templates are placed in the **...\XML Spy Suite\sps\Template\Examples** folder and are available when you select the **File | New** command and click the "Select a Document Editor template..." button.

Document Editor features:
- Free-flow WYSIWYG text editing
- Form-based data input
- Presentation and editing of repeating XML elements as tables
- Real-time validation, and consistency checking using XML Schema

XML Spy Document Editor is available in three versions:
- As a stand-alone application
- Integrated as a separate view within the XML Spy IDE user-interface (if you purchase the XML Spy Suite product)
- As a Browser Plug-In for Internet Explorer

Overview

Document Editor has two main areas: the main window, and the entry helpers at right. The graphic below shows the OrgChart template with all the markup info hidden.

- The **main window** allows you to display the document in several different views: the Document Editor view which is the default view for this type of document template, the Enhanced Grid view or Text view. The Enhanced Grid view incorporates a special view, called the Database/Table view, which collapses recurring XML data into table form.

- The **right area** contains three Entry helper windows, which allow you to insert specific elements (or attributes) depending on the current cursor position in the document.

Orgchart template document

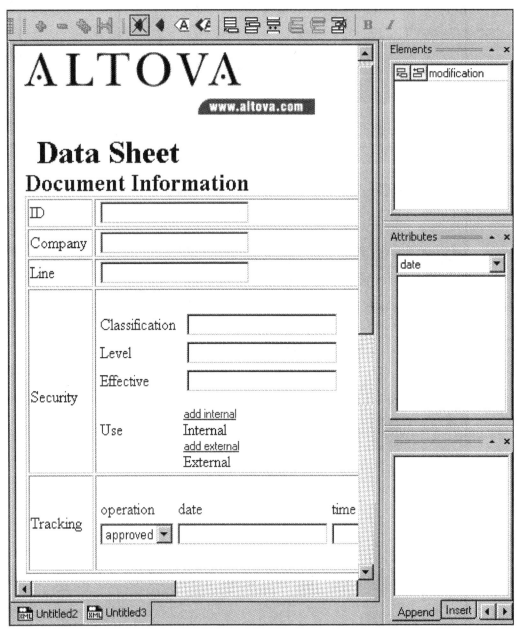

Datasheet template document

Symbols and icons

Document Editor uses easily recognizable symbols to display the various XML elements. There are different ways to customize the Document Editor view: hide all markup, show small markup, show large markup and show mixed markup.

 Clicking this icon switches to the Document Editor view in XML Spy. This view is automatically opened when you open a **template file** (*.**sps**). Clicking the icon causes a dialog box to appear if the active file is not a template file. You can then select the template file of your choice.

Template files (*.**sps**) can only be created in XSLT Designer, please see the XSLT Designer documentation for more information on how to do this.

You can of course, click the Enhanced Grid view or Text view icon, and edit your document there.

"Content" icon bar icons:

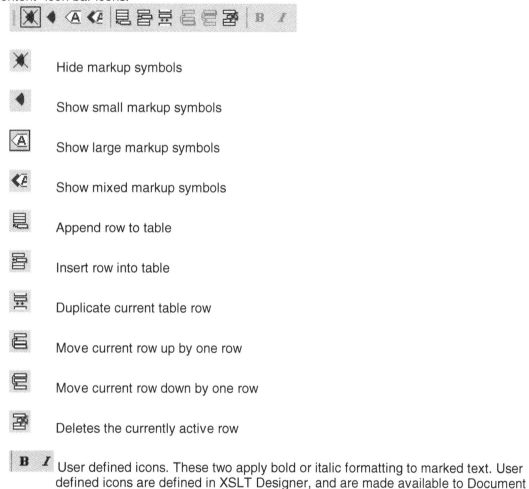

Hide markup symbols

Show small markup symbols

Show large markup symbols

Show mixed markup symbols

Append row to table

Insert row into table

Duplicate current table row

Move current row up by one row

Move current row down by one row

Deletes the currently active row

B *I* User defined icons. These two apply bold or italic formatting to marked text. User defined icons are defined in XSLT Designer, and are made available to Document Editor as icons in the icon bar.

Please see the XSLT Designer documentation for more information.

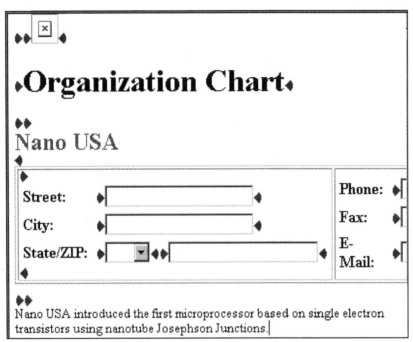

This graphic shows the OrgChart document with **small markup** symbols visible.

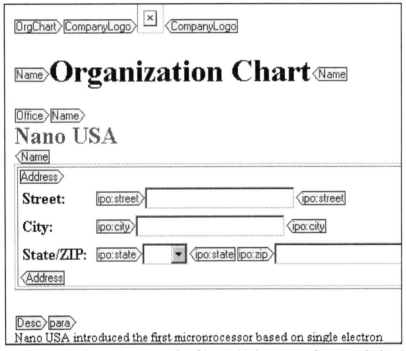

This graphic shows the same OrgChart with **large markup** symbols visible.

Document Editor view, tag symbols

Start and end tags of the (Department) **Name** element, start and end tags expanded.

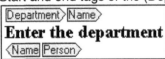

(Department) **Name** tag, contracted. To expand or contract tags, double click the specific tag.

Operation attribute, as a combo box.

Documentid element, as a text box.

The "Title" field is defined as an **optional** element in the (referenced) schema. Clicking the "add Title" text, allows you to enter data into this field.

Document Editor Browser Plug-in

The Document Editor Browser Plug-In is a unique solution that allows live XML content editing from any desktop in your enterprise, which dramatically eases deployment and reduces total cost of ownership (TCO).

This is the first browser-based XML editing solution in the entire industry, and it is based upon open standards, such as XML Schema and XSLT! It is also fully Unicode compatible!

Please see the Document Editor Plugin documentation for more information.

Document Editor Tutorial

The aim of this tutorial is to fill in the OrgChart template supplied with XML Spy IDE.

This will be achieved by:
- Entering data into the predefined tables
- Adding additional persons to the department table
- Adding a new company and filling in all the relevant data.

Prerequisites:
- The OrgChart template necessary for this tutorial is supplied with XML Spy IDE.
- Any other templates you want to edit **must** have been created using **XSLT Designer** and saved there (thus creating a ***.sps** file).

Opening a document template *.sps

To open a document template:
XML Spy Document Editor enables you to edit XML documents **based on templates created in XSLT Designer!** You cannot create a new template using Document Editor, this must be done in XSLT Designer.

1. Start XML Spy by double clicking the XML Spy icon (or your stand-alone Document Editor icon).
2. Select the menu option **File | New** and click the "**Select a Document Editor template...**" button.

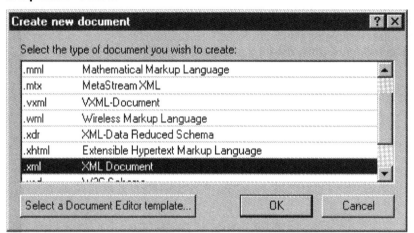

This opens the "New" dialog box.

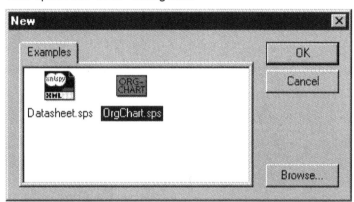

3. Double click the **OrgChart.sps** icon to open the orgchart template in Document Editor (or click the Browse... button to open a different *.sps file). Please see **File | New** for more information on how *.sps template **icons** are created.

   The orgchart template is now on screen and can be edited directly within this view. You can also edit it in the Enhanced Grid and Text view if you wish.

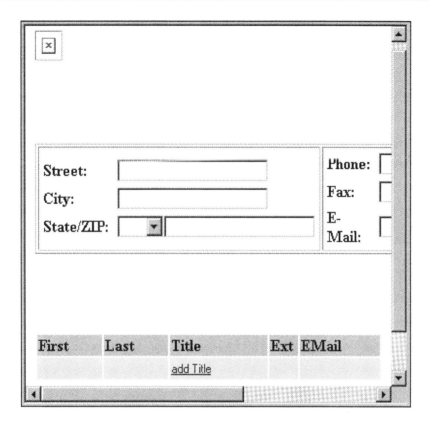

Please note:
> You cannot open a Document Editor template (***.sps** file) in the Document Editor view using the **File | Open** command. If you do so, the file will be opened in the Enhanced Grid view as a normal XML document.
>
> You have to **select** a Document Editor template created in **XSLT Designer**, using the **File | New** command in Document Editor.
>
> All *.sps templates supplied with XML Spy are placed in the folder you installed XML Spy in +...+ **Altova\XML Spy Suite\sps\Template\Examples.**

Adding data in Document Editor

This section deals with entering data in the XML document based on the OrgChart template.
The diagram below, shows you where to click in the following example.

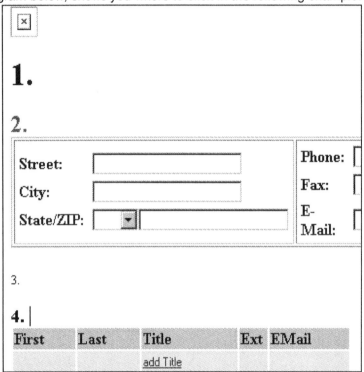

Adding data to the document:

1. Click at position 1. and enter the name of the document (e.g. Organization Chart).
2. Click at position 2. and the company name (e.g. Nano USA).

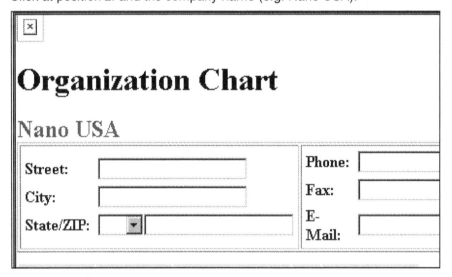

3. Press the TAB key, to place the text cursor in the address table.
4. Fill in the address data of the company, using TAB to step through all the fields.

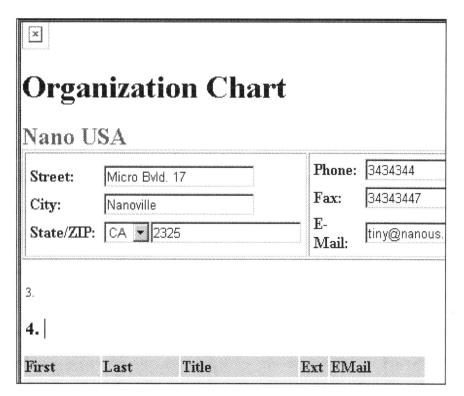

5. Click at position 3. and enter a short **company description** (between the **Desc | Para** tags - if visible). You can hit the Enter key to add a new line from anywhere within the description text.
6. Click at position 4. and enter the **Department** name.
7. Hit the TAB key and fill in the Person table, using TAB to step through the fields.

Auto- and manual validation

When entering text in the e-mail field, you will notice that it initially appears in red. Document Editor uses the schema, on which the template is based, to provide real-time validation. When the data has been entered correctly, the text changes to black.

The e-mail field is valid as soon as the address contains an @, another character, followed by a period (defined as a pattern in the schema file).

You can validate the whole document by selecting the menu option **XML | Validate**, or hitting the F8 key.

Organization Chart

Nano USA

Street:	Micro Bvld. 17		Phone:	3434344
City:	Nanoville		Fax:	34343447
State/ZIP:	CA	2325	E-Mail:	tiny@nanou:

Nano USA introduced the first microprocessor based on single electron transistors using nanotube Josephson Junctions.

Research and development

First	Last	Title	Ext	EMail
Albert	Angström	add Title	11	ang@nanous.com

Optional fields:

Pressing the TAB key in the Person table, skips the "Title" field. The Title field was defined as **optional** in the schema file, and is displayed as a link in a template document. To add data in this field, click the "add Title" text and enter your data.

Hints:

Placing the text cursor in, or above the "e-mail" field (in the Person table) causes a hint popup to appear. These hints were defined in XSLT Designer and are designed to aid users when filling in the document.

Hints can be defined for any element using the "Node Settings" function in XSLT Designer.

Orgchart with Large Markup visible.

To add a new row to the Person table:
1. When the text cursor is in the **last cell** (Email) of the Person table, hit TAB to add a new row, or
2. Right click and select **Insert | Person**.

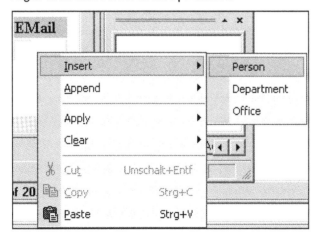

Fill in the new row with the person data.

Nano USA introduced the first microprocessor based on single electron transistors using nanotube Josephson Junctions.

Research and development

First	Last	Title	Ext	EMail
Albert	**Angström**	add Title	11	ang@nanous.com
Brad	**Buckyball**	add Title	12	bb@nanous.com

Table types

Tables in Document Editor

There are two types of table available in the Document Editor, fixed and dynamic tables.

An example of a **fixed table** is the company Address table. The structure of this type of table cannot be changed; you cannot add or delete rows or columns.

The Person table is an example of a **dynamic table**. You can change the structure of this table at will. You can insert, append, duplicate, move, and delete rows, using the respective icons. Hitting the TAB key in the last field of such a table, automatically adds a new row.

Please note:
> The two tables in this example are colored differently, this does not however, have any bearing on the type of table they are. The table type and color scheme were defined in XSLT Designer.

To add a new office to the orgchart:

1. Click the **append** Office icon (leftmost icon of the pair) in the entry helper, to append a new office.
   Empty address and person tables, as well as all other related tags, are automatically inserted at the end of the document.

   The element entry helper contains elements that can be appended or inserted to the document, depending on the current cursor position.

   You can of course, right click to open the context menu and select **Insert or Append | Office**. The context menu supplies the same options as the element entry helper.

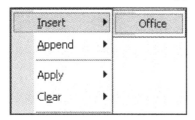

Please note:
> The context menu also allows you to apply formatting to text, or clear previously applied formatting. The options depend on where you right click.

Nano USA

Street:	Micro Bvld. 17	Phone:	3434344
City:	Nanoville	Fax:	34343447
State/ZIP:	CA ▾ 2325	E-Mail:	tiny@nanous

Nano USA introduced the first microprocessor based on single electron transistors using nanotube Josephson Junctions.

Research and development

First	Last	Title	Ext	EMail
Albert	**Angström**	add Title	11	ang@nanous.com
Brad	**Buckyball**	add Title	12	bb@nanous.com

Street:		Phone:	
City:		Fax:	
State/ZIP:	▾	E-Mail:	

First	Last	Title	Ext	EMail
		add Title		

2. Fill in the office data as before.

Organization Chart

Nano USA

Street:	Micro Bvld. 17		**Phone:**	3434344
City:	Nanoville		**Fax:**	34343447
State/ZIP:	CA ▾	2325	**E-Mail:**	tiny@nanous

Nano USA introduced the first microprocessor based on single electron transistors using nanotube Josephson Junctions.

Research and development

First	Last	Title	Ext	EMail
Albert	**Angström**	add Title	11	ang@nanous.com
Brad	**Buckyball**	add Title	12	bb@nanous.com

Nano EU subsidiary

Street:	Pico Drive 2		**Phone:**	3232445
City:	New London		**Fax:**	32324457
State/ZIP:	CT ▾	06320	**E-Mail:**	mingi@nano

Nano EU developed the theoretical foundation for the nanotube Josephson Junction revolution we see today.

Changing text attributes:

The Company description text can be made bold or italic.

1. Mark the text you want to make bold or italic, and
2. Click the **bold** or **italic** icons in the icon bar, to apply these attributes.
    The marked text is displayed as bold, and strong and/or italic tags are inserted on each side of the marked text (visible when Show large markup is active).

Desc⟩ para⟩
Nano USA introduced the first ⟨strong⟩**microprocessor** ⟨strong⟩based on single electron transistors using ⟨italic⟩*nanotube* ⟨italic⟩Josephson Junctions.
⟨para ⟨Desc

Please note:

B *I* are user-defined icons. These two apply bold or italic formatting to marked text. User defined icons are defined in XSLT Designer (Text State icons), and are made available to Document Editor as icons in the icon bar. Please see the XSLT Designer documentation for more information.

Document Editor Reference

The reference section contains a complete description of all Document Editor windows and menu commands.

Menus and Dialogs

This section describes the menu, dialog box and context menu options.

File

The File menu contains all commands relevant to manipulating files in the order common to most Windows software products.

New

The "New..." command is used to create a new type of XML document, or open a predefined Document Editor template file created by XSLT Designer. Template files can only be **opened** in Document Editor, they have to be created in XSLT Designer.

To open a Document Editor template file (*.sps)
- Click the "Select a Document Editor template..." button and select a file from the dialog box.

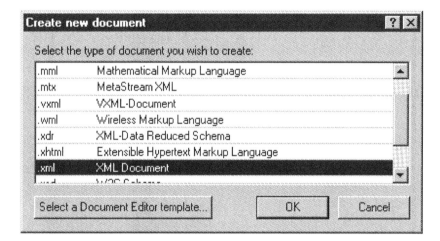

This opens the New dialog box.

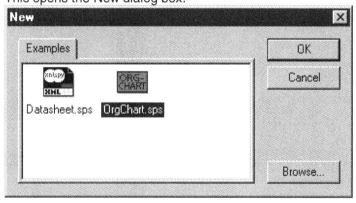

- The two *.sps icons you see here are supplied with XML Spy Suite. and are automatically placed in the folder you installed XML Spy in +...+ **Altova\XML Spy Suite\sps\Template\Examples.**
- The OrgChart icon (OrgChart.ico) is also in the Examples folder. A default icon (e.g. Datasheet.sps icon) is used, if you do not create a specific one.
- You can add **new tabs** to this dialog box, by adding a sub-folder to the Template folder

e.g. XML Spy +...+ **Altova\XML Spy Suite\sps\Template\My folder**

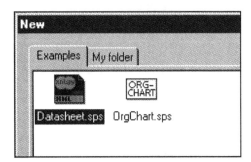

Open

The "Open..." command allows you to open any type of XML file. The familiar Windows "Open" dialog is opened and allows you to select one of these file types.

Do not use this command to open a Document Editor template file (*.sps), use **File | New** instead.

Save

The "Save" command saves the currently open Document Editor file as a normal XML file.

Save as...

The "Save As..." command shows the familiar Windows "Save as..." dialog and prompts for the name and location of the XML file to be saved.

Exit

The "Exit" command is used to quit Document Editor. If you have an open file with unsaved changes, you will be prompted to save these changes.

Document Editor

The Document Editor menu contains commands relevant to displaying document markup, as well as manipulating tables.

Assign configuration file...

This command assigns a Spy Structure file (SPS) to an XML document to enable viewing and editing in the Document Editor view.

The command opens a dialog box allowing you to specify the SPS file you wish to assign, and inserts the required SPS statement into your XML document.

Hide markup

This command hides markup symbols in the Document Editor view.

Show small markup

This command shows small markup symbols in the Document Editor view.

Show large markup

This command shows large markup symbols in the Document Editor view.

Show mixed markup

This command shows mixed markup symbols in the Document Editor view.

Append row

This command appends a row to the current table in the Document Editor view.

Insert row

This command inserts a row into the current table in the Document Editor view.

Duplicate row

This command duplicates the current table row in the Document Editor view.

Move row up

This command moves current row up by one row in the Document Editor view.

Move row down

This command moves the current row down by one row in the Document Editor view.

Delete row

This command deletes the currently active row in the Document Editor view.

Help

Document Editor includes a online help system that is based on the Microsoft HTML Help Viewer, and let you currently access the table of contents, index and search function of the supplied help file.

About Document Editor

This command displays the current Document Editor splash window.

Context menus

Context menus are opened by clicking right on some part of the user-interface. The pop-up menu that opens is determined by where you click.

The context menu supplies:
- The standard editing functions: Cut, Copy and Delete.
- Options to insert or append elements, through the Insert and Append options. The items that can be selected, are the same as the ones available in the entry helper.
- Options to apply formatting to text, or clear previously applied formatting.

Part VII

7   XML Spy Document Editor Browser Plug-in

The Document Editor Browser Plug-In is a unique solution that allows live XML content editing from any desktop in your enterprise, which dramatically eases deployment and reduces total cost of ownership (TCO).

This is the first browser-based XML editing solution in the entire industry, and it is based upon open standards, such as XML Schema and XSLT! It is also fully Unicode compatible!

The purpose of the XMLSpy Browser Plug-In is to make it possible to:
- edit an XSLT transformed XML document within an HTML page

This makes it possible for users to edit XML files in a WYSIWYG fashion without seeing the underlying raw XML code. There is also no need for extra software deployment, if you embed the plug-in into Internet Explorer. The first time a user visits your HTML page, the ActiveX control is installed and automatically activated.

The XMLSpy Browser Plugin is an ActiveX control where the COM interface is defined by the XMLSpyDocumentEditor object.

The complete object model of the Browser Plugin consists of the following parts:

XMLData
XMLSpyDocumentEditor
XMLSpyXMLLoadSave

The OBJECT tag

To use the Browser plug-in with an HTML page, the following HTML "OBJECT" tag must be used.

```
<OBJECT id=XMLSpyPlugin style="WIDTH:500px; HEIGHT:500px"
    codeBase="http://plugin.xmlspy.com/cabfiles/XMLSpyPlugin.CAB#Versi
on=2,0,0,0"
    classid=clsid:46987108-BA64-4fd1-A947-1BF7DA938FC0>
    <PARAM NAME="XMLDataURL"
VALUE="http://plugin.xmlspy.com/Altova.xml">
    <PARAM NAME="SPSDataURL"
VALUE="http://plugin.xmlspy.com/Altova.sps">
    <PARAM NAME="SchemaDataURL"
VALUE="http://plugin.xmlspy.com/Altova.xsd">
    <PARAM NAME="LicKey" VALUE="XBA760-9HF1TT-Aq9FXB-0HstC2">
    <PARAM NAME="LicCompany" VALUE="Test">
    <PARAM NAME="LicUser" VALUE="Test">
</OBJECT>
```

Please note that the values for the various parameters and attributes of the OBJECT tag, must be replaced with valid data for this sample to work (i.e. a valid XML data file name and path for the "XMLDataURL" parameter).

XMLDataURL: This is the location of the XML data file that is loaded into the plugin. This will also be the XML data file that is edited. The location of the file must be an absolute URL.

SPSDataURL: This is the location of the XMLSpy XSLT Designer generated SPS file. The location of the file must be an absolute URL.

SchemaDataURL: This is the location of the Schema file used to **validate** the XML file. The location of the file must be an absolute URL.

LicKey: This is the license key used to validate the use of the XMLSpy Browser Plugin. The example license key in the example above, cannot be used for this purpose. Please see the License information for more information.

LicCompany: This is the company name of the license key specified in the LicKey PARAM definition.

LicUser: This is the user name of the license key specified in the LicKey PARAM definition.

LicServer: This is the name of the server if you put your license information in a separate key.

LicFile: This is the file name where the key is stored.

Please see "License information" for more information about the LicServer and LicFile parameters.

A simple HTML

The HTML code below generates a page containing buttons which call simple functions using the XMLSpy Browser Plug-in. You can use this code as a template to build more complex solutions using the control.

```
<html>
<head>
<meta http-equiv="Content-Type" content="text/html; charset=windows-
1252">
<title>Minimal XMLSpyDocEditPlugIn page</title>

<SCRIPT ID=clientEventHandlers LANGUAGE=vbscript>
Sub BtnOnSave
     objPlugIn.XMLDataSaveUrl =
"http://plugin.xmlspy.com/SaveFile.xml"
     objPlugIn.Save
End Sub

Sub BtnOnClick
     objPlugIn.SchemaLoadObject.URL =
"http://plugin.xmlspy.com/OrgChart.xml"
     objPlugIn.XMLDataLoadObject.URL =
"http://plugin.xmlspy.com/OrgChart.xml"
     objPlugIn.DesignDataLoadObject.URL =
"http://plugin.xmlspy.com/OrgChart.sps"
     objPlugIn.StartEditing
End Sub

Sub OnClickFind
     objPlugIn.FindDialog
End Sub

Sub OnClickReplace
     objPlugIn.ReplaceDialog
End Sub

Sub BtnOnTestProp
     If objPlugIn.IsRowInsertEnabled Then
          msgbox "true"
     Else
          msgbox "false"
     End If
End Sub

</SCRIPT>
</head>

<body>
<OBJECT id=objPlugIn
     odeBase="http://plugin.xmlspy.com/XMLSpyPluginCabinet.cab#Versio
n=2,0,0,0"
     lassid=clsid:46987108-BA64-4fd1-A947-1BF7DA938FC0 width="600"
height="500">
     <PARAM NAME="LicServer" VALUE="http://plugin.xmlspy.com">
     <PARAM NAME="LicFile" VALUE="/key.lic">
</OBJECT>
```

```
<p><input type="button" value="Start editing" name="B3"
onclick="BtnOnClick"></p>
<p><input type="button" value="Find" name="B4"
onclick="OnClickFind"></p>
<p><input type="button" value="Replace" name="B5"
onclick="OnClickReplace"></p>
<p><input type="button" value="Save" name="B6"
onclick="BtnOnSave"></p>
<p><input type="button" value="Test property" name="B7"
onclick="BtnOnTestProp"></p>
</body>
</html>
```

Please note that the values for the various parameters and attributes of the OBJECT tag, must be replaced with valid data for this sample to work.

Row operations

Repeatable elements can be created within an XML Document. This is made possible by the specific schema file to which the XML file is assigned. The WYSIWIG environment allows you to manipulate rows and their data, individually.

An XML row may be implemented by an HTML table, but this need not always be the case. The XSLT Designer *.SPS file defines the HTML page layout. While editing XML data, an external script performs the row operations (on each row individually).

If an external script is to perform row operations then two steps must occur:
- The first step checks whether the cursor is currently in a row using a property. E.g. **IsRowInsertEnabled**, which returns a TRUE or FALSE value.
- If the return value is TRUE then the row method can be called. E.g. **RowAppend**, which has no parameters and returns no value.

The following is a list of properties and methods available that perform table operations. Each of the properties return a BOOL and each of the methods have no parameters.

IsRowInsertEnabled, RowInsert:	Row insertion operation.
IsRowAppendEnabled, RowAppend:	Append row operation.
IsRowDeleteEnabled, RowDelete:	Delete row operation.
IsRowMoveUpEnabled, RowMoveUp:	Move the XML data up one row location.
IsRowMoveDownEnabled, RowMoveDown:	Move the XML data down one row location.
IsRowDuplicateEnabled, RowDuplicate:	Duplicate the currently selected XML row.

Editing operations

When XML data is displayed as HTML data, it is possible to manipulate individual elements using standard editing operations cut, copy and paste.

Not all XML data elements can be edited however, and it is therefore necessary first to test if editing is possible. This is achieved in the same way as row operations, starting with a property to test editing capabilities and then calling the method to perform the editing operation.

The only method that does not have a test is the method **EditSelectAll**, which automatically selects all elements displayed in the document. The following is a list of properties and methods available that perform editing operations. Each of the properties returns a BOOL and each of the methods have no parameters.

IsEditUndoEnabled, **EditUndo**	Undo an editing operation
IsEditRedoEnabled, **EditRedo**:	Redo an editing operation
IsEditCopyEnabled, **EditCopy**	Copy the selected text to the Windows clipboard
IsEditCutEnabled, **EditCut**	Cut the selected text to the Windows clipboard
IsEditPasteEnabled, **EditPaste**	Paste the Windows clipboard text to the current cursor position
IsEditClearEnabled, **EditClear**	Clear the selected text from the XML document

Find and replace

When navigating through a complex document it is often difficult to find specific sections of text.

The **FindDialog()** method, opens a Find dialog box. The user can then search for a specific element. The **FindNext()** method allows the next instance of the same item to be found. The **FindNext** method can be tested using the BOOL property **IsFindNextEnabled,** to see if there is a further occurence.

A variation of the FindDialog method is the **ReplaceDialog()** method. This operation finds a specific item, and is used to replace the item with a specific value entered by the user in the Replace dialog box. If the FindNext method is then called, the next item is found and replaced.

Shortcut keys

The following shortcut keys are valid if the Document Editor browser plugin has the input focus:

CTRL + P	Print document
CTRL + Z	Undo
CTRL + Y	Redo
CTRL + X	Cut
CTRL + C	Copy
CTRL + V	Paste
CTRL + A	Select all
CTRL + F	open Find dialog box
CTRL + H	open Find-Replace dialog box

License information

There are two ways you can supply the license information for the Document Editor Plug-in.

First, use the LicUser, LicCompany and LicKey parameters of the OBJECT tag, or the properties of the plugin interface with the same names. This method is easy to set up, you just type your license data into the HTML code of your page. If you use this method, your keycode will be visible to anyone who is able to view your HTML pages.

Alternatively, store the license key in a file located on a server.

To place the license on the server:

1. Request a key from us (Altova.com) with the name of the server (e.g. "http://www.nanonull.com") where you want to put the key (and propably the plugin).

   The new key will be bound to that server.

2. Create a license file (e.g. naming it **key.lic**) containing the license code in plain text as the only content at the specific location.
   Example: "http://www.nanonull.com/key.lic"

3. In your HTML code use the following parameters in the OBJECT tag:
   <PARAM NAME="LicServer" VALUE="http://www.nanonull.com">
   <PARAM NAME="LicFile" VALUE="/key.lic">

The license information is now bound to your server and also located there.

It is not possible to take the key from the file and set the properties (LicKey, LicCompany, LicUser) of the control with this information. This will be forbidden by the control itself. You can also protect the file storing the license information with a password, if you set up your server accordingly.

Using XMLData

XMLData gives you access to the elements of the currently displayed XML file. It enables you to perform all necessary modifications to the elements of the XML structure. The main functionality of XMLData is:

1. Access to the names and values of all kinds of elements (e.g. elements, attributes)

2. Creation of new elements of all kinds.

3. Insertion and appending of new elements.

4. Erasing of existing child elements.

Structure of XMLData

Before you can use the XMLData interface, you have to know how an existing XML file is mapped into a XMLData structure. One major thing you must be aware of is, that XMLData has no seperate branch of objects for attributes.

The attributes of an element are also children of the element. The "XMLData.Kind" property, gives you the opportunity to distinguish between the different types of children of an element.

Example:

This XML code,

```
<ParentElement>
      <FirstChild attr1="Red" attr2="Black">
            This is the value of FirstChild
      </FirstChild>
      <SecondChild>
            <!--Your Comment-->
            </DeepChild>
      </SecondChild>
      This is Text
</ParentElement>
```

is mapped to the following XMLData object structure:

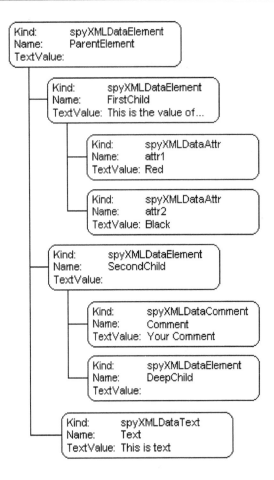

The parent of all XML elements inside of a file is the property
"XMLSpyDocumentEditor.XMLRoot". Use this XMLData object to get references to all other
XML elements in the structure.

Name and value of elements

To get and to modify the name and value of all types of XML elements use the
"XMLData.Name" and "XMLData.TextValue" properties. It is possible that several kinds of
XMLData objects and empty elements do not have a text value associated.

Creation and insertion of new XMLData objects

The creation of a new XML language entity requires the following steps:

1. Create the new XMLData object:
    Use the "XMLSpyDocumentEditor.CreateChild" method to create a new XMLData
    object. Set name and value after you have inserted the new XML entity (see point 3).

2. Find the correct location for the new XMLData object:
    To insert a new XMLData object you have to get a reference to the parent first. If the
    new child is to become the last child of the parent, use the "XMLData.AppendChild"
    method to insert the XMLData object.
    If the new child should be located elsewhere in the sequence of child objects, use the
    "XMLData.GetFirstChild" and "XMLData.GetNextChild" to move the iterator to the child

before which the new child should be inserted.

3. Insert the new child with "XMLData.InsertChild"
    The new child will be inserted immediately before the current child.

    The following example adds a third child between <FirstChild> and the <SecondChild> element:

```
Dim objParent
Dim objChild
Dim objNewChild

Set objNewChild = objPlugIn.CreateChild(spyXMLDataElement)

'objParent is set to <ParentElement>
'GetFirstChild(-1) gets all children of the parent element
'and move to <SecondChild>
Set objChild = objParent.GetFirstChild(-1)
Set objChild = objParent.GetNextChild

objParent.InsertChild objNewChild
objNewChild.Name = "OneAndAHalf"
Set objNewChild = Nothing
```

Copying of existing XMLData objects

If you want to insert existing XMLData objects at a different place in the same file you can't use the XMLData.InsertChild and XMLData.AppendChild methods. These methods only work for new XMLData objects.

Instead of using InsertChild or AppendChild you have to copy the object hierarchy manually. The following function written in JavaScript is an example for recursively copying XMLData:

```
// this function returns a complete copy of the XMLData object
function GetCopy(objXMLData)
{
        var objNew;
        objNew = objPlugIn.CreateChild(objXMLData.Kind);

        objNew.Name = objXMLData.Name;
        objNew.TextValue = objXMLData.TextValue;

        if(objXMLData.HasChildren)      {
                var objChild;
                objChild = objXMLData.GetFirstChild(-1);

                while(objChild)     {
                        try {
                                objNew.AppendChild(GetCopy(objChild));
                                objChild = objXMLData.GetNextChild();
                        }
                        catch(e) {
                                objChild = null;
                        }
                }
        }

        return objNew;
}
```

Erasing of XMLData objects

XMLData provides two methods for the deletion of child objects, "XMLData.EraseAllChildren" and "XMLData.EraseCurrentChild".

To erase XMLData objects you need access to the parent of the elements you want to remove. Use "XMLData.GetFirstChild" and "XMLData.GetNextChild" to get a reference to the parent XMLData object.

See the method descriptions of "EraseAllChildren" and "EraseCurrentChild" for examples how to erase XML elements.

DOM and XMLData

The XMLData interface gives you full access to the XML structure behind the current document with less methods than DOM and is much simpler. The XMLData interface is a minimalist approach to reading and modifying existing, or newly created XML data. You might however, want to use a DOM tree because you can access one from an external source or you just prefer the MSXML DOM implementation.

The **ProcessDOMNode()** and **ProcessXMLDataNode()** functions provided below convert any segments of an XML structure between XMLData and DOM.

To use the **ProcessDOMNode()** function:
- pass the root element of the DOM segment you want to convert in **objNode** and
- pass the plugin object with the CreateChild() method in **objCreator**

To use the **ProcessXMLDataNode()** function:
- pass the root element of the XMLData segment in **objXMLData** and
- pass the DOMDocument object created with MSXML in **xmlDoc**

```
//////////////////////////////////////////////////////////////////
// DOM to XMLData conversion

function ProcessDOMNode(objNode,objCreator)
{
      var objRoot;
      objRoot = CreateXMLDataFromDOMNode(objNode,objCreator);

      if(objRoot) {
            if((objNode.nodeValue != null) &&
(objNode.nodeValue.length > 0))
                  objRoot.TextValue = objNode.nodeValue;

            // add attributes
            if(objNode.attributes) {
                  var Attribute;
                  var oNodeList = objNode.attributes;

                  for(var i = 0;i < oNodeList.length; i++) {
                        Attribute = oNodeList.item(i);

                        var newNode;
                        newNode =
ProcessDOMNode(Attribute,objCreator);

                        objRoot.AppendChild(newNode);
                  }
            }

            if(objNode.hasChildNodes)      {
                  try {
                        // add children
                        var Item;
                        oNodeList = objNode.childNodes;

                        for(var i = 0;i < oNodeList.length; i++) {
                              Item = oNodeList.item(i);
```

```
                              var newNode;
                              newNode =
ProcessDOMNode(Item,objCreator);

                              objRoot.AppendChild(newNode);
                    }
               }
               catch(err) {
               }
          }
     }

     return objRoot;
}


function CreateXMLDataFromDOMNode(objNode,objCreator)
{
     var bSetName = true;
     var bSetValue = true;

     var nKind = 4;

     switch(objNode.nodeType)        {
          case 2:nKind = 5;break;
          case 3:nKind = 6;bSetName = false;break;
          case 4:nKind = 7;bSetName = false;break;
          case 8:nKind = 8;bSetName = false;break;
          case 7:nKind = 9;break;
     }

     var objNew = null;
     objNew = objCreator.CreateChild(nKind);

     if(bSetName)
          objNew.Name = objNode.nodeName;

     if(bSetValue && (objNode.nodeValue != null))
          objNew.TextValue = objNode.nodeValue;

     return objNew;
}


///////////////////////////////////////////////////////////
// XMLData to DOM conversion

function ProcessXMLDataNode(objXMLData,xmlDoc)
{
     var objRoot;
     objRoot = CreateDOMNodeFromXMLData(objXMLData,xmlDoc);

     if(objRoot) {
          if(IsTextNodeEnabled(objRoot) &&
(objXMLData.TextValue.length > 0))
               objRoot.appendChild(xmlDoc.createTextNode(objXMLData
.TextValue));

          if(objXMLData.HasChildren)      {
```

```
            try {
                var objChild;
                objChild = objXMLData.GetFirstChild(-1);

                while(true) {
                    if(objChild)      {
                        var newNode;
                        newNode =
ProcessXMLDataNode(objChild,xmlDoc);

                        if(newNode.nodeType == 2)      {
                            // child node is an
attribute
                            objRoot.attributes.setNamedI
tem(newNode);
                        }
                        else
                            objRoot.appendChild(newNode)
;
                    }

                    objChild = objXMLData.GetNextChild();
                }
            }
            catch(err) {
            }
        }
    }

    return objRoot;
}

function CreateDOMNodeFromXMLData(objXMLData,xmlDoc)
{
    switch(objXMLData.Kind) {
        case 4:return xmlDoc.createElement(objXMLData.Name);
        case 5:return xmlDoc.createAttribute(objXMLData.Name);
        case 6:return xmlDoc.createTextNode(objXMLData.TextValue);
        case 7:return
xmlDoc.createCDATASection(objXMLData.TextValue);
        case 8:return xmlDoc.createComment(objXMLData.TextValue);
        case 9:return
xmlDoc.createProcessingInstruction(objXMLData.Name,objXMLData.TextValu
e);
    }

    return xmlDoc.createElement(objXMLData.Name);
}

function IsTextNodeEnabled(objNode)
{
    switch(objNode.nodeType) {
        case 1:
        case 2:
        case 5:
        case 6:
        case 11:return true;
    }
```

```
        return false;
}
```

Objects

XMLData

See also

Methods
InsertChild
AppendChild

EraseAllChildren
EraseCurrentChild

GetCurrentChild
GetFirstChild
GetNextChild

IsSameNode

Properties
Name
TextValue

HasChildren
MayHaveChildren

Kind
Parent

Description

You can use the XMLData interface to manipulate the content of the currently displayed XML. This interface is a lightweight COM counterpart of the implementation used inside the plugin and XMLSpy itself.

To create a new XMLData object use the CreateChild() method of the plugin interface.

InsertChild

See also

Declaration: InsertChild(*pNewData* as XMLData)

Description

InsertChild inserts the new child before the current child (see also XMLData.GetFirstChild, XMLData.GetNextChild to set the current child).

AppendChild

See also

Declaration: AppendChild(*pNewData* as XMLData)

Description

AppendChild appends pNewData as last child to the XMLData object. See also "Using XMLData".

Example

```
Dim objCurrentParent
Dim objNewChild

Set objNewChild = objPlugIn.CreateChild(spyXMLDataElement)
Set objCurrentParent = objPlugIn.XMLRoot

objCurrentParent.AppendChild objNewChild

Set objNewChild = Nothing
```

EraseAllChildren

See also

Declaration: EraseAllChildren

Description

EraseAllChildren deletes all associated children of the XMLData object.

Example

The sample erases all elements of the active document.

```
Dim objCurrentParent

Set objCurrentParent = objPlugIn.XMLRoot
objCurrentParent.EraseAllChildren
```

EraseCurrentChild

See also

Declaration: EraseCurrentChild

Description

EraseCurrentChild deletes the current XMLData child object. Before you call EraseCurrentChild you must initialize an internal iterator with XMLData.GetFirstChild.

Example

This JavaScript example deletes all elements with the name "EraseMe". The code shows you, that it is possible to call EraseCurrentChild and GetNextChild inside the same loop to continue stepping through the child elements.

```
function DeleteXMLElements(objXMLData)
{
        if(objXMLData == null)
                return;

        if(objXMLData.HasChildren){
                var objChild;
                objChild = objXMLData.GetFirstChild(-1);

                while(objChild)     {
                        DeleteXMLElements(objChild);

                        try     {
                                if(objChild.Name == "EraseMe")
                                        objXMLData.EraseCurrentChild();

                                objChild = objXMLData.GetNextChild();
                        }
                        catch(Err)   {
                                objChild = null;
                        }
                }
        }
}
```

GetCurrentChild

See also

Declaration: GetCurrentChild as XMLData

Return Value
Returns an xml element as XMLData object.

Description

GetCurrentChild gets the current child. Before you call GetCurrentChild you must initialize an internal iterator with XMLData.GetFirstChild.

GetFirstChild

See also

Declaration: GetFirstChild(*nKind* as SPYXMLDataKind) as XMLData

Return Value
Returns an xml element as XMLData object.

Description

GetFirstChild initializes a new iterator and returns the first child. Set nKind = -1 to get an iterator for all kinds of children.

Example

See the example at XMLData.GetNextChild.

GetNextChild

See also

Declaration: GetNextChild as XMLData

Return Value

Returns an xml element as XMLData object.

Description

GetNextChild steps to the next child of this element. Before you call GetNextChild you must initialize an internal iterator with XMLData.GetFirstChild.

Check for the last child of the element as shown in the sample below.

Example

```
On Error Resume Next
Set objParent = objPlugIn.XMLRoot

'get elements of all kinds
Set objCurrentChild = objParent.GetFirstChild(-1)

Do
    'do something useful with the child

    'step to next child
    Set objCurrentChild = objParent.GetNextChild
Loop Until (Err.Number - vbObjectError = 1503)
```

Name

See also

Declaration: Name as String

Description

Used to modify and to get the name of the XMLData object.

TextValue

See also

Declaration: TextValue as String

Description

Used to modify and to get the text value of this XMLData object. See also "Using XMLData".

HasChildren

See also

Declaration: HasChildren as Boolean

Description

The property is true, if the object is parent of other XMLData objects.

This property is read-only.

MayHaveChildren

See also

Declaration: MayHaveChildren as Boolean

Description

Tells if it is allowed to add children to this XMLData object.

This property is read-only.

Kind

See also

Declaration: Kind as SPYXMLDataKind

Description

Kind of this XMLData object.

This property is read-only.

IsSameNode

See also

Declaration: IsSameNode(*pNodeToCompare* as XMLData) as Boolean

Description

Returns true if pNodeToCompare references to the same node as the object itself.

Parent

See also

Declaration: Parent as XMLData

Return value
Parent as XMLData object.
Nothing (or NULL) if there is no parent element.

Description

Parent of this element.

This property is read-only.

XMLSpyDocumentEditor
See also

Methods

StartEditing
LoadXML
Reset

Save
SavePOST
SaveXML

ValidateDocument

EditClear
EditCopy
EditCut
EditPaste
EditRedo
EditSelectAll
EditUndo

RowAppend
RowDelete
RowDuplicate
RowInsert
RowMoveDown
RowMoveUp

FindDialog
FindNext
ReplaceDialog

ApplyTextState
IsTextStateApplied
IsTextStateEnabled

MarkUpView

Print
PrintPreview

CreateChild

GetAllowedElements

GetNextVisible
GetPreviousVisible

SelectionMoveTabOrder
SelectionSet

attachCallBack

Properties

IsEditClearEnabled
IsEditCopyEnabled
IsEditCutEnabled
IsEditPasteEnabled
IsEditRedoEnabled
IsEditUndoEnabled

IsFindNextEnabled

IsRowAppendEnabled
IsRowDeleteEnabled
IsRowDuplicateEnabled
IsRowInsertEnabled
IsRowMoveDownEnabled
IsRowMoveUpEnabled

LicCompany
LicFile
LicKey
LicServer
LicUser

SchemaLoadObject
XMLDataLoadObject
DesignDataLoadObject

XMLDataSaveUrl

XMLRoot

CurrentSelection

event

validationBadData
validationMessage

Events

SelectionChanged

Description

XMLSpyDocumentEditor Class

ApplyTextState

See also

Declaration: ApplyTextState(*elementName* as String)

Description

Applies or removes the text state defined by the parameter elementName. Common examples for the parameter elementName would be strong and italic.

In an XML document there are segments of data, which may contain sub-elements. For example consider the following HTML:

```
<b>fragment</b>
```

The HTML tag <b> will cause the word fragment to be bolded. However, this only happens because the HTML parser knows that the tag <b> is bold. With XML there is much more flexibility. It is possible to define any XML tag to do anything you desire. The point is that it is possible to apply a Text state using XML. But the Text state that is applied must be part of the schema. For example in the OrgChart.xml OrgChart.sps, OrgChart.xsd example the tag <strong> is the same as bold. And to apply bold the method **ApplyTextState()** is called. But like the row and edit operations it is necessary to test if it is possible to apply the text state.

See also IsTextStateEnabled and IsTextStateApplied.

CreateChild

See also

Declaration: CreateChild(*nKind* as SPYXMLDataKind) as XMLData

Return Value
New XML node

Description

The CreateChild method is used to create new nodes which you can insert into the XML structure of the current document using the XMLData interface.

The values for the nKind parameter are as follows:

```
spyXMLDataXMLDocStruct          = 0
spyXMLDataXMLEntityDocStruct          = 1
```

spyXMLDataDTDDocStruct	= 2	
spyXMLDataXML	= 3	
spyXMLDataElement	= 4	
spyXMLDataAttr		= 5
spyXMLDataText	= 6	
spyXMLDataCData	= 7	
spyXMLDataComment	= 8	
spyXMLDataPI	= 9	
spyXMLDataDefDoctype		= 10
spyXMLDataDefExternalID	= 11	
spyXMLDataDefElement		= 12
spyXMLDataDefAttlist	= 13	
spyXMLDataDefEntity	= 14	
spyXMLDataDefNotation		= 15
spyXMLDataKindsCount		= 16

See also XMLData.AppendChild and XMLData.InsertChild

EditClear

See also

Declaration: EditClear

Description

Clears the current selection.

EditCopy

See also

Declaration: EditCopy

Description

Copies the current selection to the clipboard.

EditCut

See also

Declaration: EditCut

Description

Cuts the current selection from the document and copies it to the clipboard.

EditPaste

See also

Declaration: EditPaste

Description

Pastes the content from the clipboard into the document.

EditRedo

See also

Declaration: EditRedo

Description

Redo the last undo step.

EditSelectAll

See also

Declaration: EditSelectAll

Description

The method selects the complete document.

EditUndo

See also

Declaration: EditUndo

Description

Undo the last action.

FindDialog

See also

Declaration: FindDialog

Description

Displays the FindDialog.

See also Find and replace.

FindNext

See also

Declaration: FindNext

Description

The method performs a find next operation.

See also Find and replace.

IsTextStateApplied

See also

Declaration: IsTextStateApplied(*elementName* as String) as Boolean

Description

Checks to see if the it the text state has already been applied. Common examples for the parameter elementName would be strong and italic.

IsTextStateEnabled

See also

Declaration: IsTextStateEnabled(*elementName* as String) as Boolean

Description

Checks to see if it is possible to apply a text state. Common examples for the parameter elementName would be strong and italic.

LoadXML

See also

Declaration: LoadXML(*xmlString* as String)

Description

Loads the current XML document with the XML string applied. The new content is displayed immediately.

MarkUpView

See also

Declaration: MarkUpView(*kind* as long)

Description

By default the document displayed is using HTML techniques. But sometimes it is desirable to show the editing tags. Using this method it is possible to display three different types of markup tags:

k_XMLSpyContentMarkupHide (0)	hide the markup tags
k_XMLSpyContentMarkupLarge (2)	show the large markup tags
k_XMLSpyContentMarkupMix (3)	show the mixed markup tags.

Print

See also

Declaration: Print

Description

Print the current document being edited.

PrintPreview

See also

Declaration: PrintPreview

Description

Print preview the document being edited.

ReplaceDialog

See also

Declaration: ReplaceDialog

Description

Displays the ReplaceDialog.

See also Find and replace.

Reset

See also

Declaration: Reset

Description

Reset the data being edited. Typically called before editing a new set of XML, XSL and SPS documents.

The method does not change the view and its still possible to continue working with the currently displayed document.

RowAppend

See also

Declaration: RowAppend

Description

Appends a row at the current position.

See also Row operations.

RowDelete

See also

Declaration: RowDelete

Description

Deletes the currently selected row(s).

See also Row operations.

RowDuplicate

See also

Declaration: RowDuplicate

Description

The method duplicates the currently selected rows.

See also Row operations.

RowInsert

See also

Declaration: RowInsert

Description

Inserts a new row immediately above the current selection.

See also Row operations.

RowMoveDown

See also

Declaration: RowMoveDown

Description

Moves the current row one position down.

See also Row operations.

RowMoveUp

See also

Declaration: RowMoveUp

Description

Moves the current row one position up.

See also Row operations.

Save

See also

Declaration: Save

Description

Saves the document to the URL specified by the property XMLDataSaveUrl.

The plugin sends an HTTP PUT request to the server to save the currently displayed XML file.

SavePOST

See also

Declaration: SavePOST

Description

Saves the document to the URL specified by the property XMLDataSaveUrl.

The plugin sends an HTTP POST request to the server to save the currently displayed XML file.

SaveXML

See also

Declaration: SaveXML as String

Return Value
XML structure as string

Description

Saves the current XML data to a string that is returned to the caller.

StartEditing

See also

Declaration: StartEditing as Boolean

Return Value
True if all files were successfully loaded and displayed.

Description

Start editing the current document. It is important to set the properties of the load objects SchemaLoadObject, DesignDataLoadObject and XMLDataLoadObject first.

ValidateDocument

See also

Declaration: ValidateDocument(*showResults* as Boolean) as Boolean

Return Value
result of validation

Description

Validates the current XML data for correctness as per the XML schema data. If the parameter showResults is FALSE then the validation errors will be suppressed, otherwise validation errors are shown.

validationMessage

See also

Declaration: validationMessage as String

Description

If the validation failed (after a call to ValidateDocument) this property stores a string with the error message.

validationBadData

See also

Declaration: validationBadData as XMLData

Description

If the validation failed (after a call to ValidateDocument) this property holds a reference to the XML element which causes the error.

DesignDataLoadObject

See also

Declaration: DesignDataLoadObject as XMLSpyXMLLoadSave

Description

The DesignDataLoadObject contains a reference to the SPS document. The SPS document is used to generate the WYSIWYG editing environment and is typically generated by XMLSpy XSLT Designer.

See also SchemaLoadObject for an example.

IsEditClearEnabled

See also

Declaration: IsEditClearEnabled as Boolean

Description

True if EditClear is possible.

See also Editing operations.

IsEditCopyEnabled

See also

Declaration: IsEditCopyEnabled as Boolean

Description

True if copy to clipboard is possible.

See also EditCopy and Editing operations.

IsEditCutEnabled

See also

Declaration: IsEditCutEnabled as Boolean

Description

True if EditCut is currently possible.

See also Editing operations.

IsEditPasteEnabled

See also

Declaration: IsEditPasteEnabled as Boolean

Description

True if EditPaste is possible.

See also Editing operations.

IsEditRedoEnabled

See also

Declaration: IsEditRedoEnabled as Boolean

Description

True if EditRedo is currently possible.

See also Editing operations.

IsEditUndoEnabled

See also

Declaration: IsEditUndoEnabled as Boolean

Description

True if EditUndo is possible.

See also Editing operations.

IsFindNextEnabled

See also

Declaration: IsFindNextEnabled as Boolean

Description

True if FindNext is currently possible. False if no more occurances are left.

See also Find and replace and FindDialog.

IsRowAppendEnabled

See also

Declaration: IsRowAppendEnabled as Boolean

Description

True if RowAppend is possible.

See also Row operations.

IsRowDeleteEnabled

See also

Declaration: IsRowDeleteEnabled as Boolean

Description

True if RowDelete is possible.

See also Row operations.

IsRowDuplicateEnabled

See also

Declaration: IsRowDuplicateEnabled as Boolean

Description

True if RowDuplicate is currently possible.

See also Row operations.

IsRowInsertEnabled

See also

Declaration: IsRowInsertEnabled as Boolean

Description

True if RowInsert is possible.

See also Row operations.

IsRowMoveDownEnabled

See also

Declaration: IsRowMoveDownEnabled as Boolean

Description

True if RowMoveDown is currently possible.

See also Row operations.

IsRowMoveUpEnabled

See also

Declaration: IsRowMoveUpEnabled as Boolean

Description

True if RowMoveUp is possible.

See also Row operations.

LicCompany

See also

Declaration: LicCompany as String

Description

LicCompany stores the company name of the license information.

LicFile

See also

Declaration: LicFile as String

Description

LicFile holds the file name if you use server bound license information.

See also LicServer and License information.

LicKey

See also

Declaration: LicKey as String

Description

LicKey stores the license key.

LicServer

See also

Declaration: LicServer as String

Description

LicServer holds the server name if you use server bound license information.

See also LicFile and License information.

LicUser

See also

Declaration: LicUser as String

Description

LicUser holds the user name of the license information.

SchemaLoadObject

See also

Declaration: SchemaLoadObject as XMLSpyXMLLoadSave

Description

The SchemaLoadObject contains an reference to the XML Schema document for the current XML file. The Schema document is typically generated using XMLSpy.

Example

```
    objPlugIn.SchemaLoadObject.URL =
"http://plugin.xmlspy.com/OrgChart.xml"
    objPlugIn.XMLDataLoadObject.URL =
"http://plugin.xmlspy.com/OrgChart.xml"
    objPlugIn.DesignDataLoadObject.URL =
"http://plugin.xmlspy.com/OrgChart.sps"
    objPlugIn.StartEditing
```

The code above sets all URL properties of the load objects and calls StartEditing to load and display the files. The current content and status of the plugin will be cleared.

XMLDataLoadObject

See also

Declaration: XMLDataLoadObject as XMLSpyXMLLoadSave

Description

The XMLDataLoadObject contains an reference to the XML document being edited. The XML document is typically defined using XMLSpy, but generated using a database or another business process.

See also SchemaLoadObject for an example.

XMLDataSaveUrl

See also

Declaration: XMLDataSaveUrl as String

Description

When the XML data has been modified it is possible to save the data back to a server using an URL. This property defines the location where the XML data will be saved.

See also the XMLSpyDocumentEditor.Save and the XMLSpyDocumentEditor.SavePOST methods.

XMLRoot

See also

Declaration: XMLRoot as XMLData

Description

XMLRoot is the parent element of the currently displayed XML structure. Using the XMLData interface you have full access to the complete content of the file.

See also Using XMLData for more informations.

SelectionChanged

See also

Declaration: SelectionChanged as VT_0019

Description

This event is raised whenever the user changes the current selection.

GetPreviousVisible

See also

Declaration: GetPreviousVisible(*pElement* as XMLData) as XMLData

Description

The method gets the previous visible XML element in the document.

GetNextVisible

See also

Declaration: GetNextVisible(*pElement* as XMLData) as XMLData

Description

The method gets the next visible XML element in the document.

SelectionMoveTabOrder

See also

Declaration: SelectionMoveTabOrder(*bForward* as Boolean,*bTag* as Boolean)

Description

SelectionMoveTabOrder() moves the current selection forwards or backwards.

If bTag is false and the current selection is at the last cell of a table a new line will be added.

SelectionSet

See also

Declaration: SelectionSet(*pStartElement* as XMLData,*nStartPos* as long,*pEndElement* as XMLData,*nEndPos* as long) as Boolean

Description

Use SelectionSet() to set a new selection in the Document Editor view. Its possible to set pEndElement to null (nothing) if the selection should be just over one (pStartElement) XML element.

CurrentSelection

See also

Declaration: CurrentSelection as DocEditSelection

Description

The property provides access to the current selection in the Document Editor view.

The example code below retrieves the complete text of the current selection:

JavaScript:

```
// somewhere in your script:
GetSelection(objPlugIn.CurrentSelection);

// GetSelection() collects complete text selection
function GetSelection(objSel)
{
        var strText = "";

        var objCurrent = objSel.Start;

        while(!objSel.End.IsSameNode(objCurrent))
        {
                objCurrent = objPlugIn.GetNextVisible(objCurrent);
                strText += objCurrent.TextValue;
        }

        strText +=
objSel.End.TextValue.substring(0,objSel.EndTextPosition);
        return
objSel.Start.TextValue.substr(objSel.StartTextPosition) + strText;
        }
```

GetAllowedElements

See also

Declaration: GetAllowedElements(*nAction* as
DOCEDElementActions,*pStartElement* as XMLData,*pEndElement* as
XMLData,*pElements* as Variant)

Description

GetAllowedElements() returns the allowed elements for the various actions specified by
nAction. Valid values for nAction are:

k_ActionInsertAt	= 0
k_ActionApply	= 1
k_ActionRemoveSurr	= 2
k_ActionAppend	= 3
k_ActionInsertBefore	= 4

JavaScript example:

```
function GetAllowed()
{
        var objView = Application.ActiveDocument.DocEditView;

        var arrElements = new Array(1);

        var objStart = objView.CurrentSelection.Start;
        var objEnd = objView.CurrentSelection.End;

        var strText;
        strText = "valid elements at current selection:\n\n";

        for(var i = 1;i <= 4;i++)      {
                objPlugIn.GetAllowedElements(i,objStart,objEnd,arrEl
```

```
ements);
                        strText = strText + ListArray(arrElements) + "------
------------\n";
                }

                return strText;
        }

        function ListArray(arrIn)
        {
                var strText = "";

                if(typeof(arrIn) == "object") {
                        for(var i = 0;i <= (arrIn.length - 1);i++)
                                strText = strText + arrIn[i] + "\n";
                }

                return strText;
        }
```

VBScript example:

```
        Sub DisplayAllowed
                dim objView
                set objView = Application.ActiveDocument.DocEditView

                dim arrElements()

                dim objStart
                dim objEnd
                set objStart = objView.CurrentSelection.Start
                set objEnd = objView.CurrentSelection.End

                dim strText
                strText = "valid elements at current selection:" & chr(13)
& chr(13)

                dim i

                For i = 1 To 4
                        objView.GetAllowedElements
i,objStart,objEnd,arrElements
                        strText = strText & ListArray(arrElements) & "------
---------" & chr(13)
                Next

                msgbox strText
        End Sub

        Function ListArray(arrIn)
                dim strText

                If IsArray(arrIn) Then
                        dim i

                        For i = 0 To UBound(arrIn)
                                strText = strText & arrIn(i) & chr(13)
                        Next
                End If

                ListArray = strText
        End Function
```

attachCallBack

See also

Declaration: attachCallBack(*bstrName* as String,*varCallBack* as Variant)

Description

The Document Editor PlugIn provides events which can be handled using custom callback functions. All event handlers take no parameters and any returned value will be ignored. To retrieve information when a specific event is raised you have to read the according properties of the event object.

List of currently available events:

```
ondragover
ondrop
onkeydown
onkeyup
onkeypressed
onmousemove
onbuttonup
onbuttondown
oncontextmenu
oneditpaste
oneditcut
oneditcopy
oneditclear
```

JavaScript example:

```
// somwhere in your script:
objPlugIn.attachCallBack("ondragover",OnDragOver);
objPlugIn.attachCallBack("ondrop",OnDrop);

// event handlers
function OnDragOver()
{
        if(    !objPlugIn.event.dataTransfer.ownDrag &&
               objPlugIn.event.dataTransfer.type == "TEXT"))
        {
               objPlugIn.event.dataTransfer.dropEffect = 1;
               objPlugIn.event.cancelBubble = true;
        }
}

// OnDrop() replaces the complete text value of the XML
// element with the selection from the drag operation
function OnDrop()
{
        var objTransfer = objPlugIn.event.dataTransfer;

        if(    !objTransfer.ownDrag &&
               (objTransfer.type == "TEXT"))
               objPlugIn.event.srcElement.TextValue =
objTransfer.getData();
        }
```

event

See also

Declaration: event as DocEditEvent

Description

The event property holds a DocEditEvent object which contains informations about the current event.

DocEditSelection

See also

Properties

Start
StartTextPosition
End
EndTextPosition

Start

See also

Declaration: Start as XMLData

Description

XML element where the current selection starts.

StartTextPosition

See also

Declaration: StartTextPosition as long

Description

Position in DocEditSelection.Start.TextValue where the selection starts.

End

See also

Declaration: End as XMLData

Description

XML element where the current selection ends.

EndTextPosition

See also

Declaration: EndTextPosition as long

Description

Position in DocEditSelection.End.TextValue where the selection ends.

DocEditEvent

See also

Properties

altKey
altLeft
ctrlKey
ctrlLeft
shiftKey
shiftLeft

keyCode
repeat

button

clientX
clientY

dataTransfer

srcElement
fromElement

propertyName

cancelBubble
returnValue

type

Description

DocEditEvent interface.

altKey

See also

Declaration: altKey as Boolean

Description

True if the right ALT key is pressed.

altLeft

See also

Declaration: altLeft as Boolean

Description

True if the left AI T key is pressed.

ctrlKey

See also

Declaration: ctrlKey as Boolean

Description

True if the right CTRL key is pressed.

ctrlLeft

See also

Declaration: ctrlLeft as Boolean

Description

True if the left CTRL key is pressed.

shiftKey

See also

Declaration: shiftKey as Boolean

Description

True if the right SHIFT key is pressed.

shiftLeft

See also

Declaration: shiftLeft as Boolean

Description

True if the left SHIFT key is pressed.

keyCode

See also

Declaration: keyCode as long

Description

Keycode of the currently pressed key.

This property is read-write.

repeat

See also

Declaration: repeat as Boolean

Description

True if the onkeydown event is repeated.

button

See also

Declaration: button as long

Description

Specifies which mouse button is pressed:

0	No button is pressed.
1	Left button is pressed.
2	Right button is pressed.
3	Left and right buttons are both pressed.
4	Middle button is pressed.
5	Left and middle buttons both are pressed.
6	Right and middle buttons are both pressed.
7	All three buttons are pressed.

The onbuttondown and onbuttonup events set the button value in different ways. The onbuttonup event just sets the value for the button which has been released and raised the up event regardless which buttons are also pressed at the moment.

clientX

See also

Declaration: clientX as long

Description

X value of the current mouse position in client coordinates.

clientY

See also

Declaration: clientY as long

Description

Y value of the current mouse position in client coordinates.

dataTransfer

See also

Declaration: dataTransfer as Variant

Description

property dataTransfer

srcElement

See also

Declaration: srcElement as Variant

Description

Element which fires the current event.

This is usually an XMLData object.

fromElement

See also

Declaration: fromElement as Variant

Description

Currently no event sets this property.

propertyName

See also

Declaration: propertyName as String

Description

Currently no event sets this property.

cancelBubble

See also

Declaration: cancelBubble as Boolean

Description

Set cancelBubble to TRUE if the default event handler should not be called.

returnValue

See also

Declaration: returnValue as Variant

Description

Use returnValue to set a return value for your event handler.

type

See also

Declaration: type as String

Description

Currently no event sets this property.

DocEditDataTransfer

See also

Methods

getData

Properties

dropEffect
ownDrag
type

Description

DocEditDataTransfer interface.

getData

See also

Declaration: getData as Variant

Description

getData gets the actual data associated with this dataTransfer object. See also
DocEditDataTransfer.type for more informations.

dropEffect

See also

Declaration: dropEffect as long

Description

The property stores the drop effect from the default event handler. You can set the drop effect
if you change this value and set DocEditEvent.cancelBubble to TRUE.

ownDrag

See also

Declaration: ownDrag as Boolean

Description

The property is TRUE if the current dragging source comes from inside of the Document Editor
view.

type

See also

Declaration: type as String

Description

Holds the type of the data you get with the DocEditDataTransfer.getData method.

Currently supported data types are:

OWN	data from Document Editor PlugIn itself
TEXT	plain text
UNICODETEXT	plain text as UNICODE

XMLSpyXMLLoadSave

See also

Properties

String
URL

Description

The XMLSpyXMLLoadSave object is used to set the source for the files you need to load. You can either set the content directly via the String property or as an external location via the URL property.

See also XMLSpyDocumentEditor.SchemaLoadObject, XMLSpyDocumentEditor.DesignDataLoadObject and XMLSpyDocumentEditor.XMLDataLoadObject for more informations about how to use them.

String

See also

Declaration: String as String

Description

You can use this property to set the XML structure from a string. The URL property of the object must be empty if you want to use this property.

URL

See also

Declaration: URL as String

Description

The property should contain a valid URL for the load or save operation. Currently supported HTTP protocols are http, https, ftp and gopher.

Part **VII**

8   XSLT Designer

XSLT Designer converts XML documents into HTML without you having to know a single thing about XSLT "programming!". The XSLT Stylesheet is automatically created for you!

There are only a few steps:
- Load the Schema that forms the basis of your HTML document
- Assign a working XML document which provides preview data
- Drag and drop the specific schema elements into XSLT Designer window
- View the results in the integrated Internet Explorer window

The XSLT Stylesheet is automatically created for you!

XSLT Designer is available in two flavors:

- As a stand-alone product which allows you to create XSLT stylesheets
- As an administration module/tool which allows you to prepare XSLT Templates for further use with Document Editor.

Overview

XSLT Designer has three main areas: the two panes on the left and the main window at right.

- The **top left** pane displays a tree view of currently loaded schema file. The schema name and path is displayed in the top line.

- The **bottom left** pane (the HTML attributes window) consists of several tabs, and allows you to assign html properties to the elements or attributes in the main window.

- The **main window** is where you design your XSLT template. You can also view the automatically generated XSLT style sheet and preview the transformation results in Internet Explorer in this window.

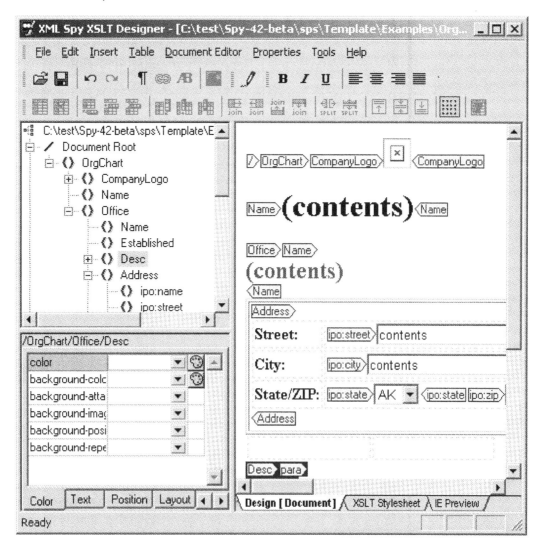

Symbols and icons

XSLT Designer uses easily recognizable symbols to display the various schema elements in the tree view, and uses tag symbols for the XSLT elements in the Design view.

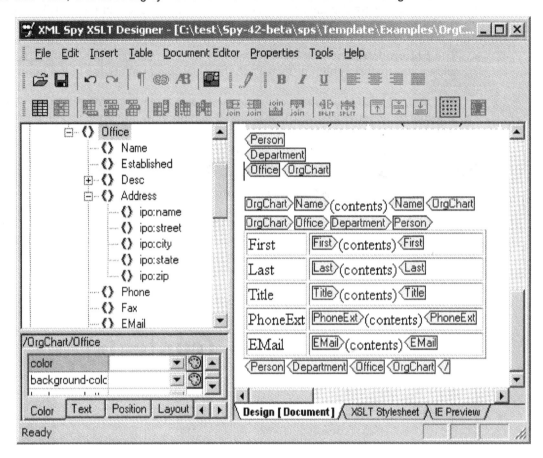

Tree view symbols and icons

Schema name and folder

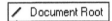

Document root.
All elements inserted from below the Document root (but not under the Global Templates) into the Design view, become local elements. Any formatting applied to them in the Design view, only takes effect in this document instance. The Design view tab contains the text **Design [Document]**.

Global templates are defined using the elements under the Global Templates element.

Element

Attribute.

Element with child/sub elements.

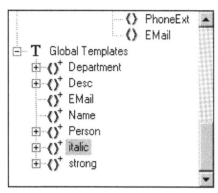

Global templates, these are equivalent to global elements in a schema.

Use Global Templates as text modifiers for the moment e.g. bold, italic or paragraph.

Formatting Global Elements:
1. Click the global template you want to apply formatting to (italic. in this case).
    The Design view now displays the italic. template. The tab also contains the name of
    the global template **Design [italic]**.

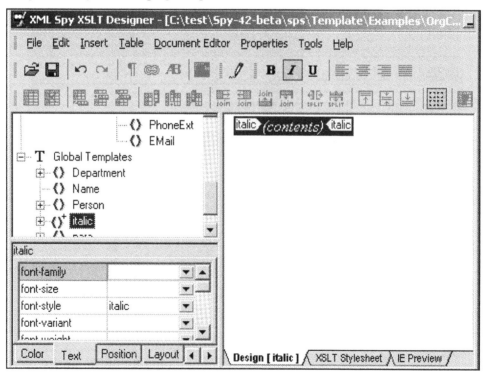

2. Define the attributes the global element is to have using the HTML properties window
    (font-style = italic).

Wherever this element appears (or is applied to) text in Designer view, it will appear in italic.

3. (Clicking the italic icon in the title bar in **Document Editor** inserts this element and changes the text to italic.)

Design view symbols and icons

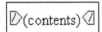

Root element tags.

The **(contents)** "text" between the two tags in the Design view, is the symbol for an XML data **placeholder**. The placeholder is filled with data when you switch to the IE Preview tab. The data is supplied by the XML file assigned to the currently visible schema visible in the tree view. Use the menu option **File | Assign working XML file...** to assign the XML file to the schema.

To delete a placeholder:
1. Click the placeholder and press the keyboard Del. key.

   This deletes the placeholder in the Design tab, and causes the XML data to be suppressed in the IE Preview.

To (re) insert a placeholder:
1. Click between the two tags where you want to insert the placeholder.
2. Click right (at the cursor position) to open the context menu, and select "Insert Contents".

   The placeholder is inserted at the cursor position.

Start and end tags of the Person element, expanded. The parent tags of the Person element (Altova) are also included.

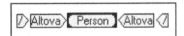

Person element tag, contracted. To expand or contract tags, double click the specific tag.

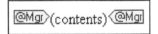

Manager attribute, start and end tag.

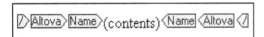

"Contents", placeholder for XML data.

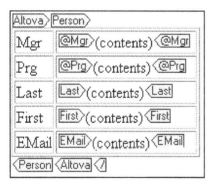

Person element inserted as a table containing both elements and attributes.

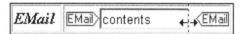

Email element "input field". Clicking right on the vertical border at the right allows you to directly change the size of this field by dragging with the mouse.

Formatting tables:
XSLT Designer allows you to directly format tables (as well as the input field) using the mouse.

- Place the cursor over any table or cell border and drag when the mouse pointer changes to the double headed arrow.

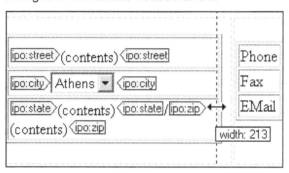

The moment you click and drag, the cell or table dimensions appear in a popup allowing you to precisely define its size.

You can also use the same method on table borders that have been hidden, by clicking the View table cell bounds icon, ⊞ and dragging on the dashed border lines that then become visible.

Marking and applying formatting in tables:
XSLT Designer offers you many ways to format your table data.
- You can apply formatting (bold etc.) to **parts** of a table eg. only some of the column headers, some cells etc., by just marking them and applying bold or any other HTML formatting for example.
- Using **drag left** allows you to **mark multiple cells** and apply formatting.
- Clicking an element tag marks the whole element, to which you can then apply the specific formatting. In the diagram above, clicking the <Altova><**Person**> element would mark the whole table.

Designer Tutorial

The aim of this tutorial is to create an XSLT stylesheet for a company which has two offices, the main US office and the EU dependency.

What the XSLT stylesheet should contain:
- The name of the Document, Orgchart in this case
- The name of the regional office
- The address data of each of the regional offices
- The office departments and a list of employees in each department.

Please note:
Designer supports **unlimited undo**, you can always go back and retrace your steps!

Creating an XSLT Stylesheet

Starting XSLT designer:

1. Start XSLT Designer by double clicking on the XSLT Designer icon.

   XSLT Designer

   You are presented with an empty environment.

2. Select the menu option **File | Open** and opon the **OrgChart.xsd** schema file supplied with XSLT Designer (in the **Examples** folder).

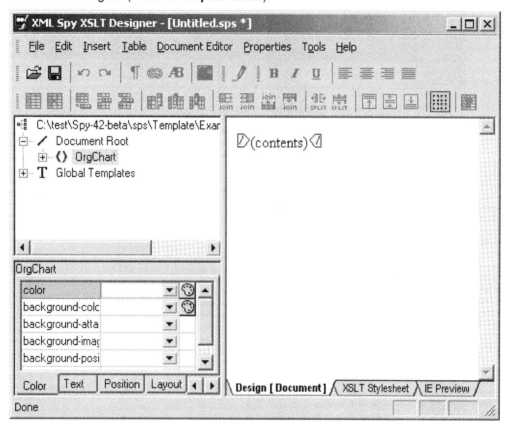

The OrgChart schema is the basis of your stylesheet. The elements and attributes it contains are used to create the XSLT stylesheet.

3. Select the menu option **File | Assign working XML file...** and open the **OrgChart.xml** file supplied with XSLT Designer.

   This file supplies the XML data through which you preview the XSLT Stylesheet. The file and folder name of the XML file now appear in the title bar.

Inserting a schema element into the Design view:

1. Click on the **plus** icon of OrgChart element in the schema tree view, to see the sub-elements.

2. Click the **Name** element and drag it into the Design window. Drop it just after the (contents) text to the left of the root element, end tag.
   A popup window appears at this point.

3. Click the **Create Contents** option in the popup.

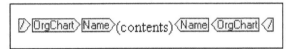

The start and end tags of the Altova and Name elements are inserted. The (Contents) text, is a **placeholder** in the Design view and is replaced by XML data in the IE Preview tab.

Previewing the XSLT stylesheet:

*   Click on the IE Preview tab to display the resulting HTML output of the XSLT stylesheet.
    In this case the orgchart title is displayed.

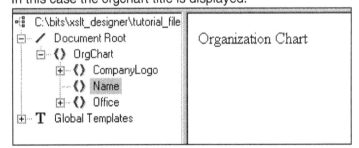

To view the XSLT stylesheet code:

*   Click the XSLT stylesheet tab to see the automatically generated XSLT code.

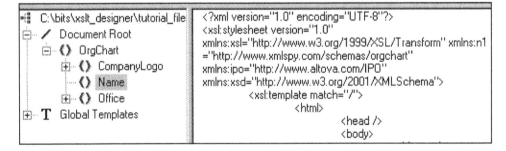

*   Click the **Design[Document]** tab, to return to the Design view.

The XSLT stylesheet can be saved by selecting the menu command **File | Save Generated XSLT file...**

Saving XSLT Designer files:

- Select the menu option **File | Save as**, and enter a name for the file (XSLT-tutorial). The file name you enter also appears in the title bar.

  The "Save" command saves the **XSLT Designer file** as a structure file, or template, (extension ***.sps**). The .sps file saves all the data visible in the Designor window, as well as the associated working XML and Schema/DTD files.

Please note:

Only template files (all *.sps files) saved from within XSLT Designer, can be edited in XML Spy Document Editor!

Inserting tables and applying HTML attributes

Applying HTML attributes to an element:

1. Click the **(Contents)** placeholder to mark it.
    The lower left pane (HTML attributes window) now shows the name of the element/attribute and displays all the HTML attributes available that can be assigned to the element. You might have to drag up the window divider to see more of the attributes.
2. Click the **Text tab**, then the **font-size** combo box and select "**large**".
    The (contents) placeholder is updated immediately, and displays the HTML attributes you select.
3. Click to set the text cursor after the Name **end** tag, and hit the Enter key.
    This moves the OrgChart end tag, to the next line.

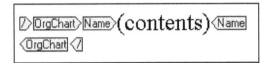

4. Click the plus icon next to the Office element (in the tree view) to expand the sub-elements.

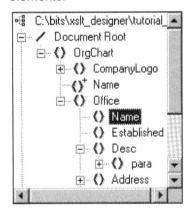

5. Click the **Name** element (under the Office element) **drag** it into the Design view, and drop it in front of the OrgChart end tag.
6. Select the **Create Paragraph** item from the popup menu.
    The start and end tags are now displayed over three lines. This is the visual indication that a paragraph is to follow each of the XML data instances in the IE Preview.

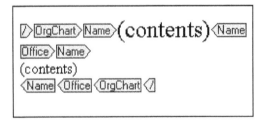

7. Click the **(contents)** placeholder and select "**medium**" from the font-size combo box in the HTML attributes window.
8. Click the **Color** tab in the HTML attributes window and select "**red**" from the color combo box. (Click somewhere else in the Design window to deselect the contents placeholder).

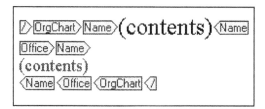

9. Click the **IE Preview** tab to see the changes made to the stylesheet.

Organization Chart
Nanonull, Inc.
Nanonull Partners, Inc.

10. Click the Design [Document] tab to return to the Design view.

Inserting fixed and dynamic tables:
1. Set the text cursor between the Name and Office **end** tags.
2. Select the menu option **Insert | Insert Table**.
3. Define a **table** of 1 row by 2 columns in the Insert Table dialog box, click OK to confirm the selections.
   A standard HTML table is inserted between the two tags. This is a fixed table and does not change with the underlying XML data.

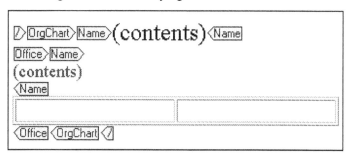

4. Place the text cursor on the **Address** tag in the tree view, and drag the Address element into the first cell of the table.
5. Select **Create Table** from the popup. This opens the "Create dynamic table" dialog box.
6. Click the "**ipo:name**" entry in the Show columns list box, to deselect it.

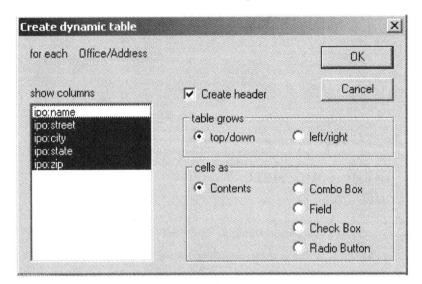

7. Click the Table grows... "**left/right**" radio button, and confirm with OK.
    This inserts a **dynamic table** within the table we just created. Dynamic tables adjust their size to the underlying XML data.

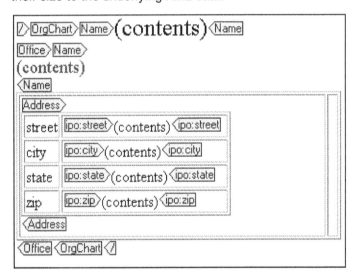

8. Click in the empty column at the far right, and select the menu option **Insert | Insert Table**. Define the table as having 3 rows and 2 columns.
9. Click in the first column (of the new table) and enter Phone, Fax and E-mail in each row.

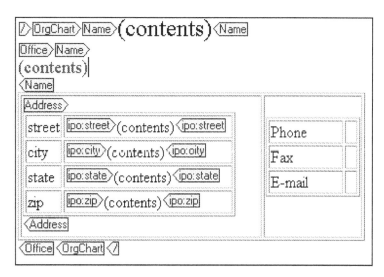

10. Click the **Phone** element in the tree view, drag it into the Design view, and drop it next to the Phone cell. Select **Create Contents** from the popup.

11. Use the same method to insert the Fax and Email elements from the tree view into the respective cells of the table. Select "Create Contents" in both cases.

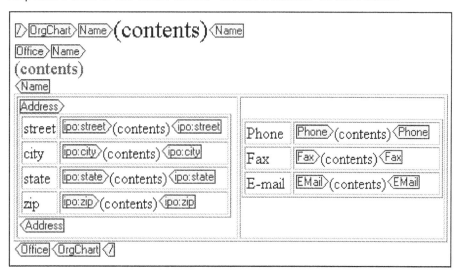

12. Click the **IE Preview tab**, to see the progress so far, then switch back to the Design tab so we can continue designing the Orgchart.

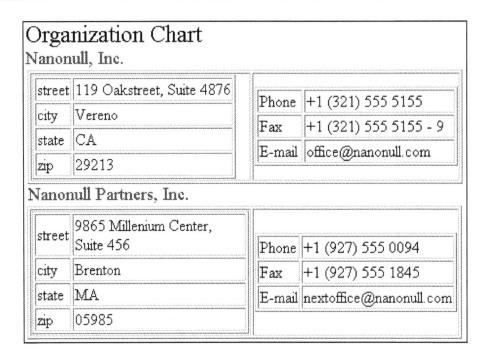

Not the most beautiful table layout, I am sure you will agree! Lets try and make it somewhat more pleasing to the eye.

Joining cells and changing tag types:
1. Click in the **zip** cell and select the menu option **Table | Join cell above**.
   Do the same thing for the **zip** row label.
2. Set the text cursor between the state and zip text, and enter a forward slash character (/). Enter the same character after the **ipo:state** end tag.

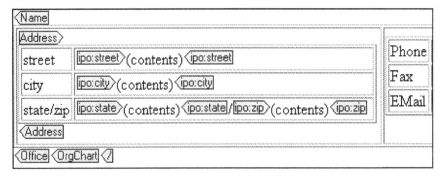

3. Right click the **ipo:city** tag, and select **Change to combo box** from the popup menu.
4. Click the "+" button, and double click in the Visible Entry field.
5. Enter a city name, e.g. Athens and hit TAB.
6. Enter the text or value that is to appear in the XML document, hit Enter to confirm. The XML Value can of course differ from the text in the Visible Entry field.
7. Click the "+" button again and enter the name of a second city (e.g. Paris).

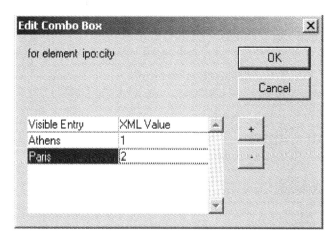

8. Click OK to confirm these entries and close the dialog box.

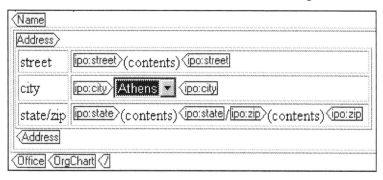

Please note:
    To edit the combo box settings: right click the combo box (not the ipo:city tags), and
    select "Edit properties..." from the popup menu.

Formatting tables:
    1. Click the **Address** tag at the top of the table, and select the menu option **Table | Table
        properties**.
    2. Click the **border** combo box, and select **0** from the drop down list, confirm the changes
        with OK.

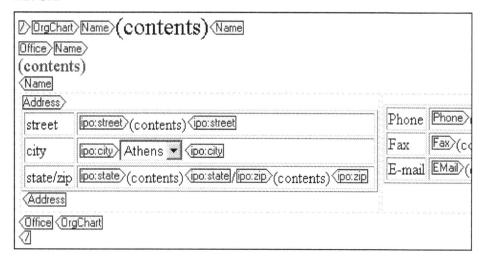

This removes the table border from the Design view, as well as in the IE Preview

window.
The table border is now displayed as a dashed line.
This enables you to click the border and resize it if you wish. Click the "View table cell

bounds" icon 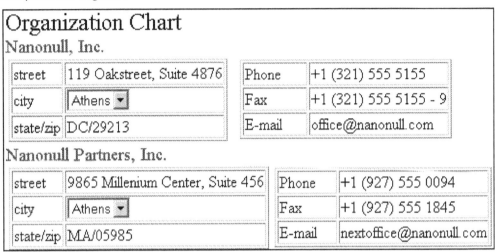 to switch the dashed line on or off.

3.   Click the **IE Preview** tab to see the changes, then click the Design tab so we can complete our orgchart.

Organization Chart

Nanonull, Inc.

street	119 Oakstreet, Suite 4876	Phone	+1 (321) 555 5155
city	Athens ▾	Fax	+1 (321) 555 5155 - 9
state/zip	DC/29213	E-mail	office@nanonull.com

Nanonull Partners, Inc.

street	9865 Millenium Center, Suite 456	Phone	+1 (927) 555 0094
city	Athens ▾	Fax	+1 (927) 555 1845
state/zip	MA/05985	E-mail	nextoffice@nanonull.com

Please note:

The City combo box entries you define here, can be selected when this template is opened and completed in Document Editor, the IE Preview displays the currently defined entries. The **XML Values** defined in the Edit Combo box, are what actually appear in the template document in Document Editor (in this case 1 for Athens and 2 for Paris).

Completing the stylesheet
Inserting company description, departments and the people they contain:
1. Set the text cursor just **in front** of the **Office** end tag and hit the Enter key (you can also use the keyboard arrow keys, to move the cursor in the design view).

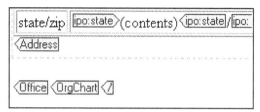

This inserts a space between the end of the table and the end tags, and also creates a paragraph in the IE Preview.
2. Click on the **Desc** tag in the tree view, drag it to the Design view and drop it in front of the Office end tag.
3. Select **Create Contents** from the popup menu.

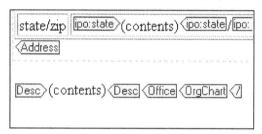

4. Click the **Para** tag in the tree view (expand the Desc. tag), drag it to the Design view and drop it in front of the **Desc** end tag. Select **Create Paragraph** from the popup menu.

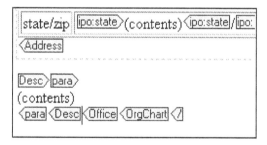

Please note:
Inserting the **para** (graph) tag in XSLT Designer, makes it possible to add a new paragraph(s) to the Description text (using the Enter key) in **Document Editor**. The para start and end tags, are automatically inserted when the Enter key is pressed in Document Editor.

Deleting paragraphs in Document editor is achieved using the Backspace and Del. keys.

5. Click between the **Desc** and **Office** end tags, and hit Enter to insert a paragraph.

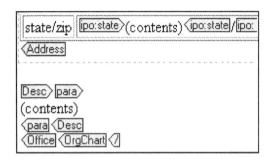

6. Click the **IE Preview** tab to see the results, and then switch back to the Design view.

Each company now has its own address data and description text.

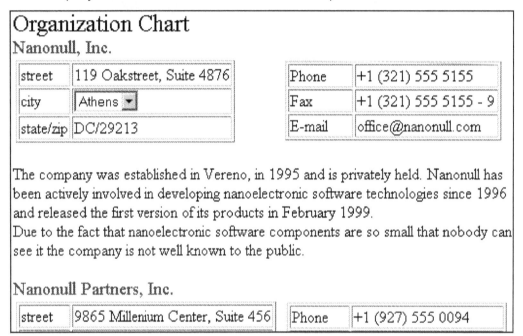

Inserting departments and people in a dynamic table:
*   Click the plus icon next to the Department element, to see the sub elements.

1. Click the **Name** element (of the **Department** parent element), drag it to the Design view, and drop it after the **Desc** end tag.
2. Select **Create Paragraph** from the popup menu that opens automatically.

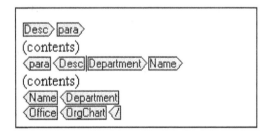

3. Place the text cursor between the Desc **end tag** and the Department **start tag**, and hit the Enter key.

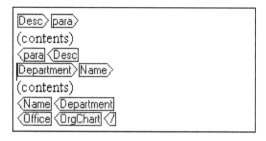

If you check the IE Preview, you will see that all the department names have been inserted after the company description text.

The company was established in Vereno, in 1995 and is
has been actively involved in developing nanoelectronic ş
since 1996 and released the first version of its products i
the fact that nanoelectronic software components are so
it the company is not well known to the public.

Administration
Marketing
Engineering
IT & Technical Support

4. Click the **Department | Name** (Contents) placeholder, and select **bold** from the **font-weight** combo box in the Text tab of the HTML attributes window.
5. Click the (Department) **Person** element in the tree view, **drag** it into the Design view and drop it between the Name and Department end tags.
6. Select **Create Table** from the popup menu that opens at this point, and confirm with OK.

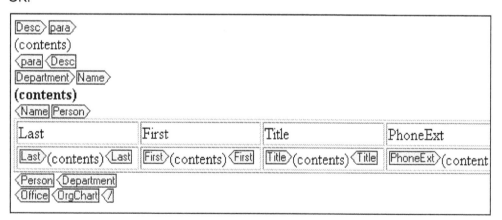

7. Click between the **Person** and **Department** end tags, and hit the Enter key.
8. Click the **IE Preview** tab to see the results, and then return to the Design view.

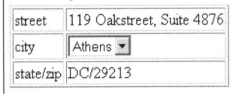

Organization Chart
Nanonull, Inc.

street	119 Oakstreet, Suite 4876
city	Athens ▾
state/zip	DC/29213

Phone	+1 (321) 555 5155
Fax	+1 (321) 555 5155 - 9
E-mail	office@nanonull.com

The company was established in Vereno, in 1995 and is privately held. Nanonull has actively involved in developing nanoelectronic software technologies since 1996 and released the first version of its products in February 1999.
Due to the fact that nanoelectronic software components are so small that nobody ca it the company is not well known to the public.

Administration

First	Last	Title	PhoneExt	EMail
Vernon	Callaby	Office Manager	582	v.callaby@nanonull.com
Frank	Further	Accounts Receivable	471	f.further@nanonull.com
Loby	Matise	Accounting Manager	963	l.matise@nanonull.com

Marketing

First	Last	Title	PhoneExt	EMail
Joe	Firstbread	Marketing Manager Europe	621	j.firstbread@nanonull.com

Changing Table properties:
1. Click in the **table header** and select the menu option **Table | Table properties...**
2. Click the **Row** tab and select **aqua** from the **bgcolor** combo box, click on OK to confirm.
3. Click in one of the table body cells and use the same method to color the rows yellow.
4. Use the same method to change the **border** combo box entry to 0 (zero), in the Table tab.

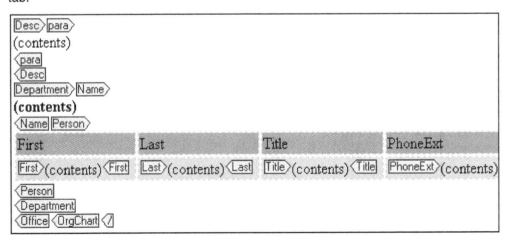

5. Click the **IE Preview** tab to see the results, and then save your work using the **File |**

Save menu entry.

Organization Chart
Nanonull, Inc.

street	119 Oakstreet, Suite 4876
city	Athens ▾
state/zip	DC/29213

Phone	+1 (321) 555 515
Fax	+1 (321) 555 515
E-mail	office@nanonull.c

The company was established in Vereno, in 1995 and is privately held. Nanonull ha
actively involved in developing nanoelectronic software technologies since 1996 an
released the first version of its products in February 1999.
Due to the fact that nanoelectronic software components are so small that nobody c
it the company is not well known to the public.

Administration

First	Last	Title	PhoneExt	EMail
Vernon	Callaby	Office Manager	582	v.callaby@nanonull.com
Frank	Further	Accounts Receivable	471	f.further@nanonull.com
Loby	Matise	Accounting Manager	963	l.matise@nanonull.com

Marketing

First	Last	Title	PhoneExt	EMail
Joe	Firstbread	Marketing Manager Europe	621	j.firstbread@nanonull.com
Susi	Sanna	Art Director	753	s.sanna@nanonull.com

To save the generated XSLT Stylesheet:
- Select the menu option **File | Save Generated XSLT file...**

The generated XSLT can now be used to create HTML output for your XML files. If you want to edit the XSLT file you can open it in XML Spy at any time.

XSLT Designer Reference

The reference section contains a complete description of all XSLT Designer windows and menu commands.

Menus and Dialogs

This section describes the menu, dialog box and context menu options.

File

The File menu contains all commands relevant to manipulating files in the order common to most Windows software products.

Open

The "Open..." command allows you to open an XML schema, DTD or .sps file. The familiar Windows "Open" dialog is opened and allows you to select one of these file types.

You may get an error message if your file is either not well-formed or invalid, in this case switch to XML Spy and try to resolve the problem there.

Opening a .sps file displays the tags in the Design view, and automatically loads all the XML files associated with this file (Schema/DTD and XML document instance).

Save

The "Save" command saves the currently open XSLT Designer file as a structure file. The file type extension is *.sps.

The .sps file saves all the data visible in XSLT Designer, as well as the associated XML and Schema/DTD files.

> Please note:
> Only template files (all *.sps files) saved from within XSLT Designer, can be edited in XML Spy Document Editor!

Save as...

The "Save As..." command shows the familiar Windows "Save as..." dialog and prompts for the name and location of the .sps file to be saved.

> Please note:
> Only template files (all *.sps files) saved from within XSLT Designer, can be edited in XML Spy Document Editor!

Assign working XML file...

The "Assign working XML file" command assigns an existing XML file to the currently open DTD or schema file.

The XML file is used to preview the XSLT file using the XML data. Clicking the IE Preview tab without having assigned an XML file, opens a message box prompting you to select one.

> Please note:
> The name and folder of the XML working file is displayed in the **title bar** of XSLT Designer! If a file has not been assigned, only the *.sps name is displayed.

Save generated XSLT file...

The "Save generated XSLT file" command allows you to save the current version of the XSLT file visible in the XSLT Stylesheet tab.

Most recently used files

The list of most recently used files, shows the file name and path information for the nine most recently used files, which you can select with the mouse.

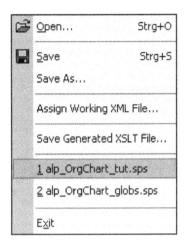

To access these files using the **keyboard**, press:
ALT+F,1 to open the File menu, and select the first file in the list.

Exit

The "Exit" command is used to quit XSLT Designer. If you have an open file with unsaved changes, you will be prompted to save these changes.

Edit

The Edit menu contains the undo and redo commands which allow you to discard or restore your previous actions.

Undo

          Hotkey: **CTRL + Z**

The "Undo" command contains support for unlimited levels of Undo! Every action can be undone and it is possible to undo one command after another. The Undo history is retained after using the "Save" command, enabling you go back to a state the document was in before you saved your changes.

Redo

          Hotkey: **CTRL + Y**

The "Redo" command allows you to redo previously undone commands – thereby giving you a complete history of the work you have completed. You can step back and forward through this history using the Undo and Redo commands.

Insert

The Insert menu provides commands enabling you to insert various items into the Design view.

Image...

The "Image..." command allows you to insert a .GIF, .JPG or .PNG graphics into the Design tab.

Paragraph

The "Paragraph" command encloses the selected element in a paragraph.

Table...

The "Table..." command inserts an empty table into the design tab. A dialog box opens allowing you to define the size of the table. The inserted table is of a **fixed type** and does not automatically change size with varying XML data in the IE Preview.

To insert a **dynamic table** please see the section **Context menus | Create... context menu | Create table.**

List...

The "List..." command inserts a list bullet for each of the elements or attributes. A dialog box opens, allowing you to specify how many list instances you want to insert.

Insert Contents

The **(contents)** "text" between the two tags is the Design view symbol for an XML data **placeholder**.

The placeholder is filled with data when you switch to the IE Preview tab. The data is supplied by the XML file assigned to the currently visible schema visible in the tree view. Use the menu option **File | Assign working XML file...** to assign the XML file to the schema.

To (re) insert a placeholder:
1. Click between the two tags where you want to insert the placeholder.
2. Click right (at the cursor position) to open the context menu, and select "Insert Contents".

The placeholder is inserted at the cursor position.

To delete a placeholder:
1. Click the placeholder and press the keyboard Del. key.

   This deletes the placeholder in the Design tab, and causes the XML data to be suppressed in the IE Preview.

Link to

The "Link to" command/icon allows you to define a hypertext link from an element in XSLT Designer.

E.g.
1. Double click the text (free standing or table header text) from where you want start.
2. Click the **Link to...** icon in the title bar.
3. Enter the address you want to navigate to e.g. http://www.altova.com
4. Click the **IE Preview** tab, and then click the header to jump to the link destination. The altova home page now appears in the IE Preview window.
5. Hit the keyboard Backspace key, to return to the transformed XML document.

Table

The Table menu provides commands enabling you to change table characteristics; append, insert, delete and join rows and columns. The table commands available to you depend on the type of table and the current cursor position.

To change table characteristics:
- You must have previously inserted a table using the **Insert | Table** menu command (a fixed table), or
- Dragged an element into the Design window and selected **Create Table** from the popup menu (a dynamic table).
- Click in a table cell and select the specific command from the menu or toolbar.

Navigating in tables:
Use the keyboard Tab as well as the arrow keys, to navigate the table cells.

Adding text in tables:
Text can be entered in any table cell, this includes the table headers as well.

Delete table

The "Delete table" command deletes the currently active table.

Append row

The "Append row" command appends a row to the end of the currently active table.

Append column

The "Append column" command appends a column to the end of the currently active table.

Insert row

The "Insert row" command inserts a row above the current cursor position in the currently active table.

Insert column

The "Insert column" command inserts a column to the left of the current cursor position in the currently active table.

Delete row

The "Delete row" command deletes the row where the cursor is currently positioned.

Delete column

The "Delete column" command deletes the column where the cursor is currently positioned.

Join cell left

The "Join cell left" command joins the current cell (current cursor position) with the cell to the left. The tags of both cells remain in the new cell, the column headers remain unchanged.

Join cell right

The "Join cell right" command joins the current cell (current cursor position) with the cell to the right. The tags of both cells remain in the new cell, the column headers remain unchanged.

Join cell below

The "Join cell below" command joins the current cell (current cursor position) with the cell below. The tags of both cells remain in the new cell, the column headers remain unchanged.

Join cell above

The "Join cell above" command joins the current cell (current cursor position) with the cell above. The tags of both cells remain in the new cell, the column headers remain unchanged.

Split cell Horizontally

The "Split cell Horizontally" command creates a new cell to the right of the currently active cell. The size of both cells, is now the same as the original cell.

Split cell Vertically

The "Split cell Vertically" command creates a new cell below the currently active cell.

Table properties

The "Table properties" command opens the Table Properties dialog box. This allows you to customize your table.

Cell content alignment

These commands allow you to format the cell content of individual cells in a table.

Align Top
This command aligns the cell contents to the top of the cell.

Center vertically
This command centers the cell contents.

Cell bottom
This command aligns the cell contents to the bottom of the cell.

View table cell boundaries

This command displays or hides table boundaries in the Design [Document] tab.

To display the table boundaries:
1. Set the table **border** to **0** (zero) in the Table Properties dialog box, in the Table tab.
2. Click the View table cell bounds icon.
   This switches the dashed table borders of all tables on or off.

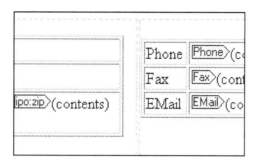

This method allows you to see hidden table borders and easily change the table size using the mouse.

- Move the mouse pointer over the dashed line, until the double-headed arrow appears, then click and drag the mouse. A popup appears showing the dimensions while you drag the mouse.

Document Editor

The Document Editor menu allows you to define special settings for further processing of the resulting HTML document with the **Document Editor**. These settings only apply when using the Document Editor!

Node Settings...

The "Node Settings..." command allows you to define the properties of each node i.e. element/attribute in the Design view, for further processing in Document Editor.

To define node settings:
1. Click a node start or end tag (element/attribute tag).
2. Select the menu option **Document Editor | Node Settings...** (or right click the tag and select "Editor Node settings..." from the popup menu).

   Note: You have to click a tag to be able to edit the node settings, clicking the (Contents) placeholder does not make this possible.

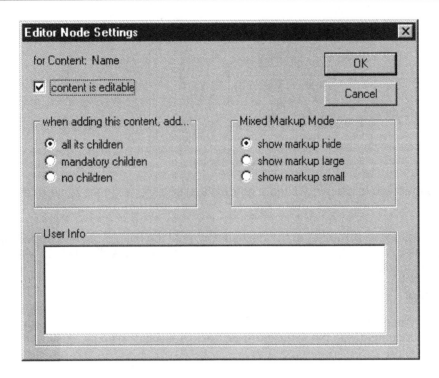

"Content is editable"
This check box lets you define if the **XML content** of this node can be edited in the Document Editor.

"When adding content, add..."
This group lets you define if existing child nodes are to be added, when you add this node in the Document Editor.

"Mixed markup mode"
This group lets you define if, and how, you want to see the markup tags in the Document Editor.

"User Info"
Text entered in this text box, appears as a tool tip hint when the mouse pointer is placed over the node in the Document Editor. Use this text box to enter explanatory text or hints on how the document is to be filled in. E.g. The Office node could have the explanatory text, "Enter the office name here!"

Text State icons

The "Text State icons" command allows you to define an icon for each global element (that can contain text) present in the schema. A global element is one that appears under the "Global Templates" element in the schema tree view. You have total freedom to apply any styles, formatting etc. to XML documents using this command.

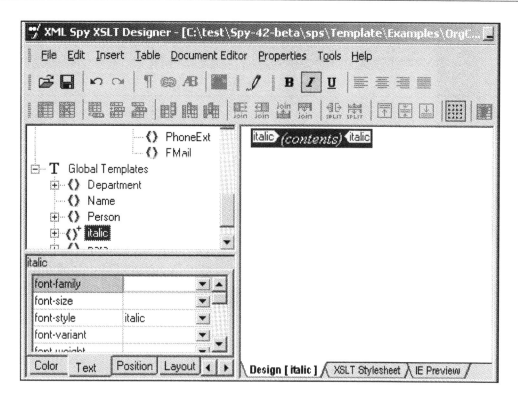

Defining text state icons

1. Make sure the element type you want to define as an icon is available as a global element in the schema (italic). The entry will be visible under Global Templates in the schema tree view in XSLT Designer.
2. Click the **italic** element under Global Templates, and define the attributes you want it to have in the HTML attributes window e.g. font-style = italic.
3. Select the menu option **Document Editor | Text State Icons**.

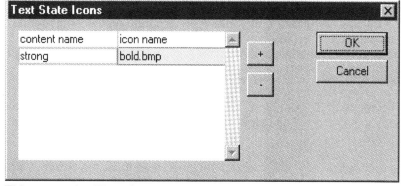

   This opens the "Text State Icons" dialog box.
4. Click the "+" button to add a new line.
5. Click the combo box that is made available at this point.
   The drop down list contains all the elements that can contain text in the Global Templates list.

© 2002 Altova Ges.m.b.H

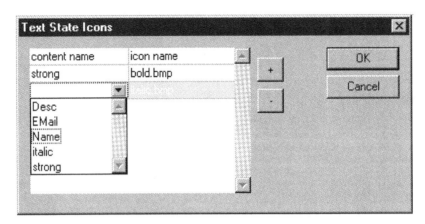

6. Click the **italic** entry and confirm with Enter.
7. Double click in the **icon name** column, and enter the name of the icon that should represent the attribute e.g. italic.bmp, in the Document Editor toolbar.

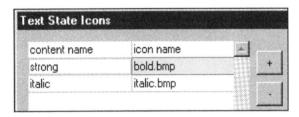

8. Click OK to confirm.

Making Text state icons available to Document Editor
1. Design the icon you want to represent "italic" in your graphic program (as a windows .BMP), and give it the same name as entered in the Text State Icon dialog box (italic.bmp)
2. Place the italic.bmp in the installation folder of XML Spy which is your installation folder +...+**Altova\XML Spy Suite\sps\Picts.**
3. Start XML Spy Document Editor and open or create a new template file (*.sps). The italic.bmp icon you defined is now visible in a toolbar.
4. Mark some text in the Document Editor and click the italic icon to apply the formatting.

Assign Template XML file

The "Assign Template XML" command allows you to define which XML file is to act as a template when you select the **File | New** menu option in the Document Editor and select a template file (*.sps).

The file you select can be any XML file and does not have to be the currently loaded one, but must conform to the schema currently in use.

Properties

The Properties menu allows you to change the properties of the various objects in XSLT Designer.

Page

The "Page" command allows you to define the current page properties. The properties defined here take precedence over the individual HTML element settings.

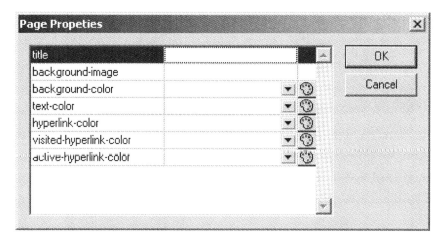

Table

The "Table properties" command opens the Table Properties dialog box. This allows you to define the specific table properties.

Selected object

The "Selected object" command, opens the dialog box of the specific object you select. This command only becomes active if you select a **combo box**, **check box** or **radio button**.

Tools

The Tools command allows you to select the customize option, from where you can customize XSLT Designer.

Customize

The customize command lets you customize XSLT Designer to suit your personal needs.

Commands

The Commands tab allows you customize your menus or toolbars.

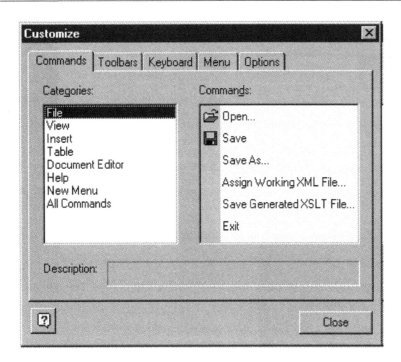

To add a command to a toolbar or menu:
1. Open this dialog using **View | Customize.**
2. Select the command category in the Categories list box. The commands available appear in the Commands list box.
3. Click on a command in the commands list box and drag "it" to an to an existing menu or toolbar.
4. An **I**-beam appears when you place the cursor over a valid position to drop the command.
5. Release the mouse button at the position you want to insert the command.

•   A small button icon appears at the tip of mouse pointer when you drag a command. The check mark below the pointer means that the command cannot be dropped at the current cursor position.
•   The check mark disappears wherever it is possible to drop the command (over a tool bar or menu).
•   Placing the cursor over a menu when dragging, opens it, allowing you to insert the command anywhere in the menu.
•   Commands can be placed in menus or tool bars. If you created you own toolbar you can populate it with your own commands/icons.

Please note:
    You can also edit the commands in the **context menus** (right click in XSLT Designer opens a context menu), using the same method. Click the Menu tab and then select the specific context menu from the Context Menus combo box.

To delete a command or menu:
1. Open this dialog using **View | Customize.**
2. Click on the menu entry or icon you want to delete, and drag with the mouse.
3. Release the mouse button whenever the check mark icon appears below the mouse pointer.
    The command, or menu item is deleted from the menu or tool bar.

Toolbars

The Toolbars tab allows you to activate or deactivate specific toolbars, as well as create your own specialized ones.

XSLT Designer toolbars contain symbols for the most frequently used menu commands. For each icon you get a brief "tool tip" explanation when the mouse cursor is directly over it. The status bar (at the bottom of the application window) displays a more detailed description of the command.

You can drag the toolbars from their standard position to any location on the screen, where they appear as a floating window. Alternatively you can also dock them to the left or right edge of the main window.

To activate or deactivate a toolbar:
1. Click the check box to activate (or deactivate) the specific toolbar.

To reset the Menu Bar
- Click the Menu Bar entry and
- Click the **Reset** button, to reset the menu commands to the state they were in when XSLT Designer was installed.

To reset all toolbar and menu commands
- Click the **Reset All** button, to reset all the toolbar commands to the state they were when XSLT Designer was installed. A prompt appears stating that all toolbars and menus will be reset.
- Click Yes to confirm the reset.

Show text labels:
This option places explanatory text below toolbar icons when activated.

Keyboard

The Keyboard tab allows you to define (or change) keyboard shortcuts for any XSLT Designer command.

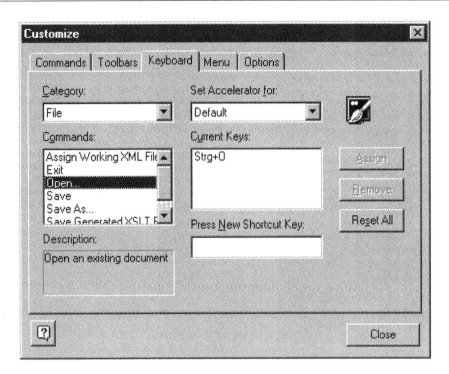

To assign a new Shortcut to a command:
1. Select the commands category using the **Category** combo box.
2. Select the **command** you want to assign a new shortcut to, in the Commands list box
3. Click in the "**Press New Shortcut Key**:" text box, and press the shortcut keys that are to activate the command.
   The shortcut immediately appears in the text box. If the shortcut was assigned previously, then that function is displayed below the text box.
4. Click the **Assign** button to permanently assign the shortcut.
   The shortcut now appears in the Current Keys text box.
   (To **clear** this text box, press any of the control keys, CTRL, ALT or SHIFT).

To deassign (or delete a shortcut):
1. Click the shortcut you want to delete in the Current Keys list box, and
2. Click the **Remove** button (which has now become active).
3. Click the Close button to confirm all the changes made in the Customize dialog box.

To reset all keyboard assignments:
1. Click the Reset All button.
   A dialog box appears prompting you to confirm if you want to reset all keyboard assignments.
2. Click Yes if you want to reset all keyboard assignments.

Set accelerator for:
Currently no function.

Menu

The menu tab allows you to customize the main menu bars as well as the context menus (right click anywhere).

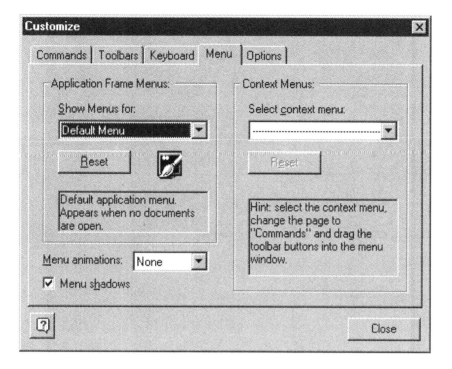

To customize a menu:
1. Select the menu bar you want to customize (Default Menu currently).
2. Click the **Commands** tab, and drag the commands to the menu bar of your choice.

To delete commands from a menu:
1. Click right on the command, or icon representing the command, and
2. Select the **Delete** option from the popup menu,

or,
1. Select **View | Customize** to open the Customize dialog box, and
2. Drag the command away from the menu, and drop it as soon as the check mark icon appears below the mouse pointer.

To reset either of the menu bars:
(Select the Default Menu entry in the combo box)
1. Click the **Reset** button just below the menu name.
A prompt appears asking if you are sure you want to reset the menu bar.

To customize any of the Context menus (right click menus):
1. Select the context menu from the combo box.
2. Click the **Commands** tab, and drag the commands to context menu that is now open.

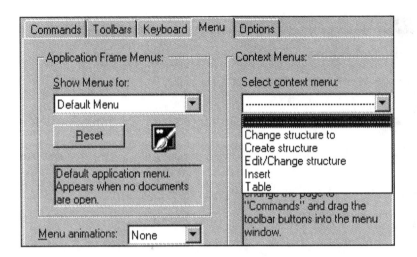

To delete commands from a context menu:
1. Click right on the command, or icon representing the command, and
2. Select the **Delete** option from the popup menu

or,
1. Select **View | Customize** to open the Customize dialog box, and
2. Drag the command away from the context menu, and drop it as soon as the check mark icon appears below the mouse pointer.

To reset any of the context menus:
1. Select the context menu from the combo box, and
2. Click the **Reset** button just below the context menu name.
   A prompt appears asking if you are sure you want to reset the context menu.

To close an context menu window:
1. Click on the **Close icon** at the top right of the title bar, or
2. Click the Close button of the Customize dialog box.

Menu animations
• Select one of the menu animations from the combo box, if you want animated menus.

Menu shadows
• Click the "Menu shadows" check box, if you want all your menus to have shadows.

Options

The Options tab allows you to set general environment settings.

Toolbar
When active, the **Show Tool tips on toolbars** check box displays a popup when the mouse pointer is placed over an icon in any of the icon bars. The popup contains a short description of the icon function, as well as the associated keyboard shortcut, if one has been assigned.

The **Show shortcut keys in Tool tips** check box, allows you to decide if you want to have the shortcut displayed in the tool tip. When active, the **Large icons** check box switches between the standard size icons, and larger versions of the icons.

Help

The Help menu contains all commands required to get help or more information on XSLT Designer, as well as links to information and support pages on our web server.

XSLT Designer includes a online help system that is based on the Microsoft HTML Help Viewer, and let you currently access the table of contents, index and search function of the supplied help file.

The Help menu also contains the Registration dialog, which lets you enter your license key-code, once you have purchased the product.

Table of contents...

This command displays a **hierarchical representation** of all chapters and topics contained in the online help system. Use this command to jump to the table of contents directly from within XSLT Designer.

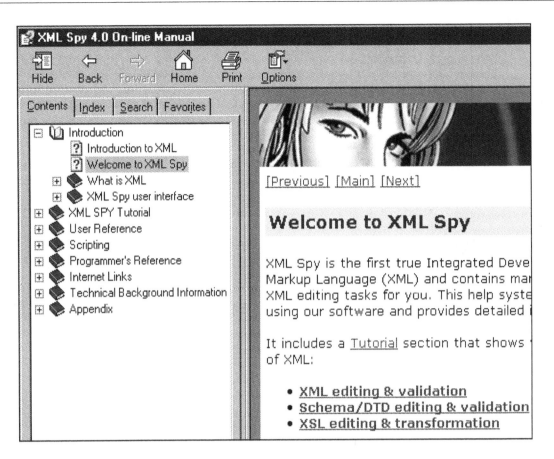

Once the help window is open, use the three tabs to toggle between the table of contents, index, and search panes. The Favorites tab lets you bookmark certain pages within the help system.

Index...

This command accesses the **keyword index** of XSLT Designer Online Help. You can also use the Index tab in the left pane of the online help system.

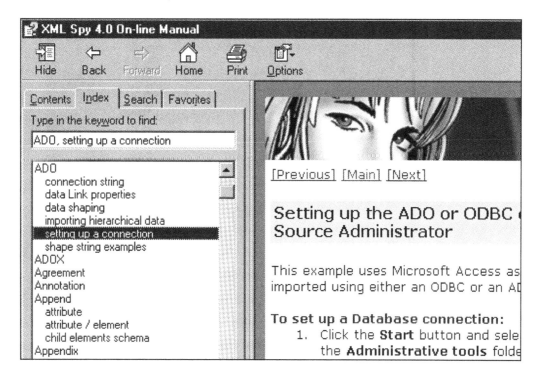

The index, lists all relevant keywords and lets you navigate to a topic by double-clicking the respective keyword. If more than one topic matches the selected keyword, you are presented a list of available topics to choose from:

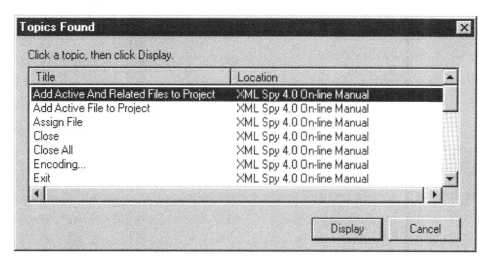

Search...

The Search command performs a **full-text search** in the entire online help system.

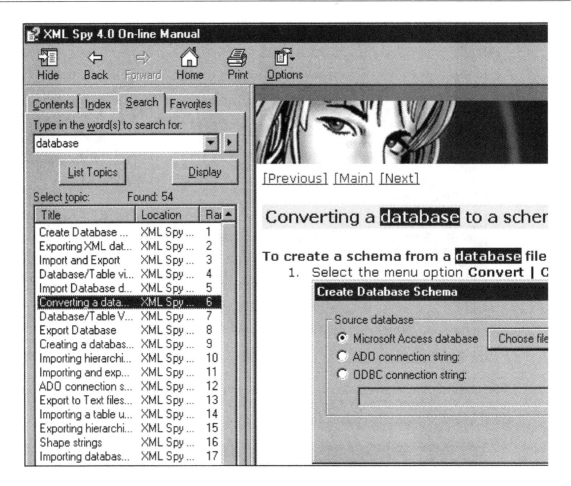

- Once you enter your search term into the query field and hit the Return key.
  The online help system displays a list of available topics that contain the search term you've entered.
- Double-click on any item in the list to display the corresponding topic.

Registration...

When you start XSLT Designer for the first time, you are automatically presented with the Registration dialog box, which lets you register your software product in order to be eligible for technical support and activate your license, which is done by entering a unique key-code to unlock the software.

FREE Evaluation Version

If you have downloaded the XSLT Designer from our web server and would like to activate your **FREE** 30-day evaluation version, please enter your name, company, and e-mail address and click on the "Request FREE evaluation key..." button. XSLT Designer then uses your Internet connection to transmit the information you have just entered to our web server, where a personal unique evaluation license will be generated for you. The license key-code, which is necessary to unlock your software, will then be sent to the e-mail address you have entered - it is therefore important, that you enter your **real e-mail address** in the registration dialog box!

Once you have clicked the request button, please go to your favorite mail software and retrieve the license key-code from our e-mail message, which you should be receiving in a matter of a few minutes (depending on transient Internet conditions).

If you requested a key-code and it didn't arrive in a short space of time, the process may have failed due to Firewall restrictions in your network. If this is the case, please send a short message with your information via e-mail to evaluate@xmlspy.com and our support staff will generate a key-code for you manually.

When you have received your evaluation key-code, please enter it into the key-code field in the registration dialog box and click on OK to start working with XSLT Designer.

Whenever you want to place an order for a licensed version of XSLT Designer, you can also use the "Order license key   " button in the registration dialog box or the Order form menu command to proceed to the Secure XML Spy Online Shop on the Internet.

Licensed Version

If you have purchased a *single-user* license for XSLT Designer, you will receive an e-mail message from us that contains your license-data and includes your name, company and key-code. Please make sure that you enter **all fields** from your license e-mail into the registration dialog box. The key-code will only be able to unlock your software installation, if the entries in the name and company fields match the name and company entered into our order form.

If your company has purchased a *multi-user* license for XSLT Designer, you will receive an e-mail message from us that contains your license-data and includes your company name and key-code.

Please make sure that you enter the company name and key-code from your license e-mail into the registration dialog box and also enter your personal name into the name field. The key-code will only be able to unlock your software installation, if the value in the company field match the company name entered into our order form.

Please note that the XSLT Designer License-Agreement does not allow you to install more than the licensed number of copies of XSLT Designer on the computers in your organization (per-seat license).

Order form...

When you want to place an order for a licensed version of XSLT Designer, use this command or the "Order license key..." button in the registration dialog to proceed to the Secure XML Spy Online Shop on the Internet, where you can choose between different single- and multi-user license packs.

Once you have placed your order, you can choose to pay by credit card, send a check by mail, or use a bank wire transfer.

Support Center...

If you have any questions regarding our product, please feel free to use this command to query to our support center on the Internet at any time. This is the place where you'll find links to the FAQ, support form, and e-mail addresses for contacting our support staff directly.

FAQ on the web

To help you in getting the best support possible, we are providing a list of Frequently Asked Questions (FAQ) on the Internet, that is constantly updated as our support staff encounters new issues that are raised by our customers.

Please make sure to check the FAQ before contacting our technical support team. This will allow you to get help more quickly.

We regret that we are not able to offer technical support by phone at this time, but our support staff will typically answer your e-mail incidents within one business day.

Components download

The Components download option, currently lets you to download the latest Microsoft XML Parser, as well as an alternate XSLT Transformation System, and will be expanded in the future.

XML Spy on the Internet...

This command takes you directly to the XML Spy web-server http://www.xmlspy.com where you can find out about news, product updates and additional offers from the XML Spy team.

Japanese distributor...

If you are located in Japan, you may prefer to contact our Japanese distributor on the Internet by using this menu command.

About XSLT Designer

This command displays the current XSLT Designer splash window and version number.

Context menus

Context menus are opened by clicking right on some part of the user-interface. The pop-up menu that opens is determined by where you click.

You can customize the context menus using the **View | Customize** option.

Change... context menu

Change...
Right clicking in the Design view, opens this context menu. If you right click a tag, you can change the tag into any one of the other types available in this list.

The Document Editor Node Settings... item, opens a dialog box enabling you to define the current node properties for further editing in the Document Editor. (Node in the Designer view means an element or attribute tag.)

The Insert Contents item only becomes active if you have previously clicked and set the text cursor, and subsequently clicked right with the cursor at that position. The (contents) placeholder is then inserted at the cursor position.

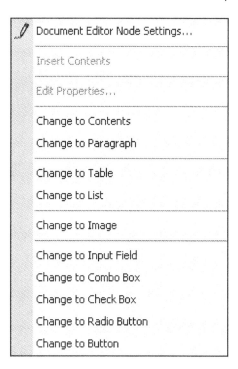

Create... popup menu

Create...
Not exactly a context menu. This menu is automatically opened when you **drag** an element from the schema tree view into the Design view pane. It allows you to decide how the schema component is to be used in the XSLT stylesheet.

Create Contents:
Selecting Create Contents inserts the respective tags, and displays them in the same line in the Design tab. The IE Preview tab displays the XML data as text in a single line without delimiters.

Create Paragraph:
This command encloses the contents in a paragraph. Selecting Create Paragraph, inserts the respective tags, and displays them over three lines. The first line contains the start tags, the second the (contents) placeholder, and the third all the end tags. The IE Preview tab displays the XML data as text, one line for each instance.

Create Table:
Selecting Create Table allows you to insert a "dynamic" table. The size of the table is determined by the XML data, and varies according to the XML file you assign (menu option **File | Assign working XML file**). A dialog box opens when you drop the element/attribute in the Design view.

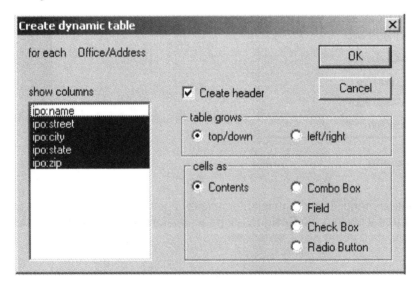

The dialog box allows you to define the table attributes:
Which columns (elements or attributes) are to appear in the table, and should a table header be created. The direction the table will expand with XML data, vertically or horizontally. The

cell types/contents of the table: Contents, Combo box, Field, Check box, Radio button.

- Contents:
  This is the default setting when inserting a table. The element/attribute tags (and content placeholders) are placed in the respective cells. The IE Preview displays the XML data as text.

- Combo box:
  The element/attribute tags are placed in the respective cell. A combo box appears between the start and end tags in the Design view (in place of the (content) place holder). The combo box values are defined in the dialog box that is automatically opened.
  The IE Preview displays a combo box for each XML data instance.

- Field:
  The element/attribute tags are placed in the respective cell. A text box appears between the start and end tags in the Designer view. The IE Preview displays a text box for each XML data instance.

- Check box
  The element/attribute tags are placed in the respective cell. A check box appears between the start and end tags in the Designer view. The check box values are defined in the dialog box that is automatically opened. The IE Preview displays a check box for each XML data instance.

- Radio button
  The element/attribute tags are placed in the respective cell. A radio button appears between the start and end tags in the Designer view. The radio button values are defined in the dialog box that is automatically opened. The IE Preview displays a radio button for each XML data instance.

Create List:
Selecting List, inserts the respective tags and displays them over three lines in the Design view. The first line contains the start tags, the second a "bulleted" (contents) placeholder, and the third the end tags. The IE Preview tab displays the XML data as bulleted text, one line for each instance.

Create Image:
Selecting image, inserts the image referenced in the image path.

Create Input Field:
Selecting Input Field inserts the element/attribute tags with a text box between the start and end tags in the Designer view. The IE Preview displays a text box for each XML data instance. Input fields can be resized by clicking the right border and dragging. A popup appears displaying the current dimensions.

Create Combo box:
Selecting Combo box, allows you to define a combo box and the values it contains for the element/attribute you insert. A dialog box opens the moment you select the Combo box entry.

Click the "Plus" button to add a list entry line to the combo box. Double click in the "Visible entry" column and enter the list entry you want to appear. Double click in the "XML value" column to add combo box return values. The visible entry is used as a descriptor, the XML value is what is actually saved.

E.g.   Visible entry   XML value

Programmer   1
Support   2
Manager   3

Click the "Minus" button to delete a row from the list entries.

Clicking OK inserts the element/attribute tags with a combo box between the start and end tags in the Design view. The IE Preview tab displays a combo box for each XML data instance.

To **reopen** this dialog box, click the combo box and select the menu option **Properties | Selected object...**

Create Check box:
A dialog box opens the moment you select the check box entry. To open this dialog box at a later time s

Click the "Plus" button to add an entry line to the "Checked values" column. Double click in the column and enter the checked value you want to appear. Double click in the "Unchecked value" text box to change the unchecked value. The unchecked value represents the unchecked status of a check box, and is the XML value when unchecked (a check box must always have a distinct state).

Click the "Minus" button to delete a row from the checked values.

Clicking OK inserts the element/attribute tags with a check box between the start and end tags in the Designer view. The IE Preview displays a check box for each XML data instance.

To **reopen** this dialog box, click the check box and select the menu option **Properties | Selected object...**

Create Radio button:
A dialog box opens the moment you select the check box entry.

Click the "Plus" button to add an entry line to the "Checked values" column. Double click in the column and enter the "Checked value" you want to appear. The checked value is the XML value that represents checked.

Click the "Minus" button to delete a row from the checked values.

Clicking OK inserts the element/attribute tags with a radio button between the start and end tags in the Designer view. The IE Preview displays a radio button for each XML data instance.

To **reopen** this dialog box, click the radio button and select the menu option **Properties | Selected object...**

Create Button:
Selecting Button inserts the element/attribute tags with a button named "Button text" between the start and end tags in the Designer view. The IE Preview displays a button for each XML data instance.

Part IX

9   Technical Background Information

This chapter contains useful background information on the technical aspects of XML Spy. If you run across a technical term in the remainder of this help system you may occasionally find a link to some of the background materials provided here.

XML Parser

When opening any XML document, XML Spy uses its built-in incremental validating parser to both check the document for well-formedness and validate it against any specified DTD, DCD, XDR, BizTalk, or XSD Schema.

The same parser is also used while editing a document that refers to a DTD, DCD, XDR, BizTalk, or XSD Schema to provide intelligent editing help and immediately display any validation error that is encountered.

This is possible through the incremental design of the new parser that is optimized for the special needs of an integrated development environment.

The built-in parser implements the new May 2nd Final Recommendation XML Schema from the W3C and we are constantly tracking the W3C Schema Group's efforts and are actively participating in all Schema-related discussions to provide you with a state-of-the-art development environment.

Schema Dialects

An important aspect of XML is the area of schemas and DTDs that define the logical structure (or content model) of an XML document - XML Spy is the ideal tool that integrates schema and DTD creation while working with XML instance documents.

XML Spy supports both editing and schema-validation of the following schema kinds:

- Document Type Definitions (DTD)
- Document Content Descriptions (DCD)
- XML-Data Reduced (XDR)
- BizTalk
- XML Schema Definition (XSD) draft April 7, 2000, CR Oct. 24 2000, May 2nd 2001 Final Recommendation

and can validate an XML instance document against any of the above schema dialects.

Since the XML Schema definition is still only available as a "last call" draft, the corresponding implementation in the built-in validating parser in XML Spy is a preliminary version. It does, however, already include - among other functions - all of the following important aspects of XML Schemas:

- simpleType & complexType
- element, attribute, attributeGroup
- group, sequence, choice, any
- all datatype facets, including user-defined patterns (!)
- notation, annotation, documentation, include

XSLT Processor

To use the full power of XSLT for XSL Transformations, you will need to download and install any XSLT transformation engine, which supports the current XSLT standard from W3C and has a command line interface.

Please note, that we provide some of the most well known XSLT engines on our Components web page http://www.xmlspy.com/components, including Microsoft XML Parser MSXML 3.0 or 4.0.

To use XSLT successfully, please make sure that your XSL Stylesheet correctly refers to the namespace defined in the final XSLT recommendation:

```
<xsl:stylesheet version="1.0" xmlns:xsl="http://www.w3.org/1999/XSL/Transform">
```

OS & Memory Requirements

XML Spy is a modern 32-bit Windows application that runs on Windows 95, 98, NT 4.0, Windows 2000 and Windows XP. It requires a fair amount of memory to be installed in the system, because it loads each document fully into memory.

On the other hand it typically requires less memory than many Java-based applications, because it is written entirely in C++ and thus does not require the overhead of a Java runtime environment.

Having documents in main memory is necessary to completely parse and analyze each document, and to also improve the viewing and editing speed during normal work. While editing a small to medium sized document (up to 512kB) is possible in as little as 2MB of RAM, opening a 5MB document can consume up to 50MB during the initial parsing process.

Memory requirements are also influenced by the unlimited Undo history. When repeatedly cutting and pasting large selections in large documents, memory can rapidly be depleted.

Internet Usage

XML Spy is an integrated development environment for XML and as such will, also initiate Internet connections on your behalf in the following situations:

a) if you click the "Request evaluation key-code" in the registration dialog the three fields in the registration dialog box are transferred to our web server by means of a regular http (port 80) connection and the free evaluation key-code is sent back to the customer via regular SMTP e-mail.

b) if you use the Open URL... dialog box to open a document directly from a URL, that document is retrieved through a http (port 80) connection.

c) if you open an XML document that refers to an XML Schema or DTD and the document is specified through a URL, it is also retrieved through a http (port 80) connection, once you validate the XML document. This may also happen automatically upon opening a document, if you have instructed XML Spy to automatically validate files upon opening in the File tab of the Tools | Options dialog.

d) if you are using the Send by mail... command, the current selection or file is sent by means of any MAPI-compliant mail program installed on the user's PC.

All this communication is, of course, only initiated in response to a direct request from you! XML is, after all, related to the Internet and thus any XML development tool must have access Internet protocols to provide an efficient environment for the everyday duties of any XML developer.

Unicode Support

Unicode is the new 16-bit character-set standard defined by the Unicode Consortium that provides a unique number for every character,

- no matter what the platform,
- no matter what the program,
- no matter what the language.

Fundamentally, computers just deal with numbers. They store letters and other characters by assigning a number for each one. Before Unicode was invented, there were hundreds of different encoding systems for assigning these numbers. No single encoding could contain enough characters: for example, the European Union alone requires several different encodings to cover all its languages. Even for a single language like English, no single encoding was adequate for all the letters, punctuation, and technical symbols in common use.

These encoding systems used to conflict with one another. That is, two encodings used the same number for two different characters, or different numbers for the same character. Any given computer (especially servers) needs to support many different encodings; yet whenever data is passed between different encodings or platforms, that data always runs the risk of corruption.

Unicode is changing all that!

Unicode provides a unique number for every character, no matter what the platform, no matter what the program, and no matter what the language. The Unicode Standard has been adopted by such industry leaders as Apple, HP, IBM, JustSystem, Microsoft, Oracle, SAP, Sun, Base and many others.

Unicode is required by modern standards such as XML, Java, ECMAScript (JavaScript), LDAP, CORBA 3.0, WML, etc., and is the official way to implement ISO/IEC 10646. It is supported in many operating systems, all modern browsers, and many other products. The emergence of the Unicode Standard, and the availability of tools supporting it, are among the most significant recent global software technology trends.

Incorporating Unicode into client-server or multi-tiered applications and web sites offers significant cost savings over the use of legacy character sets. Unicode enables a single software product or a single web site to be targeted across multiple platforms, languages and countries without re-engineering. It allows data to be transported through many different systems without corruption.

Even though XML is clearly defined to be based on the Unicode standard, XML Spy is still one of the few XML development tools that *fully* implements Unicode!

Windows NT 4.0 & Windows 2000

Starting with version 2.0 XML Spy provided full Unicode support in the Windows NT and Windows 2000 version of the software. To edit any XML document from a non-roman writing system you will, however, also need a font that supports the Unicode characters being used by that document.

Windows NT typically includes support for all common single-byte writing-systems in its Arial, Times, and Courier New fonts and will additionally include all required fonts for the writing-system in your own country (i.e. If you install the Japanese version of Windows NT you will automatically have fonts that support the Katakana, Hiragana, and Kanji writing-systems as well as the input-methods and dictionaries to enter Kanji and to switch between Katakana and Hiragana). If you wish to edit any document from a foreign writing-system, you may want to install additional Windows NT components for that writing-system or purchase special Unicode fonts for these writing-systems (such fonts are available from all leading type vendors).

Please note that most fonts only contain a very specific subset of the entire Unicode range and are therefore typically targeted at the corresponding writing system. Consequently you may encounter XML documents that contain "unprintable" characters, because the font you have selected does not contain the required glyphs. Therefore it can sometimes be very useful to have a font that covers the entire Unicode range - especially when editing XML documents from all over the world.

The most universal font we have encountered is a typeface called "Arial Unicode MS" that has been created by Agfa Monotype for Microsoft. This font contains over 50.000 glyphs and covers the entire set of characters specified by the Unicode 2.1 standard. It needs 23MB and is included with Microsoft Office 2000.

We highly recommend that you install this font on your system and use it with XML Spy, if you are often editing documents in different writing systems. This font is not installed with the "typical" setting of the Microsoft Office setup program, but you can choose the Custom Setup option to install this font.

In the "Examples" folder you will also find a new XHTML file called "Unicode-UTF8.xml" that contains the sentence "When the world wants to talk, it speaks Unicode" in many different languages ("Wenn die Welt miteinander spricht, spricht sie Unicode") and writing-systems ("世界的に話すなら、Unicode です") - this line has been adopted from the 10th Unicode conference in 1997 and is a beautiful illustration of the importance of Unicode for the XML standard. Opening this file will give you a quick impression on what is possible with Unicode and what writing systems are supported by the fonts available on your PC installation.

Windows 95/98/ME

These Windows versions do not include full Unicode capabilities on the operating system layer. Instead support for non-roman writing-systems is provided through so-called code-pages that contain all the required characters mapped to either the available byte-values in the range of 0x80 to 0xFF (in case of single-byte systems, such as Cyrillic or Hebrew) or as double-byte values, where the first most significant bit of the first byte is typically used to indicate that this is a so-called "wide character" (in case of CJK writing-systems).

We therefore provider a special Windows 95/98/ME version of XML Spy that is automatically installed whenever you are using the Setup program on these operating systems. This version of XML Spy supports the following code-pages for viewing and editing XML documents (for excellent background information about code-pages please refer to http://czyborra.com/charsets/codepages.html):

Code-page	Equivalent XML Encoding
1252	ISO-8859-1 (Western, Latin-1)
1250	ISO-8859-2 (Eastern Europe, Latin-2)
1251	ISO-8859-5 (Cyrillic)
1253	ISO-8859-7 (Greek)
1254	ISO-8859-9 (Turkish)
1255	ISO-8859-8 (Hebrew)
1256	ISO-8859-6 (Arabic)
874	ISO-8859-11/TIS-620 (Thai)
932	Shift-JIS (Japanese)
936	GB2312 (Chinese)
949	EUC-KR (Korean)
950	Big5 (Taiwanese)

Whenever you open an XML file, XML Spy detects the character-set encoding used in that file, expands the file to an internal full Unicode representation and then transforms the document to a code-page supported by Windows 95/98 in order to enable viewing and editing of the document.

In most cases this process will be entirely automatic, as the available ISO-8895-x encodings as well as some of the CJK encodings often correspond with a certain code-page. However, if you open a Unicode encoded file (e.g. UTF-8 or UTF-16) XML Spy will be unable to determine which code-page to use and will thus bring up a dialog box that asks you to specify a code-page to be used for editing.

In order to correctly view and edit a Unicode file under Windows 95/98/ME it is extremely important that you use this dialog box to:

    a) choose the correct code-page that includes all characters contained in the file and
    b) later select a font and script from the settings dialog box that also supports the same code-page.

If the file contains any characters that are not available in the selected code-page, the user will receive an error message including a detailed list of offending characters before they will be replaced by a '_' (underscore).

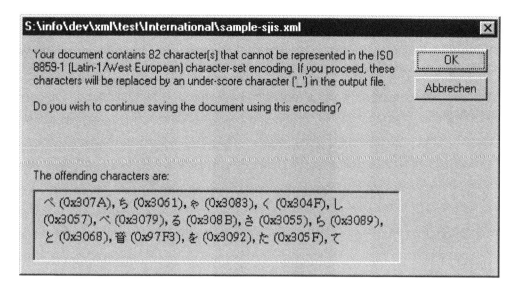

We therefore highly recommend using only the Windows NT/2000 version of XML Spy for editing XML files that make full use of Unicode!

Right-to-Left Writing Systems

Please note that even under Windows NT 4.0 any text from a right-to-left writing-system (such as Hebrew or Arabic) is not rendered correctly except in those countries that actually use right-to-left writing-systems. This is due to the fact that only the Hebrew and Arabic versions of Windows NT contains support for rendering and editing right-to-left text on the operating system layer.

RichEdit Component

XML Spy uses the Microsoft-supplied "RichEdit" component for editing documents in the Text View. The version of RichEdit that is available in Windows 98 and Windows NT 4.0 is called RichEdit 2.0 and contains many known limitations.

Windows 2000 contains a new and vastly improved version called RichEdit 3.0, that not only fixes most known bugs, but also contains special support for finer Undo-Control as well as better international capabilities with foreign writing systems.

XML Spy already contains full support for RichEdit 3.0 and takes advantage of the new features, if it detects the presence of RichEdit 3.0.

Altova is a registered MCSP (Microsoft Certified Solution Provider), we are unfortunately not allowed to distribute the RichEdit 3.0 component to our customers (RichEdit is only available as part of the operating system and is not redistributable).

We are, however, allowed to suggest that if you have access to a Windows 2000 CD-ROM you should install Windows 2000 on some machine and copy the file "riched20.dll" from the Windows\System directory of that machine to the Windows NT 4.0 or Windows 98 Windows installation (thereby replacing the old RichEdit 2.0 version) that you wish to use XML Spy on.

This will get you all the benefits of RichEdit 3.0 now and will - in our experience - not cause any compatibility problems, since the RichEdit 3.0 component is fully compatible with Windows 98 and Windows NT 4.0.

License Metering

XML Spy has a built-in license metering module that helps you in avoiding any unintentional violation of our license agreement. XML Spy can be licensed either as a single-user or multi-user software and depending on your license, this license-metering module makes sure, that no more than the licensed number of users are using XML Spy concurrently.

This license-metering technology uses your local area network (LAN) to communicate between instances of XML Spy running on different computers.

Single license

When XML Spy starts up, it sends a short broadcast datagram to find any other instance of the product running on another computer in the same network segment. If it doesn't get any response, it will open a port for listening to other instances of XML Spy. Other than that, it will do nothing at all in a single-user situation. If you are not connected to a LAN or are using dial-up connections to connect to the Internet, XML Spy will NOT generate any network traffic at all.

Multi license

If more than one copy of XML Spy is used within the same LAN, they will briefly communicate with each other on startup, to exchange their key-codes to ensure that the number of concurrent licenses purchased is not accidentally violated, as additional copies of the product are launched by more users.

This is the same kind of license metering technology, that is common in the Unix world and with many other database development tools and allows our customers to purchase reasonably-priced concurrent-use multi-user licenses (see http://www.xmlspy.com/order for our price list).

Please note, that XML Spy is at no time attempting to send any information out of your LAN, or over the Internet. We are also deliberately sending very few and small network packets so as to not put a burden on any network. The TCP/IP ports (2799) used by XML Spy are officially registered with the IANA see http://www.isi.edu/in-notes/iana/assignments/port-numbers for details) and our license-metering module is a proven and tested technology.

If you are using a firewall, you may notice communications on port 2799 between the computers that are running XML Spy. You are, of course, free to block such traffic between different groups in your organization, as long as you can ensure by other means, that your license agreement is not violated.

You will also notice, that XML Spy contains many useful functions that make use of your Internet connection, but these are unrelated to the license-metering technology.

Part **X**

10   Appendix

This appendix contains important legal information concerning your rights to use this software product. Please read carefully - this information is binding, as you have agreed to these terms upon installation of this software product.

Electronic Software Distribution

We are making XML Spy available through electronic software distribution only, because this method offers many unique benefits for our customers:

* you can freely evaluate the software before making a purchasing decision
* once you decide to buy the software, you can place your order online and immediately get a fully licensed product within minutes
* you can be sure to always got tho latoot vcrsion of our software
* we include both a comprehensive integrated online-help system and an electronic manual that you can also print out, if you prefer to read your documentation on paper

Once you download this software product, you may evaluate the XML Spy for a period of up to 30 days free of charge. During this evaluation period the software will start to remind you after about 20 days that it has not been licensed yet. The reminder message will, however, only be displayed once every time you start the program.

If you would like to continue using the program after the 30 day evaluation period, you have to purchase a license, which is delivered in the form of a key-code that you enter into the Registration dialog to unlock the product.

You can register and purchase your license on-line by directing your browser to access our web-shop at http://www.xmlspy.com/order. On this page you will get detailed pricing information (including multi-user discounts) and also find a list of authorized distributors and resellers.

If you want to share XML Spy with others, please make sure that only the installation program is ever distributed. It contains the application program, grammar description, sample files, and this online manual as well as a quick Read-Me file in one neat package. Any person that receives the XML Spy software from you is also automatically entitled to a 30 day evaluation period. After the expiration of said period, any other user must also purchase a license in order to be able to use XML Spy.

For further details, please refer to the SOFTWARE PRODUCT LICENSE at the end of this manual.

Copyright

All title and copyrights in and to the SOFTWARE PRODUCT (including but not limited to any images, photographs, animations, video, audio, music, text, and "applets" incorporated into the SOFTWARE PRODUCT), the accompanying printed materials, and any copies of the SOFTWARE PRODUCT are owned by Altova GmbH or its suppliers. The SOFTWARE PRODUCT is protected by copyright laws and international treaty provisions. Therefore, you must treat the SOFTWARE PRODUCT like any other copyrighted material.

Copyright ©1998-2002 Altova GmbH

All rights reserved.

Software Product License

THIS IS A LEGAL DOCUMENT -- RETAIN FOR YOUR RECORDS

ALTOVA SOFTWARE LICENSE AGREEMENT

Licensor:

Altova GmbH
Rudolfsplatz 13a/9
A-1010 Wien
Austria

Notice to User:
This is a legal document between you and Altova GmbH ("Altova"). It is important that you read this document before using the Altova-provided software ("Software") and any accompanying documentation ("Documentation"). By using the Software, you agree to be bound by the terms of this Agreement whether or not you decide to purchase the Software. If you do not agree, you are not licensed to use the Software, and you must destroy any downloaded copies of the Software in your possession or control. Please go to our Web site to download and print a copy of this Agreement for your files.

1.   SOFTWARE LICENSE
(a)   License Grant. Altova grants you a non-exclusive, non-transferable (except as provided below), limited license to install and use a copy of the Software on your compatible computer, up to the Permitted Number of computers. The Permitted Number of computers shall be delineated at such time as you elect to purchase the Software.

(b)   Server Use. You may install one copy of the Software on your computer file server for the purpose of downloading and installing the Software onto other computers within your internal network up to the Permitted Number. No other network use is permitted, including without limitation using the Software either directly or through commands, data or instructions from or to a computer not part of your internal network, for Internet or Web-hosting services or by any user not licensed to use this copy of the Software through a valid license from Altova.

(c)   Concurrent Use. If you have purchased a "Concurrent-User" version of the Software, you may install the Software on any compatible computers, up to ten (10) times the Permitted Number of users, provided that only the Permitted Number of users actually use the Software at the same time. The Permitted Number of concurrent users shall be delineated at such time as you elect to purchase the Software.

(d)   Backup and Archival Copies. You may make one backup and one archival copy of the Software, provided your backup and archival copies are not installed or used on any computer and further provided that all such copies shall bear the original and unmodified copyright, patent and other intellectual property markings that appear on or in the Software. You may not transfer the rights to a backup or archival copy unless you transfer all rights in the Software as provided under Section 3.

(e)   Home Use.   You, as the primary user of the computer on which the Software is installed, may also install the Software on one of your home computers. However, the Software may not be used on your home computer at the same time as the Software is being used on the primary computer.

(f)   Key Codes. You will receive a key code when you elect to purchase the Software. The key code will enable you to activate the Software after an initial thirty (30)-day evaluation period. You may not relicense, reproduce or distribute a key code except with the express written permission of Altova.

(g)   Title. Title to the Software is not transferred to you. Ownership of all copies of the Software and of copies made by you is vested in Altova, subject to the rights of use granted to you in this Agreement.

(h)   Reverse Engineering. You may not reverse engineer, decompile, disassemble or otherwise attempt to discover the source code, underlying ideas, underlying user interface techniques or algorithms of the Software by any means whatsoever, directly or indirectly, or disclose any of the foregoing, except to the extent you may be expressly permitted to decompile under applicable law, it is essential to do so in order to achieve operability of the Software with another software program, and you have first requested Altova to provide the information necessary to achieve such operability and Altova has not made such information available. Altova has the right to impose reasonable conditions and to request a reasonable fee before providing such information. Any information supplied by Altova or obtained by you, as permitted hereunder, may only be used by you for the purpose described herein and may not be disclosed to any third party or used to create any software which is substantially similar to the expression of the Software. Requests for information should be directed to the Altova Customer Support Department.

(i)   Other Restrictions. You may not loan, rent, lease, sublicense, distribute or otherwise transfer all or any portion of the Software to third parties except to the limited extent set forth in Section 3. You may not copy the Software except as expressly set forth above, and any copies that you are permitted to make pursuant to this Agreement must contain the same copyright, patent and other intellectual property markings that appear on or in the Software. You may not modify, adapt or translate the Software. You may not, directly or indirectly, encumber or suffer to exist any lien or security interest on the Software; knowingly take any action that would cause the Software to be placed in the public domain; or use the Software in any computer environment not specified in this Agreement. You will comply with applicable law and Altova's instructions regarding the use of the Software. You agree to notify your employees and agents who may have access to the Software of the restrictions contained in this Agreement and to ensure their compliance with these restrictions.   THE SOFTWARE IS NOT INTENDED FOR USE IN THE OPERATION OF NUCLEAR FACILITIES, AIRCRAFT NAVIGATION, COMMUNICATION SYSTEMS OR AIR TRAFFIC CONTROL EQUIPMENT, WHERE THE FAILURE OF THE SOFTWARE COULD LEAD TO DEATH, PERSONAL INJURY OR SEVERE PHYSICAL OR ENVIRONMENTAL DAMAGE.

(j)   License Metering. Altova has a built-in license metering module that helps you to avoid any unintentional violation of this Agreement. Altova may use your internal network for license metering between installed versions of the Software.

2.   INTELLECTUAL PROPERTY RIGHTS

Acknowledgement of Altova's Rights. You acknowledge that the Software and any copies that you are authorized by Altova to make are the intellectual property of and are owned by Altova and its suppliers. The structure, organization and code of the Software are the valuable trade secrets and confidential information of Altova and its suppliers. The Software is protected by copyright, including without limitation by United States Copyright Law, international treaty provisions and applicable laws in the country in which it is being used. You acknowledge that Altova retains the ownership of all patents, copyrights, trade secrets, trademarks and other intellectual property rights pertaining to the Software, and that Altova's ownership rights extend to any images, photographs, animations, videos, audio, music, text and "applets" incorporated into the Software and all accompanying printed materials. You will take no actions, which adversely affect Altova's intellectual property rights in the Software. Trademarks shall be used in accordance with accepted trademark practice, including identification of trademark owners' names. Trademarks may only be used to identify printed output produced by the Software, and such use of any trademark does not give you any right of ownership in that trademark. XML Spy and Altova are trademarks of Altova GmbH (registered in numerous countries). Unicode and the Unicode Logo are trademarks of Unicode, Inc. Windows, Windows 95, Windows 98, Windows NT and Windows 2000 are trademarks of Microsoft. W3C, CSS, DOM, MathML, RDF, XHTML, XML and XSL are trademarks (registered in numerous countries) of the World Wide Web Consortium (W3C); marks of the W3C are registered and held by its host institutions, MIT, INRIA and Keio. Except as expressly stated above, this Agreement does not grant you any intellectual property rights in the Software.

3.   LIMITED TRANSFER RIGHTS

Notwithstanding the foregoing, you may transfer all your rights to use the Software to another person or legal entity provided that: (a) you also transfer each of this Agreement, the Software and all other software or hardware bundled or pre-installed with the Software, including all copies, updates and prior versions, and all copies of font software converted into other formats, to such person or entity; (b) you retain no copies, including backups and copies stored on a computer; (c) the receiving party secures a personalized key code from Altova; and (d) the receiving party accepts the terms and conditions of this Agreement and any other terms and conditions upon which you legally purchased a license to the Software. Notwithstanding the foregoing, you may not transfer education, pre-release, or not-for-resale copies of the Software.

4.   PRE-RELEASE PRODUCT ADDITIONAL TERMS

If the product you have received with this license is pre-commercial release or beta Software ("Pre-release Software"), then this Section applies. To the extent that any provision in this Section is in conflict with any other term or condition in this Agreement, this Section shall supersede such other term(s) and condition(s) with respect to the Pre-release Software, but only to the extent necessary to resolve the conflict. You acknowledge that the Software is a pre-release version, does not represent final product from Altova, and may contain bugs, errors and other problems that could cause system or other failures and data loss. CONSEQUENTLY, THE PRE-RELEASE SOFTWARE IS PROVIDED TO YOU "AS-IS", AND ALTOVA DISCLAIMS ANY WARRANTY OR LIABILITY OBLIGATIONS TO YOU OF ANY KIND EXPRESS OR IMPLIED. WHERE LEGALLY LIABILITY CANNOT BE EXCLUDED FOR PRE-RELEASE SOFTWARE, BUT IT MAY BE LIMITED, ALTOVA'S LIABILITY AND THAT OF ITS SUPPLIERS SHALL BE LIMITED TO THE SUM OF FIFTY DOLLARS (U.S.$50) IN TOTAL. You acknowledge that Altova has not promised or guaranteed to you that Pre-release Software will be announced or made available to anyone in the future, that Altova has no express or implied obligation to you to announce or introduce the Pre-release Software and that Altova may not introduce a product similar to or compatible with the Pre-release Software. Accordingly, you acknowledge that any research or development that you perform regarding the Pre-release Software or any product associated with the Pre-release Software is done entirely at your own risk. During the term of this Agreement, if requested by Altova, you will provide feedback to Altova regarding testing and use of the Pre-release Software, including error or bug reports. If you have been provided the Pre-release Software pursuant to a separate written agreement, your use of the Software is governed by such agreement. You may not sublicense, lease, loan, rent, distribute or otherwise transfer the Pre-release Software. Upon receipt of a later unreleased version of the Pre-release Software or release by Altova of a publicly released commercial version of the Software, whether as a stand-alone product or as part of a larger product, you agree to return or destroy all earlier Pre-release Software received from Altova and to abide by the terms of the license agreement for any such later versions of the Pre-release Software.

5.   WARRANTY AND LIMITATION OF LIABILITY

(a)   Limited Warranty. Altova warrants that (a) the Software will perform substantially in accordance with the accompanying written materials for a period of ninety (90) days from the date of receipt, and (b) any support services provided by Altova shall be substantially as described in applicable written materials provided to you by Altova, and Altova support engineers will make commercially reasonable efforts to solve any problem issues. Some states and jurisdictions do not allow limitations on duration of an implied warranty, so the above limitation may not apply to you. To the extent allowed by applicable law, implied warranties on the Software, if any, are limited to ninety (90) days.

(b)   Customer Remedies. Altova's and its suppliers' entire liability and your exclusive remedy shall be, at Altova's option, either (a) return of the price paid, if any, or (b) repair or replacement of the Software that does not meet Altova's Limited Warranty and which is returned to Altova with a copy of your receipt. This Limited Warranty is void if failure of the Software has resulted from accident, abuse or misapplication. Any replacement Software will be warranted for the remainder of the original warranty period or thirty (30) days, whichever is longer.

(c)   No Other Warranties. TO THE MAXIMUM EXTENT PERMITTED BY APPLICABLE LAW, ALTOVA AND ITS SUPPLIERS DISCLAIM ALL OTHER WARRANTIES AND CONDITIONS, EITHER EXPRESS OR IMPLIED, INCLUDING, BUT NOT LIMITED TO, IMPLIED WARRANTIES OF MERCHANTABILITY, FITNESS FOR A PARTICULAR PURPOSE, INFORMATIONAL CONTENT OR ACCURACY, QUIET ENJOYMENT, TITLE AND NON-INFRINGEMENT, WITH REGARD TO THE SOFTWARE, AND THE PROVISION OF OR FAILURE TO PROVIDE SUPPORT SERVICES. THIS LIMITED WARRANTY GIVES YOU SPECIFIC LEGAL RIGHTS. YOU MAY HAVE OTHERS, WHICH VARY FROM STATE/JURISDICTION TO STATE/JURISDICTION.

(d)   Limitation Of Liability. TO THE MAXIMUM EXTENT PERMITTED BY APPLICABLE LAW, IN NO EVENT SHALL ALTOVA OR ITS SUPPLIERS BE LIABLE FOR ANY SPECIAL, INCIDENTAL, DIRECT, INDIRECT OR CONSEQUENTIAL DAMAGES WHATSOEVER (INCLUDING, WITHOUT LIMITATION, DAMAGES FOR LOSS OF BUSINESS PROFITS, BUSINESS INTERRUPTION, LOSS OF BUSINESS INFORMATION, OR ANY OTHER PECUNIARY LOSS) ARISING OUT OF THE USE OF OR INABILITY TO USE THE SOFTWARE OR THE PROVISION OF OR FAILURE TO PROVIDE SUPPORT SERVICES, EVEN IF ALTOVA HAS BEEN ADVISED OF THE POSSIBILITY OF SUCH DAMAGES. IN ANY CASE, ALTOVA'S ENTIRE LIABILITY UNDER ANY PROVISION OF THIS AGREEMENT SHALL BE LIMITED TO THE GREATER OF THE AMOUNT ACTUALLY PAID BY YOU FOR THE SOFTWARE PRODUCT OR U.S.$50.00; PROVIDED, HOWEVER, IF YOU HAVE ENTERED INTO AN ALTOVA SUPPORT SERVICES AGREEMENT, ALTOVA'S ENTIRE LIABILITY REGARDING SUPPORT SERVICES SHALL BE GOVERNED BY THE TERMS OF THAT AGREEMENT. Because some states and jurisdictions do not allow the exclusion or limitation of liability, the above limitation may not apply to you. In such states and jurisdictions, Altova's liability shall be limited to the greatest extent permitted by law.

(e)   Infringement Claims. Altova will indemnify and hold you harmless and will defend or settle any claim, suit or proceeding brought against you that is based upon a claim that the content contained in the Software infringes a copyright or violates an intellectual or proprietary right protected by United States or European Union law ("Claim"), but only to the extent the Claim arises directly out of the use of the Software. You must notify Altova in writing of any Claim within ten (10) business days after you first receive notice of the Claim, and you shall provide to Altova at no cost with such assistance and cooperation as Altova may reasonably request from time to time in connection with the defense of the Claim. Altova shall have sole control over any Claim (including, without limitation, the selection of counsel and the right to settle on your behalf on any terms Altova deems desirable in the sole exercise of its discretion). You may, at your sole cost, retain separate counsel and participate in the defense or settlement negotiations. Altova shall pay actual damages and costs awarded against you (or payable by you pursuant to a settlement agreement) in connection with a Claim to the extent such damages and costs are not reimbursed to you by insurance or a third party, to an aggregate maximum of US$1,000. If the Software or its use becomes the subject of a Claim or its use is enjoined, or if in the opinion of Altova's legal counsel the Software is likely to become the subject of a Claim, Altova shall attempt to resolve the Claim by using commercially reasonable efforts to modify the Software or obtain a license to continue using the Software. If in the opinion of Altova's legal counsel the Claim, the injunction or potential Claim cannot be resolved through reasonable modification or licensing, Altova, at its own election, may terminate this Agreement without penalty, and will refund to you on a pro rata basis any fees paid in advance by you to Altova. THE FOREGOING CONSTITUTES ALTOVA'S SOLE AND EXCLUSIVE LIABILITY FOR INTELLECTUAL PROPERTY INFRINGEMENT.

6.   TERM AND TERMINATION

This Agreement may be terminated (a) by your giving Altova written notice of termination; or (b) by Altova, at its option, giving you written notice of termination if you commit a breach of this Agreement and fail to cure such breach within ten (10) days after notice from Altova. Upon any termination of this Agreement, you must cease all use of the Software, destroy all copies then in your possession or control and take such other actions as Altova may reasonably request to ensure that no copies of the Software remain in your possession or control.

7.   GENERAL PROVISIONS

If there is a local subsidiary of Altova in the country in which the Software was obtained, then the local law of the jurisdiction in which the subsidiary is located shall govern this Agreement. Otherwise, this Agreement shall be governed by the laws of the Republic of Austria and, to the extent applicable, the European Union. This Agreement contains the entire agreement and understanding of the parties with respect to the subject matter hereof, and supersedes all prior written and oral understandings of the parties with respect to the subject matter hereof. Any notice or other communication given under this Agreement shall be in writing and shall have been properly given by either of us to the other if sent by certified or registered mail, return receipt requested, or by overnight courier to the address shown on Altova's Web site for Altova and the address shown in Altova's records for you, or such other address as the parties may designate by notice given in the manner set forth above. This Agreement will bind and inure to the benefit of the parties and our respective heirs, personal and legal representatives, affiliates, successors and permitted assigns. The failure of either of us at any time to require performance of any provision hereof shall in no manner affect such party's right at a later time to enforce the same or any other term of this Agreement. This Agreement may be amended only by a document in writing signed by both of us. In the event of a breach or threatened breach of this Agreement by either party, the other shall have all applicable equitable as well as legal remedies. The Software and its related documentation may not be exported or reexported in violation of the U.S. Export Administration Act and its implementing regulations or the laws of the jurisdiction in which the Software was obtained. Each party is duly authorized and empowered to enter into and perform this Agreement. If, for any reason, any provision of this Agreement is held invalid or otherwise unenforceable, such invalidity or unenforceability shall not affect the remainder of this Agreement, and this Agreement shall continue in full force and effect to the fullest extent allowed by law. The parties knowingly and expressly consent to the foregoing terms and conditions.

Index

- A -

- P -

Paragraph 517
    delete (Doc. Editor) 517
    enabling for Document Editor 517
    para tag 428
Paragraph style 207
Parameter entities 114
Parent element 172
    importing with ADO 229
Parsed entity 180
Parser 551
    XSLT 289
Parser download 299, 544
Password protection 120, 124
    URL 120, 124
Paste 132
Patterns 552
PI 162, 164, 167, 169
    Add Child 167
    Appending 164
    Convert To 169
    Inserting 162
Placeholder 502
    adding/deleting 502
Plug-in 424
PNG 185
    save graphic 185
Popup 428
    hint 428
port 562
    2799 562
    80 555
Position 247
    Character 247
    Line 247
Premium 177
Presentation 284
Pretty print 135
    in text view 135
Preview 109, 127, 202
    XSLT file 507
Price list 565
Primary 75
    & secondary key - import 75
Primary key 218

Primary/foreign key 203
    exlude 203
Print 129
    Command 127
    Preview 127
    Setup 129
Print Setup 129
Processing instruction 199
    Add Child 167
    Append 164
    Convert To 169
    Insert 162
Processing instructions 135
Program settings 280
Project 179
    Add active and related files 152
    Add External folder 152
    Add External web folder 155
    Add file 152
    Add files to project 151
    Add folder 152
    Add local/network folder 152
    add to source control 146
    Add URL to project 151
    adding files to 84
    advantages 83
    assign script to 267
    assigning DTDs 111
    assigning XSL transformations 111
    Close Project 139
    create 84
    create addtnl. folder 84
    delete file from 84
    management 138
    Menu 138
    Most recently used 159
    New 138
    Open project 138
    properties 83, 157, 176
    Reload project 139
    remove from source control 148
    save 84
    Save Project 139
    scripting 267
    scripts active 267
    unassign scripts from 267
    window 19
    source control 140

- V -

- W -

© 2002 Altova Ges.m.b.H

www.ingramcontent.com/pod-product-compliance
Lightning Source LLC
Chambersburg PA
CBHW080130060326
40689CB00018B/3733